'INDUSTRIOUS AND FAIRLY CIVILIZED'
THE GLASTONBURY LAKE VILLAGE

by
John Coles and Stephen Minnitt

1995

Somerset Levels Project
and
Somerset County Council Museums Service

reprinted 2000
with the support of Somerset County Council

We have taken the opportunity to make minor corrections here and there, and to add a post-script on dating.

ISBN 0 9507122 2 1

Design and typesetting:
Mike Rouillard,
Department of Archaeology,
University of Exeter

Printed by Short Run Press, Exeter

Published by the
Somerset Levels Project
and Somerset County Council Museums Service

Contents

DEDICATION

We dedicate this book to the
Glastonbury Antiquarian Society
for its care of the Lake Village
since 1892

Introduction and Acknowledgements

The Glastonbury Lake Village was discovered by Arthur Bulleid in March 1892. From that date until 1917 the site was under investigation: 11 years of excavation and almost 20 years of analysis and study leading to the final publications in 1911 and 1917. The two books, written by Arthur Bulleid and Harold St George Gray, revolutionised knowledge of the Iron Age of southern Britain, and exposed the values and difficulties of wetland archaeology. Since then, the Lake Village has featured in most general west European textbooks on archaeology and prehistory, and it has been the subject of several intensive studies.

In 1992, 100 years after the discovery, a small booklet was published by Somerset County Council Museums Service and the Somerset Levels Project to commemorate the centenary; it was written by three authors, John Coles, Stephen Minnitt and Armynell Goodall, one of Arthur Bulleid's daughters. In the same year, a new display was opened at the Peat Moors Visitor Centre at Westhay, Somerset, with reconstructions of Glastonbury-type houses and other exhibits. Work then began on a re-appraisal of the records of the Bulleid and Gray excavations, and previously unpublished information was made available through the Somerset Record Office and other sources. Among these were the Minute Books of the Glastonbury Antiquarian Society, owners of the site and organisers of the early work, and the Black Book of Relics compiled by Gray. Many letters, notebooks and other materials were examined in order to give access to the archaeological approaches adopted by Bulleid and Gray in their work. A new Lake Village exhibition was opened in The Tribunal, Glastonbury, by Somerset County Council Museums Service. The archive of finds was re-examined, new analyses carried out, specialists consulted, and the surviving evidence brought together for a new and extensive study. This study commenced in late 1993; this book is the result.

The book takes as its title one of Arthur Bulleid's comments about the site. It reflects his interest and his perception of what he and Gray had found. They published the bulk of the evidence in 1911 and 1917. Nineteen chapters were concerned with small finds and we have made no attempt to re-publish their data. That information is best consulted in their books. In this book we have concentrated on an analysis of the site itself and have focused more on the physical remains of the site, its Mounds and Floors, its Houses and open Spreads, its Environment and its Phases of development, and ultimately its reason for existence in the swamps of the eastern Brue Valley.

In the course of this work we have been aided by many people and organisations. In 1984 the Somerset Levels Project carried out a small investigation on and around the Lake Village, funded by English Heritage and with the permission of the Glastonbury Antiquarian Society. Our recent studies and this publication have been supported by grants from: The Hiram Walker Group Limited, Glastonbury Antiquarian Society, the Society of Antiquaries of London, the Maltwood Fund (administered by Somerset Archaeological and Natural History Society), the Marc Fitch Fund, University of Exeter Department of History and Archaeology, Somerset County Council Museums Service and the Somerset Levels Project. We gratefully acknowledge support from: the Radiocarbon Accelerator Unit of the Research Laboratory for Archaeology and the History of Art, University of Oxford, the Ancient Monuments Laboratory, London, the Department of Earth Sciences, University of Oxford, the National Museum of Denmark, the Centre for Maritime Research, Roskilde, and the Museums and Galleries Commission.

For support and advice we thank Robin Andrews, Justine Bayley, John Barrett, Rosemary Blackman, Neil Bonham, David Bromwich, Andrew Burnett, Bryony Coles, Bob Croft, Barry Cunliffe, Mark Davis, David Dawson, Caroline Earwood, Chris Evans, Don Evely, Anabel Field, Anders Fischer, Armynell Goodall, Jim Hanwell, Robert Hedges, R.J. Howell, Mogens Schou Jørgensen, Madge Langdon, Kirsten Lindhard, John Loveridge, Jes Martens, Tom Mayberry, Peter McCrone, Sean McGrail, Stephen Morland, Adrian Olivier, Dennis Parsons, Sylvia Peglar, Peter Reynolds, Val Rigby, Roger and Andrea Rogers, Roy Switsur, Malcolm Todd, Michael Tomlinson and Alan Ward.

Crucial to the project were those involved in putting the text on to wordprocessors and the preparation of the work for publication; for this we are indebted to Lawrence Bostock, Sue Clements, Joy Minnitt, Carole Price, Mike Rouillard, Tina Tuohy, Carol Turner, Anne Marie Warfield and Jennifer Warren.

All the Chapters in the book have been discussed by both authors, but responsibility for individual Chapters is as follows: Chapters 1 and 6 (SCM), Chapters 2, 4, 7 and 8 (JMC). Chapter 3 was compiled by JMC (Mound structures) and SCM (artefacts). We are grateful to Rupert Housley for contributing Chapter 5, and to various authors of sections in Chapter 6: Geraldine Barber (Palaeopathology Study Group, University of Bristol Rheumatology Unit), Richard Brunning (Somerset County Council), Julian Henderson (University of Sheffield), Catherine Mortimer (Ancient Monuments

Laboratory), Julian Richards, Fiona Roe, Juliet Rogers (Palaeopathology Study Group, University of Bristol Rheumatology Unit), David Starley (Ancient Monuments Laboratory), Tina Tuohy (University of Exeter) and Rebecca Wiggins (Palaeopathology Study Group, University of Bristol Rheumatology Unit).

We are grateful to Mike Rouillard of the Department of History and Archaeology, University of Exeter, for designing and typesetting the book.

The paper archive of the Glastonbury Lake Village excavations is in the Somerset Record Office. The reference collection of artefacts is cared for by the Somerset County Council Museums Service in Taunton and can be accessed by appointment.

We are above all indebted to the Glastonbury Antiquarian Society in whose care the site and collections have been for the past 100 years. During that time the integrity of the site has been maintained and it remains today more or less in the shape in which Arthur Bulleid found it, excavated it and left it, still wet, still with some buried timbers, and still holding promise for any future examinations.

John Coles and Stephen Minnitt

November1994.

Note: A folding plan of the site with its Mound numbers will be found inside the back cover. References to numbered Mounds are abbreviated throughout the book to M, e.g. M1, M21.

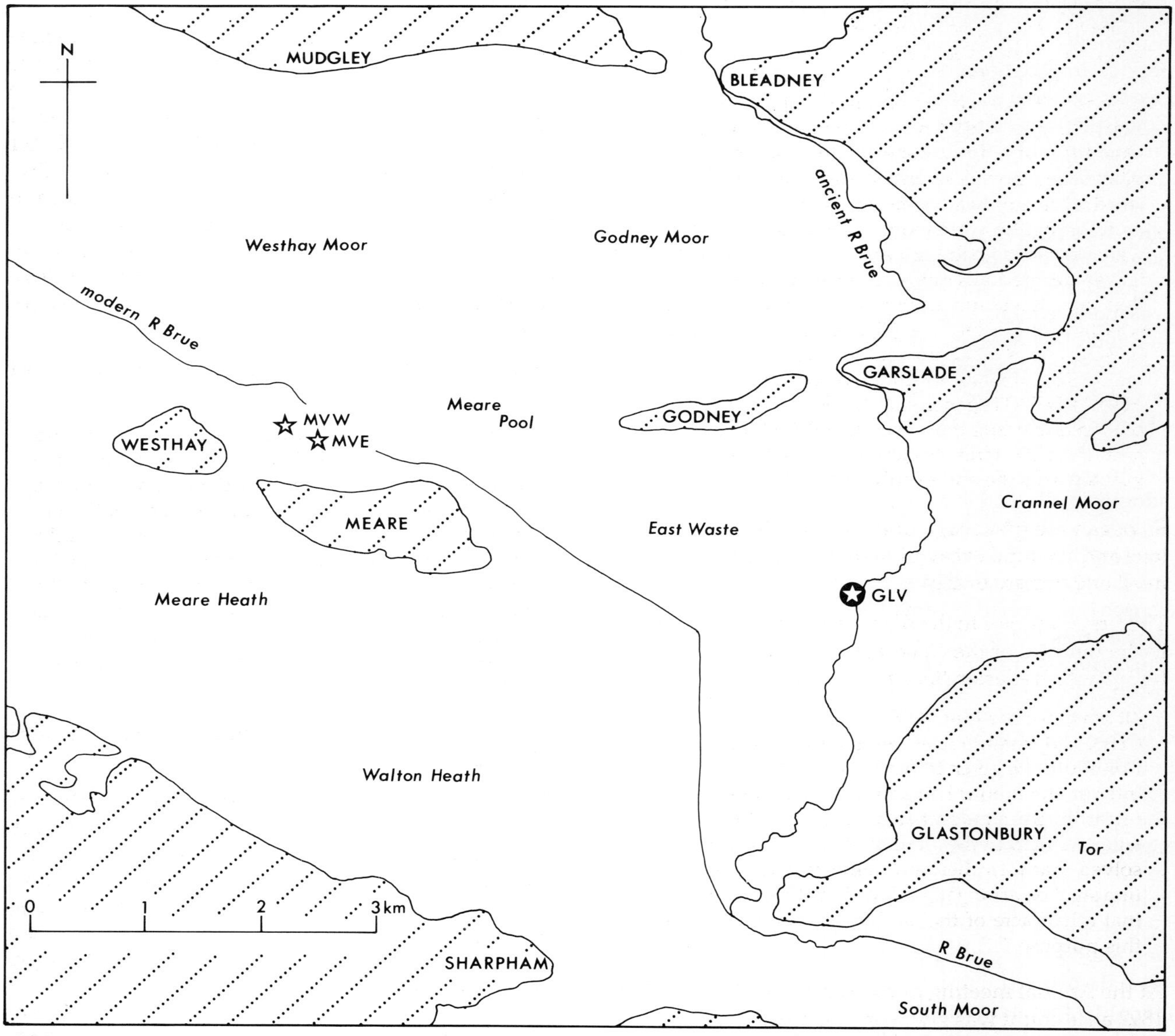

Fig.1.1 The eastern Brue Valley with the Lake Village of Glastonbury and the Meare Villages. (Higher land shown hatched) JMC

Chapter 1

The Discovery and Early Excavations

Arthur Bulleid:

> "On a Wednesday afternoon in March, 1892, when driving across the moor from Glastonbury to Godney, a field was noticed to be covered with small mounds, an unusual feature in a neighbourhood where the conformation of the land is for miles at a dead level. On the following Sunday afternoon the field was visited, and anticipations were agreeably realized by picking up from the numerous mole-hills a number of pottery fragments, a whetstone, and pieces of bone and charcoal. The same evening in course of conversation a valued friend and neighbour, Mr EDWARD BATH, became interested in the matter, and having intimated that he believed the field belonged to him, a note arrived the following morning to confirm this, with permission to dig, subject to making arrangements with the tenant. This was done, and a week or two later tentative excavations took place by digging trenches into two of the mounds. The sections exposed clay floors with hearths, supported by massive timber substructures. Quantities of pottery, bones of animals, several implements of bone and antler, and a beautifully polished jet ring or bead, were among the relics discovered during these preliminary investigations. As the water level was still high and flooded the trenches, it was deemed advisable to postpone the exploration until the summer. In the meantime the matter was brought before the Glastonbury Antiquarian Society, and a fund was started with the object of making a systematic examination of the site, and Mr EDWARD BATH generously made a gift of five acres of land (including the site of the village) to the Glastonbury Antiquarian Society. Investigations were begun towards the end of July 1892."

So began the great saga of the Glastonbury Lake Village and the total excavation of the site which was almost one hectare in area.

The first reference to the discovery of the Lake Village in the minutes of the General Committee of the Glastonbury Antiquarian Society was on 19th April 1892:

> "It was proposed by Mr E. Bath, seconded by Mr F. Clark and unanimously resolved the thanks of the Committee be given to Mr A. Bulleid for the trouble, interest and labour he had taken in discovering and unearthing the ancient remains of a prehistoric village in a field in the Godney Road ... It was also resolved that a further and more systematic exploration shall be arranged and Mr E. Bath kindly offered that a half acre of the land might be fenced off for this purpose."

At the Annual meeting of the Society on 31st October 1892 an account was given of progress that year:

> "A portion of the foundation upon which the Huts were evidently built, has been laid open, the character of the Huts has been made clear, and many bone, bronze and earthenware objects have been found. Most of these have been already placed in the Museum and the Committee think it is not too much to expect that this most valuable addition, when completed, will ensure the great popularity of that Institution not only locally but nationally. By what has already been found a clearer insight into the village life of the inhabitants two thousand years ago is obtained."

Excitement reigned in Glastonbury. Knowledge of the discovery soon spread nationally.

The early excavations

Two committees were established to oversee the excavations. One, the Expert Committee, was to comprise national figures. Those invited to join this committee in April 1893 were : J. G. Baker, Professor W. Boyd Dawkins, Sir John Evans, the Right Honourable Sir Edward Fry, Dr R. Munro, Lieutenant General Pitt-Rivers, the Rev H. H. Winwood, A. W. Franks and Bishop Hobhouse. Winwood, Franks and Hobhouse all declined but the others responded favourably to the request. There was a more local Excavation Committee which included John Morland and various other worthies.

On 28th November 1893 the Antiquarian Society heard that:

> "The digging was commenced this year in April and the examination of the five mounds opened in the previous autumn was continued. On May 1st some new ground was railed in at the east side of the village and during the past season ten more dwelling mounds have been partially excavated together with the ground round them - and about 150 feet of the village border. There still remain 50 dwelling mounds and nearly the whole of the village border, or roughly speaking three-quarters of its area, left for future examination."

Figure 1.2 shows one of the Mounds excavated in 1893 (the negative is unlabelled).

The costs of the first year's work on the Lake Village were borne by the Society. It was recognised, however, that funding a prolonged campaign was beyond its capability and external fund-raising began. In 1893 "circulars asking for pecuniary assistance" were sent to the Somerset Archaeological and Natural History Society (hereafter referred to as SANHS) and the Society of Antiquaries of London.

In 1894 Bulleid concentrated on following the palisade. The length of palisade excavated on the east side of the

Fig.1.2 Bulleid's excavation, probably of Mound 65 in 1893. He has put sticks to mark the wall lines of round houses.

site in 1893 was continued in a southerly direction by a further 90m and in a northerly direction by 30m. Altogether a total length of about 170m had been examined, approximately one third of the circuit. Bulleid also investigated an area outside the palisade but problems were encountered as a result of water levels: "in the latter part of the summer all deep digging was stopped and the more superficial work of examining the Dwelling Mounds undertaken instead." Pumps were in continual use within the settlement area to enable work to continue. £7.12.0d was spent on new pumps and fittings in 1894.

In 1895 work began on 22nd April when it was agreed to examine Mounds 29 and 12 and to continue with the western palisade once water levels allowed.

Fifteen Mounds were excavated in 1896 bringing the total investigated to 30. 150m of the western palisade and extensions outwards were also excavated. The palisade on the west side was considered less strong than on the east and included an 18m gap containing a bank of peat: "the peat wall was kept in place by a single line of upright piles driven down near its centre, the upper parts of the posts being evidently bound together with hurdle work." Some two thirds of the palisade had now been uncovered leaving only that to the north and south untouched. At this stage it was believed that there was a total of 65 Mounds.

1897 was a dry season allowing excavation up to a depth of 3m, something previously not possible. The final lengths of palisade were excavated together with the area outside up to a distance of between 3m and 30m. Eight Mounds were totally or partially excavated along with the areas between. Three hurdles were found close to a beam of morticed oak, "the first distinct proof that some of the dwellings were rectangular."

In March 1898 it was decided that a larger area than usual should be opened in view of the planned visit by the British Association in September. The decision was also taken that "after this year the excavations will be discontinued and it is thought advisable to reserve a portion of the field so that there might be some mounds left to be opened upon special occasions in the future. The excavations have been carried on so systematically that they know every foot of the ground and the plans are so complete that they can locate within a foot where any of the articles discovered had laid."

Bulleid had his own reasons for postponing further excavations, namely, the quantity of finds now accumulated and requiring processing, the poor state of the Museum in Glastonbury, and his personal circumstances. He was engaged to be married and had decided to resume the medical studies which he had previously abandoned. Bulleid wrote to his advisor Robert Munro:

> "I think it will be the better plan to stop work altogether at the end of the coming summer at least for a season or two - to give me an opportunity of preparing things for publishing - but I intend ultimately to finish the whole settlement."

The annual report for 1898 did not appear, but the Society was probably still basking in the President's report of 1897:

> "...the Society had now completed its first decade, and was growing in interest and importance every year. It had now acquired an almost European fame. The discovery of the Lake Village had conferred a lustre upon Glastonbury which no other town in England enjoyed. They held a unique position. The annals of Glastonbury had been rendered more illustrious than ever by the discovery of this ancient village. So numerous and so important were the treasures which had been brought to light by the excavations..."

Flinders Petrie was amongst the visitors to the excavations in 1898. Bulleid was on hand to describe the site; no comment appears as to Petrie's opinion of the work.

The later excavations

The Glastonbury Lake Village remained untouched from 1898 to 1904 other than by a small excavation carried out in 1902, not by Bulleid but by Harold St George Gray. Gray, formerly assistant to Lt. General Pitt-Rivers and with long experience of excavations, had just been appointed Assistant Secretary of SANHS, as well as Curator of the Society's Museum. At the request of SANHS, and with the permission of the owner of the site, the Glastonbury Antiquarian Society, Gray opened up trenches across Mounds 55 and 74, cutting into the central hearth areas.

Gray reported that: "Two new mounds were partly excavated. Cuttings were made through them wide enough to allow room enough for working..."The trenching approach to the site was thus firmly initiated (fig.1.3); Bulleid had previously operated a more open excavation except, regrettably, in his pursuit of the palisade (see Chapter 2).

Gray's work was small in scale and plans for total excavation of the site remained in abeyance. In July 1903 Boyd Dawkins wrote to the President of the Antiquarian Society encouraging completion of the excavations and their full publication. Among his suggestions was that the work should be put in the hands of Gray and that SANHS should organise the campaigns.

The Antiquarian Society Committee discussed Boyd Dawkin's letter in some detail. The conclusions were

Fig.1.3 Excavation by trenching through a Mound. Note the Floor timbers exposed, and cut off, and the hearth stones in right foreground.

that "Mr Arthur Bulleid was the prime mover in this great work of discovering and excavating the British Village and it would be impossible to put him aside and transfer the work to other hands." They did, however, recognise the importance of completing and publishing the excavations and that Bulleid was not going to be able to undertake this work alone. With Bulleid's assent Gray and SANHS were approached "... with the view to his [Gray] working at the completion of the exploration of the site of the British Village in conjunction with Mr A. Bulleid and preparing the complete record for publication, as Mr Bulleid's partner."

SANHS agreed to the proposal, their only reservation being the amount of time that Gray would have to commit if the excavations were to be completed quickly:

> "Mr Gray is equally ready to undertake the work. But, if it was done straightaway it would mean his being absent from the Museum for some months at a stretch, which would be quite impracticable. Moreover, the after-work he would have to do in the way of writing the report, preparing plans, sections, illustrations etc, would occupy him weeks or months longer; and thus still further hamper him in connection with his regular duties.
>
> But, there appears to be an easy way out of the difficulty. Why not carry on a certain portion of the work every year as has been done at Silchester, Caerwent etc. Mr Gray would then go to Godney for two or three weeks at a time - open a crannog and complete it. The work this would involve, he could do easily and thoroughly without seriously interfering with his regular duties. Moreover, he would have time to carefully think over the results as he went along, and thus, probably arrive at valuable conclusions for his ultimate summary of results."

The 1904 excavation season began in mid-May. Tom Paul and three or four men were employed. At the same time it was decided to establish another committee from the ranks of the Excavation Committee whose purpose would be to see through "the preparation and publication of a volume giving a full and detailed account of the excavation and its results at the completion of the work."

The 1905 excavations ran from 12th May to 10th June and Tom Paul was again engaged as supervisor. It was felt that the workforce should also work Saturdays for which they were to receive one shilling per week extra.

In 1906 the excavations lasted for four weeks beginning on 4th May. Dr Munro wrote offering £50 towards the work, providing that the excavations were completed the following year. This was agreed and the money accepted. Munro's money allowed 6 weeks work in 1907 and Bulleid could then write: "The systematic examination of the entire village is now complete, with the exception of a small piece of ground on which the shed stands."

It was a quite extraordinary achievement on the part of Bulleid in particular, but also of Tom Paul the leader of the labouring team and someone entrusted with more than mere trench digging.

The cost of the whole enterprise from start to finish was £697.19.0d. But among the many uncosted elements was Bulleid's own expenses. He had spent about 7 years of full-time work on excavations and immediate post-excavation and conservation procedures, at no salary and few expenses. Money was offered to Bulleid, though not always taken up, to cover his out-of-pocket expenses. In 1894, for example, he received 10 guineas. The following year he did not take the 5 guineas awarded him. The Society presented Bulleid with a cheque for £50 in 1900 as a wedding present in recognition of his services. The arrangements for Gray were equally slender. In 1906 the Antiquarian Society agreed to pay him an honorarium of 10 guineas in recognition of the valuable work that he was doing. Both men received some remuneration from the sale of the publication.

Throughout the excavations as work on a Mound came to an end it was restored as close to its original appearance as possible. The 'central picket' (see below) enabled the correct height to be achieved. Bulleid was happy that on completion of fieldwork the site closely resembled its appearance at the time of discovery.

Conservation

One of the major issues facing Bulleid from the beginning was the treatment of finds to ensure their long term survival for study and display. Bulleid himself undertook much of the work, including pottery restoration. Wood, however, was a particular problem (fig.1.4). Some unsolicited advice was received such as that sent by the Very Reverend Dean of Wells on 6 August 1893 expressing concern about the Iron Age logboat discovered the previous year 1km north of the Lake Village at Crannel Farm and excavated by Bulleid:

> "The boat will crumble up if it continues in that very dry & very hot room with S.W. front: a conservatory needing no fire. It could be put in a tank, or even in a ditch, full of water; such a place as the barton behind Mr Bath's house could spare room for, it might, being wet always, last for years. It is sadly altered since Nov. 92."

Work itemised in the 1892-3 accounts as "Preserving and Moving Boat" and costing £0.17.10d had clearly not been entirely successful.

Bulleid sought advice on the conservation of wood from a variety of authorities, continuing long after the end of the Glastonbury Lake Village excavations. Among the recommendations received was that from Lt. General Pitt-Rivers in 1893 who suggested "metallated spirits of wine" and gelatine. Charles Read of the British Museum offered silicate of soda, and Wilfrid Jackson of Manchester University Museum suggested paraffin wax. Clement Reid proposed slow

Fig.1.4 Part of a wicker basket, maximum width 710mm, height 480mm, found outside the fence N of M46.

drying in a wrapper of brown paper, after which the wood might be varnished or waxed. It is not known whether Bulleid experimented with any of these proposals.

Attention focussed upon wooden artefacts rather than structural timber. The latter received only cursory study and publication. The timber was either discarded at the time of excavation or left in situ. Bulleid's ultimate solution for the artefacts was two-fold; both involved simply keeping the wood wet rather than subjecting the pieces to conservation treatment. It must have been apparent to him that there was no guaranteed solution to the problem of wood conservation. After recording, the larger wooden artefacts such as the ladder were reburied in the waterlogged conditions of the site where they remain today. How well they have survived remains to be tested. A selection of smaller-sized artefacts was placed in glass jars containing a mixture of glycerine and water. Regular monitoring of the fluid levels would have been necessary. The advantage of this method was that the pieces could be displayed in the museum. Remarkably, many of these wooden objects survived to successfully undergo carbowax treatment in 1962, a reflection of the level of care given them in the preceding 70 years.

In spite of the Dean of Wells' concern as to the deteriorating condition of the Crannel Farm log-boat in 1893 it would seem to have received no treatment other than to be allowed to dry out slowly. Subsequent deterioration has been due more to damage resulting from a complete lack of physical protection whilst on display than the lack of conservation treatment. The boat's freeboard is reduced and many fragments doubtless reside as souvenirs.

Specialist Reports

Bulleid was aware from the start that advice and assistance were needed, not only on tackling the excavation but also on the analysis of the finds. The great importance of the site meant that he had little trouble in attracting people with the necessary expertise. Work on the finds was certainly eased with the involvement of Gray from 1902 whose particular interest lay in the artefacts but many other people were involved along the way. Some had their contributions published, others did not. The result was a multi-disciplinary approach including reports on fauna and flora, human remains, the sourcing of stone and pottery and the scientific examination of some categories of artefact. Amongst the latter was the work of J. H. Gladstone of 17 Pembroke Square, London, in 1899, in differentiating between lead and tin artefacts. Specialists persuaded to examine material from the Lake Village included C. W. Andrews (bird bones), Boyd Dawkins (human remains), J. F. Baker and Clement Reid (peat, seeds, wheat cakes and plum stones).

Bulleid wrote the pottery report. Many thumbnail drawings and notes were made of vessels in museums in southern England as he amassed background and comparative data as part of his study. He undertook a Mound-by-Mound analysis of the forms represented using criteria such as rims, ornamentation, cordons, pedestalled bases, etc. This analysis was only published in the form of an overall summary. A fabric analysis was undertaken by J. Allen Howe FGS. From the sample of 'typical pieces of Glastonbury pottery' presented to him, Howe identified 13 distinct fabrics. Bulleid investigated the relationship between fabric and form.

Gray devoted much of his research time to the production of catalogues of most of the small finds, and described, often in great detail, analogous material from British Iron Age sites.

The Museum

The formation of Glastonbury Antiquarian Society arose out of the proposal by J.G.L. Bulleid in 1885 to establish a museum in the town. The arches under the Town Hall, built for use as shambles and market stalls, were unused. The Town Council supported the idea of the museum and made this space available. The site was converted into two rooms at a cost of £300 and the museum opened. The Society's modest collection was dramatically increased by the excavation of the Lake Village. They had a responsibility to place a representative collection of material on display and a vested interest in doing so in terms of the attraction that the displays would have to visitors and the income that this would produce. As the number of finds increased with each season so too did the need for additional accommodation.

The publicity given to the discovery of the Lake Village and the display of the finds had a dramatic effect on numbers visiting the Museum:

1888 476
1889 651
1890 680
1891 816
1892 631
1893 1524
1894 1791
1895 1599
1897 2070
1906 2189

The decline in visitors in 1895 was attributed to particularly poor weather during the summer.

In February 1934 the possibility of transferring the museum displays to the Tribunal in High Street, Glastonbury, was discussed for the first time. One advantage of moving to the Tribunal was that it was in the care of the Office of Works who normally provided a custodian for their properties. The Society would thereby be relieved of this responsibility. Reservations as to the suitability of the building were expressed, notably in respect of limited space and poor lighting. It was not until 1962 that the move to the Tribunal happened.

The Tribunal, now known to be a misnomer, continues as the venue for the display of material from the Lake Village. As part of the series of events organised to mark the centenary of the discovery of the Lake Village a new display, prepared by Somerset County Museums Service, opened in July 1993.

The Collections

Storage of the finds was a continual problem. The Glastonbury Antiquarian Society was ill-prepared to accommodate the vast quantity of material from the Lake Village either in its reserve stores or display cases. The issue was frequently discussed at its committee meetings. Premises rented for storage were generally not well suited for the purpose and were changed at intervals for various reasons, but usually cost. By 1917, the monographs had appeared, and it seemed to some that the Lake Village and its artefacts required no more attention.

The subsequent history of the reserve collections is unclear. The pottery had been transferred to the Abbey gatehouse by the early 1950's. In the minutes for 9 October 1953 is the rather worrying statement "Hon. Secretary reported that permission had been rec'd from the Bath Bequest Trustees to sell pieces of broken pottery now stored in the Abbey Gatehouse."

The various moves, which included the temporary transfer of the finds to Cell 15 in the Territorial Hall, Taunton, for safety during the Second World War, and lack of professional curatorial care inevitably resulted in both loss and damage to the specimens. One of the biggest losses concerns the querns; the whereabouts of only 26% of the numbered specimens is known. The only coin has also gone astray.

Although there had been a responsibility for overseeing the collections for some time and some material, including the pottery, had already been moved to Taunton, it wasn't until 1987 that, by a loan arrangement with the Glastonbury Antiquarian Society, the Lake Village reference archive was formally transferred to the care of the Somerset County Council Museums Service. At this point the remaining reserve collections were moved to Taunton (accession number TTNCM 252/1987).

The importance of the site and wealth of finds resulted in a series of requests for specimens from other museums. In September 1898 Charles Read, Keeper of British and Medieval Antiquities and Ethnography at the British Museum attended a meeting of the General Committee of the Glastonbury Antiquarian Society to discuss the possibility of transferring artefacts to the British Museum. (Bulleid had already given 12 pieces of baked clay sling shot, some pottery and a plaster cast of axe facets in 1895 and a copy wooden bowl in 1897, all in his own name.) Pressure was brought to bear in pursuance of this particular request. Grants had been made by the British Association towards the excavations and one of the General Regulations attached to the award was that there should be "some practical acknowledgement of the help so rendered." Read argued that in this case the 'acknowledgement' should consist of the gift of finds to the national museum. This arm-twisting was refuted by John Morland who denied that any such conditions had been attached to the grant to the Society. However, both Morland and Bulleid supported the principle that material should be placed permanently in the British Museum and Bulleid was given the responsibility of selecting items which would go to the full committee for approval.

The Society, however, failed to implement the decision and Read applied further pressure. In 1904 the Society applied to the Society of Antiquaries for a grant towards excavation costs. Read, in his capacity as Secretary of the Society of Antiquaries, responded to the application on 24th November 1904: "I am directed to inform you that the Council cannot consider such a grant until it is informed what steps your Committee proposes to take towards carrying into effect its resolution of 15th September 1898."

The Society responded by stating, quite sensibly, that whilst it intended to adhere to the 1898 decision, it did not intend to part with any of the finds until the excavations had been completed and published. In May 1905 the subject was raised once again at an Antiquarian Society committee. This time it relented and "an instalment of duplicates" was to be sent to the British Museum. Bulleid's selection was approved on 6th June 1905. The director of the British Museum duly wrote expressing his gratitude and a cheque for £10 towards the Excavation Fund was received from the Society of Antiquaries. Twenty-four artefacts were selected for the British Museum and over the years 1905 and 1906 others followed (see Appendix 1.1).

The first approach regarding acquisition of Lake Village finds by SANHS was made in October 1902 to Charles Grant, chairman of the Glastonbury Antiquarian Society:

> "....when they [General Committee] meet we shall be glad if you will kindly ask them to be good enough to consider the still larger question of giving us from your ample stores a selection of articles sufficient to fill a case in our Great Hall. It seems a great pity that one of the most interesting and important archaeological discoveries made in Somerset should remain unrepresented in the County Museum; especially as the things you have packed away are serving no useful purpose where they are. Here they would afford pleasure to thousands of people and would help to foster a taste for and further knowledge on subjects which we all have much at heart."

It was agreed unanimously to lend material to SANHS though the transfer did not take place until 1905. The objects concerned are listed in Appendix 1.1.

The British Museum and Somerset County Museum were not alone in wishing to acquire material from Glastonbury Lake Village. In February 1912 a request from Mr H. Balfour for six pieces of sling shot for display in the Pitt-Rivers Museum, Oxford, was approved. In 1913 Professor Boyd Dawkins asked for a selection of the Lake Village relics for Manchester Museum. Dawkins was to be one of the contributors to the second volume of the Glastonbury Lake Village report. His request for specimens carried with it the threat that he was not prepared "to move" with his contribution until "the Society had recognised his claim." Bulleid supported the request and approval was given. However, nothing was done about it as is clear from the minutes of the Monograph Committee held on 31st May 1915:

> "Mr Gray reported that the completion of Volume II could not be effected until after the next Christmas at the earliest and that the publication of such volume was delayed because Professor Boyd Dawkins would not send in his chapter on animal bones until the Society had sent to the Manchester Museum the selection of relics which he required."

The material was sent off shortly afterwards (see Appendix 1.1).

In 1938 "a bag of pottery" was lent to the Royal Institution of South Wales, Swansea. In 1961 other material including pottery, worked bone and antler, loom weights, worked stone and flints was lent to Leeds Museum for an exhibition on the British early Iron Age; it was returned in 1992.

Not all requests were approved. In 1927 Birmingham Central Technical College was refused one ounce of lead wanted for analytical purposes. It was considered that analysis of a single piece of lead would serve no useful scientific purpose. Mr Andrews was turned down when he requested duplicate bird bones for the British Museum in 1901.

Publication

In 1894 Bulleid read a paper to SANHS at a meeting at Langport. The County Society who were to publish the paper in their Proceedings, suggested that the print-run could be extended and that the paper could form a guide to the excavations. The Glastonbury Antiquarian Society agreed to the proposal and also to enhance the guide with additional articles by Munro, Boyd Dawkins and Evans dealing respectively with the discovery of the site, the place of the Lake Village in British archaeology and Greek and Italian influences in pre-Roman Britain. A print-run of 1,000 was approved at a cost of £10.8.4d or twopence halfpenny each, Barnicott and Pearce of Taunton were the printers. The booklets sold for one shilling. It sold well and a further 1,000 were printed in 1896. A third, revised edition was published in 1899.

A Publishing Committee to deal with the full publication of the excavations was formed in 1907 and comprised Morland, Clark, Bulleid, Gray and Grant. Bulleid and Gray were to be the editors. The decisions reached at the first meeting held in 1908 were that the publication would be in one volume, with copyright belonging to Glastonbury Antiquarian Society. By 1910 it was clear that two volumes would be required. Volume 1 was published in 1911, volume 2 in 1917.

In 1911, just as the first volume appeared, *The Illustrated London News* carried a lengthy report by Arthur Bulleid

Fig.1.5 Reconstruction drawing of the Lake Village by A. Forestier.

Fig.1.6 Metalworking. Forestier's drawing of 1911

on the Lake Village. It was well-illustrated and was provocatively titled "Not the Woad-daubed Savage of the Old History Books: the Civilised Ancient Briton." This report did much to publicise the Lake Village, and several of its illustrations are reproduced in the present book (e.g. figs.1.5 and 1.6).

There were twenty-nine chapters in the two Glastonbury Lake Village volumes, 101 plates, 179 drawings and 724 pages - all for £2.2.0d. Bulleid contributed the major chapter on a description of the Lake Village, Mound-by-Mound, illustrated by his own plans and sections (fig.1.7). He also wrote about the environment, the wooden objects, the pottery, querns and stones. Lawrence Bulleid, his brother, contributed a colour frontispiece of a selection of the glass beads. Gray wrote 14 chapters on all the other finds, and various specialists (most of them Fellows of the Royal Society or other high order) supplied chapters on animals and plants. The final two chapters were by Boyd Dawkins on the inhabitants of the village, their racial and linguistic characters, and here he proposed the idea that the village had been terminated not by natural events such as flooding but by a massacre of the occupants. It took Bulleid a number of years to dispose of this theory which had no basis in any of the evidence that he had recovered so carefully.

Subsequent developments

Following the completion of the excavations at the Glastonbury Lake Village, Bulleid and Gray continued to work together in excavations at Meare, and in 1924 Bulleid wrote a small booklet *The Lake Villages of Somerset*; it was published by the Glastonbury Antiquarian Society and it was dedicated to John Morland. The booklet was enormously popular and is now in its seventh edition. Gray was annoyed that the booklet appeared under the sole authorship of Bulleid and he refused to sell it in the Somerset Society's premises at Taunton. There is no reference to it in the correspondence between the two, or in any of the excavation records.

The site remains in the possession of Glastonbury Antiquarian Society. The responsible approach taken by the Society has ensured that the field has been used in a manner appropriate to its significance. The land has been rented out for pasture; it has not been ploughed, drained or in any way improved. Excavations in more recent years have shown this policy to have resulted in a high degree of preservation of the remaining archaeology.

In 1968 and 1969 Michael Avery of Queen's University, Belfast, cut three small trenches in an attempt to locate the palisade in the north western part of the site. The excavations failed in this respect and the results of this fieldwork have yet to be published.

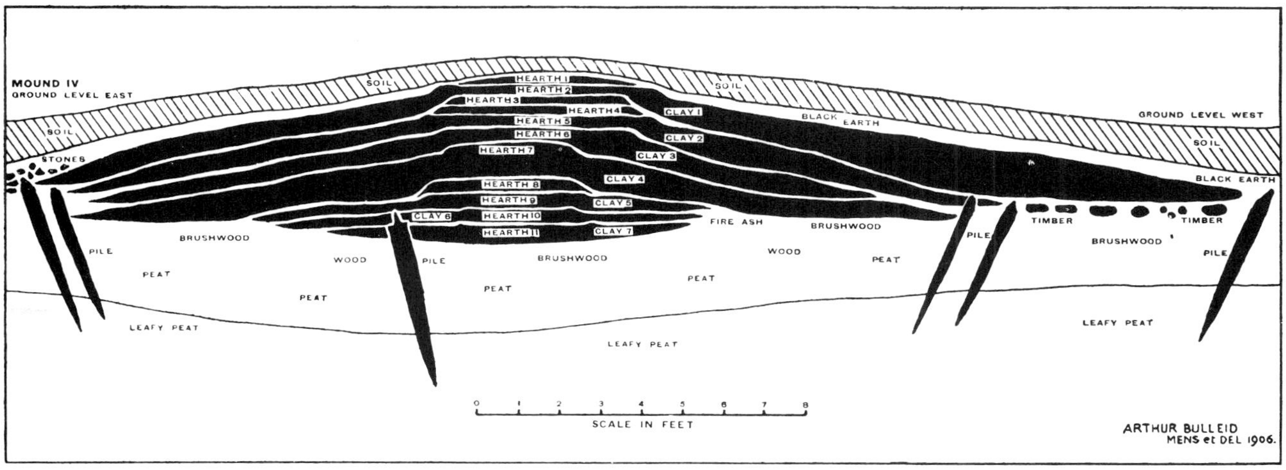

Fig.1.7 Bulleid's section drawing of Mound 4 with its Floors, hearths, foundation wood and wall posts.

In 1984 the Somerset Levels Project carried out further work on the site (Coles, Coles and Morgan 1988,57-62). Three small trenches were excavated in the north, west and east of the settlement. The purpose was to obtain samples for environmental analysis, to search for economic evidence, to examine any residues left by Bulleid and Gray and to assess the condition of the surviving archaeological deposits. The results are noted in Chapters 3, 4 and 5.

Background to the Chapter 3 finds list

One item missing from Bulleid and Gray's volumes is a complete sequential list of finds cross-referenced to their Mounds of origin. The nature of the find reports makes it very difficult to access entries on specific artefacts. Boyd Dawkins recommended that volume 2 should have such a list but the additional printing cost was considered too high. We have resurrected this idea, added corrections and new information, and it appears as Appendix 3.1. For each small find number the main publication reference by volume and page number and the Mound or nearest Mound to its findspot is given. This allows referral to more detailed information on provenance, where it exists, in both the original reports and the artefact lists in Chapter 3 of this monograph. Presentation of the data in this way also gives an overview of the variability in the level of recording between different categories of artefact. By far the most anomalous is flint where only 53 out of a total of up to 386 small finds numbers (13.7%) have any provenance or publication data.

This may be a convenient place to describe Bulleid's system of numbering the finds, as we have retained it throughout the book. Bulleid numbered all small finds from the site using an alpha-numeric system. Each object is prefixed by a letter which in most cases, but not all, denotes the raw material from which the object was made. As discoveries were made each was given an individual number. The prefixes used were as follows:

A amber
B bone
C crucibles
D baked clay (prefixed B.C. in the early years)
E bronze (prefixed Br. in the early years)
F flint
G glass
H antler
I iron
J jet
K shale
L lead and tin
M human bone
P pottery
Q querns
S stone
T tusks
W spindle whorls
X worked wood
Y unbaked clay
Z coins (including currency bars)

Our catalogue of finds by Mound in Chapter 3 provides data on provenance gathered from various sources: volumes 1 and 2 of the published report (finds reports, Mound descriptions and site plans), the interim reports published in the Proceedings of the Somerset Archaeological and Natural History Society (PSANHS) in 1902, 1904, 1905, 1906 and 1907, the small finds catalogue (Black Book of Relics), surviving excavation records and notes held by Somerset Record Office and the markings on objects and containers. The latter were particularly important for unpublished and unnumbered finds. A proportion of the collection remains unprovenanced simply because the data were not recorded or have not survived.

Prior to excavation the centre or highest point of each Mound was marked by a post. This 'central picket' was used to plan the Floors and the position of artefacts within and adjacent to the Mound. However, the finds have been re-assessed in relation to their nearest published Mound, since the central picket selected as the base point wasn't necessarily the central picket of the nearest Mound; it could instead be the one on the nearest Mound under excavation at the time. There is therefore some variation in artefact provenance between Bulleid and Gray's report and the present work. With few exceptions everything found outside a Mound is unstratified, the only data available being the distance from a nearby 'central picket'.

A number of discrepancies were found between sources of data on provenance. This was inevitable in view of the scale of the excavations and quantity of finds. Some of the discrepancies identified are listed in Appendix 1.2 (the list is not comprehensive).

From the artefactual point of view, pottery is a particular problem. There is a large quantity of it, though by no means all was saved, and it is particularly poorly provenanced and recorded. A small proportion of the pottery is individually numbered, the sequence running from P 1 onwards. The reasoning behind the allocation of find numbers to some pieces and not others is unknown. Some numbered sherds, but by no means all, were published and most, but not all, are decorated (fig.1.8). Many decorated sherds did not receive a number. The bulk of the pottery remains unprocessed. The cost and the limited potential of such an exercise, due to the lack of contextual data, meant that this large body of material was left mostly untouched in the current research. Only decorated pottery is included in the Chapter 3 finds lists.

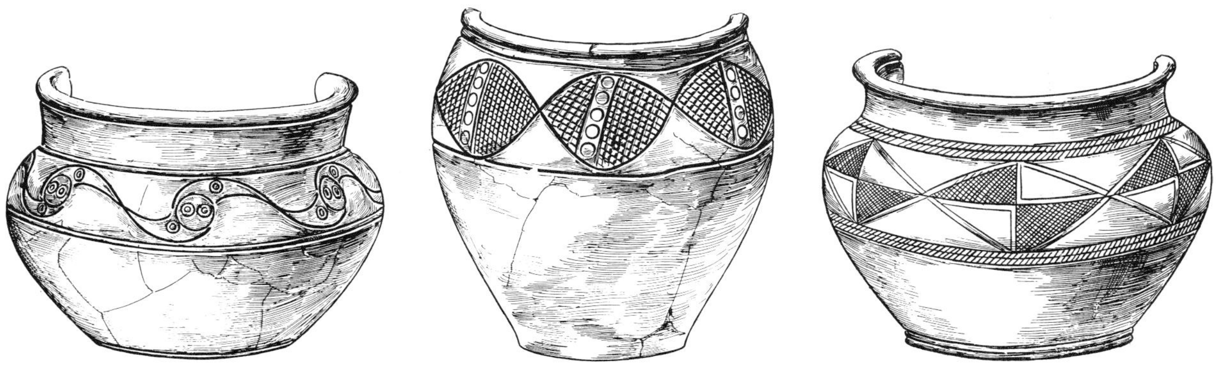

Fig.1.8 Bulleid's drawings of pottery prepared for the final report.

Appendix 1.1 Material accessed into other collections.

Note: these lists are based upon records in Taunton; whilst they are believed to be largely correct, there may be a few discrepancies.

British Museum:

B 12, B 32, B 68, B 147, B 196, B 219, B 231, B 274, B 288, B 327, B 332, B 341, B 357, B 367, B 369, B 375, B 379, B 382, B 443, C 11, E 31, E 49, E 77, E 160, E 195, E 197, F 43X3, F 57, F 70, F 207, F 241, F 365, F 368, F 370, G 13, H 4, H 76, 129, H 134, H 136, H 142, H 170, H 205, H 217, H 285, H 287, H 290, H 292, H 298, H 303, H 308, H 309, H 325, HS 25, I 76, I 88, K 23, L 6, P 163, P 170, Q 10, Q 34, S 31, S 33, S 35, T 2, W 26, W 66, W 75, WS 85, WS 108, WS 135, WS 137, WS 159, WS 177, WS 194, WS 210, WS 238, WS 240, WS 259 plus 21 pieces of baked clay, a loom weight, 11 pieces of worked bone, 3 boar tusks, a piece of worked antler, and 4 other pieces of pottery. To these were added P 79 and P 86 in 1950 and P 115, P 156 and P 157 in 1951. The last three were a loan.

Somerset Archaeological and Natural History Society (now in the care of the Somerset County Museums Service):

B 160, B 237, B 304, B 328, B 381, B 395, C 7, E 23, E 82, F 43, F 58, G 28, H 5, H 167, H 253, H 299, H 304, H 313, K 18, L 8, P 167, T 11, W 172, plus a partly perforated ball of baked clay from Mound 70.

Manchester Museum:

B 39, B 42, B 79, B 95, B 118, B 155, B 171, B 187, B 253, B 309, B 333, B 360, B 362, B 397, B 400, B 412, F 36, F 67, F 117, F 145, F 373, H 25, H 46, H 90, H 116, H 196, H 263, H 383, HS 1, HS 3, W 25, W 46, W 90, W 116, W 196, W 263, W 383, WS 136, WS 178, WS 243 and various unnumbered finds:
1 flint saw, hammerstone, 5 whetstones, 9 clay sling pellets, 14 daub fragments, 20 pot sherds, 2 pieces of worked antler, 3 boar tusks, 9 pebbles, 3 pot boilers, 1 facetted stone, 2 loom weights and a sample of peas.

Appendix 1.2 Mislocations and misattributions of relics.

B 273 is shown as SW of M4 on the plan, but the finds book states that it came from within the Mound NNE of the Central Picket (c.p.)
B 299 is plotted on the plan twice, to the NE and SE of M5
E 84 is described as coming from Floor 3 of M27 but is shown on the plan as lying outside the Mound
E 191 is shown as coming from SE of M58 whilst the finds book gives its derivation as Floor 2
H 183 is listed as coming from M9 but appears on M27 on the plan
H 336 is recorded in the finds book as having been found in M71, but the published description and plan ascribe it to M83
H 357 is derived from M79 according to the published description, but the finds book and plan state that it was M74
K 10 is wrongly written as X 10 on the plan
M 35 is listed as having been found on Floor 1 of M55 but is shown as lying to the SW of the Mound on the published plan
M 39 comes from Floor 2 of M71 according to the finds catalogue but Floor 3 in the published report
P 112 is published as coming from M72 but the finds book and plan show it to be from outside the palisade to the north of M48
P 275 is published as M30 and is published in the finds catalogue as such but the label on the sherd attributes it to M56. As the label was applied to the sherd some time after the excavations this is probably where the error lies
W 99 appears twice on the plan
W 163 is plotted twice on the plan, to the north and south of the c.p. of M33
X 66 is described as having been found outside the palisade whilst the plan appears to show it within
X 90 is shown to the south east of both M21 and M22

Appendix 1.3 Concordance of the Mound numbering systems.

Bulleid initially used an alphabetical system for identifying the Mounds. This was later replaced by Roman numerals, presumably because of the ever-increasing complexity of the original system. The former was used in some of the early reports and the latter in the 1911 and 1917 volumes. For ease of use the Roman numerals have been changed to Arabic figures in the present volume. To avoid confusion a concordance of the different systems of labelling is given overleaf.

Gray complicated the situation when he began work on the site in 1902 excavating Mounds 55 and 74. Instead of continuing Bulleid's numbering system he numbered and published these Mounds as 1 and 2 respectively.

Bulleid's Original	1911 + 1917 Monographs	Numeric (this volume)	Bulleid's Original	1911 + 1917 Monographs	Numeric (this volume)	Bulleid's Original	1911 + 1917 Monographs	Numeric (this volume)
A	I	1	GG	XXXII	32	NNN	LXIII	63
B	II	2	HH	XXXIII	33	OOO	LXIV	64
C	III	3	JJ	XXXIV	34		LXV	65
D	IV	4	KK	XXXV	35		LXVI	66
E	V	5	LL	XXXVI	36		LXVII	67
F	VI	6	MM	XXXVII	37		LXVIII	68
G	VII	7	NN	XXXVIII	38		LXIX	69
H	VIII	8	OO	XXXIX	39		LXX	70
J	IX	9	PP	XL	40		LXXI	71
K	X	10	QQ	XLI	41		LXXII	72
L	XI	11	RR	XLII	42		LXXIII	73
M	XII	12	SS	XLIII	43		LXXIV	74
N	XIII	13	TT	XLIV	44		LXXV	75
O	XIV	14	UU	XLV	45		LXXVI	76
P	XV	15	VV	XLVI	46		LXXVII	77
Q	XVI	16	WW	XLVII	47		LXXVIII	78
R	XVII	17	XX	XLVIII	48	'a'	LXXIX	79
S	XVIII	18	YY	XLIX	49	'b'	LXXX	80
T	XIX	19	ZZ	L	50	QA	LXXXI	81
U	XX	20	AAA	LI	51	HHa	LXXXII	82
V	XXI	21	BBB	LII	52	YYa	LXXXIII	83
W	XXII	22	CCC	LIII	53	Va	LXXXIV	84
X	XXIII	23	DDD	LIV	54	Vb	LXXXV	85
Y	XXIV	24	EEE	LV	55	Ea	LXXXVI	86
Z	XXV	25	FFF	LVI	56		LXXXVII	87
AA	XXVI	26	GGG	LVII	57		LXXXVIII	88
BB	XXVII	27	HHH	LVIII	58		LXXXVIX	89
CC	XXVIII	28	JJJ	LIX	59		XC	90
DD	XXIX	29	KKK	LX	60			
EE	XXX	30	LLL	LXI	61			
FF	XXXI	31	MMM	LXII	62			

Chapter 2

Critical analysis of the record

At the completion of the excavations in 1907 Bulleid and Gray were faced with a daunting task - to publish the results of eleven years work on a site clogged with structural remains, deep and complex stratigraphy, and rich in the yield of Relics. Bulleid had made pencil plans of the Mounds as they were excavated, and drawn some sections in his notebooks. Gray had his own set of notebooks and a 'Black Book' in which he entered lists of finds, arranged by the categories already noted (Bone, Glass, Antler, Whorls, etc). Pottery had been divided into Decorated and Plain, with rather little attention paid to the latter. Looking at the quantities of evidence of all kinds from our position some 90 years later, it seems that both men were to some extent overwhelmed by the prospect of putting it all in some order, and it may be that they were subconsciously aware that there were going to be difficulties with the records made during the years of excavation. The few notebooks that have survived show a rather disturbing state of disorganisation in record-taking, but both men were clearly capable of accurate planning and documentation. In this chapter we will try to conduct some sort of source critical analysis, to see the problems and thereby to gain an understanding of what can be deemed reliable in our own interpretive efforts. This will also have relevance in assessing the work of others who have tried to reinterpret the published evidence. Our own sources of information are, of course, the two large volumes of Bulleid and Gray (1911 and 1917), the Relics which have survived in identifiable condition, the various notebooks mentioned above, sketch drawings and photographs (the latter surviving as glass negatives), a large amount of correspondence, the Minute Books of the Glastonbury Antiquarian Society, various reports in the Proceedings of the Somerset Archaeological and Natural History Society, and the crucially important Black Book of Relics in which the findspots and contexts of artefacts were listed by Gray and later checked and often amended in his handwriting. The Black Book and one of the Minute Books have only recently come to light after a period of misplacement. We have taken all these sources into consideration, and have also had the benefit of small excavations on the site to gauge the character of the deposits and appreciate the difficulties of recognition in the field.

The major elements in our analysis of this site are threefold: environment, structure, context. Are the observations made by the excavators sufficiently detailed and reliable to warrant our acceptance of them as bases for reinterpretations or, indeed, to allow us to confirm original opinions about conditions, houses and activities? Current views about the environment of the Lake Village are expressed in Chapter 5 by Rupert Housley who has carried out a large series of corings and analyses in the immediate area of the site, as well as transects across the moors. The careful opinion of Harry Godwin (1981,40) was that Bulleid was a careful observer and could be relied upon. Bulleid's general ideas about the environment were not far from what we can demonstrate today, although many refinements are now possible. The other two aspects - structural evidence and the contextual evidence for the Relics - are examined now.

Structural Evidence

Bulleid's aim right from the start of the work was to excavate the entire site. After five years of work, and various difficulties which we outline in our 1992 book (Coles, Goodall and Minnitt 1992), he was as determined as ever: "I mean to finish the village . . . if it takes 20 years to accomplish . . . if I have to do the work with my own hands". By the end of 1907 he could write "the systematic examination of the whole village is now complete . . . the excavations were begun in March 1892, and have therefore been in progress sixteen years".

Although Bulleid was, by all accounts, a careful excavator and was eager to measure and record, his general plan of the site in its local setting is more a sketch than a detailed location plan. It has been difficult to identify the Lake Village Mounds that now survive (restored by Bulleid) with his plan of the site, and one attempt at this in our 1984 excavation report (Coles, Coles and Morgan 1988) was only partly successful (and not helped by two lettering mistakes in our published plan, misnumbered Mounds 4 and 85). A more determined effort has now been made and is reproduced here as figure 2.1; this uses a newly-drawn version of Bulleid's Mound plans fitted with no real difficulty onto a modern field plan, and it should be accurate to about two metres within the field.

A very surprising omission from the 1911 monograph was a contour plan of the site. Bulleid was advised by O. G. S. Crawford on how to prepare a contour plan when Bulleid and Gray were working at Meare in 1921, long after the Glastonbury excavations had ended. Gray, in 1902, working his way into the site, commented adversely on the lack of a contour plan and demonstrated the concept in his excavation report on his trenches into Mounds 55 and 74 (Gray 1902). For whatever reason, Gray did not extend his technique to the surviving or restored parts of the site when, in 1904, he became partner to Bulleid in the excavations to complete the examination of the entire settlement. Bulleid was more successful in his horizontal planning of the site; in 1892 he had instructions from C. W. Dymond on the setting of pegs over a Mound to create a complete recording system for finds as well as structures.

GLASTONBURY LAKE VILLAGE

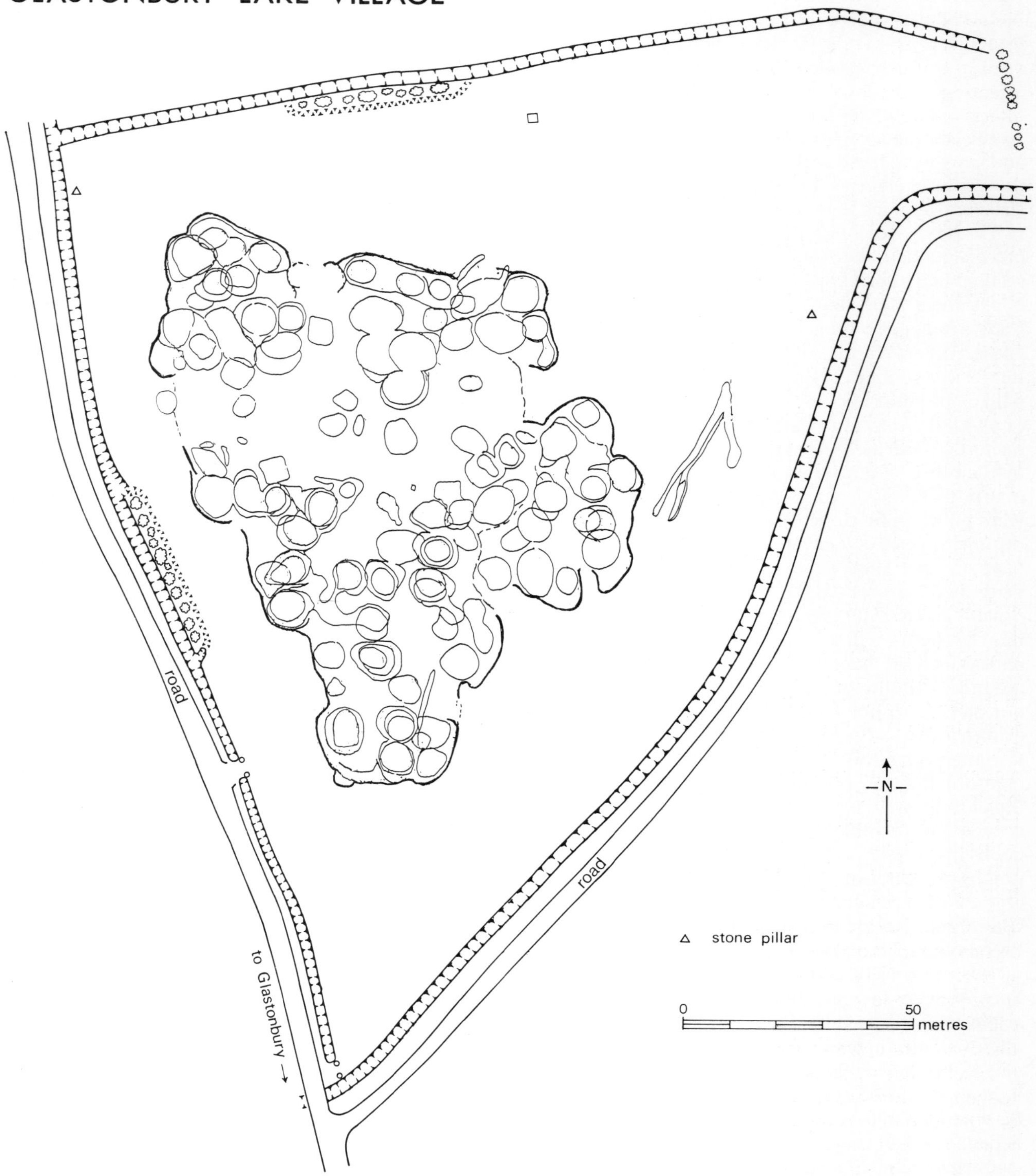

Fig.2.1 Field plan of the Lake Village with Bulleid's drawing of the site and Somerset Levels Project's modern field outline. The stone pillars marked the Antiquarian Society's boundary; the small square at the top is a sampling pit opened by the Project (see Chapter 5)

Dymond also advised on the quadrant method of excavation to give sections across Mounds. Advice from all quarters came in the matter of context (see below) but a general comment from Robert Munro as early as 1893 referred to Pitt-Rivers and the techniques developed by this experienced excavator "... leave undisturbed whatever novel objects you expose. You may have to deal with a Harbour or Bulwark of some kind or the village well. You are always on sure ground with a Mound ... put yourself unreservedly in the hands of Gen. Pitt-Rivers in regard to the method of excavating". This advice was probably a little confusing to

Bulleid; "leave undisturbed" was of course impossible, and Pitt-Rivers did not visit in time to help Bulleid establish a regime for recording both horizontal and vertical features. As we will see, the absence of much attention to the levels within each Mound seriously affects our ability to interpret the records, and makes more elaborate attempts very suspect.

There is very little information available about the excavation methodology used by Bulleid, and later by Bulleid and Gray. When Munro visited the site in the first season (September 1892) he saw two long parallel trenches cut through Mounds 62 - 65, with shorter trenches off at right angles from one of the long trenches. Although four Mounds were being examined, there were "large intervening spaces untouched". These presumably were excavated later, but seemingly in the same year (1892) as the area was thereafter untouched until 1904 when some work on the east side of these Mounds was carried out. Bulleid refers to lying on a plank for several days in cleaning up some hurdles under one Mound elsewhere on the site, and his photographs often show structural elements very clearly exposed and clearly recorded. He rarely allowed his labourers to do much of the detailed cleaning. Photographs of the site under excavation are not abundant, and many glass negatives are lost, probably destroyed. Those that survive show both open excavation, with perhaps half a Mound exposed, or more constricted trenches. Gray seems to have favoured narrow trenches at the later Meare excavations, and probably had preferred these at Glastonbury as well from 1902 onwards. The 27 sections that Bulleid drew (see below) show that a number of Mounds had a vertical cutting made. The photographs of the work also show the long scars through the deposits made by the men who worked with sharp spades, cutting vertically into the peat and clays (figs.2.2 and 2.3). It is very difficult to see how a thin clay floor could be distinguished by this approach.

The plans made by Bulleid are the basis for all efforts at interpretation of the site. They are reproduced in the 1911 book at "full size" as drawn in the field, one eighth of an inch = one foot (1/96). Bulleid put a metal post, called a central picket or c.p. on the plans, into the centre of each Mound, and used lines and a large T-square to take the field measurements, all recorded in relation to the c.p. Often he and Gray recorded finds of Relics or other debris as compass orientations from the c.p., so an object was x feet x inches x direction from the c.p. (e.g. 12' 6" NNE of c.p.). The directions only cover 16 possible orientations (N, NNE, NE, ENE, E etc) and as Mound clays were uneven in their spread, objects not detailed on Bulleid's plan cannot so easily be related to Mound edges with this scheme; some fall outside, some inside the Mounds. Most of the individual Relics, being carefully gathered by Gray in particular, are located on the plans, but general spreads or dumps are not always shown.

The principal excavator from 1892 to 1907 was Tom Paul, "whose interest in the excavation never failed from beginning to end. He removed the first turf, and was the last to leave the field upon completion of the exploration". In 1899, Bulleid was happy to acknowledge Paul as a friend as well as a labourer, and as someone who could be relied upon to take care in handling specimens in the museum as well as in the field; Gray employed him in his trenching exercise of 1902. The expertise of Paul was clearly a very important element in the continuation, year by year, of the excavations. Mound after Mound was examined, edges of floors drawn on the plan, floors distinguished only with great difficulty and sometimes not at all, and Relics seen, plotted and collected. The incomplete arcs of stakes that appear on the plans suggest that, in places, the men cut them away accidentally, or on purpose; it was deliberately done at Meare when the men felt that their progress along the trenches was going too slowly. Thin floors of clay, ash and charcoal spreads, a scatter of seeds or of potsherds, lines of stones, minute beads or disintegrating wood or iron or unbaked clay objects, all could hardly be left unharmed by the spading approach in narrow trenches, or sometimes even on more open excavated areas. There is nothing in the records to say where or when such events occurred, mostly of course because the note-takers were not aware of them.

The plan (fig.2.4) shows the entire site and the years in which its parts were examined. Exact edges of trenches or areas opened are not known from the surviving records except in the most general way and the extent of the palisade exploratory trenches of 1893-96 is not fully recorded. This trenching around the entire site was probably a disaster, in separating the surviving Mounds from the outside environmental record, as well as creating problems for subsequent seasons when the relationship of palisade to Mound edges could not be ascertained; the plans of the NW section of the site are very confused as the 1905-06 excavations do not tie into one another at the palisade. The 'limits of excavation' are shown on all of Bulleid's plans, and are entirely geometric; we think this may be a cosmetic effect produced for the publication, and suggest that the edges were less regular. However, some Relics are marked on the plans very near these edges and probably the men worked close to the programmed lines even if the full depth and precise edges were not achieved. Bulleid also sent his men to dig holes well away from the palisade, and they discovered various fragments of pottery, bone and/or worked wood at distances and directions as follows:

from Mound 1	26m South
from Mound 48	20m North East
from Mound 47	45m North

These finds were not followed up and no further mention is made of them in the assessment of the site.

The site of the Lake Village covered an area of about 8900 square metres (circa one hectare) and was dug in two separate periods 1892-98 and 1904-07. In the first

Fig.2.2 Excavation through Mound 9 with hearths exposed at various levels (2.2a) and the decorated hearth preserved (2.2b).

Fig.2.3 Excavation of a hearth with Floor timbers exposed. Note the spade marks as the several upper Floors were cut through.

period, Bulleid worked with a team of 2-6 men, usually 3, for 4-6 months each year. The men worked from 7 am to 6 pm each day, and Bulleid was generally on site both before and after these 11-hour shifts. In the second period Bulleid and Gray had a team of 8 men and worked for 4-6 weeks each year. Two-thirds of the site were excavated in the first period, one-third in the second period. The teams shifted well in excess of 1000 tonnes of deposits by hand during the work. Flooding was always a problem, and sometimes the work had to be abandoned; what it did to the clays of the Mounds and to organic material can only be guessed, but it must have been a messy business at times. Visitors were often driven away by floods or gales. Although the area of the excavations can be calculated, the overall depth of the explorations is more difficult to gauge. The palisade trenching extended to 2m in some places, and 1.5m in most. The Mounds were examined to below the clay floors, into and sometimes through the foundation timbers.

Some calculations are possible as a help in assessing the 'rate of strike' and therefore likelihood of care in the work. The average Mound was 8m diameter and had 0.645m depth of clay floor deposits. The overburden of silt was 250mm on average. The foundation could be 0.5m thick. The unmounded areas of the site were approximately 50% of the whole site. The palisade was 380m in extent and was dug to an average 1.5m depth. The amount of material moved by the small teams was enormous, some peat, some rock, some timber, much clay, and all of it waterlogged. Table 2.1 provides a small indication of the excavation progress year by year.

Table 2.1 Mound excavations by year

Year	Complete	Partial	Palisade
1892	3	3	
1893	10	1	E
1894	10	4	SE, ENE
1895	7	-	W, NW, N
1896	6	3	S, SW, NE
1897	5	-	
1898	15	2	
1902	-	2	
1904	2	5	
1905	4	7	
1906	3	6	
1907	7	7	
	72	*40*	

There is a confusion in the excavation dates for two Mounds. According to Bulleid (1911,63-64), M41 was fully excavated in 1894, and it was also partly excavated in the same year. Also, M52 was fully excavated in 1894, and in 1898 too. Table 2.1 shows that 56 Mounds were fully excavated in the first period of digging, and 16 Mounds in the second period, along with 13 and 25

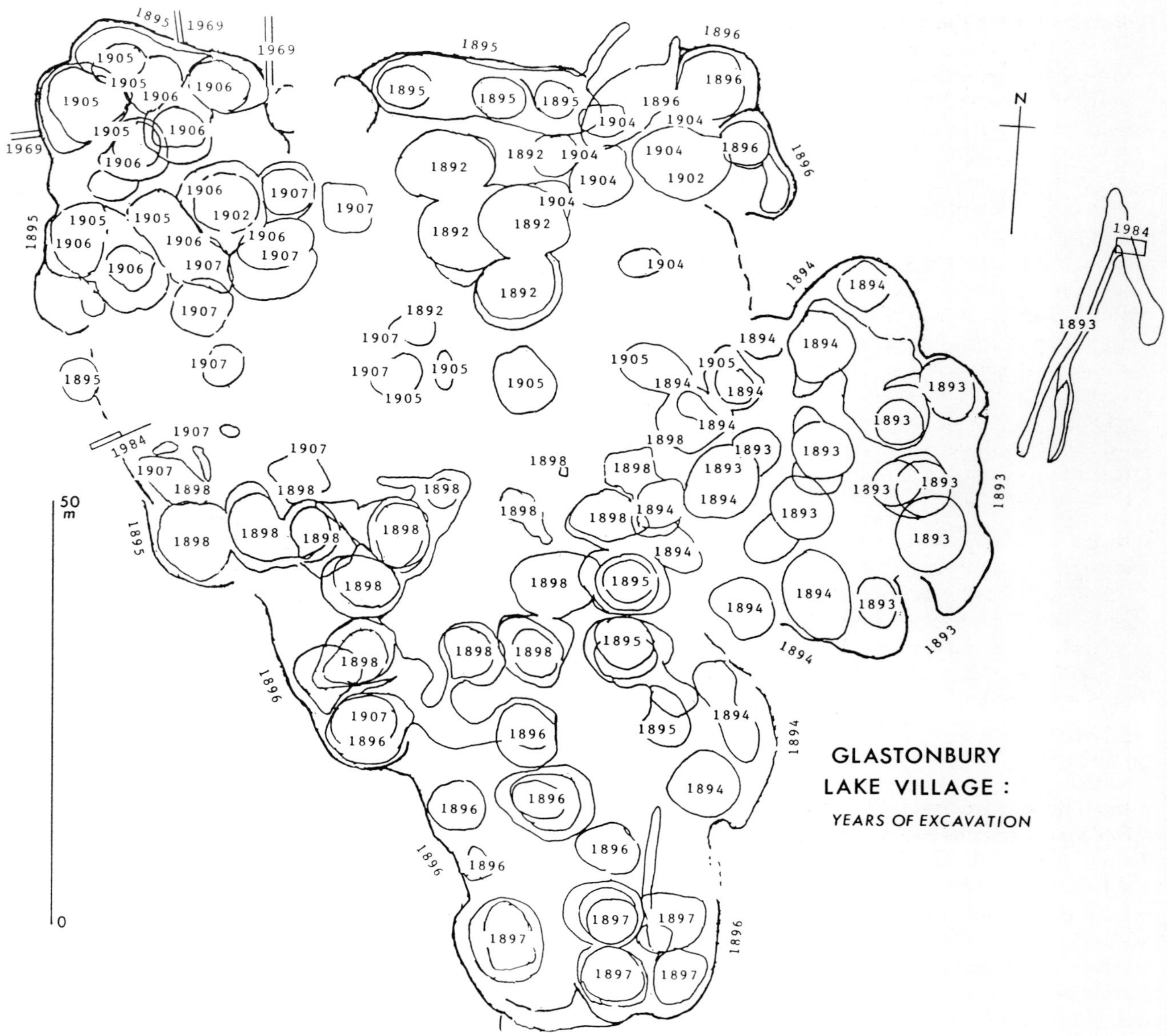

Fig.2.4 Plan of the site showing the years of excavation. JMC

partial examinations respectively, and the full palisade in the first period. In 1892-98, 100 man-weeks were worked per year; that is 700 man-weeks in the period. By calculating the number of Mounds excavated (56 + 13 partial + palisade @ 15 Mounds), we come out with a rate of 9 men for one week for one Mound. For 1904-07, 50 man-weeks per year and extras in 1907 make 220 man-weeks total. Mounds examined (16 + 24 partial) are at a rate of 8 men for one week for one Mound, but we must add the exploration of the unmounded areas in the central west and north-east areas so the rate is more like 6 or 7 men for one week for one Mound. There is not much difference in the two periods on this rather crude basis, which ignores the fact that Bulleid, in 1892-98, chose to excavate almost all of the largest most prominent Mounds, hence those with the most floors of clay and often most artefacts to recover. This reduces his 'advantage' over the 1902-07 rate, as we will see later in this chapter. It may be worth mentioning here that the Somerset Levels Project excavated a small Mound at Meare Village West in 1979, and one and a half small Mounds at Meare Village East in 1982; each Mound had little depth of deposits. The Project's rate, as compared with that of Bulleid and Gray, works out at 64 and 60 persons for one week for one Mound at the West and East sites, respectively. None of the Project's workers were full-time labourers, and Tom Paul was not there (unfortunately), so shifting overburden was very slow.

Comparisons may be invidious, but it is clear, to us at least, that the excavations of Bulleid and Gray were done at some speed, and probably too fast for adequate observation and record as well as retrieval of small Relics and separation of thin floors. Bulleid in particular was very inexperienced at the beginning, as his Committee of Advice indicates (Coles, Goodall and Minnitt 1992,13) and this inexperience shows in his strategy for the site and in his recording of Relics (see below). He was a determined worker, however, and a fast learner, and the quality of his plans and his sections are excellent for the time, and exceed those of some professional archaeologists working in the late 1890s. The quality of the excavations of 1892-98 depended upon the labourers to a very great extent, trenching at depth in wet deposits or working across an open excavation, spading around wooden pegs, posts and stakes, hurdlework fragments, palisade posts lying at angles, and around hearths of clay and floor edges, and separating thin clay floors, all the while seeing and picking up small finds and heaps of pottery, stone, bone, seeds and wood. Bulleid must have been very assiduous in creating a record of all this material, while managing the domestic operations of the site and the care of the objects. By 1896, four rooms at the top of his father's house in Glastonbury were filled to overflowing with finds.

In the second period of excavation, 1904-07, Gray brought his experience with Pitt-Rivers and others to the work. Two-thirds of the site had already been examined, and much of what remained was unmounded, according to surface indications. Most of the big Mounds were already excavated and so a wider open plan of work was probably in order; the records are very poor but it seems that trenching was the preferred option (fig.2.5), with expansions sideways as small clay spreads were encountered. The Black Book in which small finds were listed was controlled by Gray while Bulleid continued with plans and sections. In 1892-98, 28% of the Mounds examined had sections drawn; in 1904-07, the figure rises only to 34%.

It is difficult to make a wholly objective assessment of the structural record as compiled by Bulleid and Gray. The requirements, that enough elements survive to allow a reconstruction of Mound events, has many variable and complex elements. What can be done, however, is to give an impression of the quality of the records as were made, and some published, based on the detail presented and the clarity of the descriptions by Bulleid, as he was responsible for plans, sections and the ultimate report on the Mounds in the 1911 book. Where section drawings are presented and where they agree with the plans and descriptive text, where photographs enhance the report, and where the plans provide clear distinctions of Mound edges and floor separations, then we can conclude that, structurally, the quality is high. The converse is also true. A subjective assessment has been made of all aspects of the structural report, giving a value for each Mound in terms of its quality of record. Only two comments from this assessment need be made here. The first is that where section drawings were made by Bulleid, his written descriptions are better than the average text; 30% of all Mounds have sections drawn, and of these 27 Mounds, 16 have better than average texts, and only 6 poorer than average. Sections were obviously very useful to Bulleid when he came to write his long chapter on the Mounds. The second comment refers to contrasts in the two periods of excavation, Bulleid 1892-98 and Bulleid and Gray 1904-07. Subjectively, we consider

Fig.2.5 Section through Mound 74 clearly showing Floors and hearths.

Bulleid's records to be on average about the same as those compiled by Bulleid and Gray, but Bulleid alone could produce excellent descriptive texts as well as extremely poor texts, whereas he and Gray were more consistent in the 1904-07 Mound texts.

Table 2.2 Quality of Mound descriptions

Date	V. good	Good	Average	Poor	V. poor
1892		2	2		
1893	1		2	7	
1894			7	2	1
1895		2	3	2	
1896	2	3	2	1	
1897	2		1	2	
1898		1	8	7	
	5	*8*	*25*	*21*	*1*
1904			2	1	
1905		2	6		
1906		2	2	1	
1907		1	6		
	0	*5*	*16*	*2*	*0*

(Omits Mounds part-excavated in both periods)

All of these comments about the structural record have clear reflections in the contextual records. Before we examine these, however, we might conclude this section with a few more comments on the implications of the imperfections of the structural evidence. Four basic relationships on the site should be clearly exposed: 1) can we identify floors within the Mounds and small structures like hearths upon the floors? 2) can we ascertain the relationship of Mound floors to Mound foundations? 3) can we relate Mound clays and other spreads to the palisade? 4) Can we relate Mound floors and spreads to other Mounds, thereby constructing matrices for the site? The answers to these intimate questions, as they refer to individual and adjacent Mounds, appear as detailed responses in the Mound descriptions (Chapter 3) which are absolutely fundamental to any attempt to interpret the site today. The lack of clarity in many Mound records precludes a number of positive answers to these questions and it is hard to see how anyone can hope, or have hoped, to recreate the events on these mounded areas. Other records are better and, as will be seen, can be used to make statements with some justification. What can be said here with some positive emphasis is that Bulleid is generally clear about the relationship of hearths to floors, is sometimes able to identify lines of stakes as wall posts for certain floors, is rarely clear about the context of posts scattered beneath, within and beside the Mounds, and is rather vague about the connections between lowest floors of clay and foundation timber, or about the Mound edges and palisade timbers. He is sometimes very positive about Mound relationships, about the joining of clay floors, and sometimes he is maddeningly obscure and his drawn edges touch with no indication of the connections. Much of this is due to the excavation methodology, where vital relationships could not be seen or were not recorded. We turn now to the contextual evidence, especially as it relates to the artefacts.

Contextual evidence

In this section we will pay particular attention to the contexts of the finds recovered during the campaigns 1892-98 and 1904-07, as these assumed considerable importance in Bulleid and Gray's treatment of the site publication, and have been used subsequently in various interpretations. The Relics themselves were featured in 19 chapters of the 1911 and 1917 books, most of these compiled and written by Gray. The finds appear in these volumes by type, never by association with other types, and rarely by context upon Mound floors. Lists of types appear in the chapters, but in almost all cases they are incomplete. In the Mound descriptions, Bulleid comments on the number of objects recovered, and lists those thought to be most important. The full listing of all artefacts appears in the Black Book, with annotations by Gray. Other lists appear in notebooks, and descriptions of individual pieces occur in the Annual Reports in *PSANHS* 1902-07, and in Reports to the Glastonbury Antiquarian Society. The Annual Reports in *PSANHS* in particular give much more detailed descriptions of finds than appear in the 1911 and 1917 volumes, but little more detail about the Mounds and floors. Some Relics have labels attached with contexts noted. A very large amount of material, especially pottery, was boxed and labelled by Mound alone, or unlabelled. There are therefore some problems both in creating a database of all the objects found, and in assigning as many as possible to specific floors or Mounds or other positions on the site. Various people were aware of this problem at an early date. Pitt-Rivers advised Bulleid to pay special attention to pottery: it was "of great importance to preserve, tabulate and classify <u>every</u> fragment of pottery found and to note the depth. Pottery is in many cases the only reliable evidence of date attainable...". Bulleid failed to follow this advice, and Gray, trained by Pitt-Rivers, made no effort to follow it either. At the end of the excavation there were about 200 boxes of potsherds, hardly any with any assignment to stratigraphical positions in the Mounds. Boyd Dawkins, who was studying the human remains from the site, asked for "precise details of each Mound and its relics", and in 1916 commented that "omitting the position in the Mounds themselves, whether on the top most floor or at the base of 7 floors seems to me to render the information almost valueless".

The problems of context for the finds is in a great measure without solution now. The records of objects found with or near a Mound fall into five possibilities:

1) Objects associated with a Mound, ie found in Mound deposits and assigned to a specific floor.

2) Objects not assigned to a floor but found within a Mound; these cannot normally be put into the site phases of occupation as outlined in Chapter 4 (and see below).

3) Objects found outside a Mound, but near to the Mound edge, and occasionally stated to be at the same level as a certain floor; these can be phased only with caution.

4) Objects found outside a Mound and with no recorded stratigraphical relationship with a Mound; these cannot be phased.

5) Objects found in or outside the palisade, wholly without context; these cannot be phased.

By the word 'phase' we refer to Chapter 4 where an attempt is made to break up the site into stratigraphical units, joining Mound clays and individual floors, to create a 4-phase site. Where an object is assigned to a particular floor in a particular Mound, it falls into one of the phases; many objects are not assignable as we will now see.

The finds as numerically listed in the Black Book (and not in the 1911 and 1917 volumes) appear in Appendix 3.1 along with a reference to the 1911 or 1917 books and their Mound number where it can be identified. Table 2.3 shows that Bulleid and Gray, probably Gray in particular, paid a lot of attention to objects of bone and antler, bronze and iron, and very little to flint, stone or pottery (unless it was decorated). Taken as bare totals, this shows that 77% of the numbered finds were referred to in the 1911 or 1917 books, and 75% of the finds were assigned to particular Mounds. Some objects included in the Table were found outside the palisade, and thus cannot be assigned a Mound, and so the percentages are improved. Some objects were found outside the Mounds but inside the palisade, but were listed as related to the most convenient Mound, ie the one being dug at the time of discovery, so Table 2.3 is not a real guide to artefact contexts. And much pottery, bone fragments, plant remains and structural wood were never given find numbers and did not enter the Black Book. Bulleid did not collect flint or stone in the early years. So there are losses in certain categories, and the greatest is the pottery. Table 2.4 shows that no information whatsoever is given for pottery from 21 Mounds, and another 15 Mounds have the barest information. Bulleid's comments about the quantities are never numerical, and 'average' quantities are not defined although he often used the terms 'below average' or 'above average', as well as 'few', 'numerous' and 'abundant'. He only numbered 313 sherds in the finds book, and, as noted above, there are about 200 boxes of sherds from the site surviving today.

Many of the boxes (in the Somerset County Museum) have Mound numbers upon them; 191 boxes are labelled and there are 18 unlabelled boxes as well as 3 boxes with just the year of excavation. All of these boxes are not Bulleid's, but are the result of a re-boxing exercise carried out around 1969. By using Bulleid's text comments (Table 2.4) and counting the boxed sherds, it is possible to gain some idea of the distribution and quantity of pottery on the site, and this will be discussed in Chapters 6 and 8 (fig.2.6).

Table 2.3 Finds recorded, published, and attributed to Mounds

	Number	Number in 1911/17 books	Number with Mound identified
Amber	5	5	5
Bone	454	441	405
Crucibles	34	34	33
Baked Clay	81	41	51
Bronze	274	214	248
Flint	385	26	47
Glass	27	27	27
Antler	399	396	379
Iron	110	109	106
Jet	1	1	1
Shale	31	31	30
Lead & Tin	50	50	44
Human	42	42	42
Pottery	313	189	192
Querns	54	54	50
Stones	48	34	33
Tusks	14	14	14
Whorls	238	238	211
Wood	100	100	93
Unbaked Clay	20	20	1
Coin	3	3	3
Totals	***2683***	***2069***	***2015***

We should not forget the circumstances under which Bulleid worked, no finds processing team, nor conservators, nor storage space except in his father's house at first (remember the four rooms filled to overflowing by 1899). He could not cope with the mass of coarse pottery, breaking up upon recovery and seemingly without much importance or value to him.

Table 2.3 refers to find categories which provide general indications of the range of materials being used on the site, and some of the variety of artefacts in use on the site. The Table does nothing to indicate the spread of different types of objects across the site and within individual Mounds. Table 2.5 begins this process, and the matter is discussed further in Chapter 6. Table 2.5 provides a Mound by Mound listing of Relics, stratified, unstratified, outside but near Mounds, and outside the Palisade. It also notes the number of

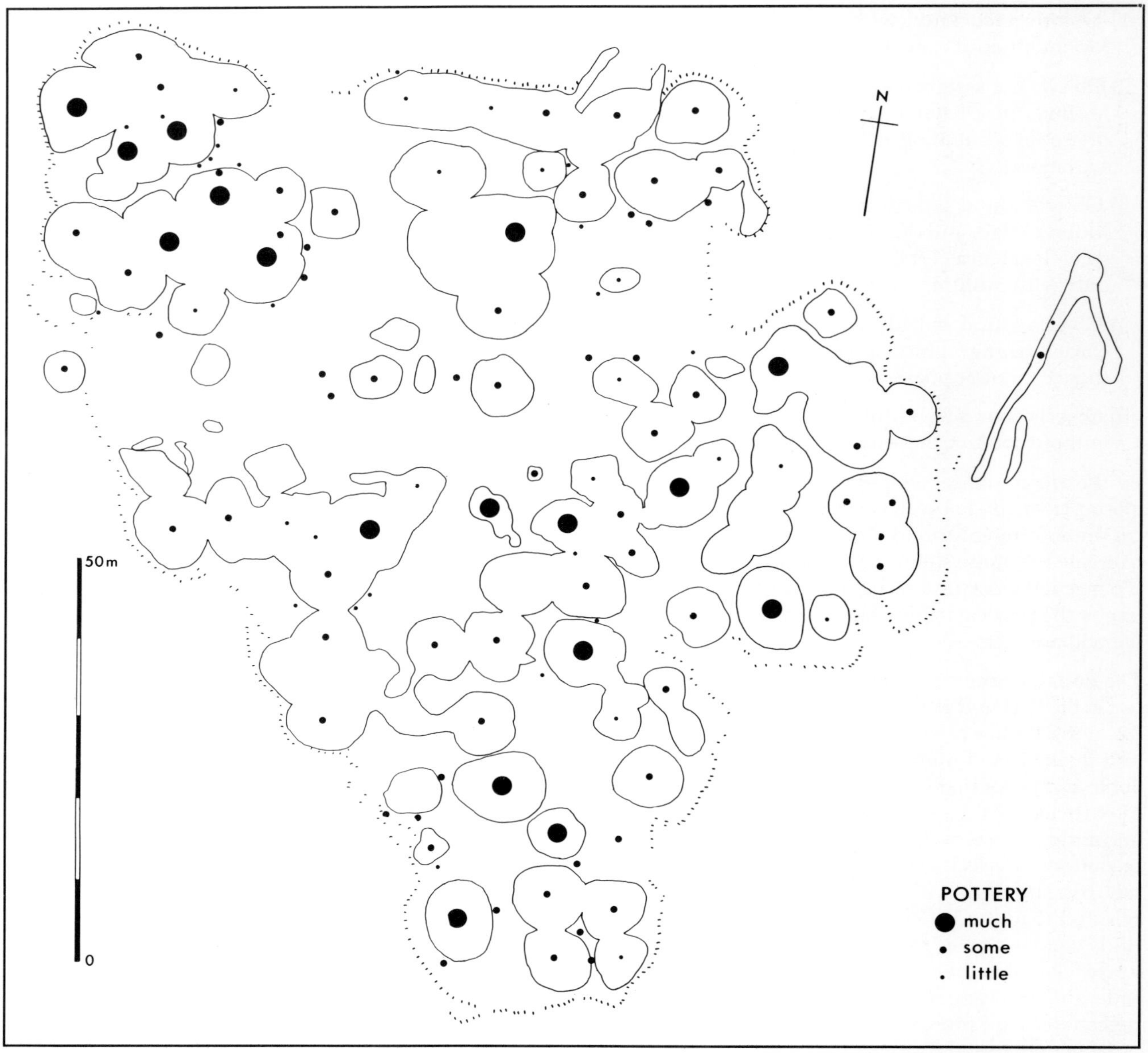

Fig.2.6 Distribution of pottery, most of it lacking context. The variation in quantities in Mounds will be evident. JMC

Table 2.4 Pottery from the Mounds

	Mounds
No information in text	21
No information in text but 1-2 numbered sherds	15
No pottery recovered	5
Very scarce	8
Below average	16
Average	2
Above average	10
Abundant	13
Total	***90***

floors recorded for each Mound. Mounds with only one floor are deemed to have all finds from the Mound stratified. The figures are taken from the Mound descriptions of Chapter 3.

Table 2.5 Mounds, Floors and Relics

Mound	Year	Floors	Unstrat.	Stratified	Ex-Mound	Ex-Palisade
1	1897	1	-	7	3	3
2	1897	2	16	1	8	3
3	1897	3	14	1	10	
4	1897	7	31	45	14	-
5	1897	7	54	44	27	47
6	1896	1	-	18	18	1
7	1894	2	19	-	4	4
8	1894	1	-	4	13	2
9	1896	9	40	32	12	-
10	1896	1	-	1	-	4
11	1896	3	4	10	5	-
12	1896	3	1	6	-	-
13	1896/1907	8	7	3	6	6
14	1898	4	3	4	1	6
15	1898	3	11	-	2	-
16	1898	3	14	7	-	1
17	1895	2	3	-	3	-
18	1895	4	49	37	11	-
19	1894	1	-	5	10	-
20	1894	5	15	1	9	-
21	1893	3	12	-	2	7
22	1893	1	-	20	8	9
23	1893	2	12	-	7	6
24	1893	2	22	-	4	-
25	1893	2	13	1	11	-
26	1894	1	-	11	6	-
27	1895	4	41	19	4	-
28	1898	1	-	2	1	-
29	1898	10	4	2	7	-
30	1898	4	13	9	5	3
31	1898	1	-	3	4	-
32	1898	2	4	-	-	-
33	1898	8	7	5	1	-
34	1898	2	-	-	-	-
35	1898	4	11	6	2	-
36	1898	3	2	-	4	-
37	1898	4	8	4	30	-
38	1898	3	14	14	4	-
39	1898	1	-	-	-	-
40	1898	1	-	2	-	-
41	1894	3	9	4	6	-
42	1893/94	4	24	12	7	-
43	1893	1	-	6	1	-
44	1893	3	33	2	16	-
45	1893	2	11	-	6	-
46	1893	2	8	5	5	7
47	1893	2	17	-	5	-
48	1894	1	-	1	4	22
49	1894	4	34	4	25	4
50	1894	1	-	2	6	-
51	1894/1905	5	3	1	3	-
52	1894/1898	2	2	1	-	-
53	1894/1905	3	5	4	6	-
54	1904	2	3	2	6	-
55	1902/1904	2	12	8	9	-
56	1896	2	8	6	5	3
57	1896	4	4	7	1	3
58	1896/1904	2	10	7	1	-
59	1895	4	2	6	2	10
60	1895	2	-	2	1	8
61	1895	2	1	1	6	5
62	1892	3	152	13	8	-
63	1892	2	22	-	3	-
64	1892	3	32	12	9	-
65	1892	3	31	5	10	-
66	1907	2	3	9	-	-
67	1906	4	5	5	4	4
68	1906	3	2	7	1	2
69	1905	2	12	20	-	3
70	1905	3	19	52	1	7
71	1905	3	17	36	5	1
72	1905/1906	3	10	12	1	-
73	1905/6/7	2	9	13	1	-
74	1902/1906	5	19	41	5	-
75	1906/1907	4	11	36	1	-
76	1906	3	6	18	-	2
77	1895	1	-	-	-	4
78	1904	3	16	4	1	-
79	1892/1904	3	1	2	3	-
80	1905	1	-	7	2	-
81	1905/1907	1	-	5	3	-
82	1905	1	-	2	-	-
83	1906	4	14	4	3	-
84	1907	2	1	7	3	-
85	1907	1	-	3	-	-
86	1907	1	-	-	-	-
87	1907	1	-	-	-	-
88	1907	1	-	1	-	-
89	1907	1	-	1	-	-
90	1892/1907	1	-	1	1	-
Totals			**1012**	**721**	**442**	**187**

These figures are based on Bulleid and Gray's small find lists only, and are inaccurate for two reasons. 1) Single numbers with multiple objects, e.g. 2 flints with one F number, are counted as one; this is a minor defect. 2) Unquantified amounts of material, e.g. box of pottery, animal bone, pebbles, with one relic number, are counted as one; this is a major defect. Nonetheless, they show several important aspects of the site contexts. From the Mounds where stratigraphy existed, and also including Mounds with only one floor, the percentage of objects recorded is 58% unstratified and only 42% stratified. A vast quantity of finds lack any indication of their position within, beneath or upon the floors. This means that it is not possible to be positive about the purpose and function of particular Mounds and particular floors. The effort to make statements about these matters will be made in Chapter 8.

Using these figures it is also possible to gauge the success or otherwise of the two periods of excavation, one (1892-98) under Bulleid's direction, and one (1902, 1904-07) with both Bulleid and Gray at the helm.

Table 2.6 Relic contexts by excavation year.

Year	Unstratified	Stratified	% Stratified
1892	237	30	11
1893	152	46	23
1894	82	34	29
1905	96	65	40
1896	79	90	53
1897	115	98	46
1898	91	58	39
Total	**852**	**421**	**33**
1902	31	49	61
1904	20	8	29
1905	72	146	67
1906	38	70	65
1907	4	25	86
Total	**165**	**298**	**64**

Two features are clear in this Table. 1) Bulleid, from 1892 to 1896, made steady improvement in his recording of contexts for finds (11% rising to 53%); thereafter there was a slight decline, and his average for the whole period 1892-98 is a modest 33%. As much unnumbered material, e.g. boxes of coarse pottery, never reached the Black Book and lacks all contextual information, his percentage falls accordingly. 2) The arrival of Gray in 1902, and the joint operations of Bulleid and Gray in 1904-07, led to significant improvements in recording contexts. The structural evidence, noted earlier in this chapter, does not conform to this pattern insofar as it only created a uniformity of modestly successful recording in contrast to Bulleid's more erratic performance.

The view is often expressed that excavators dig to find the evidence to support their current opinions. Such a process can seriously affect the recording of a site. To what extent did Bulleid, and later he and Gray, excavate the Lake Village with certain convictions about what was there to be found? To what extent were the two men concerned to keep asking questions of the site, probing for new evidence, testing their ideas?

In his earliest reports and in successive versions, Bulleid (1894, 1911, 1924) maintained his view that the Lake Village had been a permanently-occupied settlement consisting of round houses with successively repaired floors, and in which the dwellings were generally uniform in character and essentially domestic. He did not seek to distinguish phases of settlement evolution from an early presumably small occupation to a period when population was at a maximum prior to an abandonment either sudden or progressive. Although he was a wide reader and had access to a variety of ethnographic books, and had travelled to Australia as well as to other parts of the world, he does not seem to have contemplated any seasonal elements in the Lake Village, nor variation in the functions of the dwellings. He was in effect constricted by his vision of lake villages as expressed by Keller for the Swiss lake settlements, not in houses perched on posts over the lake but in the concept of a settlement in the waters, dependent on the waters and eventually overwhelmed by the waters. His approach to the excavation was designed to explore this concept - a permanently occupied site, essentially peaceful and domestic, with local industrial activity, no social stratification, no political upheavals, no extensive or organised contacts in trade or prospection, and no variation in the lives of the inhabitants. His model was perfectly reasonable, given the evidence he continued to seek, and given the fixed concepts with which he approached the site. When Gray arrived, with a determination to obtain small finds above all, he did not question Bulleid's interpretation. The reports of many Mounds are peppered with comments about the yield of artefacts: "below the average", "very numerous", "few objects of interest", "decidedly disappointing", but not so often about structural problems or the possibility of alternative explanations. This indicates where the priorities lay. Bulleid continued to be on the lookout for the curving lines of stakes that, for him, marked round houses, and where he could see only incomplete lines, or arcs of stakes, he would only admit that it had been difficult to trace the entire circuit; he does not seem to have contemplated windbreaks, shelters or penning walls - it was either a clearly-demarcated round house or it was originally a round house but the evidence had perished somehow. He did occasionally state that small clay spreads were just that and no more, but all Mounds of any considerable size were or had been round houses. In Bulleid's view, there were almost 70 such structures; in our view, less than 25 Mounds had ever supported round houses. However, just as Bulleid was constricted in his ideas about the site - dwellings, uniformity, permanence - so we are equally conditioned today to seek to explore variations, evolution and seasonality.

We can now conclude this source critical analysis with a few comments. It must be evident that Bulleid began work in 1892 with the barest idea of archaeological techniques, relying upon equally untrained labourers to dig into the largest Mounds, and satisfying himself, and his committees, with the yield of finds and the undoubted visually striking structures on site. He soon began to appreciate the importance of context and association but had little idea of how to implement the procedures to attain such records. All the while, however, he was devoting his time on site to drawing plans as accurately as he could, and sections too, and these are fundamentally important and major contributions.

And some of his Mound records are better than anything he and Gray combined could create. We suspect it was a combination of inexperience (at first) and then pressure of tasks (later) that prevented Bulleid from achieving consistently what he very clearly was capable of doing.

When Gray arrived on the scene, he brought some of the concepts of context and yet he made no real innovative impact on the working of the site other than a greater care in retrieving the objects. The improvement in contextual recording is a notable feature of the period 1904-07, but against this is the fact that by now most of the big complex Mounds had been dug and so stratigraphies were more simple to see and to record. On this argument, there should have been a greatly augmented record, but there was not.

Gray was a successful professional archaeologist who had, or soon developed, a lengthy record of excavations followed by a series of unpublished reports. Bulleid it was who drove the publication of the Lake Village forward, no matter what Gray wrote to the contrary. Without Bulleid, the site would not have emerged as the two formidable monographs of 1911 and 1917; this is only our opinion, of course.

The two volumes of report present us with only part of the detailed record of the Glastonbury Lake Village; other sources provide a much-needed augmentation of the record and without these we doubt that any efforts to develop a phasing for the site are likely to succeed. The amplification of the contextual record and its organisation into workable pieces now allow us to attempt a new interpretation of the site. But whatever and however that develops there must remain the variety of imperfections that we have outlined here, that will continue to hinder the full understanding of the Lake Village and to prevent some of the questions being asked for which we would like answers today. In this we are in full agreement with John Barrett (1987) who has touched on some of these matters in his critical analysis of the 1911 and 1917 volumes, as they relate to D. L. Clarke's interpretative efforts; to the latter we will return later in this book.

We may conclude here by stating that the Glastonbury Lake Village is a good example of archaeological 'rules': a site report can only be as good as its records allow, and site records are only as good as the observations made, and site observations are only made possible by the clarity created by the excavation techniques employed, and such techniques are often devised to answer certain questions in support of certain hypotheses. All of these matters are potential constrictions along the road to our version of 'the truth' which we fondly if naïvely believe will be close to the former reality of the situation. If we attempt in any of this to widen the passage, not by a detour but by forcing the way ahead, we have to make clear the source, position and strength of the artifices used. We will make use of some of these artifices in Chapters 4 and 8.

Chapter 3

Mound descriptions and associated finds

In this Chapter we have set out to present the data from the variety of sources mentioned in Chapter 2. The main source of information about Mound structures is Bulleid's text of 1911, greatly supplemented by close reference to his plans, and augmented by various comments in notebooks and observation from the photographs. For the finds we must rely upon the Black Book, recently rediscovered, as well as the 1911 and 1917 books, the Proceedings of SANHS, the objects themselves and a number of unpublished records.

The Chapter is a documentary and factual statement, Mound-by-Mound, each with its finds listed, including those stratified in the Floors, those only linked to a Mound, those near the Mound, and those in or outside the palisade adjacent to the Mound. The artefact lists are entirely new and for the first time it is possible to relate all the small finds to their Mounds; the lists, by type, in the 1911 and 1917 books, are incomplete as well as very user-unfriendly. The Mound descriptions are summaries of what seems to have been found by Bulleid and Gray, with comments on their interpretation and our opinions clearly stated.

We have reversed Bulleid's sequence of Mound description so that our summaries commence with the lowest

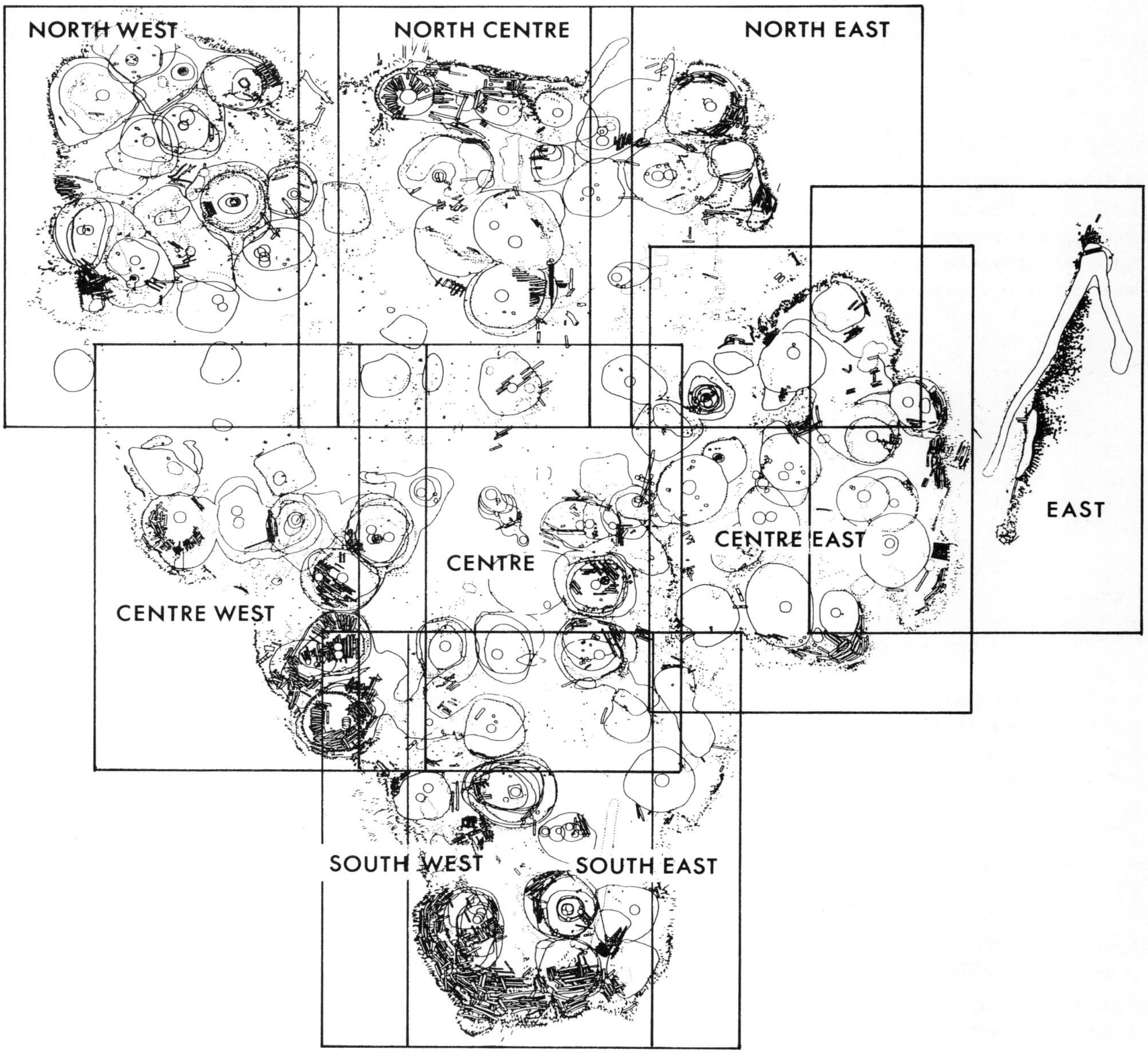

Fig.3.1 Plan of the Lake Village with areas marked. These refer to the detailed plans of Fig.3.2 - 3.10.

and earliest Mound Floor, succeeded by upper and later Floors. Then follows a brief comment on the foundation and the Relics noted by Bulleid and Gray, and lastly comes the full list of finds.

All measurements have been converted from Imperial to metric. Orientations are abbreviated as N, E, S and W. Throughout the text the word Mound is shortened to M.

Following each Mound description is a stratigraphical assessment which sets out the demonstrable relationship between the Mound Floors and those of adjacent Mounds. This is followed by our dating of each Floor, to one of four Phases: Early, Middle, Late or Final. The Phases are fully described in Chapter 4 and are the basis of all further discussions about the site, dating, distributions, activities and organisation.

All of the Mounds are illustrated in a set of plans (fig.3.2 - 3.10), preceded by a general plan (fig.3.1) which divides the site into the 9 areas. The Mound numbers assigned by Bulleid and used throughout this book appear on a fold-out plan at the end of the book.

Mound 1 (1897). (figs.3.9 and 3.10)

A spread of yellow clay at extreme S end of site. The clay, max. 330mm thick, was 7.6 x 6.1m in extent. No hearth or structural remains were noted, and no black earth covered the clay. A patch of stones S of the centre was embedded in the clay. Beneath the clay, only on the W, was a thick foundation of logs and branches, representing part of the foundation of M3, the clay floors of which spread to within 0.6m of M1. The clay of M1 abutted the palisade posts on E and S, and slightly overlay M2 clay at the extreme N. There is some trace of an old fence line abutting M3 which seems to predate M1 but this is not clear. Few relics were found. Some bone and potsherds were located about 1.8m below the clay, deep in the soft leafy peat.

Stratigraphy: Floor 1 over M2 Floor 1 (Floor 1 over Mound 2 Floor 1). Some artefacts beneath Mound

Phase: Final

Mound 1 finds

B 309	worked bone
E 152	tubular ring
F 54	burnt core rejuvenation flake
H 244	shed antler. Dated by C14 (see Chapter 6.13)
P **	decorated pottery

Mound 1 (under)

P **	pottery (unnumbered)
**	animal bone (unlisted)

Mound 1 (SW of)

X 49	knobbed post, oak

Mound 1 (NW of)

E 149	rivet head
E 151	single boss button-and-loop fastener, Wild class I

Mound 1 (NE of) outside palisade

X 1	bent wood box

Mound 1 (SE of) outside palisade

B 169	gouge-shaped object
M 6	skull and jaw with sword cuts

Mound 2 (1897). (figs.3.9 and 3.10)

Spreads of yellow clay at the S end of the site. The clay, max. 840mm thick, covered an area 7 x 7m, and consisted of 2 Floors each covered by black earth. Floor 2 had a baked clay hearth. Floor 1 (upper) had a baked clay hearth in bad condition. No other structural remains were noted. Beneath the clay on the NW was an alder stump, and under the clay on the S only was a heavy foundation of wood and stone, with a layer of blue clay with the wood; this is shown on Bulleid's plan as a patch *c* 4.5m diameter, and may have been a part of M4, or even M3 as its foundation wood extends both NE (M2) and ESE (M1). It is shown on Bulleid's section drawing. A line of posts under M2 and edging the blue clay represents an early palisade line, with traces of hurdles. A narrow causeway, made of small stones, extends under M2 clay and over the edge of Floor 1 of M4 on the W edge of M2. Part of a child's skeleton was embedded in the occupation debris. Beneath the clays were numerous potsherds, and 20-30 unbaked clay slingstones were found in a heap near the palisade line to the E of M2.

Stratigraphy: Floor 1 over M4 Floor F1. Old palisade predates M2 and M1

Phase: Final

Mound 2 finds

B 171	sawn gouge-shaped object
B 316	'bobbin', type E
B 317	point (gouge)
B 318	needle
B 412	gouge-shaped object
E 61	chain link
E 154	rivet head
E 155	brooch pin and one turn of spring
H 252	weaving comb fragment
H 253	shed antler
P 117	small undecorated pot
P 203	decorated bowl
P 211	decorated jar
P 220	decorated bowl
P **	decorated pottery
W 130	spindle whorl (clay)

Mound 2 (under)

P **	pottery, 'numerous sherds'

Mound 2 (NE of)

H 91	sawn antler
P 98	decorated bowl
**	sling shot (20-30)

Mound 2 (SW of)

B 308	pin?
B 320	needle
B 321	incomplete/broken pin

H 249	cheek piece
H 250	cheek piece

Mound 2 (NW of)

Q 31	saddle quern, upper stone

Mound 2 (E of) outside palisade

X 53	anvil-shaped block, oak, axed and adzed

Mound 2 (NE of) outside palisade

E 55	binding
X 80	dish, oak

Mound 3 (1897). (figs.3.9 and 3.10)

Spreads of yellow clay at S end of the site, abutting the palisade. The clays represent 3 Floors, each *c* 150mm thick, and the area covered was 8 x 7.5m. The lowest Floor (3) was the largest, and was irregular with a projection out to S. Floor 2 was oval, and a smaller Floor 1 was circular. The lower Floors (Floors 2 and 3) had little debris upon them, and no built hearths although a burnt area *c* 1m diameter on each probably represented fireplaces. Two large oak posts were noted near the centre of the Floors, perhaps one for each of Floors 2 and 3. A slab-paved area at the NE of Floor 1 may represent an entry. A number of posts were recorded along the SW and SE of the Floors, and others within the clay Floors. Although evidence for walled and roofed structures is slight, the position, shape and nature of M3 suggests some structure was built over and/or around the Floors. The foundation was massive, of wood and clay about 1m thick. It had 3 layers of logs laid E-W, N-S, E-W, and some logs were 6m long. The wood was covered by blue clay up to 600mm thick. This foundation spread to S outside the Floors, and represents the preparation for occupation in the S of the site, prior to any Floor spreads. The Floors of M3 overlay M4 Floor 1. A stone path running N-S for 20m had one end under Floor 1 of M3, and ran over Floor 1 of M4, but the plan is unclear about the path's relationship with Floor 2 of M3. The clay of Floor 2 directly abutted the palisade posts at the extreme S, and a line of posts also extended up the SW and W edge of M3 possibly representing an extension inwards of an early fence prior to the massive expansion outwards on the SW of the whole site. The relics from M3 were relatively few, but included a number of bone needles and splinters, concentrated at the N, and there were no recorded finds outside the palisade at the S edge of M3. No relics were assigned to specific Floors. A modern(?) glass bead was found under the Floors.

Stratigraphy: Floors 3-2-1 over M4

Phase: Floor 3 Late, Floor 2 Late/Final, Floor 1 Final

Mound 3 finds

B 297	notched and perforated ox/horse tibia
B 298a	'bobbin', type A
B 298b	'bobbin', type E
B 310	pin
B 311	needle
B **	'chips & splinters' from working
D 63	crucible
D 64	finger-marked and pricked clay
E 150	brooch, La Tène III wire brooch
F 55	knife
H 246	cheek piece
P 285	decorated bowl
P **	pottery, above average decorated
W 129	spindle whorl (baked clay)

Mound 3 (under)

G 17	modern(?) glass bead

Mound 3 (NE of)

B 312	needle
H 245	sawn antler

Mound 3 (SE of)

B 304	'bobbin', type A
E 153	perforated sheet

Mound 3 (SW of)

D 55	partly perforated ball
K 17	ring

Mound 3 (NW of)

H 238	hammer
H 239	sawn antler
P 158	lid
Q 19	rotary quern, upper stone

Mound 4 (1897). (figs.3.9 and 3.10)

Circular spreads of clay, yellow at top, colour not noted lower down, in S part of site, over an area of max. 8.5 x 9m. The clay was 1.4m thick at the centre, and represents 7 Floors; the 3 earliest (Floors 5-7) are small patches only, 3.2 x 3.6m, 2.7 x 3.4m and 2.4 x 3.0m (at base). Each of these 3 patches had one round hearth of baked clay, and Floor 5 had a second, oblong, hearth of gravel laid over the round hearth. No other structural evidence was located for these lowest Floors. Floor 4 was larger, 7.3 x 6.7m, with a central hearth of baked clay, and the Floor was edged by a more or less complete ring of post, double at the NE where hurdle work lay between the post lines. The Floor was covered with planking, laid concentrically, and this extended outside the structure to the NW where two layers of timber were laid; this may represent an entrance to a post and wattle house. Floor 3, only 5.5 x 5.8m, had one oblong raised hearth, and represents repairs to the main part of the Floor 4 house. Floor 2, 7.6 x 7.0m, follows the line of Floor 4 closely except for a small SW spread, and is a total rebuilding of the house. This had a baked clay hearth, rebuilt twice. Bulleid's section drawing shows the wall posts of Floors 4-3-2. Floor 1, of yellow clay, was the largest of all, 8.8 x 9.0m, and had one large rectangular hearth, 1.5 x 1.6m, replaced at the end by a small clay patch. An oval stone, 0.7m diameter, lay on this Floor near the SW edge, and a basin-like oven was built into the Floor off centre to the E; the oven was 600mm wide and the vertical sides were 230mm deep. It contained charcoal and fragments of baked clay fallen from the sides; there were some fragments of, seemingly, an overhanging rim, perhaps even a partial lid made of fired clay. This Floor probably represents an open clay spread, replacing the round house of Floors 4-3-2.

The 7 Floors were laid on a foundation of heavy wood in the S half, and a lighter brushwood in the N half supplemented by peat blocks distinctly unlike the natural peat around. A spread of hazelnut shells was noted on the brushwood under the clay, perhaps derived from hazel rods and branches used as brush. A narrow stone path ran N-S across the E edge of Floor 1. A scattering of posts was recorded outside the W edge of M4, perhaps relating to some sort of shelter support for Floor 1 or an external windbreak for the round house of Floor 4-3-2.

Mound 4, all Floors, lies under M2 Floor 1 and M3, and under the stone path. The relics from M4 were numerous, with many bone and antler pieces, whorls and other items not assigned to Floors.

Stratigraphy: under M2 Floor 1 and M3, under stone path. One object beneath Mound

Phase: Floor 7-6-5 Early, Floor 4-3-2 Middle, Floor 1 Late, stone path Late/Final

Mound 4 finds

B 273	'bobbin', type A
B 274	'bobbin', type E
B 275	'bobbin', type E
B 276	'bobbin', type E
B 287	polished ox metatarsal
B 289	'bobbin', type E
B 290	point (gouge)
B 291	'bobbin', type D
B 314	perforated and polished deer tarsal
B 315	needle
D 62	perforated clay ball
D **	loom weight
D **	much baked daub + thin layer ash on NE edge
E 132	brooch, one piece simple, British form (Drahtfibel)
E 139	brooch, La Tène III wire brooch
H 211	point (bone)
H 212	sawn tine
H 228	sawn tine
H 229	sawn tine
H 251	charred antler
H 254	sawn antler
HS 1028	grinding stone
I 77	adze
P 6	decorated bowl
P 204	decorated jar
P 264	decorated bowl
P **	pottery, above average decorated
Q 21	rotary quern, upper stone
S 19	haematite
W 122	spindle whorl (sandstone)
W 123	spindle whorl (sandstone)

Mound 4 (Floor 1)

B 271	needle
B 292	needle
C 16	crucible
E 133	large ring
H 207	cheek piece
H 213	sawn antler
H 226	cheek piece
I 72	ring
I 75	billhook
K 19	ring
K 20	ring
L 29	spindle whorl (lead/tin)
P 204	decorated jar
P 264	decorated bowl
Q 29	rotary quern, upper stone
S 20	whetstone
T 6	perforated boar's tusk
W 105	spindle whorl (sandstone)
W 106	spindle whorl (lias)
W 107	spindle whorl (lias)
W 109	spindle whorl (lias)
W 110	spindle whorl (lias)
W 131	spindle whorl? (ammonite)
**	oven

Mound 4 (Floor 2)

B 288	'bobbin', type A
B 319	needle
E 136	brooch, La Tène III 'Glastonbury' mock spring form
H 208	?hammer
H 209	handle
H 210	cheek piece
H 230	sawn and polished antler
I 67	spiral finger ring
I 69	point
I 70	adze
I 73	adze blade
W 108	spindle whorl (lias)

Mound 4 (Floor 3)

P 156	decorated bowl
W 132	spindle whorl (clay)

Mound 4 (Floor 4)

B 286	dice x 3
E 137	finger ring
E 144	blade-like object
Q 30	saddle quern, lower stone
S 21	pebbles x 23 ?sling stones

Mound 4 (Floor 6)

X 8	ladle

Mound 4 (clay)

I 66	binding from hide-shaped shield
**	wood chips, hazel nuts, seeds, charcoal

Mound 4 (NE of)

B 294	cut bone

Mound 4 (SE of)

B 313	needle
H 247	sawn antler
H 248	die
K 18	ring
M 28	young child's skeleton, part

Mound 4 (SW of)

B 284	point (gouge)
B 293	'bobbin', type D
D 68	loom weight fragment

F 53	arrowhead
W 124	spindle whorl? (ammonite)

Mound 4 (NW of)

B 272	'bobbin'
H 206	sawn antler
M 27	adult skull fragments and infant/foetal bones

Mound 5 (1897). (fig.3.9)

Complex clay spreads and generally oval in shape, on the extreme SW edge of the site. The clay represents 7 Floors of very unequal sizes and shapes, totalling 1.1m max. thickness, and extending 11.0 x 7.7m at max. extent. Floor 7 (the lowest) was of blue clay, an irregularly shaped spread 4.6 x 3.5m and was soon augmented by Floor 6, a small circular patch of yellow clay spread over the E edge of Floor 7, and with a raised hearth. These have no other structural features. Floor 5, 5.8 x 4.3m, was of a peaty grey ashy clay and probably represents the installation of some form of metalworking activity. The remains of a 'primitive furnace', and tuyère fragments, were found on this Floor. Floors 4 and 3 were elongated spreads of yellow (Floor 4) clay replacing and extending Floor 5 but aligned with it; each had a baked clay hearth. They may represent renewal of the 'forge' or casting place of Floor 5, and no other structural elements were recorded. Floor 2 was much larger, 10.1 x 6.1m, and extended W to near the edge of the original palisade which was now moved outwards. The Floor was also edged on the W by posts, and a circular hearth was of baked clay. The final Floor (1) was even larger, 11.0 x 7.7m, of yellow clay, with a central hearth of clay and wall posts on the W. The clay Floors of 2 and 1 had lias slabs embedded. It is likely that Floors 2 and 1 represent some form of structure rather oval in plan, with no real evidence for a full roof, but protected on the W by walling as well as by the adjacent palisade. Bulleid's section drawing shows a wall post on the E as well. The foundation of M5 was variable, brushwood on the N and heavy logs and planks on the S; here the foundation was very dense with 3 alternating rows of alder and oak timber, two parallel with the palisade, the middle row at right angle. This formed a foundation fully 1m thick with general brushwood debris filling the gaps between the logs.

M5 has no stratigraphical relationship with other Mounds. It is likely that Floors 2-1 marked the outward expansion of the palisade once it was decided to replace the open smithing area with a more expansive shelter, if not a fully roofed structure. Bulleid's plan shows a clear line of palisade posts extending in an even curve near the earlier Floors, and a more substantial line set farther outwards to respect the lines of the later Floors. The earlier line of palisade cut E towards M3 and it was only later that the palisade was massively extended W and S, to incorporate a newly-built platform of timber and logs, and finally to include what may have been a small tower or observation post at the extreme S of the site.

The relics from M5 were abundant, exceeding those of any other Mound in the whole site. Most are unstratified and include bone and antler pieces, various crucibles, iron and slag objects, decorated potsherds, quantities of wheat and peas (at all levels, according to Bulleid). Floors 5-3 had the tuyère, crucible, bronze 'lumps' and other pieces. Just outside the palisade, Bulleid recovered two barrow loads of sloestones. Much else was unstratified outside the Mound but as M5 is to some extent an isolated mound, this debris may be associated in a general sense.

Stratigraphy: none except palisade renewal

Phase: Floors 7 - 6 Early, Floors 5-4-3 Middle, Floors 2 - 1 Late

Mound 5 finds

B 280	point (gouge)
B 281	'bobbin', type D
B 282	worked rib, bow drill?
B 295	cut sheep metatarsal
B 296	'bobbin', type D
B 306	sawn ox long bone
B 307	cut ox metatarsal
D 56	perforated clay ball
D **	loom weight
E 35	nail head
E 110	spiral finger ring
E 145	belt clasp
E **	bronze fragments
F 312	flake
F **	flint flakes
H 222	sawn antler
H 223	cut antler
H 224	sawn tine
H 243	sawn antler
I 58	ring
I 71	iron lump
I 74	awl
I 78	snaffle bit
I 79	reaping hook
I 82	ring
K 16	armlet
L 27	product of lead refining?
L 28	spindle whorl (lead)
P 201	decorated jar
P 206	decorated vessel
P 208	rib-decorated vessel
P 213	decorated lug
P 216	decorated jar
P 217	decorated bowl
P 226	decorated bowl
P 227	decorated sherd
P 231	decorated bowl
P 232	decorated sherd
P 233	decorated sherd
P 237	decorated bowl
P 238	decorated jar
P 242	decorated bowl
P 247	decorated sherd
P 248	decorated jar
P 253	decorated jar

P **	large quantity of pottery, above average decorated
Q 22	rotary quern, upper stone
Q 26	rotary quern, lower stone
S 22	pebbles x 4
T 7	boar's tusk
W 114	spindle whorl (lias)
W 117	spindle whorl (femur head)
W 118	spindle whorl, unfinished (lias)
**	quantities of wheat and beans through out Mound
**	vitrified hearth lining, fuel ash slag, cinder, ironworking slag

Mound 5 (Floor 1)

E 134	spiral finger ring
H 221	cheek piece
H 233	worked tine
H 240	handle
I 68	loop
W 112	spindle whorl (lias)
W 113	spindle whorl (lias)

Mound 5 (under Floor 1)

F 51	scraper

Mound 5 (Floor 2)

C 17	crucible
E 135	rivet
E 140	punch
E 141	rivet head
E 142	brooch, La Tène III wire brooch
H 215	worked? antler. Dated by C14
H 218	weaving comb
H 219	cheek piece
H 220	handle
H 231	weaving comb
H 234	cut antler
H 235	polished and cut roe deer antler
H 236	hammer
W 120	spindle whorl (limestone)

Mound 5 (Floor 2 or 3)

E 146	decorated band
H 242	ferrule

Mound 5 (Floor 3)

E 148	rivet heads and 'numerous nondescript' pieces
H 232	handle
W 115	spindle whorl (lias)

Mound 5 (Floor 4)

E 138	spiral finger ring

Mound 5 (Floor 5)

C 18	crucible
C 19	crucible
C 20	crucible
C 21	crucible
C 22	crucible
C 23	crucible
C 24	crucible
D 57	crucible
D 78	tuyère
**	probable smithing hearth

Mound 5 (Floor 7)

F 49	scraper and core
F 50	scraper
H 237	hammer
I 76	billhook
P 157	decorated bowl
W 125	spindle whorl (lias)

Mound 5 (under)

I 81	file

Mound 5 (NE of)

B 277	'bobbin', type D
B 278	polished sheep metatarsal
B 279	'bobbin', type A
B 283	'bobbin', type D
B 285	point (gouge)
B 299	notched and perforated ox/horse tibia
H 214	perforated roe deer antler
H 216	handle
H 217	handle
H 225	handle

Mound 5 (SE of)

E 147	decorated band
F 47	scraper
H 241	handle
I 80	band
Q 17	saddle quern, lower stone
Q 27	rotary quern, lower stone
W 121	spindle whorl (clay)
W 126	spindle whorl, unfinished (lias)

Mound 5 (SW of)

C 15	crucible
E 109	punch
G 14	whirl-decorated ring bead, Guido class 7a
H 174	pointed and socketed object
Q 18	saddle quern, lower stone
**	slag

Mound 5 (NW of)

B 301	polished bone
B 302	polished horse metatarsal
E 172	lump
M 29	mandible

Mound 5 (NW of) outside palisade

H 176	sawn tine
I 60	reaping hook
I 61	point

Mound 5 (S of) outside palisade

B 246	'bobbin', type F
B 247	cut bird bone
B 248	point (gouge)
B 249	polished rib
B 250	worked sheep tibia
B 251	point (gouge)
B 252	point (gouge)
B 253	point (gouge)
E 108	hook-like twisted wire
E 131	band
F 52	blade
H 172	perforated antler
H 173	shed antler
I 56	latchlifter

I 57	band with 2 rivets
I 59	nail
M 23	right temporal bone
P 142	decorated jar
P 143	decorated vessel
P 144	decorated bowl
P 145	decorated bowl
P 146	decorated jar
W 87	spindle whorl (clay)
W 88	spindle whorl (lias)
W 89	spindle whorl (lias)
W 205	spindle whorl (clay)
X 9	handle
X 14	hand-carved tub
X 62	decorated ash
Z 3	currency bar
**	pelican and swan bones

Mound 5 (W of) outside palisade

B 254	notched and perforated ox humerus
B 255	splinter
B 300	cut and sawn bone
B 303	polished ox tibia
E 143	rivet head
H 175	handle
H 227	worked antler, spatula?
P 149	decorated bowl
W 119	spindle whorl (lias)
**	sloestones x 2 barrow loads

Mound 5 (NW of) outside palisade

I 60	reaping hook
I 61	fragment
H 176	sawn tine

Mound 6 (1896). (figs.3.9 and 3.10)

Small spreads of grey ashy clay in the S sector of the site. Only one Floor was recorded, and that in sparse detail, 6.4 x 7.0m and max. 480mm thick. The Floor supported 3 sets of 3 hearths. On the W edge of the Floor was the earliest set, consisting of a hearth of baked clay rebuilt twice and then sealed by a small thin patch of clay extending to the centre of the Floor. Upon this clay another hearth was made of baked clay, and again rebuilt twice. Upon this was spread more clay and upon this latest patch, 3 hearths were built of baked clay, now forming a cluster and presumably all capable of use together. All of the hearths were low and without built-up sides. Beside one of the uppermost hearths were 4 small holes dug into the clay, 380mm across and 200mm deep. Thin ash and charcoal layers separated all of the W and C sets and much burnt debris was scattered about especially to the W of M6. No trace of any other structures was noted, although a stout oak post remained in place off-centre. Six oak posts were recorded just off the clay Floor to the W, perhaps foundation for a shed; a spread of stones lay to their SW. The foundation of M6 was mostly brushwood but some oak planks had been dumped under the clay in the NE part. M6 is likely to represent an adjunct to M9 or M4, probably M4 in view of the entries/exits to these mounds. A stone path runs from S up to and ends just N of M6.

The relics from M6 were rather numerous for a slight mound, and although most are unstratified, they are all considered to be of a single phase of activity, during which the various hearths were built, rebuilt and moved to other places on the open clay Floor. In the presence of the hearths and the absence of any other structural evidence, M6 is likely to have been a specialised Floor for some process; no slag or metal drips were found but Bulleid noted that much pottery lay about in fragments. He presumably thought it was fired here.

Stratigraphy: none. Some planks beneath Mound

Phase: Late

Mound 6 finds

B 264	perforated scapula
B 269	gouge-shaped object
B 305	perforated scapula
D 77	ring fragment
H 198	weaving comb
H 204	sawn and perforated tine
H 205	sawn antler
I 65	knife blade
K 24	ring
L 26	pendant? (tin)
N **	beaver bones
P 222	decorated jar
P 235	decorated bowl
P **	pottery, large quantity including decorated
Q 20	rotary quern, lower stone
S 18	neolithic stone axe, group VII
T 5	boar's tusk
T 13	perforated dog canines x 2

Mound 6 (NE of)

E 156	binding
H 256	cheek piece
N **	beaver bones

Mound 6 (SE of)

B 150	'bobbin', type D
H 255	weaving comb
K 21	spindle whorl
N 5	beaver incisor
Q 25	saddle quern, lower stone

Mound 6 (SW of)

B 270	sawn ox long bone
D 59	loom weight
D 61	partially perforated ball
E 130	wire
H 201	sawn antler
H 202	sawn and perforated antler
H 203	sawn tine

Mound 6 (NW of)

H 197	hammer
K 15	armlet
W 104	spindle whorl (lias)

Mound 6 (E of) outside palisade

H 92	sawn and polished tine

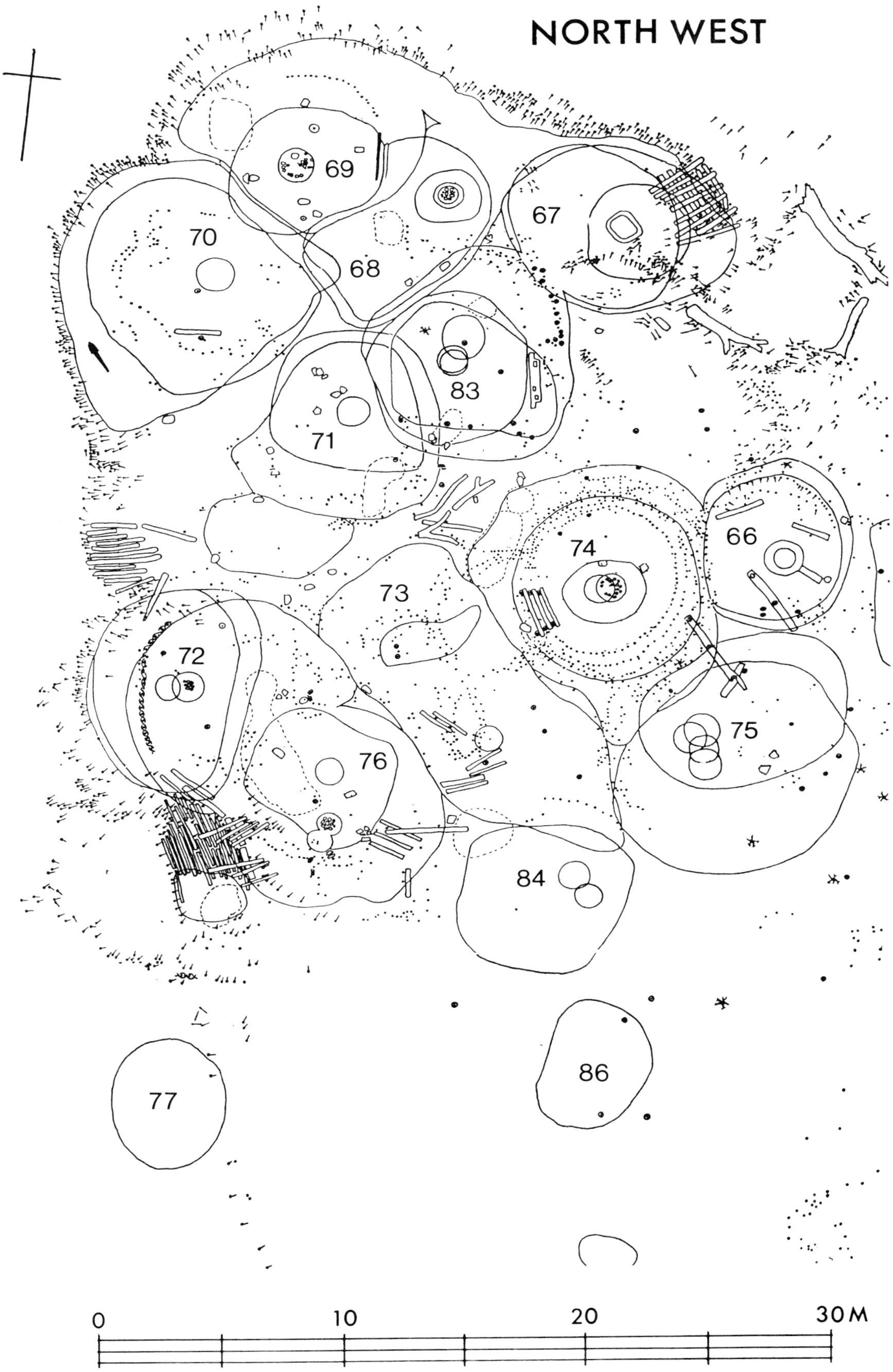

Fig.3.2 NW area plan.

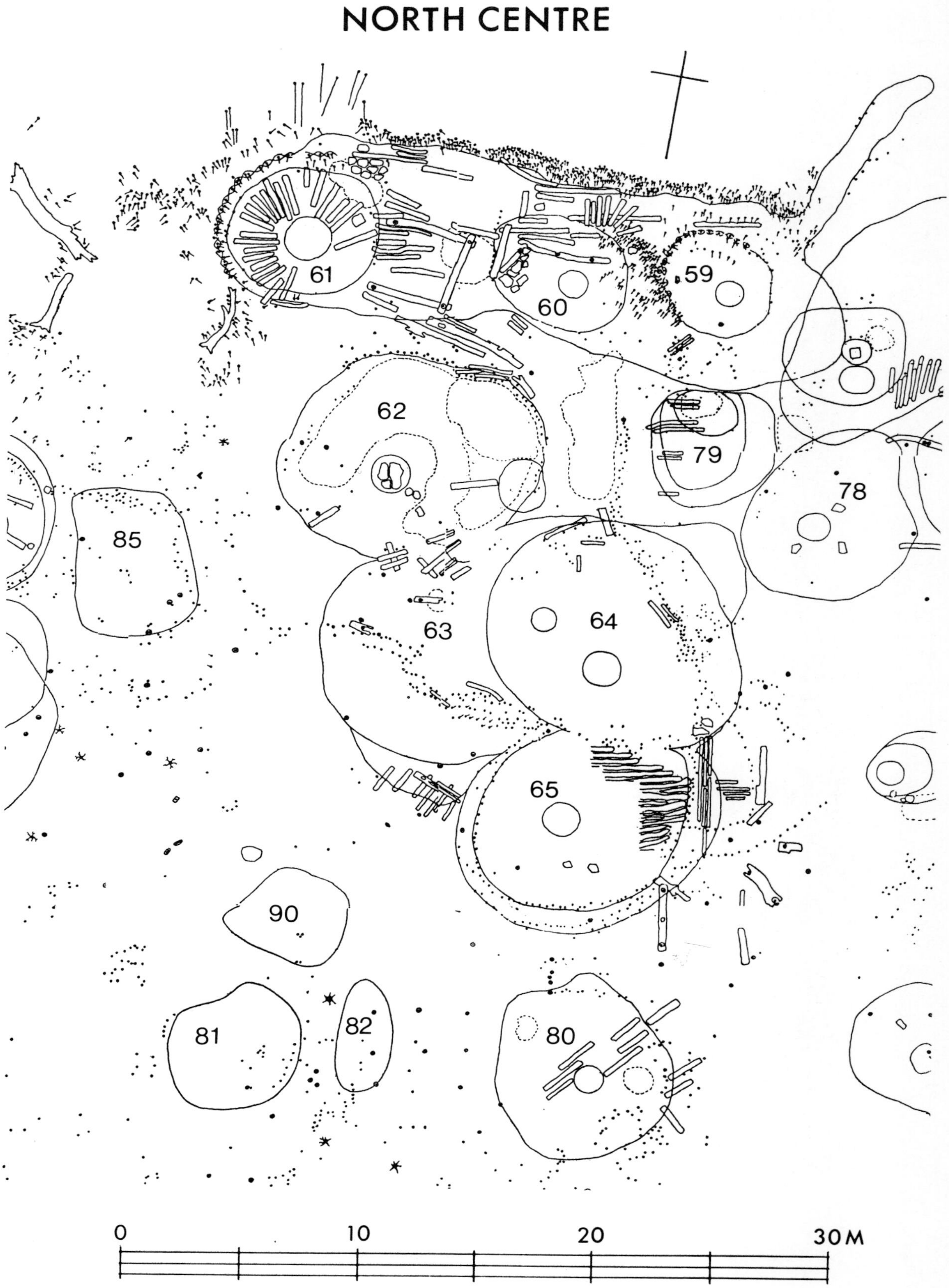

Fig.3.3 N Centre area plan.

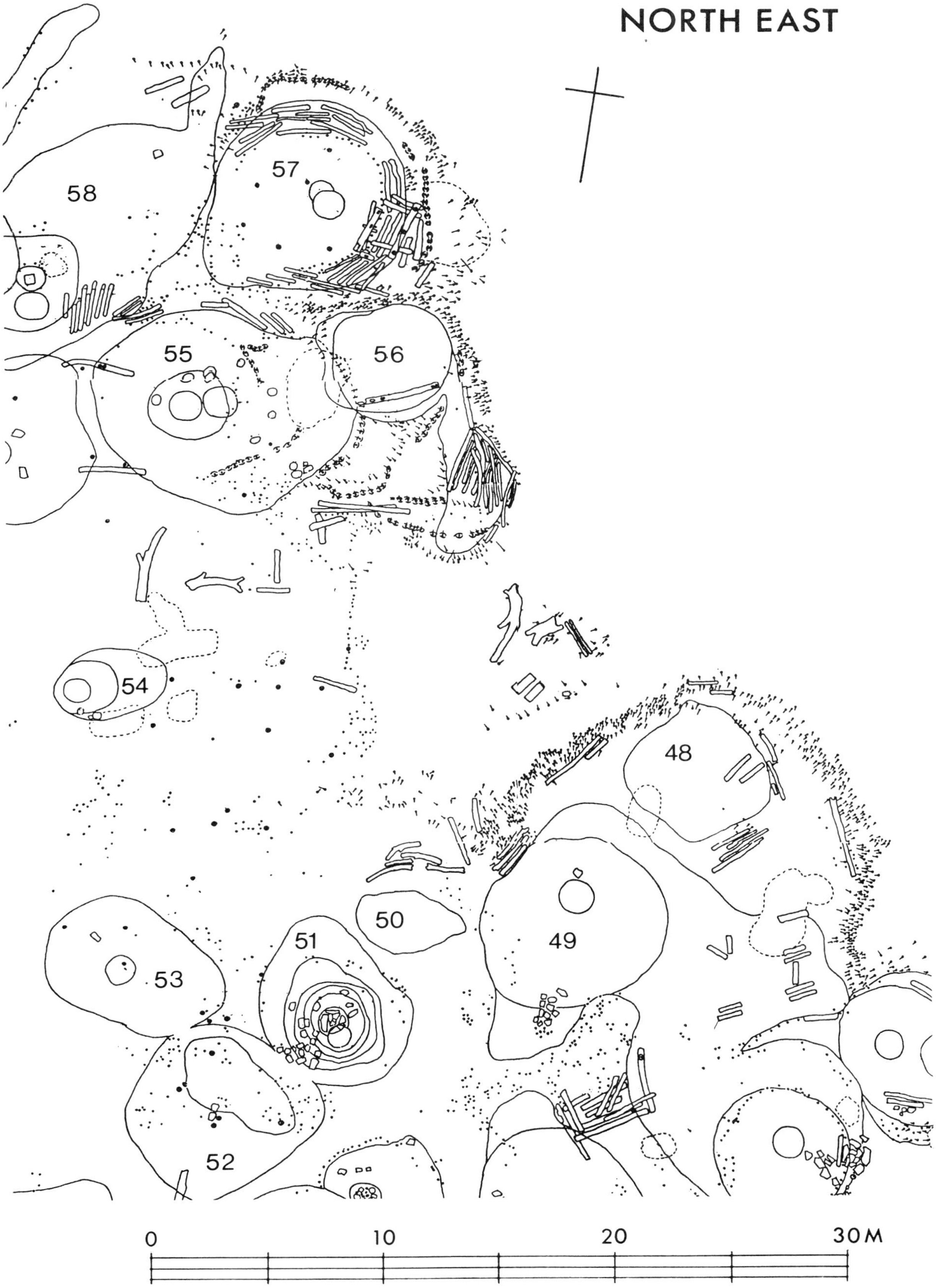

Fig.3.4 NE area plan.

CENTRE WEST

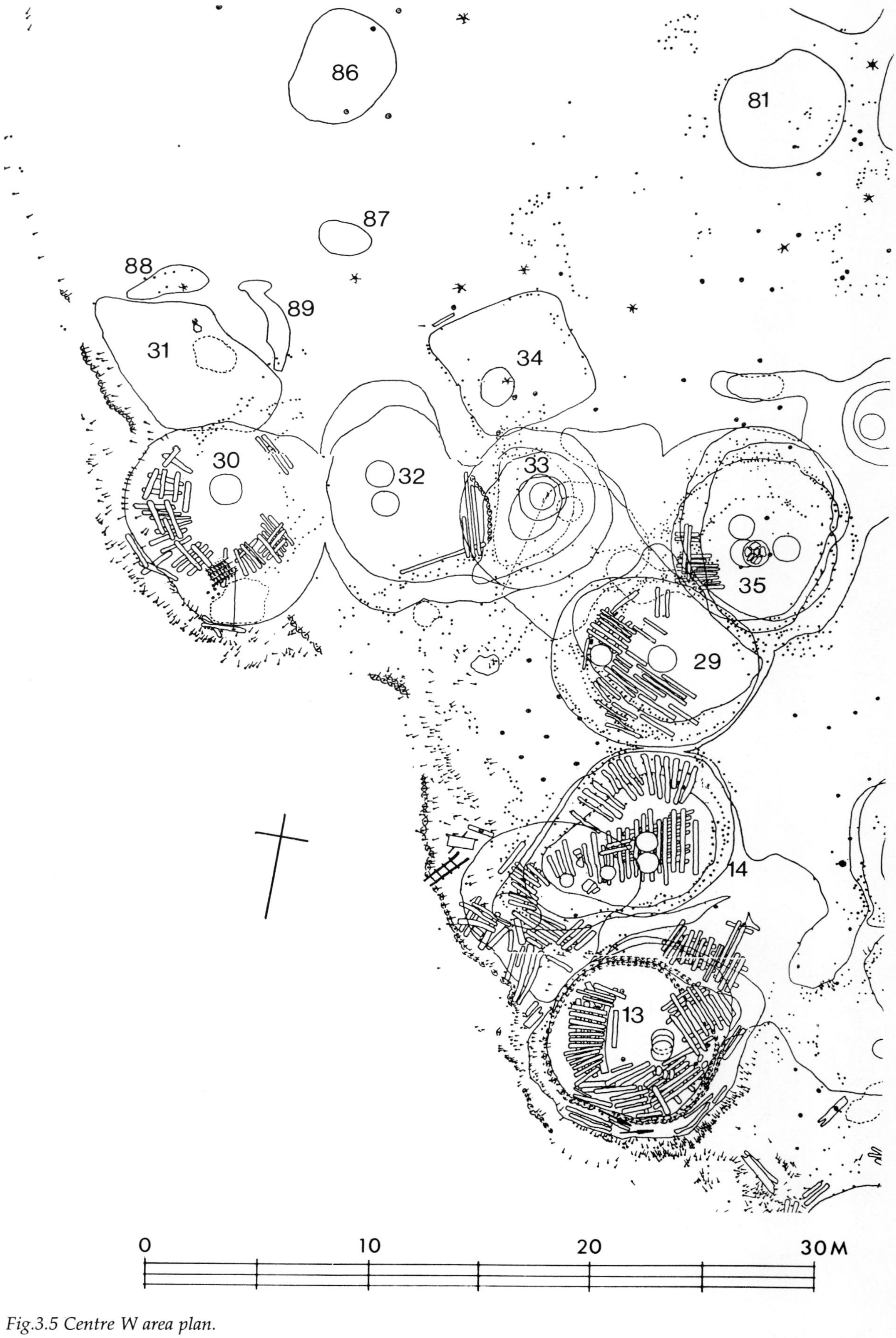

Fig.3.5 Centre W area plan.

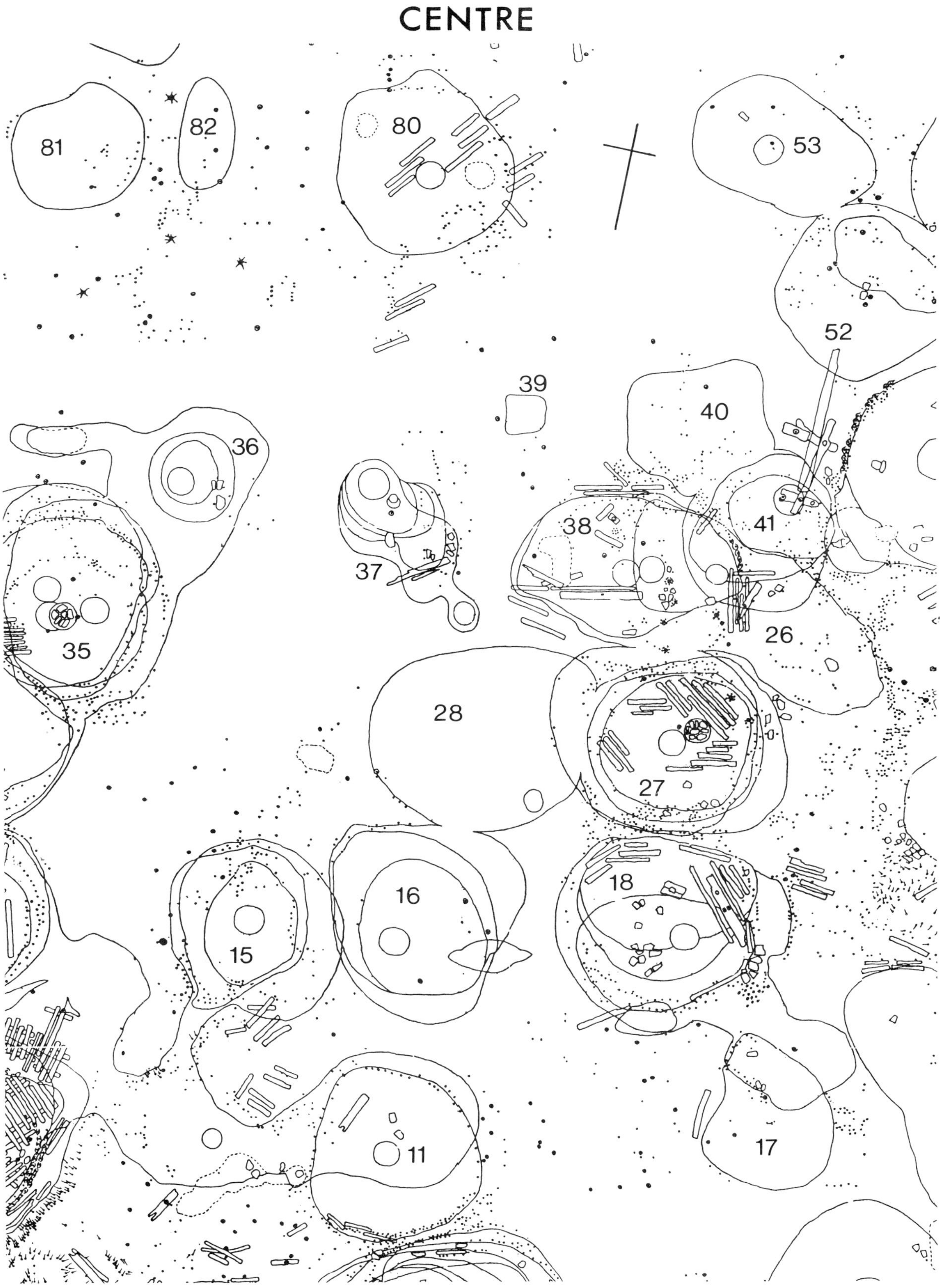

Fig.3.6 Centre area plan.

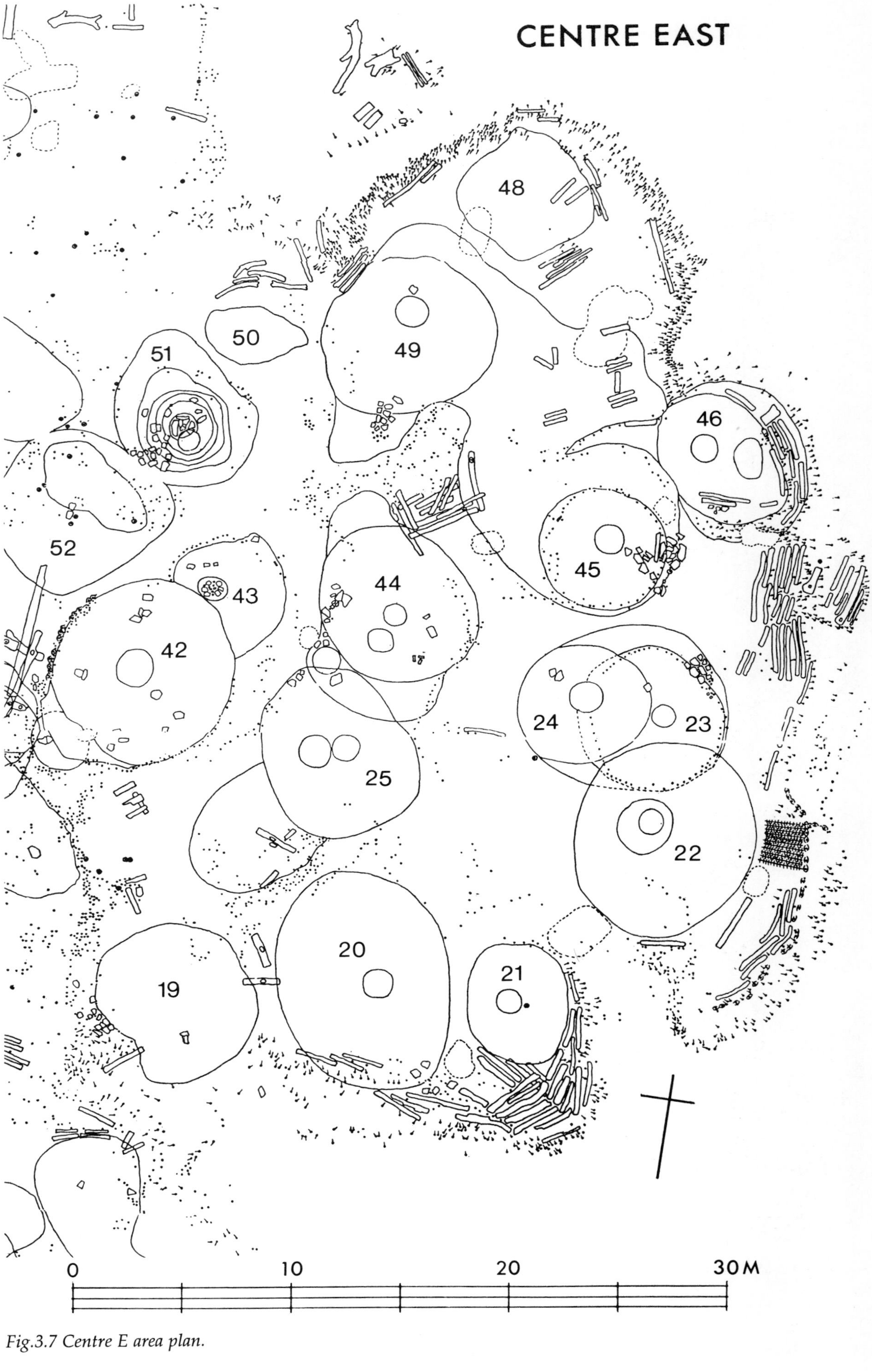

Fig.3.7 Centre E area plan.

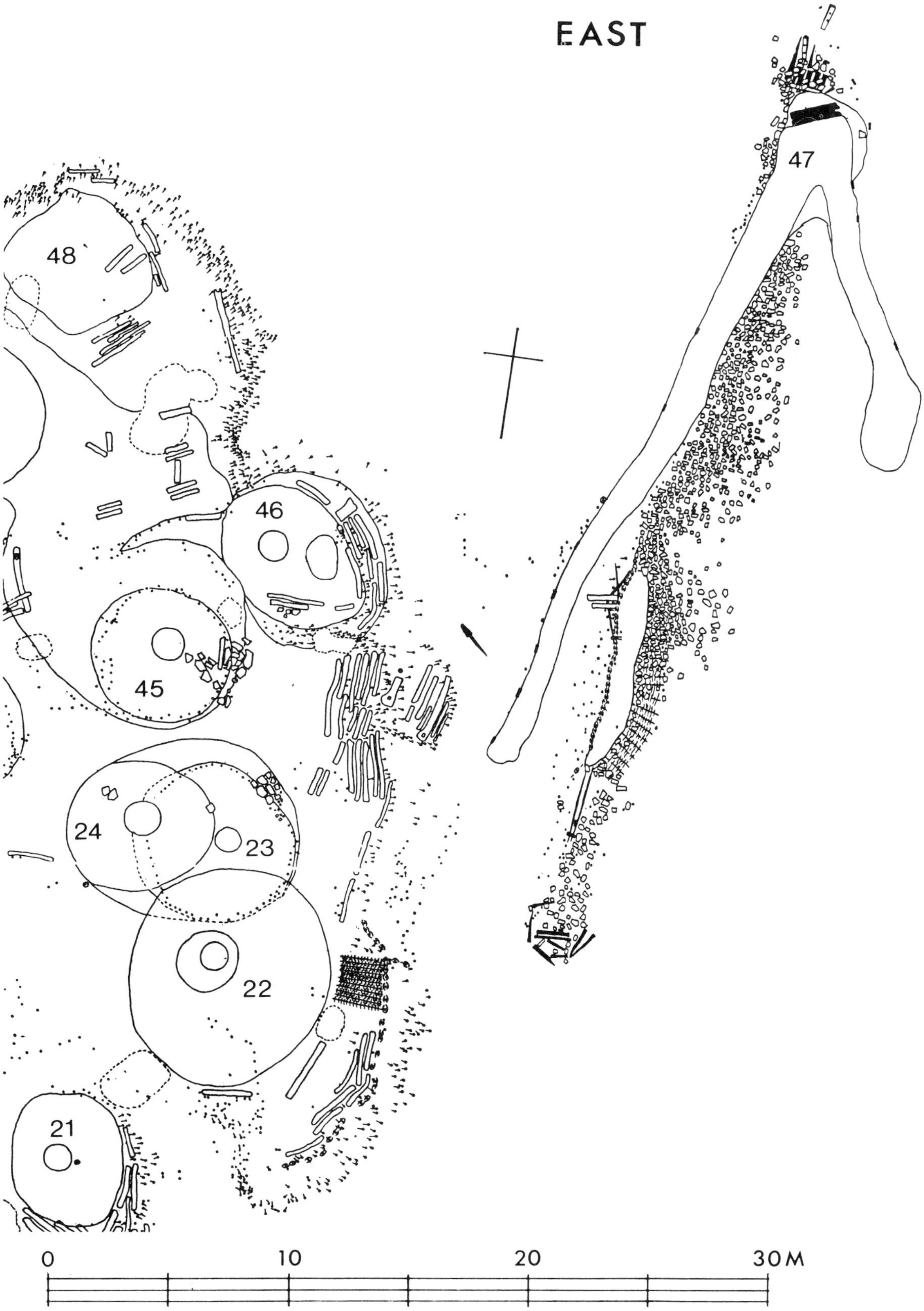

Fig.3.8 E area plan.

Fig.3.9 SW area plan.

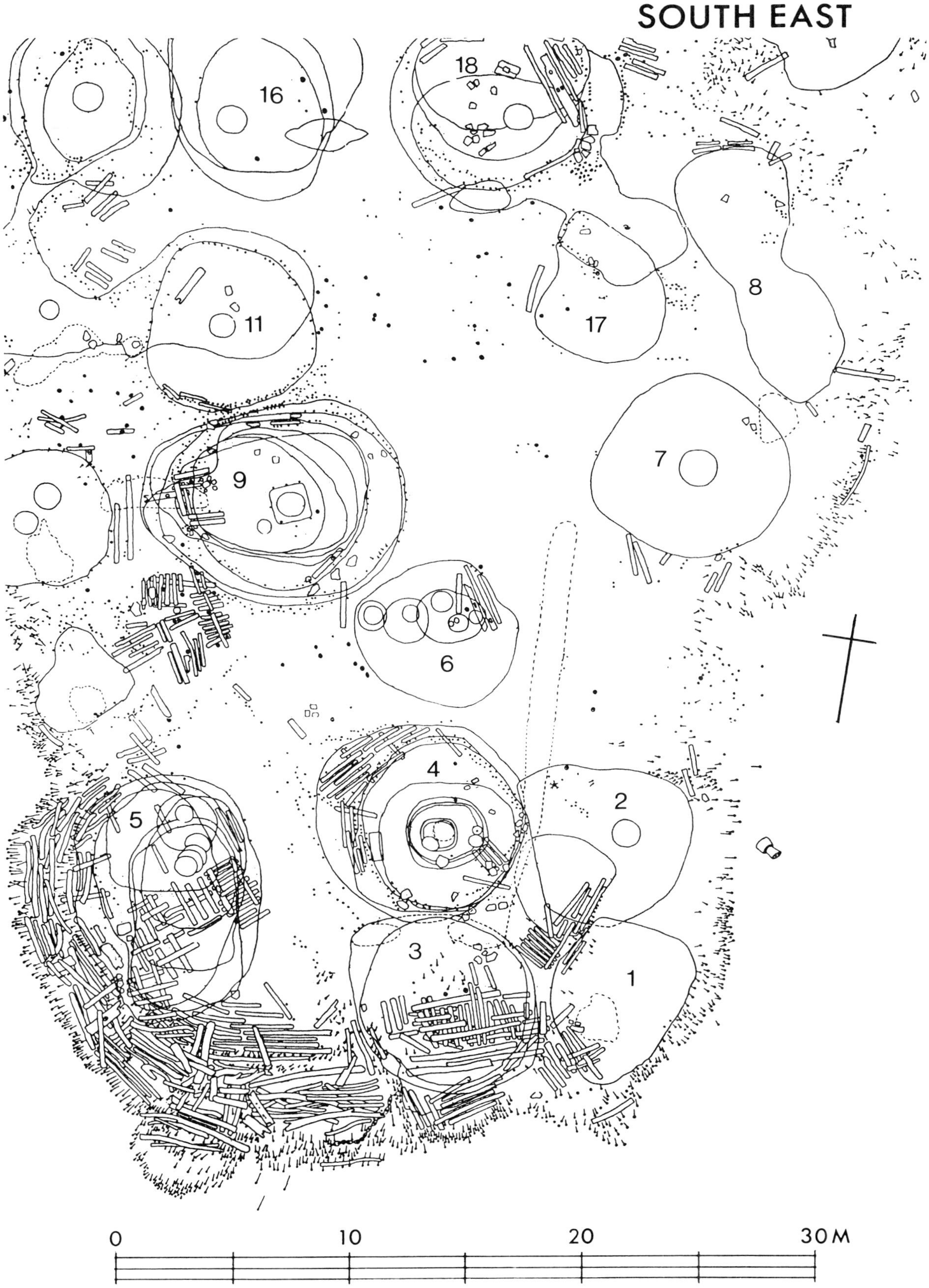

Fig.3.10 SE area plan.

Mound 7 (1894). (fig.3.10)

Spread of yellow clay on the E side of the site in its S sector. The clay represents 2 Floors and extends over a circular area 8.2m x 8.5m, max. thickness 460mm. The 2 Floors coincided and each had a circular gravel hearth; the upper Floor (1) represents a repair of the original. Black earth covered each Floor. No other structural remains were noted; a small patch of stones under a dump of clay lay beneath M7 at the NE. A few uprights were found at the S end, perhaps some slender windbreak supports. The line of palisade posts extending up from the S veers sharply away to the E as it touches M7; it is possible that it was only in this phase that any form of palisade was built in this part of the site, with M7 and M8 now occupying what had been an open entry.

The foundation consisted of 3 layers of heavy logs or planks in crisscross arrangement but these are not recorded on the plan. The relics found were all unstratified, but all probably belong to a single phase of activity.

Stratigraphy: none

Phase: Late

Mound 7 finds

B 177	notched and perforated ox/horse tibia
E 49	finger ring
E 52	rivet head
E 53	penannular ring, brooch?
E 54	spiral finger ring
E 232	penannular brooch, Fowler type B?
G 6	bead, blue annular, Guido group 6
G 7	bead, purple annular, Guido group 6
G 8	bead, globular turquoise, Guido group 7
H 283	weaving comb
H 380	sawn antler
H 381	handle
H 382	worked antler, cheek piece?
H 383	sawn antler
HS 1024	grinding stone
L 14	spindle whorl (tin)
L 15	spiral ring (lead)
L 16	ring (tin)
S 16	pebbles x 19 ?sling stones

Mound 7 (NE of)

E 38	finger ring

Mound 7 (SE of)

B 146	point
X 54	handle cross-piece, ash

Mound 7 (NW of)

L 50	tin rod, copper alloy terminals

Mound 7 (E of) outside palisade

W 52	spindle whorl (lias)
X 93	knobbed pile, oak

Mound 7 (SE of) outside palisade

B 147	point (gouge)
E 39	handle

Mound 8 (1894). (fig.3.10)

An elongated spread of yellow clay on the E side of the site just N of M7, 11.0m N-S and 5.0m W-E with a narrowing in the middle. There was no hearth, and no signs of any structure. The foundation was brushwood. The palisade line turns smoothly around M8 leading into a major entry to the N but the palisade posts look haphazard. The relics were few in number, but just off the Floor to the E, between the Floor and the palisade, were found 17 pieces of a wooden frame, perhaps a skin-stretcher.

Stratigraphy: none

Phase: Late

Mound 8 finds

B 144	point (gouge)
B 166	polished sheep metatarsal
I 27	ring
P **	decorated pottery

Mound 8 (NE of)

B 131	unfinished pin
B 151	point (gouge)
P 97	decorated jar
X 70	handle, oak

Mound 8 (SE of)

B 143	polished ox metatarsal
B 145	pointed splinter
B 149	point
X 66	framework, 17 pieces, ash and oak

Mound 8 (SW of)

E 56	binding

Mound 8 (NW of)

M 8	skull, sword cuts
W 50	spindle whorl (clay)
X 88	knobbed pile

Mound 8 (SE of) outside palisade

P 100	decorated bowl
W 51	spindle whorl (lias)
Y **	sling shot, large number

Mound 9 (1896). (figs.3.9 and 3.10)

Complex spreads, mostly of yellow clay, central to S part of site. The clays represent 9 Floors and cover an area 9.0 x 11.3m, max. thickness 1.8m; this was a substantial mound, and its top was 630mm above the level of the field in 1892. The lowest Floors (9-8) were of blue clay, and were pear-shaped with narrower end to the W. Curved lines of wall posts extended back from a W entrance based on horizontal and vertical planks, and a short stone path was laid into this entry. A hearth of baked clay was noted just inside the structure which is interpreted as an oval house 7.9 x 6.8m with a timber-framed porch. Floors 7-6-5 were smaller, consisting only of spreads of yellow clay which sealed the previous occupation layer and were in effect preparatory to the major reconstruction of Floor 4; several large posts believed by Bulleid to relate to Floor 5 are more likely to be of Floor 4. Floor 4 re-established the oval or pear-shape of the structure now erected. This was 9.1 x 6.4m with a rectangular baked clay 'hearth', repaired once, and rather uncertain evidence of any real roofed structure built over this Floor. The abundance of posts spread around the W end of the Mound, and posts within the clay, suggest that Floor 4 may have had some form of protection. The entry to the W was maintained and a clay spread (M12) was laid down as part of the arrangement. The earlier 'hearth' of Floor 4 was oblong, 1.6 x 1.4m, and raised 100mm above the Floor, with smoothed slightly curved sides and its top impressed by 67 circles, made by pressing a pot or other rim into soft clay prior to hardening by heat; the circles are 140mm diameter, with the imprint 9mm wide and up to 6mm deep. They were clearly disposed over the surface of this 'hearth', which is more likely to have been a table or presentation area, although Bulleid noted a thin layer of ash on the table. It was soon sealed by a layer of clay baked and undecorated, providing a further raised flat area. Associated with these structures was an adjacent oven, a basin-like hollow cut into the Floor and with smooth fire-cracked base and sides. The Floor clay was burnt around this oven. Floors 3-2-1 marked a transformation of M9. The area covered by clay was extended in all directions to cover a more rounded area 11.0 x 8.8m at max.; Bulleid's plan and sections show the extensions clearly. Floor 3 had a gravel hearth, replaced by a baked clay hearth, both of rectangular shape and built over the now sealed hearths of Floor 4. Floor 2 is a repair with renewed hearth and Floor 1 is a further minor adjustment of the clay spread but augmented by stone paving here and there. Floors 3-2-1 were associated with lines of wall posts and oak posts were also noted in the interior, less easily related to specific Floors. The oval house of Floors 3-2-1 probably had a W entrance in continuation with the earlier structures. Bulleid recorded a number of timbers lying just to the SW of Floors 3-2-1, consisting of horizontal timber and vertical oak posts. The shape of this is roughly rectangular and it may have been an assembly area during the work on M9. There is not much evidence to suggest it is stratigraphically earlier than M9 or M10, nor that it ever formed a roofed structure. It may well have been a loading bay for M9 (see M10). The foundation beneath all this weight of clay of M9 was rather slight, mostly brushwood and peat blocks, but at the W the porch and entrance was more heavily supported by planks (see Floors 9-8).

The relics from M9 were numerous and some were assigned to particular Floors. The bulk of finds are not stratified and include many whorls, decorated pottery, bone and antler pieces, bronze rings and part of a rotary quern. With 9 Floors identified, it is a pity so many relics are not tied to individual phases.

Stratigraphy: none, except path to M12. One object beneath Mound

Phases: Floors 9-8 Middle, Floors 7-6-5-4 Late, Floors 3-2-1 Final

Mound 9 finds

B 257	notched and perforated horse/ox tibia
B 258	'button'
B 259	sawn bone
B 261	'bobbin', type E
B 263	polished ox metatarsal
B 265	notched and perforated horse/ox tibia
B 267	polished ox bone
D 25	decorated pottery base
D 60	triangular baked clay block
D **	part perforated clay ball
E 221	bronze sheet
F 380	scraper
G 16	bead, blue ring bead, Guido group 6 ivb
H 181	ferrule
H 183	point
H 187	weaving comb fragment
H 188	sawn tine
H 196	sawn antler
H 199	ferrule
H 385	tine
H 387	worked antler
K 14	ring
L 25	weight (lead)
P 255	decorated jar
P 260	decorated jar
P 261	decorated jar
P 293	decorated sherd
P 295	decorated sherd
P **	pottery, large quantity, above average decorated
Q 11	rotary quern, lower stone
T 14	dog canine
W 92	spindle whorl (shale)
W 94	spindle whorl (lias)
W 96	spindle whorl (femur head)
W 98	spindle whorl (femur head)
W 100	spindle whorl (sandstone)
W 101	spindle whorl (femur head)
W 103	spindle whorl (clay)

Mound 9 (Floor 1)

E 121	bar
S 8	disc (sandstone)
W 34	spindle whorl (sandstone)
W 102	spindle whorl (sandstone)

Mound 9 (Floor 2)

B 266	needle
E 119	rod
E 126	rivet heads x 2
H 191	cheek piece
H 194	weaving comb
W 97	spindle whorl (clay)

Mound 9 (Floor 2 or 3)

H 193	cheek piece
H 195	worked antler
I 64	ring

Mound 9 (Floor 3)

E 124	brooch, La Tène III wire brooch
E 128	brooch, La Tène III wire brooch
E 129	brooch, La Tène III

H 185	weaving comb, unfinished
H 186	weaving comb

Mound 9 (Floor 4)

W 91	spindle whorl, unfinished (sandstone)
X 30	worked wood, oak

Mound 9 (Floor 5)

H 184	worked antler
L 24	spindle whorl (tin)
P 154	decorated jar

Mound 9 (Floor 6)

X 79	rectangular, perforated slab, oak

Mound 9 (Floor 5 or 6)

H 200	cheek piece

Mound 9 (Floor 7)

H 190	worked antler
I 62	gouge

Mound 9 (Floor 8)

H 372	cheek piece
I 63	billhook

Mound 9 (Floor 9)

H 189	cheek piece
W 99	spindle whorl (clay)

Mound 9 (under)

X 10	ladle

Mound 9 (NE of)

B 260	point (gouge)
B 262	point (gouge)
E 122	ring, harness?
E 123	finger ring
E 125	ring, harness?
H 192	sawn tine
M 26	charred adult, part

Mound 9 (SE of)

G 15	bead, blue ring bead, Guido group 6

Mound 9 (NW of)

D 58	ring
E 117	rivet head
E 120	finger ring
M 25	skeleton, young child

Mound 10 (1896). (fig. 3.9)

Small spread of yellow clay dumped at the edge of the palisade and adjacent to the timber and post platform at the SW of M9. The clay covered an irregular area 4.6 x 4.3m max, thickness 230mm. A sandstone rubble surface covered part of the spread. No hearth was seen, and the foundation was brushwood. Few relics were found. The extensive timberwork to NE of M10 links this Mound with M9 in some imprecise way; if the timber was some sort of loading or unloading bay, or stance, then M10 could represent a debris jettison zone from where debris was flung over the palisade.

Stratigraphy: none other than the timbers to NE

Phase: Late

Mound 10 finds

Mound 10 (NW of)

E 111	finger ring

Mound 10 (W of) outside palisade

F 48	core
H 177	worked tine
H 178	cheek piece
M 24	child's parietal bones (2)

Mound 11 (1896). (figs.3.6, 3.9 and 3.10)

Spreads of yellow clay directly N of M9 on the W side of the site. The clay represents 3 Floors over an area 7.9 x 7.0m, max. thickness 500mm. Floors 3-2 were virtually the same, Floor 2 being a renewal of Floor 3. Each had a central hearth of baked clay, and Floor 2 had some stone slabs on the clay perhaps representing a stone hearth (Bulleid) or rough paving. A line of wall posts around these Floors suggests a round house, with no clear entrance apparent. Floor 1 marks the disappearance of the structure, replaced by a spread of clay that covered the N two thirds of Floors 3-2 and extended W as a sinuous spread linking parts of M13, M14, M15 and M16; this is discussed under M13 as it is well-stratified here. To the E of M11 were various groups of oak posts, some extending into M17. Bulleid offers no description of these and they may represent drying racks or windbreaks; they respect Floor 1 and may be related. The foundation under M11 was brushwood, and one beam lying loose. The relics were few in number apart from quantities of coarse pottery mostly found near the S and SW.

Stratigraphy: Floor 1 joins M15 Floor 1 and M13 Floor 4 and M14 Floor 1, and lies under M16 Floor 1 and Floor 3

Phase: Floors 3-2 Middle, Floor 1 Late

Mound 11 finds

P 254	decorated bowl
P 256	decorated sherd
P 258	decorated bowl
P **	decorated pottery

Mound 11 (Floor 1)

E 157	brooch, La Tène III 'Glastonbury' mock spring form
P **	decorated bowl

Mound 11 (Floor 2)

E 116	tweezers
E 118	brooch pin and one turn of spring
G 18	zig-zag decorated bead, blue, Guido group 5
H 180	sawn burr
H 182	ferrule
J 1	jet bead/ring
L 23	lump/dribble (lead/tin)
W 93	spindle whorl (sandstone)

Mound 11 (NE of)

Q 33	rotary quern, lower stone

Mound 11 (SE of)

E 127	spiral finger ring

Mound 11 (SW of)

E 115	binding
W 90	spindle whorl (sandstone)

Mound 11 (NW of)

P 159	decorated lid

Mound 12 (1896). (fig.3.9)

Small spread of yellow clay just inside the W palisade, and attached by a path to M9. The area of clay was 6.5 x 6.0m, max. thickness 760mm, and 3 Floors were recorded. Floors 3 and 2 each had a baked clay hearth and were replaced by Floor 1, of slightly larger size, with a damaged hearth and a paving of rubble on the S which possibly relates to a rubble path off to the E which was spread over M9 Floor 8. Around the edge of Floor 1 was a sparse line of posts, incomplete, which Bulleid considered to be the wall of a round house; this is not certain, and a series of baffles or windbreaks may be more likely. The foundation was brushwood with a few logs laid alongside the palisade up to which the clay extended. The relics were very few. M12 is probably an adjunct to M9, linked to it by a stone path, and the hearths of M12 perhaps form part of the M9 activities.

Stratigraphy: Rubble path under Floor 1 on E lies over M9 Floor 8 and under M9 Floors 1-3

Phases: Floor 3 Middle, Floor 2 Late, Floor 1 Final

Mound 12 finds

P **	cordoned bowl
W 191	spindle whorl, unfinished (sandstone)

Mound 12 (Floor 1)

B 256	point (gouge)
E 112	binding, 3 perforations
K 11	armlet
K 13	armlet

Mound 12 (Floor 2)

E 113	needle
E 114	ring-headed pin

Mound 13 (1896 and 1907). (fig.3.5)

Complex spreads of various clays at extreme W edge of site in central area. The clays represent 8 Floors, max thickness 2.8m (the thickest of any mound as Bulleid's section shows) and covering an area 9.8 x 9.1m. Floors 8-7-6 were of blue clay but are not marked on the plan, nor dimensions given, and no hearths were found; the presumption is that these were simple spreads. Floor 5 was of grey clay and had no hearth but was a circular spread, probably an open stance for the structure of M14 just to the N. Floor 4 was of grey and blue clay and had heavy timbers embedded in it, probably the inception of the Floor 3 structure (see below). Floor 4 was in reality a very extensive spread of clay, without structural elements, that extended from M13 E to form the top Floor (1) of M11, M15 and M14. This clay was deliberately shaped to form rounded patches or spreads on all these mounds, reflecting their previous shapes while providing linking clay walks or working areas between; between M13 and M11 a hearth was built on the spread. The clay was also extended NE of M13 to provide an open stance for both M13 and M14. Many posts were embedded beneath and presumably through the clay, probably edging it in places particularly towards M15, and a spread of planks lay off the clay near M15. The clay extended over a large area, 30m from M11 to the palisade, and 15m from M11/13 to M14/15. On M13, this Floor was covered by timber which formed some sort of wooden flooring for a round house, Floor 3, a major structure and one that represents one of Bulleid's 'ideal' houses. A baked clay hearth and stone slab were placed inside the NE entrance, which was marked by two squared vertical posts; the remainder of the wall posts were roundwood. Hurdlework was noted all around the perimeter except at the entrance. The entry was paved with 2 layers of planking, and, as noted above, planks were embedded in the clay around the S and W parts of the Floor; that on the W radiated from the centre of the Floor. On Bulleid's plan there is a heap of timber just to the N of M13 which may be some sort of platform outside the house. Some unused sugar-loaf-headed piles lay outside the wall, and horizontal hurdles were noted inside the wall lying upon the timbers; the hurdles might represent unused panels laid flat as flooring. Floor 2 was a renewal of the flooring of this house and another hearth was built; some hurdlework was replaced. Floor 1 was a large spread of yellow clay which extended over the dismantled remains of the Floor 3-2 structure; Floor 1 was spread over the previous wall lines and had no structural elements other than a small hearth. It presumably was an open stance, as had been Floors 5 and 4.

The foundation of M13 was brushwood with a few pieces of timber including a perforated plank from a loom according to Bulleid. An alder stump was noted in the foundation deposits. M13 formed an integral part of a small complex of mounds at the centre West of the site, placed just inside the palisade; M13 is closely related to M14, 11 and 15. The palisade makes a sharp curve around M13 and posts extend NE along the line of the Floors while another line of posts cuts off to the S to continue the external palisade line; the NE line represents an early palisade, while the S line is a later extension of the palisade as the site expanded to the S.

The relics were few in number with only one object stratified on a Floor, and wooden pieces beneath the mound. Outside the palisade were found many seeds, fish scales, chips and pieces of wood, animal bones and pottery.

Stratigraphy: Floor 4 joins M11 Floor 1, M15 Floor 1 and M14 Floor 1. As Floors 3-2 overlie Floor 4, the house represented by Floors 3-2 is relatively late in date. Two wooden objects beneath Mound

Phase: Floor 8-7-6 Early, Floor 5 Middle, Floor 4-3-2 Late, Floor 1 Final

Mound 13 finds

B 221	point (gouge)
B 234	worked bone
F **	flakes x 3, 1 retouched
P 257	decorated bowl

P **	decorated pottery
W 116	spindle whorl (clay)
X 68	knobbed piles x 2

Mound 13 (Floor 2)

H 364	handle

Mound 13 (under)

X 74	worked oak
X 82	rectangular frame

Mound 13 (NE of)

E 158	brooch, La Tène III 'Glastonbury' mock spring type
E 159	button-and-loop fastener, Wild class I

Mound 13 (SE of)

H 179	weaving comb
K 12	armlet
X 24	tub, stave-built

Mound 13 (SW of)

X 81	handle, oak

Mound 13 (SW of) outside palisade

B 121	knife marked rib
X 52	knobbed object
**	seeds, fish scales, wood chips, animal bones, sling shot

Mound 13 (NW of) outside palisade

X 15	perforated peg
X 25	lid
X 75	handle

Mound 14 (1898). (fig.3.5)

Spread of mostly yellow clay near the W edge of the site. The clays represent 4 Floors, over an area 12.2 x 8.5m, max. thickness *c* 1m. Although numbered as M14, the blue clays of Floor 4 are well outside those of Floors 3-2-1, and extend to the palisade here. A small hearth was found, and this Floor must represent not M14 itself but a partial adjunct to an open stance at M13 immediately to the S. However, Floor 4 is directly overlain by Floor 3, most of which was spread to the NE of Floor 4 in a pear-shape with narrow end on the middle of Floor 4. A baked clay hearth lay near the centre of Floor 3 and some stone slabs formed a firm entry on the W. The clay was laid on a heavy base of timber and brushwood about 380mm thick, laid in two layers, and some pressed into the blue clay of Floor 4. Around Floor 3 was a line of wallposts, parts charred, and the Floor had pieces of hurdles and baked clay with finger marks. This was probably a round house, burnt down soon after construction. Floor 2 is an expansion and rebuilding of this house, with the debris partly cleared away and the structure built to the same pear-shape but larger. The line of wall posts for this Floor 2 house is less clear than that for Floor 3. The central flooring was augmented by radiating planks on the N side and a paved clay hearth was central to the house. A smaller clay hearth lay nearer the entrance. The plan shows that Floor 2 clay was connected with other clay spreads to the N, on M29, 35 and 36. This was an important observation by Bulleid and provides one of the main planks for the sequence proposed here. Floor 1 is part of the wider spread of clay seen on M11, 13 and 15. It extended well outside the now dismantled structure and spread E and S to create a wide and open series of stances, one of which (at M13) was used as a base for a structure - to replace that at M14.

The foundation of M14 was rather slight in the E, brushwood and a few logs, but was heavier in the W half, and near the palisade there were 5-6 layers of timber, probably dumped to help firm up the planned edge to the site. The palisade had firm hurdle work for 12m along M14. The relics from M14 were few in number, and only 3 objects are stratified, including a bronze disc from Floor 1. Between the palisade and Floor 4 were found a wooden ladder and a door, doubtless once among the furniture of the round house of Floors 3-2. A rectangular structure lay to the NW of M14 (see M29 description).

Stratigraphy: Floor 1 joins M13 Floor 4, M15 Floor 1 and M11 Floor 1. Floor 2 joins M29 Floor 2, M35 Floor 2 and M36 Floor 1 and is thus under M33 Floors 3-2-1

Phase: Floor 4-3 Early, Floor 2 Middle, Floor 1 Late

Mound 14 finds

B 322	weaving comb
F 58	flake
P **	decorated pottery

Mound 14 (Floor 1)

E 162	circular ornament
E 163	wire

Mound 14 (Floor 2)

E 178	fastening

Mound 14 (under)

**	wood chips, charcoal

Mound 14 (SW of)

X 28	saw-shaped object

Mound 14 (SW of) outside palisade

X 3	stave-built tub, oak
X 4	handle, oak
X 56	door-like object, oak

Mound 14 (NW of) outside palisade

X 46	notched and perforated object, oak
X 55	ladder, ash
**	'charred bread'

Mound 15 (1898). (fig.3.6)

Spread of yellow clay near centre of site. The clays represent 3 Floors, covering an area 7.0 x 6.0m max. thickness 740mm. Floor 3 (lowest) was only a small patch 5.3 x 4.0m but provided a base for 5 hearths, superimposed and not side by side; the lowest hearth was made of gravel, the upper 4 of baked clay. Each had a thin layer of ash upon its flat surface. A line of posts along the E edge of Floor 3 may represent some form of shelter or drying rack. Floor 2 was a larger spread of clay with an 'incomplete' hearth, and Floor 1 was larger still with another hearth, again of baked clay and 'incomplete' - whether this means unfinished or damaged is not made clear by Bulleid. Floor 1 clay extends from

M15 in a narrow tongue to link with Floors on other Mounds, M11, M13 and M14 (see M13 for description of this Floor).

The foundation of M15 was brushwood with some timber. There were many posts driven into the foundation particularly at the narrowing of the clay at S but also over and beyond the N part. Some of these may have been the base of shelters or racks but a very large pile, 230mm diameter, was driven into the foundation just off the clay to the W and perhaps the posts are in some way connected to this impressive pile the height of which is unknown. There was also a series of oak posts to the NW of M15, in 2 parallel rows which may have been part of a rectangular structure. N of the clay, some woodwork debris was found deep in the peat. The relics associated with M15 were few in number.

Stratigraphy: Floor 1 joins M11 Floor 1, M14 Floor 1 and M13 Floor 4. Floor 1 lies over M16 Floors 3 and 1

Phase: Floor 3 Early, Floor 2 Middle, Floor 1 Late

Mound 15 finds

B 350	'bobbin', type D
B 351	'bobbin', type E
B 352	needle
B 353	polished ox metatarsal
B 354	splinter
B 363	charred bone
I 84	file
K 22	ring
P 307	decorated bowl
P **	decorated pottery
W 154	spindle whorl (lias)

Mound 15 (NE of)

S 26	neolithic axe, group VII

Mound 15 (SE of)

W 135	spindle whorl (sandstone)

Mound 16 (1898). (figs. 3.6 and 3.9)

Spread of mostly yellow clay near centre of site. The clay represents 4 Floors, over an area 8.5 x 8.2m, max. thickness 635mm. Floor 4 was a small patch of grey clay only 3.5 x 1.3m, and has no real relationship with M16, being set well to the E; it hardly deserves the cachet of Floor. Floor 3 was a large oval spread with 'incomplete' hearth. Floor 2 was smaller, again with an 'incomplete' hearth; along the edges of the Floor, and on the Floor, was a large amount of baked clay rubble with hurdle and timber imprints, interpreted by Bulleid as the residue of a 'dwelling' destroyed by fire. The plan shows only 2 posts on the edge of Floor 2, and 3 larger posts set near the edge of the clay, so any structure may have been rather slight and was certainly small in size, 5.8 x 5.2m; this Floor is better interpreted as an open stance, or perhaps a small enclosed space without roofing. Floor 1 was a larger clay spread which extended onto M28 and was covered by part of M15. Floor 1 had another 'incomplete' hearth. All the Floors were covered by black earth, representing some kind of occupation deposit.

The foundation was brushwood, and 3 alder stumps were incorporated *in situ*.

Stratigraphy: Floor 1 joins M28, Floors 3-2-1 lie under M15 Floor 1

Phase: Floor 4-3 Early, Floor 2-1 Middle

Mound 16 finds

B **	worked bone
B **	worked bone
B 268	'bobbin', type C
B 347	'bobbin', type E
B 348	'bobbin', type D
B 349	'bobbin', type D
B 427	'bobbin', type D
B 430	'bobbin', type E
B 434	'bobbin', type E
C 32	crucible
F 64	flakes x 3
H 386	handle
H 388	sawn antler
P 289	decorated bowl
P **	Roman bowl sherd

Mound 16 (Floor 1)

E 175	finger ring
W 153	spindle whorl (sandstone)

Mound 16 (Floor 2)

E 174	button-and-loop fastener, Wild class I
H 267	weaving comb
W 152	spindle whorl (sandstone)
W 155	spindle whorl (sandstone)

Mound 16 (Floor 3)

H 268	sawn antler

Mound 16 (N of)

E 165	finger ring

Mound 17 (1895). (figs.3.6, 3.9 and 3.10)

Small spread of clay near E edge of the site. The clay represents 2 Floors over an area 6.7 x 5.5m, max. thickness 300mm. The mound was low and irregular in shape. Floor 2 had no hearth and no black earth; it was merely a small spread of yellow clay. Floor 1 was unrelated to M17, being an extension of clay from M18 and described there. There was a cluster of posts just off the E edge of Floor 2, perhaps drying rack supports, and several sets of heavier oak posts to the W, perhaps the remains of some platforms or shelters.

The foundation was a thin brushwood layer under Floor 2. The relics were few in number; an iron dagger was found beside the cluster of posts.

Stratigraphy: Floor 1 joins M18 Floor 1

Phase: Floor 2 Middle, Floor 1 Late

Mound 17 finds

B 222	ferrule?
B 359b	'bobbin', typeE
P **	decorated pottery

Mound 17 (NE of)

L 18	rod
I 32	dagger blade fragment

Mound 17 (SW of)

L 30	fragments x 2

Mound 18 (1895). (fig.3.6)

Complex spreads of mostly yellow clay in central part of site. The spreads represent 4 asymmetrical Floors in an area 10.0 x 8.3m, max. thickness 1.2m. Floor 4 was of grey clay, in 2 distinct layers with black earth between; only one of these layers (N) is shown on the plan although both appear in Bulleid's section and his text makes the extent to the S clear. A baked clay hearth was central to the combined layers. The clay floor was covered by burnt clay with marks of timber and hurdles, and pieces of charcoal and part-burned timber; a line of wall posts was recorded, the tops of some posts burned. A flooring of timber was laid on the debris, the planks concentric to the floor area. All of this evidence indicates a round house soon burnt, and its Floor renewed by planking. This served as the base for Floor 3, of yellow clay, which extended only over the S part of the Mound, the N part with planks left uncovered. The hearth was rebuilt, twice, and the floor had more planks laid upon it although these do not appear in the section. It is probable that Floor 3 marks a re-erection of a round house. Floor 2 was another spread of yellow clay used as a base for plank flooring and a hearth, renewed once again. Some stone paving was also noted. This Floor probably represents a repair of the structure as it respects the wall post line. A heap of ash 1.8m diameter was dumped just S of the structure. The entrance to the structure of Floors 4-3-2 was to the SE where stone slabs and a sill of squared oak were placed. The hearth, always in the same position, was part way in from the entrance. Floor 1 was of yellow clay spreading over and beyond the house Floors, and represents a change here from structure to open area. The clay spread SE and became Floor 1 of M17. A baked red marl hearth was noted in the usual place on M18, and some posts edged the expanded clay at the S, and also along the E edge where a line of posts, horizontal planks and thick oak piles perhaps represent some platform or other structure beside the clay spread of Floor 1. There were many posts recorded to the N of M18 where it nearly touched M27.

The foundation of M18 was brushwood laid on a simple base of timber and logs. The relics found were numerous, and included many peas and barley on Floors 4,2 and 1. Much pottery came from the Mound, and some burnt human bone was scattered about. Many objects are unstratified.

Stratigraphy: Floor 1 joins M17 Floor 1, and M18 abuts M27 but no join or overlap was noted

Phase: Floor 4 Early, Floor 3-2 Middle, Floor 1 Late

Mound 18 finds

B 197	point (gouge)
B 205	modelling tool?
B 207	notched ox/horse femur
B 212	point (gouge)
B 213	'bobbin', type D
B 214	'bobbin', type D
B 215	'bobbin', type E
B 216	'bobbin', type D
B 218	cut and polished sheep metatarsal
B 219	perforated ox humerus
B 220	needle
D 67	loom weight
H 156	worked tine
H 157	worked tine
H 158	sawn antler
H 159	worked tine
H 160	cheek piece
H 161	sawn tine
I 41	billhook
I 43	awl
M **	tibia and charred bone fragments
P 189	decorated bowl
P 200	decorated bowl
P 207	decorated vessel
P 209	decorated bowl
P 210	decorated sherd
P 212	decorated base
P 214	decorated bowl
P 215	decorated bowl
P 218	decorated sherd
P 219	decorated sherd
P 221	decorated bowl
P 223	decorated bowl
P 224	decorated sherd
P 225	decorated jar
P 228	cordoned jar
P 230	decorated sherd
P 234	decorated sherd
P 239	decorated bowl
P 240	decorated bowl
P 241	decorated bowl
P 243	decorated bowl
P 244	decorated bowl
P 245	decorated jar
P 252	decorated jar
P **	pottery, above average decorated
W 74	spindle whorl, unfinished (sandstone)
W 80	spindle whorl (lias)
W 128	spindle whorl (clay)

Mound 18 (By entrance)

B 194	needle

Mound 18 (Floor 1)

B 195	polished sheep metatarsal
B 208	needle
E 87	tweezers
E 93	brooch, La Tène III, Nauheim
E 94	pulley-like ring
W 73	spindle whorl (pottery)
**	peas and wheat

Mound 18 (Floor 2)

B 209	toggle
B 210	needle
B 211	disc
D **	loom weights, 'several'
E 95	spiral
E 96	rivet

H 141	hammer
I 40	knife
I 42	socketed spearhead
L 19	spindle whorl (lead)
M 12	tibia fragment
P **	one box of pottery
**	peas and wheat

Mound 18 (Floor 3)

I 37	finger ring
P **	'many pieces of coarse pottery'
**	slag

Mound 18 (Floor 4)

B 217	perforated horse/ox tibia. Dated by C14
H 162	cheek piece
I 39	fragments of 4 rings
L 20	spindle whorl (lead/tin)
L 21	lump (tin)
M 13	charred cranial fragments, femur and long bone fragments
W 75	spindle whorl (lias)
W 76	spindle whorl (limestone)
W 77	spindle whorl (lias)
W 78	spindle whorl (lias)
W 79	spindle whorl (lias)
**	peas and barley

Mound 18 (under)

X 77	rectangular, perforated slab, oak
**	charcoal

Mound 18 (NE of)

B 189	notched and perforated ox/horse tibia
B 190	sawn bone
K 7	ring
X 12	hemisphere

Mound 18 (SE of)

B 192	needle
B 193	needle
B 196	perforated ox humerus

Mound 18 (SW of)

E 160	spiral finger ring
E 161	penannular brooch, Fowler type B
Q 32	saddle quern, upper stone
W 134	spindle whorl? (clay)

Mound 19 (1894). (fig.3.7)

Single spread of yellow clay near E edge of site, covering an area 7.6 x 7.3m, max. thickness 280mm. The Floor had some black earth upon it, and had no hearth nor any other structural elements apart from stone slabs at the SW; these perhaps provide a working or storage platform beside the Floor, but it is more likely that they are the residue of a paved entry through the original palisade. To the SW of M19, the S line of the palisade ends at the stones, and Bulleid recorded numerous posts in a line running from here N, thus to the W of M19 and E of M26, possibly veering NE to the S of M42 - 43. This was an early palisade, before the whole E part of the site was constructed. When the expansion occurred, M19 was formed, to act as one of the entries to the enlarged site, the new palisade picking up its line to the E of M19.

The foundation was brushwood with a few logs; 2 perforated oak beams lay to the E, between M19 and M20. The relics on and near M19 were few in number.

Stratigraphy: none

Phase: Final

Mound 19 finds

B 135	'bobbin', type D
B 136	'bobbin', type D
B 137	point (gouge)
E 62	brooch pin
E 77	binding

Mound 19 (NE of)

B 75	point (gouge)
E 73	rivet

Mound 19 (SW of)

B 132	'bobbin', type D
B 138	gnawed bone
B 139	point (point)
M 5	mandible fragment

Mound 19 (NW of)

B 133	'bobbin', type D
B 134	point (gouge)
B 165	point (gouge)
E 48	brooch, one piece simple, flat bow arched profile

Mound 20 (1894). (fig.3.7)

Large spread of yellow clay at the S edge of the E segment of the site. The clay represents 5 Floors, over an area 10.4 x 8.5m, max. thickness 1.0m. Each Floor was covered by black earth, and each had a hearth of baked clay; the hearth of Floor 3 was larger than the others and had a stone slab centre. Bulleid's plan shows only one spread and presumably the 5 Floors represent periodic renewal of the original Floor 5 surface. There was no trace of any wall posts, but at the N a line of posts spread out from the edge towards M25 (see M25 description). M20 was probably an open stance, protected only on the S by the palisade; some tent-like structure is a possibility. On the S, M20 spread out to the palisade and at the SE edge some stone slabs may have provided an exit through a break in the fence to an area supported by planks, perhaps for a flat or raised platform at the SE end of the palisade (see M21).

The foundation of M20 was a thick brushwood layer over timbers in the S, and more sparsely laid elsewhere. Two perforated oak beams 1.5m long lay off to the W between M20 and M19. The relics included many coarse potsherds near the beams, and some near the SE stone slabs.

Stratigraphy: none, but clay spreads into palisade posts

Phase: Floors 5-4-3 Late, Floors 2-1 Final

Mound 20 finds

B 140	gnawed bone
B 141	splinter
B 142	worked bone
B 167	polished horse bone

B 168	'bobbin', type B
E 74	brooch, one piece simple brooch, continental form
G 9	bead, blue with white spirals, Guido class 6
H 95	ring
H 96	cheek piece
H 97	cheek piece
H 111	weaving comb fragment
H 366	toggle
H 396	sawn and perforated tine
K 10	armlet
P 40	decorated bowl

Mound 20 (under)

D **	loom weight

Mound 20 (NE of)

B 163	'bobbin', type D

Mound 20 (SE of)

E 82	spiral finger ring

Mound 20 (SW of)

D 46	ball, perforated
D 47	ball, perforated

Mound 20 (NW of)

B 60	gnawed bone
E 214	corroded bronze
E 224	brooch pin and part of spring (between Mounds 20 and 42)
E 233	brooch pin and part of spring (between Mounds 20 and 42)
H 104	worked tine

Mound 21 (1893). (figs.3.7 and 3.8)

Small spread of yellow clay at the extreme SE corner of the E sector of the site. The clays represent 3 Floors over an area 5.8 x 4.6m, max. thickness 460mm. Floor 3 (lowest) was merely a series of small clay dumps with no built hearth although some stone rubble may have been used as such. Floor 2 was more evenly spread, and had a baked clay hearth. A large oak pile near the hearth may relate to this Floor. Floor 1 had no hearth although a spread of black earth and charcoal was noted. There were no wall posts, nor entrance paving. The foundation was brushwood with timber laid parallel to the palisade but most of this seems to have been outside the Mound between M21 and the palisade. The palisade line lay very close to M21 and respected it, curving evenly N and NNW to end in a single row of posts which formed a N edge to M21. There the palisade ended with a gap of 2.4m paved with small stones leading downslope (SE) to a natural landing place or 'drink'. By its position, M21 probably relates to M22 across the entry slope. At the S and SE edge of M21 the rows of timber provided a solid base for a likely platform at the edge of the palisade. Among the objects found outside the palisade are a bone box and the famous bronze bowl, the latter found 3m from the palisade and probably deliberately deposited there.

Stratigraphy: none; close relationship with palisade

Phase: Floor 3 Late, Floors 2-1 Final

Mound 21 finds

E 103	penannular brooch, Fowler type B
H 105	worked crown
H 106	handle
P 55	decorated jar
P 185	decorated jar
P 186	decorated bowl
P 190	cordoned vessel
P 287	decorated bowl
P 300	decorated sherd
P 305	decorated bowl
W 12	spindle whorl (shale)

Mound 21 (SE of)

W 33	spindle whorl (shale)

Mound 21 (SW of)

B 26	point (gouge)

Mound 21 (SE of) outside palisade

B 27	'bobbin', type D
B 52	'dice box'
B 61	gnawed bone
E 7	rod
E 18	spiral finger ring
E 19	bowl
X 90	wicker basket

Mound 22 (1893). (figs.3.7 and 3.8)

Spread of dirty clay and ash on E edge of the site. Only 1 Floor was noted over an area 9.4 x 8.5m, max. thickness 460mm, but beneath the clay was a baked clay hearth with a clay surround 2.4m across, replaced by a gravel hearth; the associated Floors were not recorded. Floor 1 had an incomplete red marl hearth. No wall posts or entry were found. A line of posts extended from the S onto the area of M22 but whether covered by clay or driven through clay is not known. The foundation was brushwood, and this extended from the E edge of M22 to the palisade, about 3m in width and over a distance of about 10m along the palisade line. Some timber was also laid parallel to the palisade and a hurdle fence 13m long separated the palisade posts from this brushwood and timber foundation. Two of the hurdles had fallen inwards or been laid flat, and had then been pinned in place by 2 rows of pegs. The hurdles were each 2m tall and only 1m wide, with oak sails. M22 was probably a wide open stance set beside the entrance through the palisade and facing M21. M22 overlay M23 clays. The relics recovered were numerous. Among the palisade posts or beyond were an iron billhook and iron saw; these might well represent the tools for hurdle-making.

Stratigraphy: M22 overlies M23

Phase: Floor 1 Final, lower hearths Late

Mound 22 finds

B 1	'bobbin', type A
B 5	point (gouge)

B 37	'bobbin', type D
B 63	'bobbin', type A
C 1	crucible
D 1	not described
D 2	not described
E 1	mirror handle?
F 40	flint, no data
G 11	blue bead with white spirals, Guido class 6
H 2	ferrule
H 3	modelling tool?
H 4	hammer head
H 5	cylindrical piece of antler
H 6	tine tip
H 13	weaving comb
H 16	point
K 6	armlet
L 17	spiral ring (tin)
M 3	teeth x 2
P 309	decorated bowl
W 3	spindle whorl (sandstone)

Mound 22 (NE of)

H 1	shed roe deer antler
H 27	ferrule
K 5	armlet
W 1	spindle whorl (clay)

Mound 22 (SE of)

B 35	'bobbin', type D
M 4	tooth
Q 6	rotary quern, upper stone

Mound 22 (SW of)

B 38	'bobbin', type E

Mound 22 (E of) outside palisade

B 2	notched and perforated ox/horse tibia
B 3	'bobbin', type A
H 8	sawn tine, unfinished handle?
H 10	weaving comb
H 11	weaving comb
H 12	perforated antler
I 1	saw
I 9	billhook
P 13	decorated sherd

Mounds 23 and 24 (1893). (figs.3.7 and 3.8)

M23. Spread of dirty clay on the E edge of the site. The clays represent 2 Floors, the later Floor covering an area 9.8 x 7.6m, the earlier Floor 6.7m diameter, max. thickness 430mm. Floor 2 was circular with a baked clay hearth and was covered by black earth. Around its edge was a line of wall posts set 230-380mm apart, with a paved entrance at NE 1.5m wide; this was one of Bulleid's classic round houses. Floor 1 marks a complete removal of this structure. The clay spread more widely to N and W with a baked clay and gravel hearth, but no wall posts or entrance recorded; Floor 1 was an open stance.

M24. This Mound is nothing more than an upper Floor for M23. Bulleid records it as having 2 Floors, but the lower Floor, his number 2, is M23 Floor 1. Upon this, on the W part only, a new Floor was laid over an area of 6.0m diameter; this Floor is M24 Floor 1. It had a large raised hearth nearly 1.5m diameter paved in the centre with sandstone rubble. No wall posts were recorded and this Floor was probably an open stance, effectively a renewal and contraction of M23 Floor 1. The foundation beneath M23 and M24 was brushwood; this extended E to the palisade, with added timbers. The relics from M23 and M24 were numerous but all were unstratified.

Stratigraphy: M23 Floor 1 = M24 Floor 2, therefore M24 Floor 1 over M23 Floor 1

M22 over M23 Floors 1-2, and therefore over M24 Floor 2. M22 Floor 1 almost touches M24 Floor 1

Phase: M23 Floor 2 Middle, Floor 1 Late
M24 Floor 2 Late, Floor 1 Late

Mound 23 finds

B 6	perforated tarsal
B 7	notched and perforated horse/ox tibia
B 8	'bobbin', type A
B 9	'bobbin', type A
B 53	part of large metatarsal/carpal
B 57	'bobbin', type D
C 2	square-sided vessel
E 78	thin sheet bronze
H 14	weaving comb handle
H 15	cheek-piece
H 26	worked antler
I 8	rivet
P **	cordoned bowl

Mound 23 (NE of)

B 32	'bobbin', type E
B 50	point (gouge)
D 24	disc
I 7	strip
W 27	spindle whorl (shale)

Mound 23 (SE of)

B 34	'bobbin', type D
B 51	'bobbin', type D

Mound 23 (E of) outside palisade

B 4	'bobbin' x 2, type D
B 31	point (gouge)
H 7	cheek piece
I 31	ring
N 2	otter bones
P 10	decorated jar

Mound 24 finds

B 10	'bobbin', type A
B 11	point (gouge)
B 13	point (gouge)
B 24	'bobbin', type E
B 28	toggle
B 29	worked fragment
C 4	crucible
C 7	crucible
E 3	band
E 25	harness ornament
E 75	punch
H 19	potters tool?
H 23	weaving comb, unfinished

H 24	needle
H 25	weaving comb butt end?
S 2	disc (lias)
S 6	small pebbles x 12
T 1	perforated boar's tusk
W 6	spindle whorl? (ammonite)
W 7	spindle whorl (lias)
W 8	spindle whorl (lias)
**	swan bone

Mound 24 (SW of)

E 76	tube, probably part of a ring
S 3	disc (lias)
W 23	spindle whorl (lias)

Mound 24 (NW of)

H 80	socketed, pointed and decorated object

Mound 25 (1893). (fig.3.7)

Spread of clay (no colour given) near E edge of the site. The clay represents 2 Floors and an additional spread to the SW; the central Floors cover an area 8 x 7m, the extension about 5 x 5m, max. thickness of clay 480mm. Floor 2 had a large stone paved hearth, and the hearth of Floor 1 was of baked clay and gravel. The hearths were in slightly different positions, not a simple repair. Bulleid's plan suggests that the SW extension belonged to Floor 2. The clays of M25 lay over the SW extension of M44. No wall posts or entrance were detected. M25 was probably an open stance for M44 with a joint shelter wall on the E. Some stone slabs lay at the NW edge of the Floors, and there were many posts just off the E edge of the extension, and also in or beneath the clay here. This complex of posts, separating M25 and M20, does not seem to represent an old palisade line but may indicate some linear structure built prior to the clay spreads. There were several planks, one of them perforated, probably beneath the extension clay (although not mentioned in the report), which might be part of some earlier structure.

The foundation of M25 was brushwood. A human humerus was found under the clay of the main Floors, presumably under the clays of M44 as well but this is not clear.

Stratigraphy: Floors 2-1 lie over M44 Floor 3, and abut M44 Floors 2-1

Phase: Floor 2 Late, Floor 1 Final. The posts and beams beneath might be Middle Phase

Mound 25 finds

B 22	'bobbin', type D
B 23	gnawed bone
B 44	point (gouge)
B 48	'bobbin', type E
B 49	point (gouge)
D 15	no data
D 16	clay disc
E 5	brooch, La Tène III 'Glastonbury' mock spring form
H 20	toggle
H 28	cheek piece
I 5	pyrites
P **	decorated pottery
W 21	spindle whorl (sandstone)

Mound 25 (under)

M 2	humerus

Mound 25 (SW of)

B 45	knife marked bone
B 46	gnawed bone
B 47	knife-cut rib
B 152	needle
B 154	point (gouge)
B 162	point (gouge)
B 176	'bobbin', type A
D 48	reel-shaped object
E 72	rivet head
H 93	sawn antler
H 112	sawn tine

Mounds 26 (1894) and 27 (1895). (fig.3.6)

M26. Amorphous spread of yellow clay near centre of site. The clay covered an area 5.5 x 5.8m, max. thickness 460mm, and was in effect an extension of Floor 1 of M27 (see below) and 38. No hearth or other structural elements were noted.

M27. Complex series of yellow clay spreads, representing 4 Floors, over an area 10 x 8m with extension to N, max. thickness 1.3m. Floor 4 (lowest) was smaller, 6.0 x 6.3m, and its clay floor was covered by planking laid W-E. A paved hearth lay off-centre, beside a heavy vertical post; the hearth was renewed with a baked clay hearth, and black earth covered the floor. Numerous wall posts were noted but spread out unevenly around the Floor, and stone slabs at the NE may mark the entrance. Near the NE edge of Floor 4, 2 large oak posts, 1.2m apart, were driven through the clay. They were about 1m long and 150 - 230mm diameter; around each were about 6 small stakes set only 75mm from the post, and 7 or more of these settings were recorded from this area of the site, 3 on M38 and 4 on M27. They are discussed below. Floor 4 was one of Bulleid's classic round houses with plank floor and centre post. Floor 3 was a rebuilding of this house, now larger in size, 6.4 x 7.3m, also plank-floored but in NW-SE alignment. The hearth was repositioned to the centre of the structure, first with a stone slab centre and then renewed by a baked clay hearth. The wall post line was again rather unevenly represented. Floor 2 covered 7.3 x 8.5m but followed the configuration of Floor 3 except at the W where the clay was spread out beyond M27 into M28. The floor was plank-covered with black earth upon it, and the hearth was a direct renewal of the Floor 3 hearths, clay with stone slab centre. It is likely that Floor 2 also represents a structure and a W entrance seems more demonstrable than for Floors 3-4. Floor 1 marks a change in use, consisting of a wide spread of clay extending well beyond the edges of Floors 4-3-2, over an area 8.6 x 8.0m, and spreading N and NE (M26) onto and over M38 and part of M41. This Floor marks a clearing-away of structures here on the site and replacement by a wide open stance. Floor 1 on M27 had a hearth of clay with stone centre. No wall post lines were noted but a dense line of posts ran S-N along the E edge of the M26 clay, marking an old palisade which respects M26 and clings closely to M26 edges, ending at M38 - M41. Under Floor 1 clays of M27, M26 and M38 were at least 3 of the small post and stake settings, 2 were beneath the upper Floors (at least) of M27, and 2 were under the clays of M38. These are of uncertain purpose, but may have been posts supporting some material (food, textile) requiring protection from animals, or posts for hives, or posts and stakes masking some ceremonial practice of unknown character. The foundation of M26 and M27 was brushwood except at the E edge of M26 where timber lay next to the old palisade.

The relics from M26 were few in number. M27 yielded many objects, particularly potsherds from Floors 4-3-2, especially Floor 4. A horse skull with a small stake driven through it lay near the SE edge of M27. Most objects were unstratified.

Stratigraphy: M26 Floor 1 joins M27 Floor 1 and M38 Floor 1. M27 Floor 2 joins M28 Floor 1 and M16 Floor 1

Phase: M26 Floor 1 Late
M27 Floor 4 Early, Floor 3-2 Middle,
Floor 1 Late

Mound 26 finds

B 157	sawn pig tibia
B 324	'bobbin', type E
E 68	tweezers
H 258	shed antler
H 365	worked antler
H 390	sawn antler fragment
P **	decorated pottery
**	peas and beans

Mound 26 (under)

E 167	binding
**	charcoal

Mound 26 (NE of)

B 174	awl
D **	sling shot x 40
E 64	ring
W 55	spindle whorl (bone)

Mound 26 (SE of)

B 164	'bobbin', type E
E 44	bracelet

Mound 26 (SW of)

I 36	links x 2 of a snaffle-bit

Mound 27 finds

B 180	'bobbin', type D
B 181	cut/sawn bone
B 182	'bobbin', type E
B 183	sawn bone
B 184	point (gouge)
B 185	knife-cut bone
B 186	awl
B 187	notched ox/horse tibia
B 191	sawn bone
B 199	'bobbin', type D
B 200	'bobbin', type D
B 201	'bobbin', type E
B 202	'bobbin', type D
B 203	'bobbin', type D
B 204	'bobbin', type D
B 206	'bobbin', type A
B 428	knife-cut bone
B 448	point (gouge)
E 86	thin sheet bronze
E 90	band
E 92	link
H 131	sawn antler
H 132	cheek piece
H 135	sawn tine
H 137	handle
H 138	sawn tine
H 143	handle
H 144	cheek piece
H 145	sawn tine
H 147	sawn antler, handle?
H 148	point
H 151	sawn tine
H 152	sawn antler
H 153	cheek piece
H 379	sawn antler
I 38	ring end of object
P 292	decorated jar
T 4	perforated boar's tusk
W 66	spindle whorl (femur head)
W 68	spindle whorl (limestone)
W 69	spindle whorl (lias)

Mound 27 (Floor 1)

H 133	sawn tine
H 134	sawn antler
H 139	cheek piece
H 140	sawn antler
H 142	worked antler
W 71	spindle whorl (limestone)

Mound 27 (Floor 2)

E 83	needle
E 88	spiral finger ring
H 136	ferrule
H 146	weaving comb
H 154	weaving comb fragment
P **	pottery in quantity

Mound 27 (Floor 3)

E 84	band
H 150	handle
P **	pottery in quantity

Mound 27 (Floor 4)

B 198	perforated horse/ox tibia. Dated by C14
P **	pottery in quantity including decorated
W 70	spindle whorl (sandstone)

Mound 27 (under)

**	horse skull with pile through frontal bone

Mound 27 (NE of)

E 89	rivet head

Mound 27 (SE of)

H 114	handle

H 149	sawn tine
**	beans

Mound 27 (SW of)

H 155	sawn antler

Mound 28 (1898). (fig.3.6)

Simple spread of yellow clay in centre of site. The single Floor covers an area 10 x 8m, max. thickness 460mm. A small hearth of baked clay lay at the SE edge, and no wall posts were seen. The Floor joined M27 Floor 2 on the E and M16 Floor 1 on the S. M28 was probably an open stance for the M27 structure. The foundation was brushwood and a few pieces of timber, and upon this, prior to the clay Floor, was black earth with potsherds, the residue of the earlier Floors of M27. On the W edge of the Floor, and beyond the clay, were several oak posts noted in the M15 description. There were very few relics found.

Stratigraphy: Floor joins M16 Floor 1 and M27 Floor 2

Phase: Middle

Mound 28 finds

H 259	sawn and burnt antler, probably a hammer

Mound 28 (under)

E 166	nail

Mound 28 (NW of)

B 342	point (gouge)

Mound 29 (1898). (fig.3.5)

Complex spreads of yellow clay near the W edge of the site about midway. The clays represent 10 thin floors over an area about 9 x 8m, max. thickness 1.1m. Floor 10 (the lowest) was irregular, 8 x 6.5m, with a lobe to the NNE. The NW half was covered by planks, and there was no hearth. This Floor was renewed by 7 other Floors, each smaller in extent and thickness than Floor 10, and presumably aligned more or less with Floor 10 although none appears on the plan. Floor 8 was a patch 4.0m across, Floor 5 was 7.0m across and Floor 3 about 8.0m across. Timber flooring was noted for Floor 9 but the others were solely of clay. Hearths of baked clay were rebuilt in the same central position, Floor 8 with 2 hearths, the other Floors 1 each except Floor 3 which had a central hearth and a small hearth on the extreme W edge of the Floor. Several lines of wall posts were recorded but they were not assigned to any particular Floor; the plan shows 3 lines along the S and SW edge of the Floors, and 1-2 lines at N. In the NW the wall lines ended with a pair of squared oak boards vertically-driven, leaving a doorway 1.3m wide with an entry of horizontal layers of timber. It appears that Floors 10-3 represent one major structure, renewed and repaired several times with new hearths on newly-laid thin clay spreads, some clay spreading out beyond on the W and NW, and parts of the walling replaced by new uprights.

Floor 2 was about 8m across and extended well S of the former wall lines, with a baked clay hearth; no wall posts were recorded. This Floor probably was a phase of dismantling of the structure and the clearing away of debris to be replaced by an open stance that joined clay spreads in M14, M35 and M36. Floor 1 was also large, 8.2m diameter but now assumes a separate shape, with a clear wall post line around the S half and much of the N half as well although here there is some mixing with Floor 10-3 wall posts.

The foundation was brushwood. To the SW of M29 and NW of M14 was a setting of 9 heavy oak posts in 3 rows, probably representing the supports for a large rectangular structure 3 x 3m with smaller post settings beside. This structure was perhaps a raised granary or a platform for other storage or observation. It lay immediately on the edge of M29, with the W hurdlework palisade beyond, and an entry through the palisade to the N.

The relics were not numerous.

Stratigraphy: Floor 2 joins M14 Floor 2, M35 Floor 2 and M36 Floor 1. M29 overlay M33 Floor 8

Phase: Floors 10-3 Early, Floor 2 Middle, Floor 1 Late

Mound 29 finds

B 355	worked ox metatarsus
C 34	crucible
P 308	decorated bowl
W 156	spindle whorl (sandstone)

Mound 29 (Floor 1)

G 21	whirl-decorated ring bead, Guido class 7

Mound 29 (Floor 3)

B 362	weaving comb

Mound 29 (SW of)

E 164	binding
E 171	rivet head

Mound 29 (NW of)

E 170	band
E 179	rivet
M 32	tooth
T 8	perforated boar's tusk
W 136	spindle whorl (lias)

Mound 30 (1898). (fig.3.5)

Spreads of clay, some yellow, on the W edge of the site near the centre. The clay represents 4 Floors over an area 10 x 9m, max. thickness 1.3m. The Floors are not separated on the plan. Floor 4 was 6.3m across and had a baked clay hearth renewed 6 times, resulting in the upper hearths being raised well above the Floor level. Timber from some form of flooring had been used to level matters up. Floor 3 had only 1 hearth of baked clay. On the S edge were found some hurdle fragments lying flat, and the original supporting posts survived in a line across the SE part of the Floor with others in the N half. Probably some form of shelter or windbreak was once in place here; Bulleid noted that no complete line of wall posts, nor entrance, existed. Floor 2 was larger, 7.6m diameter, and had hurdles along the S edge and a central hearth of baked clay. Floor 1 was equally large but extended from just N of the hearth and out beyond the previous Floors to the S, out to the palisade; its hearth was thus asymmetric to the Floor. Floor 1 spread E to join M32 Floor 2, and probably represents an open stance once the shelter of Floor 2 was removed.

The foundation was of compressed rush and brushwood and blue clay lay between the Mound and the palisade. Under the W and S parts of the Mound, the foundation was of layers of timber in crisscross alignment, firming up the soft peats at the edge.

The relics included a large amount of pottery and various pieces of worked wood, including wheelspoke, oak axle, oak wheel, mallet and handle; all of these wooden objects came from beneath the Floors.

Stratigraphy: Floor 1 joins M32 Floor 2. M30 overlies M31

Phase: Floor 4-3-2 Late, Floor 1 Final

Mound 30 finds

B 360	point (gouge)
B 361	needle
D **	loom weight
I 87	knife
K 26	armlet
P 192	decorated bowl
P 268	decorated jar
P 275	cordoned bowl
P **	decorated pottery
**	beaver bones

Mound 30 ?

E 185	brooch, La Tène III flat bow
E 186	brooch, La Tène Type III wire brooch
E 187	brooch, La Tène III, Knotenfibel/ Aylesford type

Mound 30 (under Floor 1)

H 278	handle

Mound 30 (Floor 2)

H 277	sawn antler

Mound 30 (under)

W 164	spindle whorl (shale)
X 18	handle cross-piece
X 22	axle, oak
X 23	wheel, oak
X 69	wheel spoke
X 83	morticed plank, oak
X 94	handle

Mound 30 (S of) outside palisade

P 202	decorated bowl

Mound 30 (SE of)

B 223	'bobbin', type E
X 6	hook-shaped and perforated object
X 27	mallet head

Mound 30 (SW of)

E 100	mirror
E 101	tweezers

Mound 30 (SW of) outside palisade

X 17	bent wood box
X 21	tub base, oak

Mound 31 (1898 and 1907). (fig.3.5)

Simple spread of clay on W edge of site, representing one Floor, over an area 9.5 x 5m, max. thickness 230mm. No hearth was found but a patch of charcoal was noted off-centre. The Floor was roughly trapezoidal in shape. A ragged line of posts was recorded at the S edge of M31 and N edge of M30 where the 2 Mounds overlapped. These posts probably represent windbreaks or partitions separating the two spreads. The small clay patches of M89 and M88 were adjacent to M31. This spread probably represents an open stance for the activities on M30, as well as a staging post for materials (clay, wood, stone) on the edge of the open space between the centre W and NW mound complexes. The foundation was brushwood continuous with that of M30, and slightly denser near the palisade which consisted of hurdles for 5m opposite M31. To the N, this fence ended and was replaced by a bank of peat and posts, probably once a landing stage. Few relics were found, one rotary quernstone, and a potin coin lying in the post complex of M31 and M30. Some baked clay slingshots were found near M31 and the palisade.

Stratigraphy: M31 clay underlies M30 (probably Floor 2)

Phase: Late

Mound 31 finds

Q 14	rotary quern, lower stone
**	beans in quantity on E side
**	charcoal concentration near NE edge

Mound 31 (NE of)

S 43	whetstone
S 44	whetstone

Mound 31 (SE of)

E 184	lump
Z 1	potin coin

Mound 31 (W of)

D **	sling shot

Mound 32 (1898). (fig.3.5)

Spread of yellow clay near W edge of site. The clays represent 2 Floors over an area 11 x 6m, max. thickness 460mm. On Bulleid's plan these Floors are labelled 2 and 3, but should be 1 and 2 as described in the text. Floor 2 (lower) was 7.9 x 5.3m, and had a grey marl hearth. This Floor extended E into M33 but its relationship is unclear; it is probably earlier than M33 at least in part. Floor 1 (upper) was larger, 11 x 6m, and again extended E where it was obscured by M33; it also joined M30 Floors but which is not clear. Floor 1 had a clay and gravel hearth. The plan shows a curved wall of hurdles on the E but this was considered part of M33, as were the planks beside the hurdle wall although they are on the side of M32. The stratigraphical relationships here were complex and unresolved. M32 appears to be an open stance for M30 and M33 both of which had some slight structural elements, but the whole complex probably represents open or partly sheltered working areas for the houses of M29 and M35. The foundation of M32 was brushwood. The relics were few in number.

Stratigraphy: Floor 1 probably joins M30 Floor 1 and/or Floor 2 and joins M33 Floor 1 or 2 or 3

Phase: Floor 2 Late, Floor 1 Final

Mound 32 finds

E 97	tweezers
E 98	spiral finger ring
E 99	brooch, one piece simple, British form (Drahtfibel)
Q 38	saddle quern, lower stone

Mound 33 (1898). (fig.3.5)

Complex spreads of clay near W edge of central part of site. The clays represent 7 Floors over an area 7.5 x 6.5m, max. thickness 760mm; Floor 8 was a separate spread to the SE and has no real part in the formation of M33. Floor 8 was an oblong spread of clay 6.5 x 4.5m with an incomplete baked clay hearth near its NW edge. A line of posts extends from SW of Floor 8 through or under Floor 8 and off to the NE and M35 but there is nothing to suggest that Floor 8 was anything but a spread of clay laid as preliminary to the establishment of occupation at M33 and M29. Floors 7 and 6 were very small patches of clay dumped on the edge of Floor 8, only 3 x 2 and 2 x 2m in extent, and almost wholly occupied by clay hearths; they were replacements to the hearth of Floor 8. Floors 5 and 4 were expansions of clay around hearths put over the earlier hearths; Floor 5 was 6 x 4m, Floor 4 was 7 x 5m. Floors 3-2-1 continued the trend, hearths in the same place, and clay spread over a larger area, 7.5 x 6.5m. The complex of M33 is effectively a major hearth, with surrounds of clay, periodically renewed. The clays overlapped with those of M32, M29, M34 and M35 although only at the extreme edges and Bulleid had difficulties in this area in distinguishing Floors and relationships. There were no lines of wall posts nor entrances recorded, but a distinct hurdle wall 3m long was noted on the W of M33; this wall was bowed to the E, that is towards the centre of M33. It may have served as a substantial windbreak for the hearths but its connection with any Floors is uncertain; its base was beneath the clays of Floors 1-4. The foundation of M33 was brushwood but to the W of the hurdle wall, in the W edge of the Mound, some planks were recorded. These may have been more closely related to M32, and the hurdle wall as well, than to M33. Various posts were noted in the Mound, a group at the N particularly dense and a thin line of these down the W side of Floor 5 might represent a shelter support.

The relics were not numerous. The skeleton of a dog was found under the Mound but its position is not recorded.

Stratigraphy: Floor 8 underlies M29, Floors 3-2-1 probably overlie M34 Floor 2, Floor 1 probably joins M32 Floor 1 and thus M30 Floor 1

Phase: Floor 8 - 5 Early, Floor 4 Middle, Floors 3-2 Late, Floor 1 Final

Mound 33 finds

B 359a	'bobbin', type E
E 181	spiral finger ring
E 182	bar
E 183	rivet head
H 274	handle
P **	decorated pottery
W 162	spindle whorl (sandstone)

Mound 33 (Floor 1)

H 275	cut and perforated tine
H 276	cut tine
L 35	ring (tin)

Mound 33 (Floor 2)

I 85	knife

Mound 33 (under)

**	dog skeleton

Mound 33 (SW of)

W 163	spindle whorl (Ham Stone)

Mound 34 (1898 and 1907). (fig.3.5)

Small patch of yellow clay in W part of site adjacent to the major open area. The clays represent one main Floor (Floor 2), over a square area 6 x 6m, thickness 200mm and a small patch (called Floor 1) only 2 x 1.5m in area dumped onto Floor 2. A line of posts was recorded along the W side of Floor 2, and around the E and NE edge as well and several oak piles were noted in the Floor area. To the N of M34 a series of posts were recorded, in an irregular line. It is likely that some form of protected stance was here, perhaps a holding pen for animals with a guiding fence line to the N for driving. The many posts at the N edge of M33, with rebuilt hearths beyond, might be butchering supports. The foundation was 'unimportant'. There were several alder stumps to the N and E of the Mound and one under the clays. No relics are recorded from this Mound. Bulleid and Gray used the edge of their cutting here in 1907 to bury pieces of timber not taken for conservation.

Stratigraphy: Floor 2 underlies M33 Floor 1

Phase: Floor 2 Late, Floor 1 Final

Mound 34 finds

None

Mound 35 (1898). (figs.3.5 and 3.6)

Spreads of clay near the W edge of the site. The clays represent 4 Floors, over an area 10 x 8m although Floor 2 is larger. The maximum thickness is 840mm. Floor 4 was circular in shape, 7.3 x 7.6m, with a central baked clay hearth renewed twice. A wall line of posts surrounded the Floor, with timber laid at the SW where an entrance may have existed; this was probably a round house. Floor 3 was 8.6 x 6.4m with a gravel hearth, and wall post line not completely seen or recorded. A post beside the hearth may have been a cooking support rather than the roof post conjectured. Floor 2 was a very wide spread of clay joining M29 and M36. It overran the edges of Floors 4 and 3 and represents a transition from structure to open stance. A baked clay hearth had been repaired 4 times. The hearth was off to the E of the hearths for Floors 4 and 3. Floor 1 was 8.8 x 7.0m with a stone slab hearth and stout post on its edge. A short line of posts on the E side is not repeated elsewhere on the edge of this Floor; however, there are other lines of posts and it may be that, with the new position of the hearth, Floor 1 was a small house with the clay extending N beyond the structure. Two lines of posts converge to the N of the hearth and follow the curve of the S part of the Floor 1 clay, particularly on the E side. There is also a cluster of posts on the N part of the clay spreads, as well as several large oak posts noted for M36.

The foundation was brushwood and a few logs. The relics included numerous potsherds, and a human skull lay on Floor 4, its brain cavity 'filled with clay'.

Stratigraphy: Floor 2 joins M36 Floor 1 and M29 Floor 2; Floor 2 underlies M33 Floors 1-3

Phase: Floor 4-3 Early, Floor 2 Middle, Floor 1 Late

Mound 35 finds

B 344	'bobbin', type E
B 356	sharpened bone
B 357	'bobbin', type E
B 358	'bobbin', type E
P 184	decorated jar
P **	decorated pottery
Q 37	rotary quern, lower stone
W 157	spindle whorl (baked clay)
W 158	spindle whorl (pottery)
W 159	spindle whorl (lias)
W 160	spindle whorl (sandstone)

Mound 35 (Floor 1)

H 272	weaving comb, fragmentary

Mound 35 (Floor 2)

H 271	weaving comb
P **	much pottery

Mound 35 (Floor 3)

H 273	toggle
P **	much pottery

Mound 35 (Floor 4)

M 34	skull

Mound 35 (NE of)

E 180	pin
K 25	ring

Mound 36 (1898). (fig.3.6)

Spread of yellow clay in W part of site adjacent to open area. The clays represent 3 Floors, although the 2 lowest Floors are only small patches. Max. thickness 460mm. Floor 3 was 2.7 x 2.4m, and had a clay hearth. Floor 2 was 4.3 x 4.0m, with a clay and stone slab hearth. Other slabs lay on the E edge of the patch. Another patch was laid to the W. Over these small clay patches a wide spread of Floor 1 clay extended S and W to cover all of M35 (Floor 2), M29 (Floor 2) and M14 (Floor 2). No hearth for Floor 1 was noted, but the hearths on the other Mounds would have been in operation. This Floor marks a wide open stance in this part of the site, on the edge of the open area. On the E side of Floor 1 was a rectangular setting of posts 2 x 1m, and to NW were a number of large oak posts in a setting which may have supported a platform at the inner end of the open area, or a boundary or fence. The foundation was brushwood. The relics were few in number.

Stratigraphy: Floor 1 joins Floor 2 of M35, M29 and M14

Phase: Floor 3-2 Early, Floor 1 Middle

Mound 36 finds

P 249	decorated sherd
P **	decorated pottery

Mound 36 (NW of)

L 32	weight? (lead)
S 27	disc (sandstone)
W 150	spindle whorl (lias)

Mound 37 (1898). (fig.3.6)

Small spread of mostly yellow clay near centre of site. The clays represent 4 Floors, increasing in area from 3.5 x 3.0m (Floor 4) to over 8.0 x 3.5m (Floor 1). Maximum thickness of clay 1.3m. Floor 4 was a patch with a hearth renewed twice, and a sunken oven beside it. Floor 3 was 4.2 x 3.7m and its clay hearth was also repaired twice. Floor 2 was a further spread of clay to the SE, now 5.5 x 4.3m with a hearth repaired once, and an oven beside. All these hearths were in the same position. Floor 1 was an expansion SE to produce an elongated stance with a hearth at the NW end, and a large oven at the SE end 610mm diameter and 115mm deep. No wall posts were noted but several short lines of posts were off the clay to the E. In the light of the finds of loom weights and other objects, it may be that these lines mark the places of looms or other textile equipment. The foundation was brushwood except for the Floor 4 extension where a platform of logs 1.6m square held the clays. A large oak post through Floors 4 and 3 probably marks a support for the hearth operations, rather than a 'dwelling-post'. M37 is probably a specialised area for activities on M27 and/or M38.

The relics were numerous, particularly coarse potsherds. Bulleid considered that textiles had been produced and used here on the basis of the loom weights, combs, bobbins and needles. These objects were found scattered both within and outside the mound.

Stratigraphy: none

Phase: Floor 4 Early, Floors 3-2 Middle, Floor 1 Late

Mound 37 finds

B 337	'bobbin', type E
D 42	perforated disc
D **	loom weights, 9 from Mound
G 20	bead, blue with white spirals, Guido class 6

P 272	decorated dish
P **	decorated pottery
T 9	boar's tusk
**	beaver bones

Mound 37 (Floor 1)

W 151	spindle whorl (femur head)

Mound 37 (Floor 2)

B 345	needle
W 145	spindle whorl (lias)

Mound 37 (Floor 3)

D **	loom weights, several

Mound 37 (NE of)

B 333	'bobbin', type E
D 69	loom weight
E 173	brooch, La Tène II, arched bow form, mock spring variant
F 57	worked flint
H 262	weaving comb
I 86	spearhead

Mound 37 (SE of)

B 343	needle
G 25	bead, blue annular, Guido group 6
M 33	child's skeleton

Mound 37 (SW of)

B 329	weaving comb
B 330	needle
B 331	needle
B 334	pin/piercer?
B 335	needle
B 336	'bobbin', type E
B 340	notched and perforated ox/horse tibia
B 341	point (gouge)
H 264	weaving comb
H 269	sawn antler
Q 35	saddle quern, upper stone
Q 36	saddle quern, upper stone
W 148	spindle whorl (sandstone)
W 149	spindle whorl, unfinished (sandstone)

Mound 37 (NW of)

B 338	'bobbin', type D
B 339	'bobbin', type D
F 59	scraper
H 265	weaving comb
H 270	cheek piece fragment?
N 6	beaver jaw
W 146	spindle whorl (clay)
W 147	spindle whorl (sandstone)

Mounds 38 and 39 (1898). (fig.3.6)

M38. Spreads of clay, some yellow, other unknown, in centre of site. The spreads represent 3 Floors, over an area 9.5 x 6.5m, max. thickness 840mm. Floor 3 (lowest) was 9.4 x 6.1m and had a clay hearth, probably renewed twice. Floor 2 was a smaller spread, only 5 x 4m, placed to the E side of Floor 3 and only touching the hearth of Floor 3. Floor 2 hearth of clay, renewed once, was placed just beside that of Floor 3. Along the E side of Floor 2 was a hurdle line and posts continued NW and W. Bulleid noted that baked clay with hurdle and timber impressions were found near the burnt wall posts of the N edge. The hurdle line and N wall post line follow the edge of Floor 3, and Floor 2 may be a repair of the E part of this structure. No entrance features were found, and no wall posts were seen on the W or S; perhaps there was some enclosing shelter, unroofed, but some large oak posts in the Floors might mark roof supports to an open-sided structure. Floor 1 was 9.4 x 6.4m and joined M27 Floor 1 and M26 in a wide spread of clay, probably an open stance. Floor 1 had a hearth of clay central to M38 - M26. The foundation of M38 was brushwood but in the W this was supplemented by sandstone rubble. A large oak beam with a row of mortice holes, probably a break for hurdles, lay to the S. On the E was a large alder post 250mm diameter driven through the brushwood; around it were 9 small stakes 65mm diameter and 760mm long, one of the group of these settings noted in M27. M38 had 4 of these, one with 9 stakes, 2 with 7 stakes, 1 with 5 stakes.

The relics included much pottery, many sherds under Floor 3 in the top of the brushwood along with bone objects, a glass bead, and saddle quern. Clay slingshot were found beside Floor 5. A human skull lay under Floor 3.

M39. A small patch of clay 1.8m square to NW of M38, with no features and no relics.

Between M38 and M39 and N of M39 were a number of oak posts set well apart; these may be tethering posts or otherwise connected to functions at the inner edge of the open area on the site.

Stratigraphy: M38 Floor 1 joins M27 Floor 1 and M26. M38 underlies M41 Floors 1-2. M39 none

Phase: M38 Floor 3-2 Middle, Floor 1 Late
M39 Late

Mound 38 finds

B 323	point (gouge)
E 176	penannular brooch
E 177	rivet
H 257	awl
H 261	hook shaped worked tine
L 33	lead 'ore'
L 34	lead 'ore'
P 196	decorated jar
P 274	decorated bowl
P 291	decorated bowl
P 357	spouted bowl
P **	decorated pottery
W 137	spindle whorl (lias)
W 140	spindle whorl (sandstone)

Mound 38 (Floor 2)

E 168	brooch, La Tène III
D **	sling shot, large number
W 138	spindle whorl, unfinished (sandstone)
W 139	spindle whorl (sandstone)
W 141	spindle whorl (lias)
W 142	spindle whorl (lias)

Mound 38 (Floor 3)

B 326	sawn and longitudinally perforated ox tibia. Dated by C14

F 56	retouched flake, Mesolithic

Mound 38 (under)

B 328	point (gouge)
G 19	green pin-head
M 30	skull, part
P **	pottery, much
Q 34	saddle quern, upper & lower stones
W 143	spindle whorl (lias)

Mound 38 (NW of)

B 327	point (gouge)
B 332	'bobbin', type E
H 263	weaving comb
W 144	spindle whorl? (ichthyosaur vertebra)

Mounds 40 (1898) and 41 (1894). (fig.3.6)

M41. Spreads of clay, mostly yellow, in the central part of the site. The clays represent 3 Floors of unequal sizes, max. 7.0 x 6.4m, max. thickness 610mm. Floor 3 was 3.6 x 4.3m, with a clay hearth off-centre. Floor 2 was 5.7 x 6.0m, with a gravel hearth built over the earlier hearth. Floor 1 was 7.0 x 6.4m and had a hearth in the same place, well off-centre near the N edge of the Floor. Floor 1 extended NW to form M40 which was an oblong spread 6 x 5m with clay max. thickness 450mm; no hearth existed, and this was merely an extension from M41.

The foundation of M41 was brushwood but at the SW edge, under Floor 1 and part of Floor 2, were timbers projecting S under M26 as well. At the N of M41 and under the lowest hearth was an oak beam 4.5m long overlying another beam, both held in place by an oak post driven through a hole in each beam. Almost one metre below the beams was part of a logboat 6.4m long with its N end under M52. A short wide beam lay pegged down beside the logboat. A line of posts extended on the E of the Mound, probably an old palisade line. A spread of posts extended across the S part of M40 and other scatters were noted in M40; these may mark small fence lines or supports prior to the clay deposition. This area is likely to have been on the edge of an open stretch of reeds and water, sufficient for floating logs, and perhaps logboats, into the site prior to its foundation and clay deposition. The depth at which the fragment of boat lay and the pegged beams suggest that perhaps a landing stage or other slipway existed here, with an early palisade extending S and, near M54, a N palisade line marking the E edge to an early phase of the site. This is discussed elsewhere in this report.

The relics found in M41 were not numerous.

Stratigraphy: M41 Floor 1 joins M40 Floor. M41 abuts M42. M41 Floors 1-2 overlie M38

Phase: M41 Floor 3 Late, Floors 2-1 Final
M40 Final

Mound 40 finds

E 169	spiral finger/toe ring
I 83	rivet

Mound 41 finds

B 325	'bobbin', type E
E 51	chain, 5 links
E 69	rivet head
H 119	worked antler
I 33	sickle
I 34	iron object
I 35	bolt
M 31	tooth
P 270	decorated bowl

Mound 41 (Floor 1)

H 260	point

Mound 41 (Floor 2)

E 50	spiral finger ring

Mound 41 (Floor 3)

E 66	binding

Mound 41 (under)

X 57	logboat (part), oak

Mound 41 (SE of)

E 43	needle
E 63	fragment
E 65	rivet head
H 99	die
H 101	weaving comb
H 110	cheek piece

Mound 42 (1893-94) and 43 (1893). (fig.3.7)

M42. Spread of yellow clay in central E part of site. The clays represent 4 Floors over an area 9.3 x 8.0m, max. thickness 1.1m. The Floors were more or less the same size and shape, and Bulleid did not separate them out, other than noting that all had a hearth of clay in the same place, that Floor 3 had a small patch of clay off the SW edge, and Floor 2 had a wider patch again off the SW edge with planks lying upon it. The hearth of Floor 1 had stone rubble within its clay. Bulleid stated that no complete line of wall posts was noted, but he records a line of posts up the SE edge, and a hurdle wall runs for 4.5m along the W edge. Various stone settings are noted on Floor 1.

M43. A small spread of yellow clay, 280mm thick, over an area 5.0 x 4.0m attached to the NNE edge of M42, with a clay and stone hearth at the junction. There is no indication about the stratigraphical relationship of this spread to M42 Floors, just that it was 'joined'. A line of wall posts extended along the W edge but not beyond. It is probable that M42 and its adjunct M43 were open stances, but protected by hurdles on the NW sides. There is a possibility that the E part of M42 was also walled or sheltered but this is not clear, and it is as likely that the posts here marked a palisade extension, soon abandoned. The foundation of M42 and M43 was brushwood, with timber only at the SW under the small extensions. The relics from M42 were numerous, but little was found in M43. Much pottery was found in M42 as well as bronze fibulae, several combs, whorls and antler pieces. Clay slingshots are noted from M42 and 43 and many peas on the E side of both Mounds.

Stratigraphy: M42 abuts M41. M43 is attached to M42

Phase: M42 Floor 4 Late, Floor 3 Late/Final, Floors 2-1 Final
M43 Late

Mound 42 finds
'By far the larger number of relics were found on floor 1, and included nine long-handled weaving combs'

B 71	point (gouge)
B 120	weaving comb
B 128	gnawed bone
D 23	perforated ball
D **	sling shot, large number
E 41	rivet
E 60	chain link
E 79	brooch, La Tène III flat bow
E 85	brooch spring, La Tène III (found during backfilling)
H 30	sawn tine
H 31	sawn tine
H 53	hammer
H 54	unworked antler
H 90	worked antler
P 303	decorated sherd
P **	pottery, above average amount, including decorated
Q 8	rotary quern, lower stone
S 4	disc (lias)
S 5	disc (sandstone)
W 10	spindle whorl (lias)
W 11	spindle whorl (sandstone)
W 15	spindle whorl (lias)
W 82	spindle whorl (lias)
**	peas in quantity on E side

Mound 42 (Floor 1)

H 32	weaving comb
H 33	weaving comb
H 63	weaving comb
H 65	weaving comb
H 66	weaving comb
H 68	weaving comb
I 17	billhook
I 19	knife
I 44	billhook
I 45	knife
I 46	implement
I 47	file

Mound 42 (SE of)

B 127	'bobbin', type D
B 129	needle
B 130	needle

Mound 42 (NW of)

H 69	weaving comb
W 22	spindle whorl (lias)
W 67	spindle whorl (femur head)
**	beans

Mound 43 finds

D **	sling shot
H 40	sawn tine
H 73	weaving comb
S 14	haematite
W 18	spindle whorl (sandstone)
**	peas in large numbers

Mound 43 (NE of)

W 14	spindle whorl (lias)

Mound 44 (1893). (fig.3.7)

Spread of clay 'not of the purest kind' near the E edge of the site. The clays represent 3 Floors over an area 7.0 x 7.0m with extensions both N and S. Max. thickness 460mm. Floor 3 was 10.7 x 7.0m and was clay and black earth mixed. The hearth was at the SW edge of this elongated clay spread and was 1.3m diameter with pieces of sandstone at centre. Some stone slabs at the W edge of Floor 3 might mark some paving or entry and along the E edge of this Floor a line of posts was recorded, presumably some sheltering wall. Floor 2 was a circular spread about 7.0m diameter with a gravel hearth set to S of centre. Floor 1 was a renewal of Floor 2 with a clay and stone hearth more central. These Floors could relate closely to M25 which overlies Floor 3 and abuts Floors 2-1. The line of posts on the E edge appear to relate more to Floor 3 than to Floors 2 and 1. A large number of posts are off the Mound to the N, between M44 and M49. Beneath the clay of the Floors, at the N, several wooden objects were found amidst or below the brushwood foundation. Among the pieces were various oak beams with holes and other features, and a wooden spring trap. The brushwood surface had black earth upon it.

The relics were numerous, including parts of 7 pots found close together. Few objects were stratified. An adult human skull lay to the W of the Mound.

Stratigraphy: Floor 3 underlies M25 Floors 1-2. Floors 2-1 may relate directly to M25 Floors 1-2

Phase: Floor 3 Middle, Floor 2 Late, Floor 1 Final

Mound 44 finds

B 15	'bobbin', type E
B 16	pierced tubular bone
B 17	pin
B 18	'bobbin', type D
B 21	point (gouge)
B 36	polished sheep metatarsal
B 79	pin
C 3	crucible
C 6	crucible
D **	loom weights x 3
D **	sling shot
E 2	penannular bracelet
E 4	penannular ring, brooch?
E 80	fused bronze lump
H 18	cheek piece
H 21	cheek piece
H 22	ferrule
H 34	weaving comb
H 35	worked tine
H 81	pin
I 6	finger ring
L 11	bar (lead/tin)
P 15A	decorated bowl
P 183	decorated vessel

P 259	decorated jar
P **	decorated pottery
Q 7	saddle quern, upper & lower
Q 10	rotary quern, upper stone
S 1	cylinder
T 2	perforated boar's tusk
W 9	spindle whorl (clay)
W 39	spindle whorl (lias)
W 83	spindle whorl (clay)

Mound 44 (Floor 1)

B 25	perforated and decorated rib, bow drill?

Mound 44 (under)

**	fire ash

Mound 44 (NE of)

B 64	notched and perforated ox/horse femur
H 29	hammer
Q 3	rotary quern, upper stone
Q 4	rotary quern, upper stone
X 36	composite object, trap?, oak
X 38	mortised plank, oak
X 39	mortised plank, oak
X 78	perforated oak panel
X 89	plank, square-cut tenon either end and central hole, oak
X 97	morticed beam, oak

Mound 44 (SE of)

A3	amber bead
B 14	weaving comb
G 4	bead, yellow/brown annular, Guido group 6

Mound 44 (SW of)

A 2	amber bead
M 1	adult skull

Mound 44 (NW of)

B 19	gnawed bone

Mound 45 (1893). (figs.3.7 and 3.8)

Spreads of yellow clay at E edge of the site. The clays represent 2 Floors, the earlier Floor 5.8m diameter, the later Floor 9 x 8m, max. thickness 630mm. Floor 2 was circular, with a near-central hearth of baked clay. To the E of the hearth the Floor was roughly paved with slabs leading to an E entrance. A complete line of wall posts was recorded, with an entrance gap of 1.2m marked by a paved entry, an outer door step of stone and an inner threshold step of wood. This was one of Bulleid's classic round houses and was the plan chosen to illustrate his text on 'The Dwellings' in the monograph; for some reason, this plan of M45 was drawn as a reversed image. One feature on the site plan is that the line of posts does not follow the clay Floor edge in every sector, the clay extending 0.5m beyond the wall line on the W. Floor 1 is a major change; the house was removed and a large spread of clay deposited over the area, submerging the wall line and entrance. This clay extended N and W and formed the lower Floor (2) of M49. No hearth was noted for this Floor on M45 although there was some clay discolouration near the centre. A line of posts extended along the N edge of this spread and bent around to follow the clay E to M46. The clay of M45 Floor 1 and M49 Floor 2 covered an area 21m NW-SE and 8-10m SW-NE; it was irregular and encompassed all of M45 Floor 2 and M49 Floor 1. A large number of posts were noted on the W, and various planks were found, presumably under the Floor, on the NE part as well as a patch of small stones marked as 'over clay'. Long perforated planks lay partly beneath the clay on the W (see M44). M45 Floor 1 and M49 Floor 2 form a large open stance, probably with a shelter wall on part of the E edge but otherwise unprotected and with no substantial hearths. It may be that this open stance augmented or replaced the landing stage of M47 (the Causeway) off to the E.

The foundation of M45 was brushwood with some timber.

Stratigraphy: Floor 1 joins M49 Floor 2, overlies M46 Floors

Phase: Floor 2 Late, Floor 1 Final

Mound 45 finds

B 12	point (gouge)
B 30	point (gouge)
B 40	'bobbin', type D
B 41	point (gouge)
B 124	splinter
B 126	worked bone
C 5	crucible
H 17	worked tine
P **	decorated pottery
W 16	spindle whorl (sandstone)
W 26	spindle whorl (sandstone)

Mound 45 (SE of)

B 125	'bobbin', type D

Mound 45 (SW of)

B 42	point (gouge)
B 43	'bobbin', type D

Mound 45 (NW of)

H 122	cheek piece
H 130	sawn antler
P 126	decorated sherd

Mound 46 (1893). (figs.3.7 and 3.8)

Spreads of clay at E edge of site. The clays represent 2 Floors, over an area 7.0 x 6.5m max. thickness 460mm. Floor 2 was an oval spread 6.5 x 5.0m with a large baked clay hearth paved with stone slabs and surface 150mm above the clay Floor. Several pieces of timber and stone lay at the S edge of the Floor, but no wall posts were noted. Floor 1 was larger and had an incomplete hearth, with black earth over the clay. The thick foundation was brushwood on timber on peat on brushwood, resting on blue clay and logs laid parallel to the E edge and penetrated by a number of posts. Some of these posts apparently were sealed by the Mound and Bulleid thought they were some form of an early fence. This seems unlikely. The palisade line from the S appears to turn W at the S edge of M46, and picks up again to N of the Mound. The space between was probably never fully closed off by palisade; instead, M46 Floor 2 was a landing stage for the Causeway (M47) and only thereafter became closed off; Floor 1 became an open stance behind the final palisade which respected the E edge of M46. The causeway fell out of use and the entrance was blocked off. The planks and posts to the S may have also had a role in the use of the causeway (see M47). Under the E part of the Mound, many objects were found, presumably the debris dropped prior to M46; these included whorls, an iron dagger, 37 pieces of a wooden frame, wickerwork and, under the clay at NE, a decorated pot and an axle-box. A human skullbone was found outside the palisade.

Stratigraphy: Floors underlie M45 Floor 1

Phase: Floor 2 Late, Floor 1 Final

Mound 46 finds

B 33	'bobbin', type D
B 123	splinter
H 37	handle
P 56	decorated jar
P 313	decorated sherd
P **	decorated pottery
Q 2	rotary quern, lower stone
W 5	spindle whorl (limestone)

Mound 46 (under)

I 2	dagger
W 4	spindle whorl (lias)
W 13	spindle whorl (limestone)
W 17	spindle whorl (lias)
X 59	wheel hub, oak

Mound 46 (SE of)

W 46	spindle whorl (femur head)
W 47	spindle whorl (femur head)

Mound 46 (NW of)

B 119	gouge-shaped ox metatarsal
B 122	knife-marked bone
B 172	'bobbin', type E

Mound 46 (N of) outside palisade

B 20	'bobbin', type E
B 173	awl
P 17	decorated bowl
M 7	occipital bone
X 64	wicker basket

Mound 46 (E of) outside palisade

P 47	decorated bowl
X 65	framework, 37 pieces

Mound 47 (1893). (fig.3.8)

Causeway or landing stage off E edge of the site. Two main elements were built. a) A gravel and clay bank 32m long and 1-2m wide, with an extension 15m long; b) 30m of lias blocks and some clay lying to S and E of the bank. Bulleid described these as a) Causeway and b) Embankment. The Causeway was of yellow clay, rubble and timber posts. It extended out from a timber and post structure just S of M46, and ran N to a wide point where a shorter arm extended SSE. Recent excavations suggested that this Causeway was an elevated timber walkway, held by the clay and rubble bank and supported by timber uprights and horizontal boards. At the N end an oak beam may have formed part of a landing stage. See also page 118.

The Embankment was of lias blocks with some timber, and a S section was of lias and clay held in place by hurdles and timber walling with morticed posts and horizontal rails. The Embankment was overlain by the Causeway at the N end. The S end of the Causeway and the rubble and clay sector of the Embankment lie adjacent to the plank and post structure S of M46. This structure is only 2m from the Causeway, and it is likely that it was an integral part of the elaborate landing stage at the E edge of the site, at a time when transport by water was possible and regular. Loads and traffic would have docked within the Causeway-Embankment or at the N end or E edges, from where passage was made to the S end of the Causeway. It is conceivable that a bridge existed here, linking the platform to the Causeway. An alternative was to dock directly at the E edge of the site, onto the spread of clay at M46 in the shelter of the Causeway and palisade. This landing was closed off in the Final phase of occupation but the platform could have remained in use with the Causeway. The relics found on or near the Causeway and Embankment included a number of lead weights.

Stratigraphy: Embankment under Causeway

Phase: Embankment Middle
Causeway Late

Mound 47 finds

L 41	net sinker (lead)
L 43	net sinker (lead)
P **	decorated pottery

Mound 47 (Centre East)

L 2	net sinker (lead)
L 9	net sinker (lead)

Mound 47 (N end)

I 18	spoon augur
L 3	net sinker (lead)
L 4	net sinker (lead)
L 5	net sinker (lead)
L 6	net sinker (lead)
L 7	net sinker (lead)
L 8	net sinker (lead)
L 31	net sinker (lead)
L 40	net sinker (lead)
L GLV84	net sinker (lead)
L GLV84	net sinker (lead)

Mound 47 (S end)

L 1	net sinker (lead)

Mound 47 (E of)

Q 1	rotary quern, lower stone
X 86	knobbed pile, oak

Mound 47 (SE of)

I 4	knife

Mound 48 (1894). (figs.3.4, 3.7 and 3.8)

Spread of yellow clay at NE of site. The clay represents one Floor, 5.5m oblong, max. thickness 350mm. No hearth or wall posts were noted, and the Floor had little dark earth. The foundation was of timbers laid parallel to the palisade line which extended around the E and N edges of the Mound. Planks were also found S of the Mound. A patch of small stones lay under the clay of M48 and the adjacent M49. M48 was probably a small stance for M49, tucked against the palisade where it created a sharp curve towards a major entrance.

The relics found were mostly outside the palisade.

Stratigraphy: none

Phase: Late

Mound 48 finds

F 43	knife, scraper, flake and two cores

Mound 48 (NE of)

B 161	perforated ox/horse tibia

Mound 48 (SE of)

B 170	'bobbin', type D

Mound 48 (NW of)

B 156	point (gouge)
P 110	

Mound 48 (E of) outside palisade

B 148	modelling tool?
B 158	'bobbin', type E
B 159	'bobbin', type D
B 160	ox metatarsal, polished
E 40	finger ring
I 28	sickle
S 15	disc (sandstone)
T 3	boar's tusk

Mound 48 (N of) outside palisade

H 94	sawn and polished antler
H 126	worked tine
I 30	sickle
M 7a	right parietal bone
M 7b	left parietal bone
M 11	charred human and animal bone
P 112	decorated bowl
P 122	decorated bowl
P 123	small 'cup-shaped vessel'
P 263	decorated bowl
W 53	spindle whorl (lias)
W 63	spindle whorl (lias)
X 48	stopper, oak
Z 2	currency bar

Mounds 49 and 50 (1894). (figs.3.4 and 3.7)

M49. Spread of clay near E edge of site. The clays represent 4 Floors, over an area 8.0 x 8.0m with extensions N and S, max. thickness 1.0m. Floor 4 was 6.5m diameter with roundwood on the S side possibly flooring but more likely foundation. The baked clay hearth was not central to the Floor. Floor 3 was 8.0m diameter and had a clay hearth and a dark earth and ash deposit on the Floor. Floor 2 was a wider spread extending over Floor 3 to the S and N, and to the E where it formed part of Floor 1 of M45. This was an open stance extending towards the palisade. Floor 2 had a baked clay hearth built over the hearth of Floor 3, and a small paved area of stone slabs was near the S edge, presumably of Floor 2. Floor 1 was 7.9m diameter with a clay hearth once more in place over hearths of Floors 2 and 3, and black earth covered the Floor. No clear lines of wall posts were noted and it would seem that Floor 3 was a renewal of Floor 4, Floor 2 marked an important alteration in shape and function, and Floor 1 was a strengthening of the hearth area. A dense scatter of posts was noted to the S of M49, between M49 and M44, as if some form of structure or barrier existed here. Both these Mounds had lobes of clay extending towards these posts and a framework of timber lay deep in the peat adjacent to the posts.

M50. A small spread of yellow clay immediately W of M49 with no hearth or other structural evidence. This was probably only a small patch providing firm ground between M49 and M51.

The foundation of M49 was brushwood upon timber and the S part of the Mound had particularly strong timber foundation. At the NW of M49 and N of M50 planking lay between the clay and the palisade which here was sharply turned inwards, the rows of multiple posts ending. From this point the palisade turned N and was very slight.

The relics found on or near M49 were very numerous, particularly pottery. Few objects were assigned to Floors.

Stratigraphy: M49 Floor 2 joins M45 Floor 1. M50 none

Phase: M49 Floors 4-3 Late, Floors 2-1 Final
M50 Final

Mound 49 finds

B 371	weaving comb fragments
E 45	spiral finger ring
E 46	spiral finger ring
E 47	awl with bone handle
E 58	binding
E 67	rivet heads x 2
E 70	binding
E 71	rivet
E 226	fragments
E 227	ring
H 107	weaving comb
H 109	weaving comb
H 117	weaving comb fragments x 2, charred
H 124	handle
H 125	worked antler
H 127	worked antler
H 128	worked antler
K 8	armlet
K 9	armlet
P 105	decorated jar
P 106	decorated bowl
P 107	decorated sherd
P 127	decorated vessel

P 128	decorated jar
P 193	decorated jar
P 194	decorated jar
P 198	decorated jar
P 290	decorated bowl
P 294	decorated sherd
P 298	decorated sherd
P 301	decorated sherd
P 302	decorated sherd
P **	much pottery including decorated
W 56	spindle whorl (sandstone)
**	beans

Mound 49 (Floor 1)

E 42	penannular brooch, Fowler type B
E 81	tweezers

Mound 49 (Floor 2)

E 59	brooch fragments
G 10	bead, blue annular, Guido group 6

Mound 49 (NE of)

B 178	notched and perforated horse/ox tibia
H 116	antler with knife cuts
M 10	skull fragment
P 109	decorated sherd

Mound 49 (SE of)

B 175	perforated ox metacarpal
B 179	bone with knife marks
H 98	sawn antler
H 100	perforated disc
H 113	polished antler
H 115	shed roe deer antler, slight knife cuts
H 120	cheek piece
H 121	weaving comb
H 129	handle
M 9	skull fragment
P 99	decorated sherd
P 111	decorated bowl

Mound 49 (SW of)

H 118	shed roe deer antler
P 101	decorated jar
P 129	decorated jar
W 64	spindle whorl (shale)
W 65	spindle whorl (shale)

Mound 49 (NW of)

B 155	notched and perforated ox/horse tibia
F 42	microdenticulate, Mesolithic/early Neolithic
P 104	decorated vessel

Mound 49 (N of) outside palisade

F 41	leaf-shaped arrowhead
F 45	core
H 102	worked tine
L 13	spindle whorl (tin)

Mound 50 finds

P 276	decorated bowl

Mound 50 (SE of)

H 103	sawn tine
H 108	weaving comb

Mound 50 (NW of)

F 369	retouched flake
H 294	weaving comb
H 295	handle?, unfinished
Y 2	disc

Mounds 51 (1894, 1905), 52 (1894, 1898), 53 (1894,1905). (figs.3.4, 3.6 and 3.7)

M51. Spread of clay at centre E of site. The clays represent 5 Floors over an area 7.5 x 6.4m, with the earlier Floors very small. Floor 5 was 2.4 x 2.1m, and was merely a base for a stone hearth with stone paving around. Floor 4, 3.2 x 2.7m, had another stone hearth built over Floor 5. Floor 3, 3.7 x 3.4m, had a similar hearth on the plan but the text says no hearth was found. To the SW of Floor 3, a small patch of yellow clay 5.5 x 3.0m was laid, forming the base of M52 (Floor 2). Floor 2 of M51 was 4.9 x 4.3m with a baked clay hearth placed in a different position off-centre to the clay. Floor 1 was 7.3 x 6.4m with a clay hearth built on that of Floor 2. The clay of Floor 1 extended S and then W to form Floor 1 of M52 and M53, creating a unit of 3 distinct spreads joined at narrow points along the edges. M53 was not directly joined to M51. M52 Floor 1 was 7.5 x 7.0m and no hearth was found. M53 Floors 1-3 were the same size and shape and inseparable at the edges, 7.5 x 5.0m. The upper Floor 1 had no hearth, Floor 2 had a gravel hearth like those of M51 Floors 5-4-3, and Floor 3 had a baked clay hearth renewed 3 times. These 3 Mounds form a unit beginning with two separate hearth areas (M51 and M53), then linked by the open spread of clay (M52). No clear sign of any wall posts was noted but many posts were found in or under the N part of M52, near the hearths and paving of M51. Some oak posts of larger size were scattered through M52 and M53, and the complex of posts may mark some working platforms or racks related to the well-built hearths.

The foundation of these Mounds was brushwood with some timber for M51 and M52, brushwood for M53. The timber was heavier in the E of M52 and S of M51. Some charcoal and wood chips were noted in the foundation wood on the N of M51. The relics were sparse, including peas on M51 NW margin, and on the brushwood of M52 S side, and between M52 and M42.

Stratigraphy: M51 Floor 1 joins M52 Floor 1 and M53

Phase: M51 Floor 5 Middle, Floors 4-3 Late,
Floor 2-1 Final
M52 Floor 2 Late, Floor 1 Final
M53 Floor 3 ? Late, Floors 2-1 Final

Mound 51 finds

H 123	sawn antler
P **	'a few fragments of pottery'
**	animal bone including horse teeth

Mound 51 (under)

**	wood chips

Mound 51 (NW of)

F 370	retouched flake
P **	cordoned bowl
X 60	stave-built tub, oak

**	peas

Mound 52 finds

H 266	ferrule
Q 54	rotary quern, upper stone

Mound 52 (under)

**	beans, large quantity

Mound 52 (S of)

**	beans

Mound 53 finds

D **	loom weight fragments
D **	perforated ball
F **	flakes x 4 and natural nodule
P **	decorated pottery
WS 1128 ?	polisher

Mound 53 (Floor 2)

H 296	split and charred antler with knobbed ends, as H 335
F 372	flake

Mound 53 (Floor 3)

E 198	decorated sheet

Mound 53 (under)

F 371	flake

Mound 53 (NE of)

B 379	perforated head of femur
W 166	spindle whorl (sandstone)
W 167	spindle whorl (sandstone)

Mound 53 (SW of)

H 335	split and charred antler with knobbed ends as, H 296

Mound 53 (NW of)

Q 41	rotary quern, upper stone
W 169	spindle whorl, unfinished (sandstone)

Mound 54 (1904). (fig.3.4)

Small patch of yellow clay at N part of site. The clay represents 2 Floors over an area 5.0 x 3.0m, max. thickness 300mm. Floor 2 was 2.7 x 2.1m and was essentially merely a base for a baked clay hearth renewed once. Floor 1 was a larger patch of clay with a hearth built over the earlier hearths. Around the Mound were several spreads of stones which Bulleid considered to be pathways. M54 is an isolated patch and might have been a special place for activities that had to be kept away from the dwellings. A line of posts extends out towards M54 from M65, and another more diffuse line from the joining M64; perhaps these marked some channelling of activity to M54. To the SE of M54 a wide scatter of heavy oak posts was noted, some set 1-2m apart and these may have supported platforms just inside a major E entrance to the site, fenced by a line of posts but not densely palisaded as is N and S of this putative entry.

The foundation of M54 was felled wood and brushwood. The relics were few. Black earth was noted extending from M54 across to the fence line, containing charcoal, pottery, bone and baked clay rubble. Various objects were found among the oak posts, including a wooden tub.

Stratigraphy: none

Phase: Floor 2 Late, Floor 1 Final

Mound 54 finds

P **	decorated pottery
Q 40	saddle quern, upper stone
S **	whetstone

Mound 54 (under)

P **	pottery
**	animal bones

Mound 54 (NE of)

A 4	amber bead

Mound 54 (SE of)

B 377	perforated bone
B 378	perforated bone
E 197	rivet head
S 38	spindle whorl, unfinished (sandstone)
S 39	disc (sandstone)

Mound 55 (1902 and 1904). (fig.3.4)

Spread of 'indifferent' yellow clay at N of site. The clays represent 2 Floors, one a small patch, over an area 11 x 9m, max. thickness 380mm. Floor 2 was 3.4 x 3.0m and was a base for a baked clay and stone hearth. Floor 1 was a large oval spread 11 x 9 m with a smaller hearth of clay. Blocks of red sandstone were placed in an arc around the hearth, one of them resting on a layer of ash; they may have been seats. Behind them were the posts and fragments of hurdles probably associated with this Floor, and with a large patch of small stones beyond to the E. A line of posts extended from the hurdles up to the NW edge of the clay and other hurdlework was *in situ* off the Mound to the SE. This is a complex area of the site; the probable main E entrance to the settlement lay immediately S of M55, and the clays of M56 overlay Floor 1. Baked clay rubble was noted along the W, N and NE edges. Both Gray, who cut a trench through the Mound in 1902 (treating it like a barrow), and Bulleid considered that a complete round house had existed here; this is most unlikely. The foundation was brushwood with the bases of the hurdles embedded. Timber was laid under and along the N and NE edges of the Mound. There were many posts at the SE margin, possibly part of a palisade or fence. At the W edge, two planks 3m long lay between M55 and M78; they were 5m apart. One was pegged into the peat; the other had large pegs beside it. An alder post was upright beside the N plank.

The relics recovered included a number assigned to the Floors. M55 was Gray's 'Mound 1' of 1902.

Stratigraphy: Floor 1 underlies M56 Floors 1-2. M55 abuts M78 and M58

Phase: Floor 2 Middle, Floor 1 Late

Mound 55 finds

B 373	'bobbin', type E
D **	sling shot
D **	sling shot
F 361	nodule

F 368	flake
F **	flakes x 5 and core
H 289	sawn antler
H 324	weaving comb
L 36	lump (tin)
P **	decorated pottery
S **	sling stone

Mound 55 (Floor 1)

E 190	belt link
E 194	tubular harness? ring
E 195	ring
Q 39	rotary quern, lower stone

Mound 55 (Floor 2)

D 70	ball
H 286	worked antler
P 162	decorated sherds (2)
T 11	perforated boar's tusk

Mound 55 (NE of)

P 165	decorated bowl

Mound 55 (SE of)

D **	sling shot
H 169	sawn tine
P **	decorated pottery
X 7	ladle
X 35	disc of oak with central hole

Mound 55 (SW of)

G 22	bead with yellow chevron decoration, Guido class 11
K 28	armlet
M 35	parietal bone

Mound 56 (1896). (fig.3.4)

Complex spread of yellow clay and woodwork on E edge of site. The clays represent 2 Floors over a small area 5.5m across, max. thickness 750mm. The whole Mound was tilted down to the E as the palisade slipped outwards. Floor 2 had a small clay hearth. This Floor had dipped and a wooden platform made of 3 layers of split wood, some squared, had been laid upon it, thicker on the E, in efforts to level up the surface prior to the clay of Floor 1. Floor 1 had a clay hearth and had tilted down as the palisade slipped outwards. A line of hurdlework on the E edge of Floor 2 marked a firm edge to this Floor, which also had a wall line of posts on the W and S. It was heavily encompassed on the E and N by palisade posts and it is likely that Floor 2 had supported a small structure here at the E entrance to the site. The Floor was elongated by a lobe of clay 8m long and 1-2.5m wide extending S, held on the E by palisade posts. The W edge of Floor 2 overlapped M55 with a patch of stone between the clays.

To the S of M56, W of the lobe extension, and E of M55, the area of peat and black earth was divided by several lines of hurdles, aligned E-W and SW-NE; these formed pens or separating areas, perhaps for animals arriving at the E entrance.

The foundation of M56 was substantial. Brushwood lay upon a leafy layer which covered 3 complete hurdles, all pegged down; the hurdles were about 3.2 x 1.9m in size. Also in the foundation were mortised oak beams and planks and a knobbed pile. Bulleid considered these all to represent 'without doubt' a dismantled rectangular structure, which seems possible but by no means certain. It is as likely that when the site was extended to the NE, the exceptionally soft peats required special foundations and multiple posts for clay spreads, houses and palisade. The careful foundation directly underneath M56 Floor 2 supports the suggestion that some form of house or other structure was thereupon built, although the above-ground evidence is not conclusive. The foundation for the lobe extension was also substantial, with timbers laid over much of the wider area near the S end where posts and hurdlework were in place.

The relics from M56 were few in number, mostly decorated sherds. Around the area and sunk or buried in the soft peats were some wooden objects, including part of a tub, a ladle and a massive disc 0.7m diameter. A child's skull and some bones were found under the S edge of the Mound.

Stratigraphy: overlies M55

Phase: Floor 2 Late, Floor 1 Final

Mound 56 finds

F 44	scraper
P 277	decorated bowl
P 278	decorated sherd
P 281	decorated sherd
P 282	decorated sherd
P 283	decorated bowl
P 304	decorated bowl
**	lower bones of 4 horse legs

Mound 56 (under)

M 21	child's skull & bones
X 31	morticed beam, oak
X 32	morticed beam, oak
X 33	morticed plank, oak
X 34	morticed plank, oak
X 37	knobbed pile, oak

Mound 56 (SE of)

B 242	'bobbin', type D
B 243	'bobbin', type A
B 244	'bobbin', type D
H 167	handle
X 2	lathe-turned bowl, ash

Mound 56 (SE of) outside palisade

B 240	point
B 241	pointed bone implement
H 168	handle

Mound 56 (S of)

**	beans

Mound 57 (1896 and 1904). (fig.3.4)

Spread of yellow clay at NE edge of site. The clays represent 4 Floors, over an area 8.5 x 8.0m, max. thickness 1.1m. An 'extensive' layer of blue clay lay beneath Floor 4, but this is not marked on the plan, nor are any individual Floors. Floor 4 was 5.8m across and had a baked clay hearth at the centre of the Floor, which had subsided due to its weight. Floor 3 had brushwood incorporated in the clay and had a wide raised hearth of clay with stone rubble. Along the NE and S margin of this Floor, Bulleid noted a line of wall posts but if these are associated with Floor 3, Floor 3 must be wider than the 4.0m noted in the text. The posts extend in a more irregular way around the SW and W margins of the Floor, and a circle of 5 oak posts within the putative house might mark some internal supports; they appear to relate to Floor 2. Floor 2 was 9.1m across and Floor 1 7.6m across; neither had a hearth and they probably represent renewals of Floor 3 as the clays sunk into the soft peat and foundation, with the heavy posts put in to support an unstable roof.

The foundation was of brushwood, blue clay and logs, with the wood laid along the N, E and S sides of the Mound, and extending outside to the palisade. The wood included perforated beams of oak, pegged to the peat, on the E side which may have formed the base of a walkway outside the house and alongside the palisade hurdles. The palisade was rather thin here, with hurdles providing a slender fence and a patch of brushwood beyond, perhaps a place for disposal of rubbish and body products. The palisade posts to the S of M57 turn sharply in between M56 and M57 as if M57 was an extra structure in some way set apart from the rest of the Mounds in this area of the site. The relics were not numerous.

Stratigraphy: abuts M58

Phase: Floors 4-3-2 Late, Floor 1 Final

Mound 57 finds

B 245	'bobbin', type E
E 106	chain
P 279	decorated bowl
P 280	decorated base

Mound 57 (Floor 2)

H 170	weaving comb
H 171	hammer
H 284	cheek piece

Mound 57 (under 2nd clay layer)

F 46	scraper

Mound 57 (Floor 4)

M 22	child's skeleton, on floor nr. NW edge of hearth
**	moss and brushwood mixed with clay of floor on N & E

Mound 57 (under)

F 364	flake
W 86	spindle whorl (sandstone)

Mound 57 (NW of)

X 51	block with tenon and mortice hole

Mound 57 (E of) outside palisade

Q 15	rotary quern, lower stone

Mound 57 (N of) outside palisade

X 63	wheel hub, ash?
X 67	spoke

Mound 58 (1896 and 1904). (fig.3.4)

Spread of clay at NE of site. The clay represented one large spread (Floor 2) and a small patch (Floor 1). Floor 2 was an elongated oval of dirty yellow clay over an area 13.0 x 7.0m, with a lobe to the N. A gravel hearth was near the S end, and a scatter of posts was noted along the E side. The lobe of clay to the N extended out to the thin line of the palisade which effectively ended here. Floor 1 was 4.9 x 4.3m and was deposited on the S end of Floor 2; it had a clay hearth. The foundation was of timber and brushwood. Floor 2 was in effect an entry/exit at the N of the site, lying between two stout palisade ends, one at M57 and one at M59. It had no structure in the form of walling but was merely an open spread of clay well supported by the foundation. The relics were not numerous. Peas and wheat were scattered over the E and S parts of the Mound.

Stratigraphy: Floors 2-1 overlie M59. M58 abuts M57. Overlap with M78 unclear

Phase: Floor 2 Late, Floor 1 Final

Mound 58 finds

E 105	penannular ring
E 107	binding from hide-shaped shield?
F 362	flake
F 363	flake
F **	flake, denticulated edge?
G 13	bead, blue
Q 16	rotary quern, upper stone
S 31	pebble
S 32	pebble
S 33	pebble
W 85	spindle whorl (clay)

Mound 58 (Floor 2)

B 374	splinter
E 191	spiral finger ring
H 285	'modelling' tool
P 163	decorated bowl
**	beans and wheat

Mound 58 (under)

K 27	turned bowl rim
P 138	decorated jar

Mound 58 (NW of)

X 72	notched and perforated object

Mound 59 (1895). (fig.3.3)

Spreads of clay at N edge of site. The clays represent 4 Floors, the uppermost (Floor 1) measuring 8m wide with extensions N and W. Max. thickness 750mm. Floor 4 was of dirty clay 5.2m diameter with no hearth and a line of hurdles at the N edge. Floor 3 was yellow clay 4.6m diameter with a baked clay hearth and wall post line with hurdles around all the Floor except at the S; this was probably a small round house. Floor 2 was 4.9m across, with a clay hearth, and was a renewal of the Floor 3 structure. Floor 1 marked a change in this area, with the removal of structures and replacement by a very large spread of clay over M59, M60 and M61. This spread was 26.0 x 7.0m in extent, with a long extension to the N. It is described under M61. There was a thick line of piles immediately to the W of M59; this represents a palisade line that once extended S past M79 and M64, and forming an old E palisade that ran S past M41, M26 and M19. M59 was one of the few structures outside this palisade when the latter was in use. The foundation of M59 itself was substantial; Bulleid considered that a very soft peat existed here, effectively a wet depression which was filled by domestic debris of pottery, bone and wood; it was the village dump. Upon this a number of logs and timber was laid, on the N, with brushwood laid all over the area. The layer of compressed rush which sealed this may have been of natural origin, representing a few years' interval once the hollow had been filled and made good. Thereafter the clays of Floor 4 were laid down.

The relics included pottery and a human clavicle.

Stratigraphy: Floor 1 joins M60 and M61 Floor 1 and underlies M58 Floors 2-1. Floor 1 abuts M79

Phase: Floor 4 Early, Floors 3-2 Middle, Floor 1 Late

Mound 59 finds

G 12	bead, blue with white spirals, Guido class 6

Mound 59 (under)

B 239	'bobbin', type D
D **	sling shot, large quantity
I 55	doubled iron band
P **	pottery
X 45	block with cup-shaped depression
**	animal bones

Mound 59 (NE of)

X 20	hand-carved tub

Mound 59 (NW of)

X 16	bent wood box

Mound 59 (N of) outside palisade

B 235	point (gouge)
B 236	polished horse bone
B 237	perforated ox humerus
B 238	'bobbin', type D
D **	sling shot, large number
H 165	weaving comb
H 166	sawn tine
I 53	saw with wooden handle
M 20	clavicle, gnawed
X 11	handle
X 13	lathe-turned bowl

Mound 60 (1895). (fig.3.3)

Spread of clay at N edge of site. The clays represent 2 Floors, the upper (Floor 1) continuous with that of M59 and M61. Max. thickness 750mm. Floor 2 was of blue clay 6.0 x 4.5m, and was covered by brushwood. A hearth of baked clay was near centre and a paved area was at the W edge. Black earth was thick over all the floor, including presumably the brushwood, and contained peas, wheat and barley. No wall posts were found and this small Floor was probably an open working area for M61. It also was at the extreme NE corner of the site in its Middle phase, when the E palisade lay just off the E edge of M60. Floor 1 overlay all of this and is described under M61.

The foundation of M60 was brushwood and timber, with major pieces laid parallel to the palisade. Under the Mound a 4.0m plank was pegged down by 2 oak posts. The relics were few in number.

Stratigraphy: Floor 1 joins M59 and M61 Floor 1

Phase: Floor 2 Middle, Floor 1 Late

Mound 60 finds

Mound 60 (Floor 2)

**	beans, barley and wheat in quantity

Mound 60 (under)

I 54	gouge and wooden handle

Mound 60 (SE of)

I 16	three rings, harness?

Mound 60 (N of) outside palisade

B 230	knife-cut and polished rib
B 231	notched and perforated ox/horse tibia
B 232	weaving comb
B 233	'bobbin', type E
D **	sling shot, large number
H 164	sawn antler
W 84	spindle whorl (femur head)
X 47	stopper, oak
**	beans, large quantity

Mound 61 (1895). (fig.3.3)

Spread of clay at N edge of site. The clays represent 2 Floors, the upper (Floor 1) joining M60 and M59. Max. thickness 1.0m. Floor 2 was 6.4 x 5.5m and was of yellow clay, partly covered by timbers 1.5 - 1.8m long laid radially. A large gravel hearth 1.2m diameter was at the centre, and an area of small stones and blocks of sandstone at the NE may mark an entrance. Peas were found strewn over the SW sector of this Floor. Around the edge there were some posts but these were not numerous; it is likely, however, that this Mound had some form of structure to it, possibly a round house. The entrance in effect was also an exit through the palisade which had a distinct gap here although several very long palisade posts lay outside the normal line of posts.

The foundation of M61 was brushwood and timber and between M61 and M60 were various beams including 3 pegged together to form 3 sides of a square 3.5 x 3.3m in size, probably an early shed here on the N edge of the site.

Floor 1 of M61, M60 and M59 was one large spread of clay, 26m W-E and about 7m wide; a thin extension 9.0m long went N from the E end of this spread. The posts of the palisade were clustered thickly along the N edge of Floor 1. There were 2 'incomplete' hearths noted, at centre and W (M60 and M61). The W end of the Floor terminated in a stout hurdle fence about 10m long; outside this the palisade posts extended W for 4m and then a ragged line of posts stretched S as if to protect the W end of the M59, M60 and M61 complex. Beyond this, to the W, was another major entry to the site, protected in the same way on its other side. Floor 1 of these Mounds represented a clearing-away of structures, reinforcing of the palisade, extension of the site to the NE and the provision of a large open stance between 2 entries. The long walkway of clay leading N from M59, past the palisade, was strengthened by a number of posts and probably served either as a landing stage for rafts and boats, or as a place outside the settled area for defecation, or both.

The relics found on and around M61 were few in number.

Stratigraphy: Floor 1 joins M60 and M59 Floor 1

Phase: Floor 2 Middle, Floor 1 Late

Mound 61 finds

E 104	ring

Mound 61 (Floor 2)

**	beans, large quantity

Mound 61 (SW of)

I 48	sickle
I 49	billhook
I 50	adze
I 51	adze
X 85	lathe-turned bowl
**	horse bones

Mound 61 (N of) outside palisade

B 229	point (gouge)
D **	sling shot, large number
I 52	saw
X 5	lathe-turned tub
X 26	lid
X40	hand-carved tub, oak

Mound 62 (1892). (fig.3.3)

Spreads of yellow and grey clay near N edge of site. The clays represent 3 Floors, over an area 9 x 8m, max. thickness 1.3m. Floor 3 was of grey clay, diameter 7.6m, with a baked clay hearth and a covering of brushwood. Floor 2 was 9.1m diameter, of yellow clay covered by baked clay rubble with hurdle, timber and finger marks, ash and charcoal. A line of wall posts extended around the E and N edges, the tops of the posts charred. The hearth was slightly off centre to the SW, away from the walling, and had a stone slab surface embedded in a clay surround 1.8m diameter. The hearth had been renewed 3 times by clay and stone, the latter disintegrated. A thick deposit of ash 2.4 x 2.1m in extent was at the E edge of the Floor. Several stout posts were noted at the SW edge of the Floor but may relate to an earlier 4-post structure dismantled as the Floors were laid down. Floor 2 probably marks a substantially-built shelter, with N and E walling, hearth set forward of the walling, and subsequently burnt down. The rubble extended in a great arc around the hearth except for the extreme S. Floor 1 of yellow clay was 7.9m diameter, and joined M63 and M64 as a wide spread of clay; a clay hearth was incomplete, and the surface had black earth over it. No sign of a wall or entrance was noted for this Floor.

The foundation was of brushwood and timber, the logs arranged W-E; one of them was a morticed beam of oak. The 4 stout oak posts at the SW edge may mark an earlier shed or platform 3 x 2m approximately. Off the E edge of the Mound a large patch of stones about 6m long may mark an inner walkway for an early palisade line. The relics from M62 were numerous, almost all unstratified. Floor 2 had crucibles, a tuyère, fragments of baked clay blocks (perhaps a furnace) and baked clay daub. From the Floors in general came bobbins, needles, combs, crucibles, clay balls, clay slingshots in great abundance, bronze fibulae, glass beads, antler handles and combs, an iron spearhead, handle and file, shale, and various whorls. Pottery is barely mentioned.

Stratigraphy: Floor 1 joins M63 and M64 (Floors uncertain). Floor 2 underlies M63 Floors 1-2

Phase: Floors 3-2 Middle, Floor 1 Late

Mound 62 finds

B 39	'bobbin', type E
B 54	splinter
B 55	weaving comb fragment
B 62	weaving comb
B 66	perforated ox/horse tibia
B 67	perforated ox/horse tibia
B 72	point (gouge)
B 73	point (gouge)
B 78	needle fragment
B 102	'bobbin', type E
B 103	'bobbin', type E
B 104	'bobbin', type E
B 105	'bobbin', type E
B 106	'bobbin', type E
B 107	'bobbin', type F
B 108	'bobbin', type D
B 109	perforated sheep tibia
B 110	'bobbin', type E
B 111	'bobbin', type E
B 115	needle
B 116	needle
B 117	needle
D 27.1	sling shot
D 27.2	sling shot
D 27.3	sling shot
D 27.6	ball
D 27.7	sling shot
D 27.8	sling shot
D 27.10	sling shot
D 27.13	sling shot
D 27.16	sling shot
D 27.17	sling shot
D 27.25	sling shot
D 27.32	sling shot
D 27.34	sling shot
D 27.38	sling shot
D 27.43	sling shot
D 27.45	sling shot

D 27.47	sling shot
D 27.48	sling shot
D 27.49	sling shot
D 27.52	sling shot
D 27.54	oval disc
D 27.58	ball
D 27.60	ball
D 27.61	sling shot
D 27.62	sling shot
D 27.73	disc
D 27.74	disc
D 27.76	sling shot
D 27.77	sling shot
D 27.78	sling shot
D 27.80	lump
D 27.81	fragments
D 27.83	sling shot
D 27.84	sling shot
D 27.86	sling shot
D 27.87	sling shot
D 27.90	sling shot
D 27.91	sling shot
D 27.92	sling shot
D 27.94	sling shot
D 27.95	sling shot
D 27.96	sling shot
D 27.98	sling shot
D 27.99	disc
D 27.100	ball
D 28.1	perforated lump
D 28.7	ball
D 28.8	sling shot
D 28.9	sling shot
D 28.12	sling shot
D 28.13	sling shot
D 28.14	sling shot
D 28.15	sling shot
D 28.16	sling shot
D 28.17	sling shot
D 28.19	sling shot
D 28.20	sling shot
D 28.22	sling shot
D 28.23	sling shot
D 28.26	sling shot
D 28.27	sling shot
D 28.29	sling shot
D 28.39	sling shot
D 28.41	sling shot
D 28.45	sling shot
D 28.46	sling shot
D 29	loom weights x 6
D 36	lump
D 37	baked clay with depression
D 38	perforated slab
D 39	ball
D 40	nail-head shaped baked clay
D 41	baked clay with depression
D 44	block with hole on one side
D 45.1	perforated ball
D 45.2	perforated ball
E 9	fragment
E 13	ball
E 20	brooch, one piece simple brooch British form, (Drahtfibel)
E 21	brooch, La Tène III wire brooch
E 24	brooch pin
E 28	rivet head
E 30	rivet head
E 36	dross (tin)
G 1	bead, blue with white spirals, Guido class 6
G 3	bead, translucent green annular, Guido group 6
G 5	bead, blue with white spirals, Guido class 6
H 9	weaving comb fragment
H 38	handle
H 41	tine tip
H 43	worked tine
H 44	polished tine tip
H 51	sawn tine
H 55	sawn tine
H 57	handle ?
H 60	sawn and perforated antler
H 62	weaving comb
H 64	weaving comb
H 70	weaving comb
H 72	weaving comb
H 79	handle
H 83	worked antler
H 84	worked tine
H 370	handle
I 3	file
I 10	ferrule
I 13	sword handle?
I 20	spearhead
I 23	ring
K 2	armlet
K 3	ring
P 250	decorated sherd
Q 9	rotary quern, upper stone
S 7	disc (sandstone)
W 24	spindle whorl (sandstone)
W 28	spindle whorl (sandstone)
W 31	spindle whorl (sandstone)
W 35	spindle whorl (lias)
W 37	spindle whorl (sandstone)
W 38	spindle whorl (lias)
W 40	spindle whorl (lias)
W 44	spindle whorl (clay)
W 45	spindle whorl (clay)
W 187	spindle whorl (femur head)
W 189	spindle whorl (clay)
W 201	spindle whorl (clay)
W 202	spindle whorl (clay)
**	beans

Mound 62 (Floor 2)

C 8	square-sided vessel
C 9	crucible

C 10	crucible fragment
C 11	crucible
C 12	crucible
C 13	square-sided vessel
C **	crucibles
D 30	tuyère
D 31	moulded blocks, metalworking hearth?
D 32	moulded blocks, metalworking hearth?
D 33	moulded blocks, metalworking hearth?
D 34	daub, quantity of

Mound 62 (under)

X 84	morticed plank

Mound 62 (SE of)

E 12	bracelet
H 75	'pottery stamp'
H 78	charred antler

Mound 62 (NW of)

E 26	brooch, La Tène III 'Glastonbury' mock spring form
E 91	ring
H 87	charred antler
H 88	charred antler
H 89	charred antler

Mound 63 (1892). (fig.3.3)

Spreads of yellow clay at N of site. The clays represent 2 Floors, over an area approximately 10 x 8m, max. thickness 600mm. Floors 2 and 1 were more or less the same, with no hearth on either and no black earth separating the clays. An extension of clay to the S must be Floor 2 if the plan is to be believed. The clays overlay M62 Floor 2 rubble and joined Floor 1. The foundation was brushwood, with a few mortised oak beams and stout posts in the NW part of the Mound. These posts may mark an earlier platform or other structure. Some laid timbers at the S of the Mound, under Floor 2, also have stout oak posts around. A wide and dense line of posts extended across the Mound, beneath the clays, from E to W, possibly linking with posts under M65 and a scatter between M63 and M85. These look like some form of barrier at the edge of the open area of the site prior to the development of the N and NE part and may be an old palisade line extending from M67.

Stratigraphy: Floors join M62 and M64 (Floors unclear). Floors 1-2 overlie M62 Floor 2. Floors 1-2 probably join M62 Floor 1 and M65 (Floors unclear)

Phase: Late
Wooden structure beneath clay ?Middle

Mound 63 finds

B 58	decorated ox metatarsal
B 69	point (gouge)
B 80	splinter
B 113	needle
D 26	ring
E 10	shoe-like ornament
E 29	rivet
F **	scraper
H 48	sawn and cut tine
H 61	weaving comb
H 67	weaving comb
H 77	cheek piece
I 14	strip
L 10	bar (lead/tin)
P 63	decorated bowl
Q 5	rotary quern, upper stone
W 42	spindle whorl (lias)
W 43	spindle whorl (clay)
W 198	spindle whorl (clay)
W 199	spindle whorl (clay)
W 200	spindle whorl (clay)
**	weasel skeleton

Mound 63 (SW of)

H 49	knife-cut tine
W 95	spindle whorl (clay)

Mound 63 (NW of)

H 59	handle

Mound 64 (1892 and 1904). (fig.3.3)

Spreads of yellow clay at N part of site. The clays represent 3 Floors, over an area 11.0 x 9.5m with an extension to NE, max. thickness 1.2m. Floor 3 was the largest spread, its S edge joined to M65 (Bulleid's text says Mound XLV but he must mean LXV). Some floor boards were noted, a hearth was off-centre, and the Floor covered by blackearth. Floor 2 was smaller in extent, 7.3m N-S, and is marked in Bulleid's plan as an extension to NNE of the main Floor area; its area W-E is unknown, but the clay hearth was 1.5 x 1.8m diameter and if over the Floor 3 hearth, the Floor 2 hearth was at the SW edge of Floor 2. This is not at all clear in the text. Floor 1 joined M65 at the S and had a small red marl hearth. No wall post lines were noted. The foundation was brushwood overlain by bracken and rush containing much pottery and bone, and a small patch of 'fireash' was associated. A dense line of posts under the E part of the Mound is an old palisade running N to M59 - M60.

The relics were numerous, particularly pottery. Floor 3 had 8 iron objects including a saw, bit, ring, ferrule, band and chain. The Floor also had much pottery, and peas near the N edge.

Stratigraphy: Mound joins M62, M63 and M65 (Floors mostly unclear). Floor 1 probably joins M65 and Floor 3 probably joins M65

Phase: Floors 3-2 Late, Floor 1 Final

Mound 64 finds

A 1	amber bead
B 59	perforated disc of human skull
B 68	polished bone
B 70	point (gouge)
B 82	splinter
B 83	splinter
B 84	polished bone
B 85	knife-cut rib
B 114	needle
C 14	crucible
E 15	brooch pin

E 22	brooch, La Tène III 'Glastonbury' mock spring form
H 50	sawn tine
H 52	sawn antler
H 71	weaving comb
H 82	needle
H 85	weaving comb, unfinished
H 86	perforated antler
H 292	sawn antler
K 1	disc
K 4	disc
L 22	weight (lead)
N 7	beaver teeth
P 30	decorated sherd
P 32	decorated bowl
P **	pottery, large amount
S 34	disc (sandstone)
W 19	spindle whorl (clay)
W 29	spindle whorl (lias)
W 36	spindle whorl (lias)
W 192	spindle whorl (clay)
**	beans

Mound 64 (Floor 2)

B 376	needle
T 10	boar's tusk

Mound 64 (Floor 3)

I 11	saw
I 12	bridle bit
I 15	spiral finger ring
I 21	chain fragment
I 22	rivets x 6
I 24	wire
I 25	ferrule
I 26	band

Mound 64 (under)

P **	'numerous fragments of pottery'
**	animal bones

Mound 64 (NE of)

B 81	point (gouge)

Mound 64 (SE of)

B 86	knife-cut rib
B 87	knife-cut rib
P 26	decorated jar

Mound 64 (SW of)

H 36	weaving comb blank
W 133	spindle whorl (antler)

Mound 64 (NW of)

B 65	notched and perforated ox/horse femur
E 23	penannular brooch, Fowler type B
Q 12	rotary quern, upper stone

Mound 65 (1892). (fig.3.3)

Spreads of yellow and grey clay at N of site. The clays represent 3 Floors, over an area 11.0 x 9.0m, max. thickness 1.0m. Floor 3, of grey clay, was 8.5 x 7.6m, and had a baked clay hearth; no black earth was seen and Floor 3 merged with Floor 2 above. Some hurdle work was noted about 2.5m SE of the hearth (not shown on plan) and may have been an internal wall. The edge of the Floor had a clear line of wall posts. Floor 2 was a renewal of this Floor and had 4 hearths, built over the original hearth, the lowest 3 of baked clay, the upper hearth of red marl. Two lias slabs lay on the Floor, perhaps seats, and large parts of the Floor were covered by split wood boards laid in concentric circles parallel to the margin of the Floor. Floor 1 had a clay hearth and was covered by black earth with bones, many of pig. Along the margin of the Floor were wall posts in "an incomplete line". Bulleid does not make clear on the plan or in the text if Floor 1 was larger or smaller than Floors 2-3; the wall post lines suggest Floor 1 was an expansion. From the E edge of the Mound a line of posts ran ENE towards M54, perhaps linked with another line from M64 to create a funnel effect.

The foundation was substantial. On the W part, brushwood and some logs were found. On the E part, alder logs were laid side by side W-E as shown by the plan, but these were underlain by N-S logs, themselves over W-E logs, and brushwood below. A mortised oak beam 3m long lay at the SE edge of the Mound, pegged by 2 oak posts and fragments of other beam lay nearby. Various stout oak posts off to the E may mark an earlier wooden platform. The problem with this area of the site, M62-M65, is that it was almost all excavated in Bulleid's first year of work, 1892, when little had been learned about stratigraphy and context. Plans are unclear, sections few, texts uncertain.

The relics were numerous. Peas were found under the Floors near the oak beams, and also at the NE. Pig bones lay under the Floors. Much pottery was found, and hazelnut shells near 'the hearth' (which hearth ?).

Stratigraphy: Floor 1 probably joins M64 Floor 1. Floor 2 probably joins M64 Floor 3

Phase: Floor 3 Middle, Floor 2 Late, Floor 1 Final

Mound 65 finds

B 88	knife marked bone
B 91	knife marked bone
B 92	knife marked bone
B 94	knife marked bone
B 95	knife marked bone
B 96	knife marked bone
B 97	'polishing bone'
B 98	'bobbin', type E
B 99	'bobbin', type E
B 100	'bobbin', type E
B 112	needle
E 14	thin sheet bronze
E 27	wire
E 31	rivet
E 32	rivet
E 33	rivet head
E 34	rivet head
E 37	sheet bronze
G 2	bead, blue globular, Guido group 7
G 27	green/blue slag?
H 39	sawn tine
H 42	worked tine
H 46	worked tine
H 47	worked tine

H 56	cut beam
H 58	perforated antler
P **	much pottery including decorated
W 2	spindle whorl (sandstone)
W 25	spindle whorl (sandstone)
W 32	spindle whorl (lias)
**	peas and hazel nuts

Mound 65 (Floor 1)

E 16	finger ring
E 17	spiral finger ring

Mound 65 (under Floor 1)

**	animal bones, mainly pig

Mound 65 (Floor 3)

E 8	terret, 'simple' type
**	beans, large quantity

Mound 65 (NE of)

B 89	knife-marked bone
B 90	knife marked bone
H 74	'pottery stamp'
**	peas

Mound 65 (SE of)

B 93	knife marked bone
F **	flakes x 3
W 20	spindle whorl (lias)
**	peas

Mound 65 (SW of)

H 45	handle

Mound 65 (NW of)

B 101	'bobbin', type E

Mound 66 (1907). (fig.3.2)

Spreads of clay at NE of site. The clays represent 2 Floors, over a small area 7.3 x 5.9m, max. thickness 450mm. Floor 2 was the larger, and had a hearth of baked clay, renewed three times with the second renewal of gravel, the others of clay. The Floor was covered by black earth. Floor 1 was 6.1 x 5.5m with a smaller hearth placed over the earlier hearths. Two lines of wall posts were noted at the N and NE edge and just inside the edge of Floor 1, probably marking the remains of walling around both Floors; the clays placed to make the Floors extend beyond the walls. At the S edge a cluster of posts was noted, and along the W edge the wall line of posts is clear. Here on the W the clay of Floor 2 joins M74 Floors 1-2.

The foundation was brushwood with some timber. A mortised oak beam 3m long was pegged into the peat beneath, and an alder stump, and horse jaw, lay near the N edge. Stout oak posts were noted at the S end.

The relics were not numerous.

Stratigraphy: Floor 2 joins M74 Floors 1-2

Phase: Floor 2 Late, Floor 1 Final

Mound 66 finds

D **	sling shot
F **	flakes x 2
HS 1018	hammerstone
S **	sling stone

Mound 66 (Floor 1)

F **	flake
P **	decorated pottery

Mound 66 (Floor 2)

D **	loom weight fragment
H 360	cheek piece
H 361	awl handle
H 362	hammer

Mound 66 (under)

X 73	stopper, oak
**	lower jaw of horse
**	crane bones
**	lower jaw of ox

Mound 67 (1906). (fig.3.2)

Spreads of yellow clay (Floors 3-1) and grey clay (Floor 4), at NE edge of site. The clays represent 4 Floors, over an area 7.6 x 7.6m, max. thickness 840mm. The Floors lay beside the palisade. Floor 4, 7.0 x 6.0m joined M83 Floor 1 and spread out to the palisade; no hearth was noted but the Floor had black earth upon it. At the NE, some timber was placed on the Floor before the yellow clays of Floors 3 and 2 were deposited; this timber was an attempt to level up the surface that had begun to collapse at the palisade. Floor 3, of yellow clay, was 9.0 x 6.7m, and had timber upon its E surface for the same reason. Floor 2 was a wider spread of clay, extending W along the palisade to join M69 Floor 2 although Bulleid's section drawing does not show this westward extension; its E end is not recorded on plan and it may have merged with Floor 3 in some unclear way. Floor 1 was only 4.0 x 4.1m, with a square hearth paved with stone slabs. No wall post lines were noted on this Mound. The foundation was of timber and brushwood, thicker at E and NE where the palisade lay. Under the SE part of the Mound, posts of an earlier palisade were found, of a time when the extreme NW of the site was not yet developed. On the E, Bulleid recorded water beetle and freshwater shells. To the S, off the Mound, the soft peats had pottery, wood and bones, including a horse skull, and bronze plate fragments. The palisade was rather dense, with a thick line of posts along the N edge of the Mound, curving SE around the Mound and then becoming more sparse. About 3m SE of the Mound, the dense line of posts picks up again and extends S to M66. Between M67 and M61 was a major entrance to the site. There are a large number of posts in the area of M67 which relate to 2 old palisade lines as well as the final palisade, and these may disguise short lengths of post-supported hurdles that were not connected to any major fence line.

The relics from M67 were sparse, including potsherds.

Stratigraphy: Floor 4 joins M83 Floor 1-2 and M68 Floor 3. Floor 2 joins M69 Floor 2

Phase: Floor 4 Middle, Floors 3-2 Late, Floor 1 Final

Mound 67 finds

D **	sling shot
F 198	nodule

F **	flake with retouch
P 187	decorated sherd
P 188	decorated jar

Mound 67 (Floor 2)

E 248	rivet head
K 30	armlet
P 173	decorated jar

Mound 67 (under)

E 249	sheet
F **	scraper

Mound 67 (SE of)

H 338	weaving comb
H 339	sawn tine

Mound 67 (S of)

**	wood chips, animal bones including horse skull, pottery

Mound 67 (NW of)

Q 13	rotary quern, upper stone

Mound 67 (N of) outside palisade

M 18	vertebra
M 19	skull
X 41	plank, oak
X 42	mallet

Mound 68 (1905 and 1906). (fig.3.2)

Spreads of clay at NW edge of site. The clays represent 3 Floors over an area 10.0 x 5.0m, max. thickness 430mm. Floor 3 joined M67 Floor 4 and M83 Floor 1 and Bulleid states that it extended up to the edge of the palisade. The plan is unclear. Floor 2 was a renewal, and although the text speaks of a comparable spread, the plan shows Floor 2 to be nowhere near the palisade and confined to an area 8.0 x 4.5m which extended farther W than Floor 3 but was much more restricted to the N. No hearths were noted on either Floor 3 or Floor 2. Floor 1 was a small patch of clay 2.8 x 2.3m at the N end of Floor 2, with a clay and stone-slab hearth. No wall posts were noted on this Mound. The foundation was brushwood lying over some timber. The plan also shows a line of posts running W-E across the centre of the Mound, probably an old palisade line. The relics were few. Some Roman sherds were found on the Mound surface just under the flood soil, and one sherd came from "the black earth belonging jointly to Floors 1 and 2".

Stratigraphy: Floor 3 joins M67 Floor 4 and M83 Floor 1. Floor 2 may join M69 Floor 2

Phase: Floor 3 Middle, Floor 2 Late, Floor 1 Final

Mound 68 finds

F **	flakes x 3
WS 1110	polisher

Mound 68 (Floor 1)

W 179	disc (sandstone)

Mound 68 (Floor 2)

D 72	kiln support?
H 302	weaving comb fragment
P 174	decorated sherd
W 180	spindle whorl, unfinished (sandstone)

Mound 68 (NE of)

X 50	notched and perforated object, alder

Mound 68 (soil above)

P 166	Roman pottery
P 175	Roman pottery

Mound 68 (N of) outside palisade

B 227	point (gouge)
B 228	'bobbin', type A

Mound 69 (1905). (fig.3.2)

Spreads of clay at NW edge of site. The clays represent 2 Floors, over an area 9.7 x 8.5m, max. thickness 730mm. Floor 2 was about 8 x 8m and may have joined M67 Floor 2, although the plan of this part of the site has a disconcertingly abrupt disconformity between M69 and M68. A hearth of baked clay was S of centre and a patch of stone rubble 2.7 x 1.8m lay near the NW edge. A curved line of posts in the N part may mark a windbreak or other small structure. This Floor was an open stance, laid down along with spreads to the E, when the site was expanded to its full NW extent. It had a black earth cover. The palisade posts edged the clay at W and N. Floor 1 was 6.1 x 5.3m and was spread over the S part of Floor 2; a baked clay hearth had various small stones embedded in the clay, and 6 slabs of stone were found between 1.6 and 2.5m from the hearth, presumably seats. No line of wall posts was found, although an oak plank 2.1m long was placed on edge at the E edge of the Floor. Floor 1 overlapped M70 Floor 2 and was covered by Floor 1 of the same Mound.

The foundation was brushwood on timber and had collapsed under the weight of the hearth. The relics included Roman pottery "in and around this mound, but at a higher level than the Late-Celtic relics". Part of a child's skeleton was found among the palisade posts to the N.

Stratigraphy: Floor 1 overlaps M70 Floor 2 and underlies M70 Floor 1. Floor 1 may join M67 Floor 2; the M68 relationship is unclear

Phase: Floor 2 Late, Floor 1 Final

Mound 69 finds

B **	worked bone
D **	sling shot
D **	sling shot
P 288	decorated sherd
P **	decorated pottery
WS 1102	whetstone
WS 1104	whetstone
WS 1105	whetstone
WS 1112 ?	whetstone
WS 1114	polisher
WS 1118	whetstone
WS 1127	whetstone

Mound 69 (Floor 1)

B 380	worked bone
B 381	perforated and notched horse/ox tibia
B 382	perforated and notched horse/ox tibia
D **	sling shot x 2

E 199	binding
E 200	binding
E 202	rivet head
E 206	terret
H 297	worked antler
H 298	cheek piece
H 299	cheek piece
H 300	tine worked to a point
H 301	worked antler
L 37	ring fragment (tin)
P **	one box of pottery
Q 42	rotary quern, lower stone
S 40	whetstone
S **	hammerstone
W 168	spindle whorl (lias)
**	dogs teeth x 3

Mound 69 (N of) outside palisade

B 226	worked and charred sheep bone fragment
M 16	child's skeleton, part
M 17	child's skeleton, part

Mound 70 (1905). (fig.3.2)

Spreads of clay at NW edge of site. The clays represent 3 Floors, over an area 12.0 x 10.5m, max. thickness 950mm. Bulleid's text refers to 2 clay Floors only, but beneath the well-defined Floor 2 was a thin spread of ash and charcoal over an area 7.0 x 5.5m, with a central hearth set in a patch of clay 2.1m diameter. This hearth was renewed 6 times by baked clay hearths and slight clay surrounds. Various relics were found with these hearths including 2 infant skeletons with the uppermost hearth of this series.

Floor 2 was 12.0 x 10.5m and the clay at the N lay between M69 Floors 2 and 1. At the W the clay was neatly edged by the palisade posts which were rather thin at this position. On the Floor were a series of boards laid parallel NNE-SSW, and a hearth of baked clay.

The plan shows a single or double arc of posts around the N, W and S of the Floor but set well inside the spread, to form a structure about 6m across N-S, and open to the E. This structure may even have been associated with the earlier hearths as the section shows several posts underneath Floor 2. Floor 1 was 9.1 x 9.3m, of yellow clay, with a baked clay hearth.

The foundation was brushwood with some timber. Under the SW part of Floor 2 a large knobbed post was found. The relics were numerous. Many of the relics were found within the area partly ringed by posts which suggests that some form of containing wall had existed.

Stratigraphy: Floor 1 overlies M69 Floor 1. Floor 2 underlies M69 Floor 1. Floor 1 abuts M71 Floor 1

Phase: 'Floor 3' Middle, Floor 2 Late, Floor 1 Final

Mound 70 finds

B 401	disc
B **	'bobbin'
F **	flakes x 2
H 389	antler point
P **	much pottery including decorated
Q **	quern fragment
S **	polisher x 2
S **	sling shot x 2
WS 1108 ?	polisher
WS 1109	polisher
WS 1113	whetstone
**	barley, large quantity
**	beans

Mound 70 (Floor 1)

B 383	perforated and notched horse/ox tibia
E 201	vessel rim
H 310	point
K 29	armlet

Mound 70 (Floor 2)

E 211	brooch, La Tène III, 'Glastonbury' mock spring
E 223	needle
E 237	binding
H 308	sawn antler
P **	one box of pottery

Mound 70 ('Floor 3')

B **	worked, decorated and charred
D **	loom weights, several
H 331	charred antler
H **	worked
M 36	humerus
M 37	child's skeleton, part
M 38	child's skeleton, part
**	wheat and barley, seeds, charcoal, animal bones

Mound 70 (under clay, possibly the same context as 'Floor 3')

B 384	perforated bird bone, decorated
B 385	'button'
B 386	bead
B 387	bead
B 388	bead
B 389	bead
B 390	bead
B 391	bead
B 392	bead
B 393/1	bead
B 393/2	bead
B 393/3	bead
B 393/4	bead
B 393/5	bead
B 393/6	bead
B 393/7	bead
D **	loom weights x 10
D **	balls x 4 (3 part perforated)
D **	perforated ball
E 236	hook
G 23	fused blue glass
H 303	cheek piece
H 304	cheek piece
H 305	cheek piece
H 306	weaving comb fragment, burnt
H 307	worked burnt antler
H 309	weaving comb fragment
H 311	weaving comb fragment

H 312	weaving comb fragment
H 313	weaving comb fragment, burnt
H 314	weaving comb fragment, burnt
H 315	tool for ornamenting pottery(?)
H 316	weaving comb fragment
I 89	unidentified fragment
I 90	hammerhead
I 91	point
I 92	knife
T 12	perforated dog canine tooth
W 171	spindle whorl (clay)
W 172	spindle whorl (limestone)
X 61	knobbed pile, oak
**	charred sheep/goat bones

Mound 70 (SW of)

B 395	point (gouge)
WS 1115	polisher

Mound 70 (W of) outside palisade

B 225	polished ox metatarsal
E 102	finger ring
H 163	sawn antler
L 12	weight (tin)
M 15	skull
N 4	beaver skull
P 132	Roman sherd

Mound 71 (1905 and 1906). (fig.3.2)

Spreads of clay near NW edge of site. The clays represent 3 Floors, over an area 7.9 x 6.7m, max. thickness 450mm, with a S extension of clay. Floor 3 is said to have been the largest spread, 7.6m N-S with a separate patch 5.8 x 3.0m at the S edge; this created an elongated Floor, very irregular in shape. On Bulleid's plan, Floor 3 is not marked, but the S patch is shown and seems to be earlier than the adjacent clay. The hearth if present was left unexposed. Timber flooring was noted on the E and a patch of rubble was on the SE part of the Floor. An infant skeleton was found in the clay. Floor 2 seems to have been a renewal of the earlier spread, and possibly a wider expansion although the text is contradictory. It had a clay and gravel hearth, the NE was covered by timber flooring, and there was a line of wall posts around the S and SE sides. Black earth was noted on the W and SW of the Floor. This was probably a round house or shelter. Floor 1 was a smaller spread of clay about 6.0 x 5.5m, a renewal of the Floor around the hearth and perhaps a rebuilding. Floors 2 and 1 overlapped M83, and Floor 3 may have as well if it extended that far E. The foundation was timber laid NE-SW, with some variation in alignment. Bones and wood chips lay on the W and spread outwards to the palisade some 5m away. Most of the relics were found in the W part of the Mound.

Stratigraphy: Floors 1-2 overlie M83

Phase: patch Early, Floor 3 Middle?, Floor 2 Late, Floor 1 Final

Mound 71 finds

D **	loom weight fragment
D **	sling shot
D **	rolled clay
F **	flint flakes x 2, retouched flake/scraper
H 330	burnt antler fragment
P 169	decorated bowl
P 311	decorated bowl
P **	decorated pottery
S **	polisher
WS 1101	whetstone
WS 1111	rubber
WS 1120	polisher
WS 1125	smoother
WS **	whetstone
WS **	whetstone
WS **	whetstone
**	slag

Mound 71 (Floor 1)

B 372	needle
B 397	knife-cut rib
E 235	fragment
E 238	fragments
E 239	brooch, La Tène III, Knotenfibel
H 317	sawn tine
H 318	hammer
H 319	knife cut antler
H 320	handle
P **	one box of pottery
W 176	spindle whorl (lias)

Mound 71 (Floor 2)

B 394	bow drill?
B 398a	'bobbin', type E
B 398b	'bobbin', type D. Dated by C14
B 399	polished horse bone
C 25	crucible
D **	perforated ball
E 240	rivet head
E 241	rivet heads
E 242	binding fragments
E **	fused fragments
H 321	sawn antler
H 322	sawn antler
L 38	lead ore
M 39	child's skeleton
W 173	spindle whorl (sandstone)
W 174	spindle whorl (lias)
**	charcoal
**	grain

Mound 71 (Floor 3)

E **	numerous corroded pieces

Mound 71 (under)

B 396	polished deer metatarsal
H 323	worked antler
H 329	cheek piece
I 93	adze
**	animal bones, wood chips

Mound 71 (SE of)

D 79	plug?
I 94	bar
Q 46	rotary quern, upper stone
Q 47	rotary quern, upper stone

Mound 71 (E of) outside palisade

X 29	hand-carved tub, oak

Mound 72 (1905 and 1906). (fig.3.2)

Spreads of yellow clay at W edge of site. The clays represent 3 Floors, over an area 8.8 x 11.0m, max. thickness 800mm. One of the Floors (Floor 3) included Floors 1-2 of M76 just to the E. Floor 3 also joined M73 Floor 1 according to Bulleid although the plan does not indicate this. Floor 3 was 9.1 x 8.5m and had a raised hearth of clay with stone slab centre. At the W edge, the Floor sloped down towards the palisade, and a line of hurdles formed a stout edge about 2m from the palisade. Peas and grain were scattered around the hearth and elsewhere on the Floor. The overall spread of clay was 16 x 9m. Floor 2 was 9.1 x 6.4m and had a clay hearth renewed by a clay and pebble hearth; the Floor was covered by black earth and peas were scattered about. The Floor was eccentric to Floor 3, and extended W to the palisade. Floor 1 was a further extension W, out to the palisade, and was 8.5 x 5.8m in area, with a hearth. Both Floor 2 and Floor 1 were oval and had no wall posts although a scatter of posts was noted on the E sector of the Mound.

The foundation was slight on the E, but timber on the W helped support brushwood laid parallel to the palisade. Some slag lay on the brushwood and worked oak was included in the timber. The palisade posts were rather diffuse here, with a packing of timber just N of the Mound and an expansion of the palisade to the S (noted under M76).

Stratigraphy: Floor 3 joins M76 Floors 1-2, and may join M73 Floor 1 (unclear)

Phase: Floor 3 Middle, Floors 2-1 Late

Mound 72 finds

D **	sling shot
F 383	flakes x 5 and core
H 333	sawn antler
H 334	weaving comb fragment, charred
H 345	worked antler
P **	decorated pottery
S **	hammerstone
S **	sling shot
WS **	whetstone
WS **	polisher

Mound 72 (Floor 2)

E 246	brooch, one piece simple, 'Nauheim derivative'
E 257	bead
F 383	flake
F **	nodule
H 332	smoothed fragment
**	peas

Mound 72 (Floor 3)

E 261	tweezers
Q 49	rotary quern, upper stone
**	peas and grain

Mound 72 (under)

E 247	binding from hide-shaped shield
X 96	morticed plank, oak
**	slag

Mound 72 (SW of)

H 347	worked antler

Mound 72 (W of)

D 50	sprue cup

Mound 73 (1905, 1906 and 1907). (fig.3.2)

Spreads of yellow clay near W edge of site. The clays represent 2 Floors, Floor 1 15.5 x 6.0m, max. thickness 450mm. Floor 2 was a small patch 4.5 x 1.6m. Floor 1 was extremely large, and its W edge joined M72 Floor 3 and M76 Floor 1 according to Bulleid. At the S, Floor 1 overlay M84. At the E, Floor 1 underlay M74 and M75. These were important observations. Floor 1 had a baked clay hearth and thick black earth. No certain lines of posts were noted but many posts were scattered over the area including a trend running S-N and then off to NE and M74. The foundation was brushwood with logs at the S and timber on the E. Much pottery lay under Floor 1 as did a human skull fragment.

Stratigraphy: Floor 1 joins M72 Floor 3 and M76 Floors 1-2. Floor 1 overlies M84. Floor 1 underlies M74 and M75

Phase: Floor 2 Early, Floor 1 Middle

Mound 73 finds

B 346	needle
B 402	point (gouge)
B 403	'bobbin', type D
C 33	crucible
E 259	penannular brooch, Fowler type B
I 110	rod fragment
P **	decorated pottery
S **	sling stone

Mound 73 (under)

B **	gnawed bone
C **	crucible
D **	loom weight and fragments
D **	sling shot
E 245	finger ring
E 260	rivet
E 262	belt link
F **	flakes/bladelets x 7
H 346	split and stabbed tine
H 359	cheek piece
I **	ring fragment
M 40	cranium fragments
P **	quantity of coarse pottery

Mound 73 (NW of)

B 400	needle

Mound 74 (1902 and 1906). (fig.3.2)

Spreads of clay in NW part of site. The clays represent 5 Floors, over an area 10.0 x 9.8m, max. thickness 1.2m. Floor 5 was a patch of yellow clay, 3.7m diameter, around a hearth which was renewed 4 times. All were of baked clay, 1.3 x 1.6m across. Although Bulleid describes this as a Floor, he also provides details about a 'substructure' which in fact represented the wooden floor laid around the clay and hearth, the clay partly overlapping the timber. The wooden floor, laid upon a foundation (see below), was 5.9 x 5.8m across, and consisted of alder logs (with some bark) 1.8 - 3.7m long. These were aligned NE - SW except for two segments at the SW which neatly fitted into a stout entry constructed of timbers and posts. Around the edge of the alder Floor was a ring of wall posts set 150-380mm apart, the diameter of the round house thus formed being 5.8m. Understanding the complex nature of this Mound was not eased by a trench cut through the Mound by Gray in 1902, and Bulleid's lack of enthusiasm for the venture was clear (Gray 1902 105 f.n.10). Beside this house were 2 rectangular structures to NE and SE, marked by stout oak posts, the SE posts pinning several oak beams into the underlying peat; these may have preceded the Floor 5 house. Floor 4 was 7.0m across and was covered with brushwood laid parallel to the edge and some timber radiating from the hearth which had been renewed 3 times. The hearths were about 1.0m across and of clay or gravel. One of the hearths was square and had a moulded rim; this may not have been a real hearth. Floor 4 represents a renewal of the Floor 5 structure, and a line of wall posts indicates a wall replacement. Floor 3 was 8.5m across, slightly larger than Floor 4 although the plan shows the 2 Floors as identical. Floor 3, of yellow clay, had a baked clay hearth renewed once by blue clay, and floor timbers in the N part; it represents another renewal of the same structure with another line of wall posts. There is no indication from the text or plan that allows a separation of the several wall post lines into the numbered Floors. Three lines are clear at the S, E and N although the many additional posts at the N confuse the issue. At the W, the entrance seems to have been maintained. Floor 2 marked an alteration, with a wider spread of yellow clay about 9.7m across. A hearth of blue clay was renewed once by yellow and red clay with a stone centre, and black earth was found over the W part of the Floor. Floor 1 of yellow clay was a renewal of Floor 2, with a baked clay and stone hearth, and heap of ash on the W edge. No wall post lines were noted near the edges of Floor 2 and 1, which merged with M66 Floor 2 and overlay M75 Floors 1 and 2. A scatter of posts extended S from the S edge of Floor 3 along a lobe of Floors 1-2 clay.

The foundation was brushwood and timber, with heavy beams laid N-S; an alder stump was *in situ* in the peat at the SE edge just off the Floor 5-3 margin. Morticed beams were pegged in nearby, perhaps related to Floor 5. To the NW, various branches and stems lay between M74 and M71.

The relics were numerous, including many stratified objects. The abundance of hearths, crucibles, bronze drips, and hammerstones suggest some sort of metal working operation during Floors 4 and 3 activity. M74 was Gray's 'Mound II' of 1902.

Stratigraphy: Floors 1-2 overlie M75 Floors 1-2. Floors 1-2 join M66 Floor 2

Phase: Floor 5 Early, Floors 4-3 Middle, Floors 2-1 Late

Mound 74 finds

B **	worked sheep tarsal
C 28	crucible
D **	sling shot x 3
E 263	rivets holding bronze to wood
F **	flakes x 4
H 326	weaving comb fragment
HS 1004	hammerstone
HS **	hammerstone
I 95	bridle bit
I 97	knife blade
I 98	file
I 99	knife blade
P **	decorated pottery
Q 51	rotary quern, upper stone
Q **	quern fragment
S **	grinding stone
S **	polisher
WS 1121 ?	whetstone
WS **	whetstone
**	2-3 cat jaws

Mound 74 (Floor 1)

H 340	weaving comb fragment
W 177	spindle whorl, unfinished (sandstone)

Mound 74 (Floor 2)

E 243	rivet
F **	flake
H 325	weaving comb
H 342	weaving comb, unfinished
H 343	worked antler
H 344	hammer
W 182	disc (sandstone)
**	cat skull

Mound 74 (Floor 3)

E 264	finger ring
F **	knife
H 349	sawn tine
H 356	weaving comb
H 357	sawn antler. Dated by C14
I 102	file
P **	one box of pottery
Q 50	rotary quern, upper stone
S 42	disc (sandstone)
**	otter skull

Mound 74 (Floor 4)

C 29	crucible
E 265	spiral finger ring
E 266	'dross'
H 354	handle
I 101	point
W 185	spindle whorl (sandstone)

Mound 74 (Floor 5)

B **	'bobbin'
E 244	brooch, La Tène III 'Glastonbury' mock spring form
E 253	lump
F 376	scraper
I 100	knife

Mound 74 (under)

B 405	needle
B 406	perforated and polished bone. Dated by C14
E 267	band
H 327	weaving comb
H 351	hammer
H 355	weaving comb
I 105	knife blade
Q 52	rotary quern, lower stone
W 186	spindle whorl (lias)
X 44	ladle

Mound 74 (NW of)

B **	bone with 5 incised lines
D 74	disc
E 254	needle
E 255	rivet head
H 341	cheek piece

Mound 75 (1906 and 1907). (fig.3.2)

Spreads of yellow clay in NW part of site. The clays represent 4 Floors, over an area 10.0 x 9.75m, max. thickness 600mm. The evidence suggests that a Floor 5 existed, mostly of brushwood with a hearth, rebuilt 5 times in more or less the same position. The hearths were of baked clay (the 2 lowest), succeeded by 2 clay and stone hearths, then a baked clay hearth and a gravel hearth. These were sealed by Floor 4, a small patch of clay surrounding the gravel hearth. Floor 3 was also small and had a clay hearth. Neither Floor 3 nor Floor 4 had distinguishable edges as each was black earth and clay mixed. No structural evidence was noted other than the hearths. Floor 2 was 9.7 x 8.8m and had a clay hearth placed off-centre to the NW. Floor 1 was 8.2 x 6.1m and only partly overlapped Floor 2, extending N beyond Floor 2 edge where it underlay M74. No wall posts were noted and this was an open stance adjacent to M74. The foundation was brushwood on the W, with logs on the E. An alder stump *in situ* lay beneath Floor 2 at the S, and other stumps were in the peat off the Mound to the E and SE. Some stout oak posts were beneath Floor 2 and also in the peat off to the E. It is likely that some of these represent a structure contemporary with Floor 5 (see M85), as 4 posts form a shallow arc to the E of the Floor. The large morticed beams under Floor 2 and M74 and M66 may be related to this episode.

The relics included a large quantity of pottery outside the E margin. The relics in general conform to those of M74 with its suggested metalworking function

Stratigraphy: Floor 1 underlies M74 Floors 2-1. Floor 2 overlies M73 Floor 1

Phase: Floors 4-3 Early, Floors 2-1 Middle

Mound 75 finds

D **	sling shot
D **	sling shot
E 274	penannular brooch, Fowler type Aa
F 384	flakes x 3
S **	sling stones x 3
S **	hearth stone
WS 1122	pebble with used end
WS 1124 ?	whetstone
WS **	whetstone

Mound 75 (Floor 2)

A 5	amber bead
B 409	'button'
F **	retouched flake
E 57	brooch, La Tène II, arched bow form
E 269	hook
E 271	lumps
E 273	sheet
I 107	file?
N 8	beaver bones
P 179	decorated sherd
W 72	spindle whorl (sandstone)
WS **	whetstone
WS 1107	grinding stone

Mound 75 (Floor 3)

B 407	sawn bone. Dated by C14
E 268	lumps with charcoal adhering
I 106	tanged object

Mound 75 (Floor 4)

B 408a	'bobbin', type D
B 408b	'bobbin', type D
C 30	crucible
E 272	finger ring
F **	flake
H 358	sawn and perforated tine
H 363	cheek piece
L 49	bar (tin)
P 180	decorated sherd
**	small pieces of slag nr SW margin

Mound 75 (under, probably a Floor 5)

B 410	sawn bone
B 411	'bobbin', type D
F **	flakes x 2
I 108	bolt
K 31	armlet
P **	pottery, mostly undecorated
**	lower jaw of ox
**	dense ironworking slag
**	smithing hearth bottom
**	fuel ash slag
**	vitrified hearth lining
**	cinder
**	ironworking slag
**	animal bones
**	charcoal

Mound 75 (NE of)

F 378	scraper

Mound 76 (1906). (fig.3.2)

Spreads of yellow clay (upper Floors) at W edge of site. The clays represent 3 Floors, over an area 9.1 x 8.5m, max. thickness 600mm. Floor 3 was 6.1m across and partly underlay M72 Floor 3; it was of marl, clay and ash and was covered by charcoal and ash. A hearth of grey marl was renewed twice; the uppermost hearth had a raised rim and the hollow had ash and 'slag'. Floor 2 was more or less indistinguishable from Floor 1 above; they were 9.1 x 8.5m in size and merged with M73 Floor 1 and M72 Floor 3. The hearth of Floor 2 was of stone and clay and was replaced by a Floor 1 hearth of red marl; these hearths were S of the centre of the Floors. No wall post lines were noted on the N and E, but a scatter of posts curved around the SW of the Floors 2 and 1 hearths, well inside the clay spreads.

The foundation was timber on W and SW with brushwood under all the Mound. On the SW the foundation contained pottery and bones. A large patch of stones is shown on the plan and probably lay under the Floors. The SW margin was contained by the palisade posts and outside a line of these posts was a platform of timber laid NW-SE, partly covered by a clay patch with rubble. This platform was contained by a line of posts. Outside this an area of brushwood 6.0 x 5.5.m was enclosed by a further arc of posts. To the S of M76 the palisade posts were sparse, marking the N end of the W gap (see M77).

Outside the palisade was a human skull.

Stratigraphy: Floors 1-2 join M73 Floor 1 and M72 Floor 3

Phase: Floor 3 Early, Floors 2-1 Middle

Mound 76 finds

B 432	'bobbin', type E
B **	knife-cut bone
D **	sling shot x 3
F **	flakes x 6, core, flake from ground flint tool
P **	decorated pottery
WS 1103	pebble with used end
**	smithing hearth bottom x 3
**	vitrified hearth lining
**	fuel ash slag
	all probably from Floor 2 or 3

Mound 76 (Floor 1)

E 256	'dross and fragments'
H 352	weaving comb

Mound 76 (Floor 2)

B 404	'bobbin', type E
C 26	crucible
C 27	crucible
E 258	lump
H 353	knife-cut antler
I 96	gouge
W 183	spindle whorl (sandstone)
W 184	spindle whorl (pottery)
**	ironworking slag
**	vitrified hearth lining
**	acorn

Mound 76 (Floor 3)

C **	'several crucible fragments'
E **	dross
**	fuel ash slag
**	small piece of slag from surface of a hearth
**	'much ash'

Mound 76 (under)

H 348	handle
H 350	weaving comb
P **	pottery
**	animal bones including skull of *Bos longifrons*
**	wood chips

Mound 76 (SW of) outside palisade

B 224	point (gouge)
X 43	axle box

Mound 77 (1895). (fig.3.2)

Patch of blue clay on W edge of site. The clay represents a single spread 5.5 x 4.7m, max. thickness 300 mm. laid upon brushwood. The clay was dumped S of M76 outside an inturned palisade. From here to the S, for 10m, the palisade was not present. In its place was a bank of reeds and roots 2.3m wide and 1.0m high, pinned down by long posts driven through the centre of the bank with smaller posts along the W (outer) edge which supported hurdlework. The S end of the bank had a clay patch (M31) with hurdlework to its W, a continuation of the palisade. M77 was probably an accidental dump of clay en route into the site, or a marker for the N edge of the W gap in the palisade. No structural evidence was noted, nor were there any relics or blackearth discovered. The peat outside the clay had several pieces of worked wood but these were near the palisade to the N and represent jettisoned material from M76 and its various palisade extensions.

Phase: Late

Mound 77 finds
None

Mound 77 (NE of) outside palisade

X 19	knob, ash
X 87	spokes x 4

Mound 77 (NW of) outside palisade

M 14	skull
W 81	spindle whorl (shale)

Mounds 78 (1904) and 79 (1892 and 1904) (fig.3.3)

Spreads of clay near N edge of site. The clay of M78 represents 3 Floors according to Bulleid, but the section and text barely supports this. The area of clay was 7.3 x 7.3m, max. thickness 600mm. The clay spread was irregular, with a clay hearth, renewed twice, just S of centre. The Floors were divided only by thin and disconnected lenses of ash and debris. Some oak timbers were noted on the surface of the middle Floor (Floor 2). No wall posts were found but baked clay with marks of hurdles and fingers was seen along the E and NE margin. Three slabs of lias lay around the hearth, perhaps seats. The foundation was brushwood. Two morticed planks underlay the Mound and extended under M55.

The clay of M79 was 5.5 x 5.2m, max. thickness 530mm. Three Floors were identified. Floor 3 was a patch 2.7 x

1.8m, replaced by Floor 2, 5.2 x 4.9m, and Floor 3, 4.3 x 3.5m, with no hearths although ash was noted on each Floor. No wall posts were found. The foundation was brushwood with some planks laid W-E on the peat. The clay of Floor 2 abutted that of M78, and also M59.

These 2 Mounds were open stances linking the northern series (M60-59) with the complex to the S(M64). The relics were not numerous.

Stratigraphy: M78 Floors underlie M64 Floor 2 (according to section but not plan), and abut M79 and M55. The relationship with M58 is not made clear although an overlap existed. M79 abuts M59 and M78

Phase: M78 Floor 3-2 Late, Floor 1 Final
M79 Floor 3-2 Late, Floor 1 Final

Mound 78 finds

B 375a	'bobbin', type F
B 375b	'bobbin', type E
D 71	perforated ball
D **	perforated ball
D **	sling shot
D **	sling shot
E 193	chain link
E 196	nail
F 365	scraper
F 366	scraper .
F 367	flakes x 5 and ?projectile point tip
H 290	handle
H 293	worked antler
P **	decorated pottery
S 35	disc (sandstone)
**	field mouse skeleton

Mound 78 (Floor 1)

E 192	terret, 'Arras' type
H 287	cheek piece
H 291	weaving comb
S 36	spindle whorl, unfinished (sandstone)

Mound 78 (SE of)

S 37	spindle whorl, unfinished (sandstone)

Mound 79 finds

D **	sling shot

Mound 79 (Floor 1)

H 288	point

Mound 79 (Floor 3)

I 88	adze

Mound 79 (SW of)

B 77	perforated bone

Mound 79 (NW of)

E 11	brooch pin
W 30	spindle whorl (lias)

Mounds 80, 81 and 82 (1905 and 1907). (figs.3.3, 3.5 and 3.6)

Spreads of yellow clay near centre of site. M80. The clay represents one Floor, over an area 8.0 x 7.3m, max. thickness 330mm. A baked clay hearth was at the centre with 2 patches of stone near the edges. The foundation was brushwood and timber laid NE-SW. Clusters of posts at the S and E and a short line of oak posts on the N may mark small windbreaks; a scatter of oak posts to the W may have supported some platform or other structure prior to the clay deposition. M81. The clay represents 2 Floors, over an area 5.3 x 5.9m, max. thickness 380mm. No hearth was found, and blackearth was spread over the surface; on the N, only one Floor was found. A short line of posts was noted on the E and SE, and also on the W, presumably windbreaks. Baked clay with hurdle and finger marks on the SE may mark some windproof shelter.

M82. The clay represents a patch 4.9 x 2.1m, max. thickness 150mm. Various oak posts were recorded to E and SW of the patch, and a wider scatter was found S of M81 and M82; these may mark some extensive platform or enclosure. A short double line of posts S of M82 and M80 might represent a small pen 1.0 x 0.7m; a glass bead was found nearby. Also in the peat were a number of willow and alder stumps S of M81 and M82. These 3 clay spreads were probably temporary holding areas for materials brought in during a major expansion of the settlement.

The relics were very sparse.

Stratigraphy: none

Phase: M80 Late
M81 Late
M82 Late

Mound 80 finds

F 373	flake, worked
F **	flakes x 10
Q 43	rotary quern, upper stone
Q 44	rotary quern, lower stone
S 41	incised mudstone/shale
W 214	disc (sandstone)
**	peas

Mound 80 (SE of)

W 170	spindle whorl (shale)

Mound 80 (SW of)

G 24	bead, green annular, Guido group 6

Mound 81 finds

F **	flakes x 2
W 111	spindle whorl (horse skull)
W 178	spindle whorl (pottery)
WS 1100	polisher

Mound 81 (Floor 2)

H 328	worked antler

Mound 81 (NE of)

S 45	whetstone

Mound 81 (SE of)

Q 45	rotary quern, upper stone
W 175	spindle whorl (sandstone)

Mound 82 finds

F **	flake
WS **	whetstone

Mound 83 (1906). (fig.3.2)

Spreads of yellow clay at NW of site. The clays represent 4 Floors, over an area 9.4 x 8.2m, max. thickness 1.0m. Floor 4 was 6.4 x 5.5m and irregular in shape, with a baked clay hearth raised about 50mm above the Floor. Ash covered the E part of the Floor. Floor 3 was 6.7 x 6.4m and the baked clay hearth was built directly over the earlier hearth. Two patches of stone lay at N and S edges of the Floor. Floor 2 was larger, 9.4 x 8.2m, and the clay hearth was larger than the preceding hearths, and overlapped them. Traces of hurdles were noted on the E and NE of the Floor, and a line of posts extended inside the edge of the clay in this part. Some of these posts are likely to have been part of an old palisade line but Floor 2 may have had a shelter if not a complete building. A heavy oak post in the centre of the Floor may have been support for some form of roofing, but its position is within the large clay hearth; it is unlikely both were in use at the same time. Floor 1 was a renewal of Floor 2, including the hearth. Floors 2 and 1 are said to have been overlapped by M67, M68 and M71 in the text on M83; the text on M68 states that M68 Floor 3 joins M83 Floor 1. Both cannot be correct. The plan suggests that M68 Floor 3 may have joined M83 Floor 3 but its edge extends beyond M68 and is lost, as the plan admits. The solution chosen is to link M83 Floors 1-2 with M67 Floor 4 and M68 Floor 3 and agree that the upper Floors of M67 and M68 overlap M83.

The foundation of M83 was brushwood with some timber. An alder stump *in situ* was in the peat, and a heavy oak beam with mortice holes lay on the E edge of Floor 4; at its N end an oak board was vertical in the peat. To the SE of the Mound the peat contained wood chips, pottery and bones.

The relics were not numerous, and included much pottery to the E.

Stratigraphy: Floors 1-2 join M67 Floor 4 and M68 Floor 3. M67 and M68 upper Floors overlap M83

Phase: Floors 4-3 Early, Floors 2-1 Middle

Mound 83 finds

B **	knife-cut rib
D 73	ball
D **	sling shot
D **	rolled clay
E 250	binding
E 252	brooch, La Tène III wire brooch
F 375	scraper
F 377	scraper
F 381	end scraper
F **	flakes x 7
H 336	weaving comb fragment
P **	pottery, much
Q 48	rotary quern, lower stone
W 181	disc (sandstone)

Mound 83 (Floor 1)

L 39	spindle whorl (lead)

Mound 83 (Floor 3)

F 382	scraper

Mound 83 (Floor 4)

H 337	weaving comb

Mound 83 (under)

F 374	scraper

Mound 83 (SE of)

E 251	toggle
F **	flakes x 5
P 310	decorated bowl

Mound 84 (1907). (fig.3.2)

Spread of yellow and grey clay near W edge of site. The clays represent 3 Floors, over an area 6.0 x 7.0m, max. thickness 230mm. A small patch of clay 2.2m across, with a stone hearth, was not labelled as a 'Floor' in the text. It was succeeded by Floor 2, another patch of clay of uncertain extent with 2 small baked clay hearths near the E edge, only slightly overlapping; they could have been in use together but it is more likely that they formed a succession.

There is a confusion between text and plan in the positions of the hearths, and it is likely that the Floor 3 hearth directly underlay the S hearth of Floor 2. Blackearth covered the central part of Floor 2 and a scatter of peas and potsherds was noted. Floor 1 was 7.0 x 6.0m and had no hearth; it was overlain by M73 Floor 1. The foundation was brushwood and no wall posts were found, nor any scatter of posts. The relics were few.

Stratigraphy: Floor 1 underlies M73 Floor 1

Phase: Early

Mound 84 finds

G 26	bead, blue, Guido group 7iv

Mound 84 (Floor 1)

D 76	bead

Mound 84 (under Floor 1)

D **	loom weight
S **	polisher
WS 1123	polisher

Mound 84 (Floor 2)

D 75	bead
P **	much undecorated pottery near hearths
**	peas

Mound 84 (E of)

E 270	spiral finger ring
Q 53	saddle quern, upper stone
W 54	spindle whorl, unfinished (sandstone)

Mound 85 (1907). (fig.3.3)

Spread of yellow clay in N part of site. The clay represents one Floor, oblong in shape, 6.4 x 5.6m, max. thickness 350mm. Blackearth covered the Floor. Along the E and N edges was a scatter of posts and may have marked some form of shelter. A large number of posts were spread outside the Mound, to N, E and S. At the SE edge of the Floor and outside were a number of oak posts that may have represented some enclosure set between M75 and M63, and it may be that M85 with its numerous posts was part of such enclosures if animals were being held and marshalled. The foundation was brushwood with timber laid E-W. A large number of alder and willow stumps *in situ* were noted in the peat to the S of M85, as was the skull of a horse. The relics were few.

Stratigraphy: none

Phase: Late

Mound 85 finds

F 385	knife and flake

Mound 85 (under)

X 76	handle?
**	pelican bones

Mounds 86-90 (M86-89 1907, M90 1892 and 1907). (figs.3.2, 3.3, 3.5 and 3.8)

Patches of yellow clay in NW part of site. They were not recognised as Mounds before excavation. The areas of clay and max. thickness were: M86 5.6 x 4.6m, 130mm; M87 2.2 x 1.5m, 150mm; M88 3.2 x 1.5m, 130mm; M89 3.2 x 1.5m, 70mm; M90 5.2 x 4.3m, 160mm. Each spread was a single 'Floor', with no hearth or wall posts. Blackearth was scattered over the clay of M86 and M87. M86 had 4 oak posts under or near the clay. M88 had a short line of posts across the N edge, perhaps a windbreak. M89 had several posts across its S end, part of a short alignment from M30 and M31, perhaps an early palisade line. The foundations were slight, only brushwood with a few pieces of timber (M86), alder stumps *in situ* under (M88) or near (M87) the clay. The relics were very few in number, none for M86, M87; M88, M89 and M90 each had 2 flints, and M89 also had several potsherds.

Stratigraphy: none

Phase: Late

Mound 88 finds

F **	flint flakes x 2 (1 burnt)

Mound 89 finds

F **	flint flakes x 2

Mound 90 finds

F **	flakes x 2

Mound 90 (NE of)

H 76	cheek piece

Appendix 3.1 Find numbers, main publication reference (by volume and page) and Mound number. *See page p.16.*

AMBER

A 1	II,356	M64
A 2	II,356	M44
A 3	II,356	M44
A 4	II,356	M54
A 5	II,356	M75

BONE

B 1	II,423	M22
B 2	II,417	M22
B 3	II,423	M22
B 4a	II,424	M23
B 4b	II,424	M23
B 5	II,421	M22
B 6	II,427	M23
B 7	II,417	M23
B 8	II,423	M23
B 9	II,423	M23
B 10	II,423	M24
B 11	II,420	M24
B 12	II,421	M45
B 13	II,420	M24
B 14	II,285	M44
B 15	II,425	M44
B 16	II,428	M44
B 17	II,411	M44
B 18	II,424	M44
B 19	II,431	M44
B 20	II,425	M46
B 21	II,421	M44
B 22	II,424	M25
B 23	II,431	M25
B 24	II,425	M24
B 25	II,413	M44
B 26	II,420	M21
B 27	II,424	M21
B 28	II,406	M24
B 29	II,433	M24
B 30	II,421	M45
B 31	II,421	M23
B 32	II,425	M23
B 33	II,424	M46
B 34	II,424	M23
B 35	II,424	M22
B 36	II,414	M44
B 37	II,424	M22
B 38	II,425	M22
B 39	II,425	M62
B 40	II,424	M45
B 41	II,420	M45
B 42	II,420	M45
B 43	II,424	M45
B 44	II,420	M25
B 45	II,431	M25
B 46	II,431	M25
B 47	II,431	M25
B 48	II,425	M25
B 49	II,421	M25
B 50	II,420	M23
B 51	II,424	M23
B 52	II,407	M21
B 53		M23
B 54	II,431	M62
B 55	I,285	M62
B 56	II.412	
B 57	II,424	M23
B 58	II,428	M63
B 59	II,405	M64
B 60	II,431	M20
B 61	II,431	M21
B 62	II,431	M62
B 63	II,423	M22
B 64	II,417	M44
B 65	II,417	M64
B 66	II,415	M62
B 67	II,416	M62
B 68	II,414	M64
B 69	II,420	M63
B 70	II,420	M64
B 71	II,420	M42
B 72	II,421	M62
B 73	II,421	M62
B 74	II,420	
B 75	II,421	M19
B 76	II,421	
B 77		M79
B 78	II,411	M62
B 79	II,432	M44
B 80	II,431	M63
B 81	II,421	M64
B 82	II,431	M64
B 83	II,431	M64
B 84	II,431	M64
B 85	II,431	M64
B 86	II,431	M64
B 87	II,431	M64
B 88	II,431	M65
B 89	II,431	M65
B 90	II,431	M65
B 91	II,432	M65
B 92	II,432	M65
B 93	II,432	M65
B 94	II,431	M65
B 95	II,431	M65
B 96	II,432	M65
B 97	II,414	M65
B 98	II,425	M65
B 99	II,425	M65
B 100	II,425	M65
B 101	II,425	M65
B 102	II,425	M62
B 103	II,425	M62
B 104	II,425	M62
B 105	II,425	M62
B 106	II,425	M62
B 107	II,425	M62
B 108	II,424	M62
B 109	II,428	M62
B 110	II,425	M62
B 111	II,425	M62
B 112	II,410	M65
B 113	II,411	M63
B 114	II,410	M64
B 115	II,410	M62
B 116	II,410	M62
B 117	II,410	M62
B 118	II,417	
B 119	II,429	M46
B 120	I,285	M42
B 121	II,431	M13
B 122	II,431	M46
B 123	II,431	M46
B 124	II,431	M45
B 125	II,424	M45
B 126	II,433	M45
B 127	II,424	M42
B 128	II,431	M42
B 129	II,411	M42
B 130	II,411	M42
B 131	II,432	M8
B 132	II,424	M19
B 133	II,424	M19
B 134	II,420	M19
B 135	II,424	M19
B 136	II,424	M19
B 137	II,421	M19
B 138	II,431	M19
B 139	II,421	M19
B 140	II,431	M20
B 141	II,431	M20
B 142	II,431	M20
B 143	II,414	M8
B 144	II,420	M8
B 145	II,431	M8
B 146	II,431	M7
B 147	II,420	M7
B 148	II,412	M48
B 149	II,430	M8
B 150	II,424	M6
B 151	II,420	M8
B 152	II,411	M25
B 153	II.430	
B 154	II,420	M25
B 155	II,417	M49
B 156	II,420	M48
B 157	II,433	M26
B 158	II,425	M48
B 159	II,424	M48
B 160	II,414	M48
B 161	II,417	M48
B 162	II,421	M25
B 163	II,424	M20
B 164	II,425	M26
B 165	II,421	M19
B 166	II,414	M8
B 167		M20
B 168	II,423	M20
B 169	II,429	M1
B 170	II,424	M48
B 171	II,429	M2
B 172	II,425	M46
B 173	II,430	M46
B 174	II,430	M26
B 175	II,414	M49
B 176	II,423	M25
B 177	II,415	M7
B 178	II,417	M49
B 179	II,432	M49
B 180	II,424	M27
B 181		M27
B 182	II,425	M27
B 183		M27
B 184	II,421	M27
B 185	II,432	M27
B 186	II,430	M27
B 187	II,417	M27
B 188	II,411	
B 189	II,417	M18
B 190		M18
B 191	II,433	M27
B 192	II,411	M18
B 193	II,411	M18
B 194	II,410	M18
B 195	II,414	M18
B 196	II,417	M18
B 197	II,421	M18
B 198	II,415	M27
B 199	II,424	M27
B 200	II,424	M27
B 201	II,425	M27
B 202	II,424	M27
B 203	II,424	M27
B 204	II,424	M27
B 205	II,413	M18
B 206	II,428	M27
B 207	II,417	M18
B 208	II,411	M18
B 209	II,406	M18
B 210	II,411	M18
B 211	II,428	M18
B 212	II,421	M18
B 213	II,424	M18
B 214	II,424	M18
B 215	II,425	M18
B 216	II,424	M18
B 217	II,417	M18
B 218	II,414	M18
B 219	II,417	M18
B 220	II,410	M18
B 221	II,421	M13
B 222	II,427	M17
B 223	II,425	M30
B 224	II,420	M76
B 225	II,414	M70
B 226	II,427	M69
B 227	II,421	M68
B 228	II,423	M68
B 229	II,420	M61
B 230	II,428	M60
B 231	II,415	M60
B 232	I,285	M60
B 233	II,425	M60
B 234		M13
B 235	II,421	M59
B 236		M59
B 237	II,417	M59
B 238	II,424	M59
B 239	II,424	M59
B 240	II,431	M56
B 241	II,413	M56
B 242	II,424	M56
B 243	II,423	M56
B 244	II,424	M56
B 245	II,425	M57
B 246	II,425	M5
B 247	II,433	M5
B 248	II,421	M5
B 249	II,415	M5
B 250	II,433	M5
B 251	II,420	M5
B 252	II,420	M5
B 253	II,420	M5
B 254	II,417	M5
B 255	II,431	M5
B 256	II,421	M12
B 257	II,417	M9
B 258	II,406	M9
B 259		M9
B 260	II,421	M9
B 261	II,425	M9
B 262	II,421	M9
B 263	II,414	M9

B 264	II,415	M6
B 265	II,417	M9
B 266	II,433	M9
B 267	II,415	M9
B 268	II,423	M16
B 269	II,430	M6
B 270	II,433	M6
B 271	II,411	M4
B 272		M4
B 273	II,423	M4
B 274	II,425	M4
B 275	II,425	M4
B 276	II,425	M4
B 277	II,424	M5
B 278	II,414	M5
B 279	II,423	M5
B 280	II,420	M5
B 281	II,424	M5
B 282	II,414	M5
B 283	II,424	M5
B 284	II,421	M4
B 285	II,420	M5
B 286	II,409	M4
B 287	II,414	M4
B 288	II,423	M4
B 289	II,425	M4
B 290	II,420	M4
B 291	II,424	M4
B 292	II,411	M4
B 293	II,424	M4
B 294	II,433	M4
B 295	II,427	M5
B 296	II,424	M5
B 297	II,417	M3
B 298a	II,423	M3
B 298b	II,425	M3
B 299	II,417	M5
B 300		M5
B 301	II,414	M5
B 302	II,414	M5
B 303	II,415	M5
B 304	II,423	M3
B 305	II,415	M6
B 306	II,433	M5
B 307	II,433	M5
B 308	II,433	M2
B 309	II,431	M1
B 310	II,433	M3
B 311	II,411	M3
B 312	II,411	M3
B 313	II,432	M4
B 314	II,428	M4
B 315	II,410	M4
B 316	II,425	M2
B 317	II,421	M2
B 318	II,411	M2
B 319	II,411	M4
B 320	II,410	M2
B 321	II,433	M2
B 322	I,285	M14
B 323	II,420	M38
B 324	II,425	M26
B 325	II,425	M41
B 326	II,433	M38
B 327	II,420	M38
B 328	II,420	M38
B 329	I,286	M37
B 330	II,411	M37
B 331	II,411	M37
B 332	II,425	M38
B 333	II,425	M37

B 334	II,433	M37
B 335	II,411	M37
B 336	II,425	M37
B 337	II,425	M37
B 338	II,425	M37
B 339	II,425	M37
B 340	II,417	M37
B 341	II,420	M37
B 342	II,421	M28
B 343	II,411	M37
B 344	II,425	M35
B 345	II,411	M37
B 346	II,411	M73
B 347	II,425	M16
B 348	II.424	M16
B 349	II,424	M16
B 350	II,424	M15
B 351	II,425	M15
B 352	II,411	M15
B 353	II,414	M15
B 354	II,431	M15
B 355	II,427	M29
B 356	II,431	M35
B 357	II,425	M35
B 358	II,425	M35
B 359a	II,425	M33
B 359b	II,425	M17
B 360	II,420	M30
B 361	II,410	M30
B 362	I,286	M29
B 363	II,433	M15
B 364	II,433	
B 365	II,423	
B 366	II,423	
B 367	II,425	
B 368	II,414	
B 369	II,425	
B 370	II,433	
B 371	I,286	M49
B 372	II,411	M71
B 373	II,425	M55
B 374	II,431	M58
B 375a	II,425	M78
B 375b	II,425	M78
B 376	II,410	M64
B 377	II,429	M54
B 378	II,429	M54
B 379	II,433	M53
B 380	II,433	M69
B 381	II,417	M69
B 382	II,417	M69
B 383	II,417	M70
B 384	II,429	M70
B 385	II,406	M70
B 386	II,405	M70
B 387	II,405	M70
B 388	II,405	M70
B 389	II,405	M70
B 390	II,405	M70
B 391	II,405	M70
B 392	II,405	M70
B 393	II,405	M70
B 394	II,414	M71
B 395	II,421	M70
B 396	II,415	M71
B 397	II,431	M71
B 398a	II,425	M71
B 398b	II,424	M71
B 399		M71
B 400	II,411	M73
B 401	II,433	M70

B 402	II,420	M73
B 403	II,424	M73
B 404	II,425	M76
B 405	II,410	M74
B 406	II,429	M74
B 407		M75
B 408	II,424	M75
B 409	II,406	M75
B 410	II,433	M75
B 411	II,424	M75
B 412	II,430	M2
B 413	II,427	
B 414	II,411	
B 415	II,433	
B 416	II,425	
B 417	II,425	
B 416	II,424	
B 417	II,425	
B 418	II,424	
B 419	II,425	
B 420	II,425	
B 421	II,424	
B 422	II,431	
B 423	II,431	
B 424	II,431	
B 425	II,431	
B 426	II,424	
B 427	II,424	M16
B 428	II,432	M27
B 429	II,424	
B 430	II,425	M16
B 431	II,424	
B 432	II,425	M76
B 433	II,425	
B 434	II,425	M16
B 435	II,425	
B 436	II,425	
B 437	II,424	
B 438	II,424	
B 439	II,424	
B 440	II,424	
B 441	II,424	
B 442	II,424	
B 443	II,424	
B 444	II,424	
B 445	II,424	
B 446	II,421	
B 447	II,421	
B 448	II,421	M27
B 449	II,421	
B 450	II,421	
B 451	II,417	
B 452	II,431	
B 453	II,431	
B 454	II,432	

CRUCIBLES

C 1	I,305	M22
C 2	I,305	M23
C 3	I,305	M44
C 4	I,305	M24
C 5	I,305	M45
C 6	I,305	M44
C 7	I,305	M24
C 8	I,306	M62
C 9	I,306	M62
C 10	I.306	M62
C 11	I,306	M62
C 12	I,306	M62
C 13	I,306	M62
C 14	I,306	M64
C 15	I,306	M5
C 16	I,307	M4
C 17	I,307	M5
C 18	I,307	M5
C 19	I,307	M5
C 20	I,307	M5
C 21	I,307	M5
C 22	I,307	M5
C 23	I,307	M5
C 24	I,307	M5
C 25	I,307	M71
C 26	I,307	M76
C 27	I,307	M76
C 28	I,308	M74
C 29	I,308	M74
C 30	I,308	M75
C 31	I,308	
C 32	I,308	M16
C 33	I,308	M73
C 34	I,308	M29

BAKED CLAY

D 1		M22
D 2		M22
D 3		
D 4		
D 5		
D 6		
D 7		
D 8		
D 9		
D 10		
D 11		
D 12		
D 13		
D 14		
D 15		M25
D 16	II,558	M25
D 17	II,570	
D 18	II,570	
D 19		
D 20		
D 21		
D 22		
D 23	II,561	M42
D 24	II,558	M23
D 25	II,559	M9
D 26		M63
D 27		M62
D 28		M62
D 29	II,570	M62
D 30	I,309	M62
D 31	M62	
D 32	M62	
D 33	M62	
D 34	M62	
D 35		
D 36	II,559	M62
D 37	II,561	M62
D 38	II,559	M62
D 39	II,561	M62
D 40		M62
D 41	II,561	M62
D 42	II,561	M37
D 43	II,559	
D 44	II,559	M62
D 45		M62
D 46	II,561	M20
D 47		M20
D 48	II,559	M25
D 49	I,308	

D 50	I,308	M72
D 51		
D 52		
D 53		
D 54		
D 55		M3
D 56	II,559	M5
D 57	I,308	M5
D 58	II,559	M9
D 59	II,570	M6
D 60		M9
D 61		M6
D 62	II,559	M4
D 63	I,308	M3
D 64	II,559	M3
D 65		
D 66		
D 67	II,570	M18
D 68	II,571	M4
D 69	II,570	M37
D 70	II,559	M55
D 71		M78
D 72	II,560	M68
D 73	II,561	M83
D 74	II,560	M74
D 75	II,560	M84
D 76	II,560	M84
D 77	II,561	M6
D 78	I,309	M5
D 79	II,560	M71
D 80	II,560	
D 81	II,561	

BRONZE

E 1	I,223	M22
E 2	I,217	M44
E 3	I,236	M24
E 4	I,208	M44
E 5	I,197	M25
E 6		
E 7	I,238	M21
E 8	I,231	M65
E 9	I,238	M62
E 10	I,239	M63
E 11	I,239	M79
E 12	I,217	M62
E 13	I,239	M62
E 14	I,236	M65
E 15	I,197	M64
E 16	I,212	M65
E 17	I,212	M65
E 18	I,212	M21
E 19	I,179	M21
E 20	I,197	M62
E 21	I,198	M62
E 22	I,198	M64
E 23	I,208	M64
E 24	I,198	M62
E 25	I,229	M24
E 26	I,198	M62
E 27	I,236	M65
E 28	I,234	M62
E 29	I,234	M63
E 30	I,234	M62
E 31	I,234	M65
E 32	I,234	M65
E 33	I,234	M65
E 34	I,234	M65
E 35	I,235	M5
E 36	I,238	M62
E 37	I,236	M65
E 38	I,212	M7
E 39	I,239	M7
E 40	I,212	M48
E 41	I,234	M42
E 42	I,208	M49
E 43	I,224	M41
E 44	I,217	M26
E 45	I,213	M49
E 46	I,213	M49
E 47	I,225	M49
E 48	I,198	M19
E 49	I,213	M7
E 50	I,213	M41
E 51	I,233	M41
E 52	I,234	M7
E 53	I,208	M7
E 54	I,213	M7
E 55	I,233	M2
E 56	I,233	M8
E 57	I,199	M75
E 58	I,233	M49
E 59	I,236	M49
E 60	I,233	M42
E 61	I,233	M2
E 62	I,199	M19
E 63	I,239	M41
E 64	I,227	M26
E 65	I,234	M41
E 66	I,233	M41
E 67	I,234	M49
E 68	I,226	M26
E 69	I,234	M41
E 70	I,233	M49
E 71	I,234	M49
E 72	I,234	M25
E 73	I,235	M19
E 74	I,199	M20
E 75	I,225	M24
E 76	I,227	M24
E 77	I,233	M19
E 78	I,236	M23
E 79	I,199	M42
E 80	I,238	M44
E 81	I,226	M49
E 82	I,213	M20
E 83	I,224	M27
E 84	I,239	M27
E 85	I,199	M42
E 86	I,236	M27
E 87	I,226	M18
E 88	I,213	M27
E 89	I,234	M27
E 90	I,236	M27
E 91	I,227	M62
E 92	I,220	M27
E 93	I,199	M18
E 94	I,239	M18
E 95	I,239	M18
E 96	I,234	M18
E 97	I,226	M32
E 98	I,214	M32
E 99	I,199	M32
E 100	I,223	M30
E 101	I,226	M30
E 102	I,214	
E 103	I,208	M21
E 104	I,227	M61
E 105	I,227	M58
E 106	I,233	M57
E 107	I,232	M58
E 108	I,239	M5
E 109	I,225	M70
E 110	I,214	M5
E 111	I,214	M10
E 112	I,233	M12
E 113	I,224	M12
E 114	I,219	M12
E 115	I,233	M11
E 116	I,226	M11
E 117	I,234	M9
E 118	I,199	M11
E 119	I,239	M9
E 120	I,214	M9
E 121	I,240	M9
E 122	I,227	M9
E 123	I,214	M9
E 124	I,200	M9
E 125	I,227	M9
E 126	I,234	M9
E 127	I,214	M11
E 128	I,200	M9
E 129	I,200	M9
E 130	I,217	M6
E 131	I,236	M5
E 132	I,200	M4
E 133	I,218	M4
E 134	I,214	M5
E 135	I,234	M5
E 136	I,200	M4
E 137	I,214	M4
E 138	I,215	M5
E 139	I,200	M4
E 140	I,225	M5
E 141	I,235	M5
E 142	I,200	M5
E 143	I,235	M5
E 144	I,240	M4
E 145	I,218	M5
E 146	I,236	M5
E 147	I,240	M5
E 148	I,235	M5
E 149	I,235	M1
E 150	I,200	M3
E 151	I,219	M1
E 152	I,228	M1
E 153	I,237	M3
E 154	I,235	M2
E 155	I,200	M2
E 156	I,233	M6
E 157	I,200	M11
E 158	I,201	M13
E 159	I,219	M13
E 160	I,215	M18
E 161	I,208	M18
E 162	I,240	M14
E 163	I,236	M14
E 164	I,233	M29
E 165	I,215	M16
E 166	I,215	M28
E 167	I,233	M26
E 168	I,201	M38
E 169	I,215	M40
E 170	I,237	M29
E 171	I,235	M29
E 172	I,238	M5
E 173	I,201	M37
E 174	I,219	M16
E 175	I,215	M16
E 176	I,209	M38
E 177	I,235	M38
E 178	I,218	M14
E 179	I,235	M29
E 180	I,225	M35
E 181	I,215	M33
E 182	I,240	M33
E 183	I,235	M33
E 184	I,238	M31
E 185	I,201	M30
E 186	I,202	M30
E 187	I,202	M30
E 188	I,233	
E 189	I,202	
E 190	I,229	M55
E 191	I,215	M58
E 192	I,232	M78
E 193	I,233	M78
E 194	I,228	M55
E 195	I,228	M55
E 196	I,235	M78
E 197	I,235	M54
E 198	I,237	M53
E 199	I,233	M69
E 200	I,233	M69
E 201	I,181	M70
E 202	I,235	M69
E 203	I,228	
E 204	I,236	
E 205	I,215	
E 206	I,232	M69
E 207	I,235	
E 208	I,235	
E 209	I,235	
E 210	I,237	
E 211	I,202	M70
E 212	I,202	
E 213	I,202	
E 214	I,238	M20
E 215	I,202	
E 216	I,237	
E 217	I,202	
E 218	I,202	
E 219	I,235	
E 220	I,237	
E 221	I,237	M9
E 222	I,235	
E 223	I,224	M70
E 224	I,202	M20
E 225	I,237	
E 226	I,238	M49
E 227	I,228	M49
E 228	I,240	
E 229	I,225	
E 230	I,240	
E 231	I,215	
E 232	I,209	M7
E 233	I,202	M20
E 234	I,233	
E 235	I,238	M71
E 236	I,218	M70
E 237	I,233	M70
E 238	I,240	M71
E 239	I,202	M71
E 240	I,235	M71
E 241	I,235	M71
E 242	I,235	M71
E 243	I,235	M74
E 244	I,203	M74
E 245	I,215	M73
E 246	I,203	M72
E 247	I,232	M72
E 248	I,235	M67
E 249	I,237	M67
E 250	I,233	M83

E 251	I,220	M83
E 252	I,203	M83
E 253	I,238	M74
E 254	I,224	M74
E 255	I,235	M74
E 256	I,238	M76
E 257	I,240	M72
E 258	I,238	M76
E 259	I,209	M73
E 260	I,235	M73
E 261	I,226	M72
E 262	I,229	M73
E 263	I,237	M74
E 264	I,216	M74
E 265	I,216	M74
E 266	I,238	M74
E 267	I,237	M74
E 268	I,238	M75
E 269	I,218	M75
E 270	I,216	M84
E 271	I,238	M75
E 272	I,216	M75
E 273	I,237	M75
E 274	I,209	M75

FLINT

F 1 - F 17 no data		
F 18	II,606	
F 19 - F39 no data		
F 40	M22	
F 41	II,606	M49
F 42	II,606	M49
F 43a	II,607	M48
F 43b	II,607	M48
F 44		M56
F 45	II,607	M49
F 46		M57
F 47	II,606	M5
F 48	II,607	M10
F 49	II,606	M5
F 50		M5
F 51		M5
F 52		M5
F 53	II,606	M4
F 54		M1
F 55	II,607	M3
F 56	II,607	M38
F 57		M37
F 58	II,607	M14
F 59	II,606	M37
F 60 - F 63 no data		
F 64		M16
F 65 - F 89 no data		
F 90	II,607	
F 91 - F 197 no data		
F 198		M67
F 199 - F 201 no data		
F 202	II,607	
F 203 - F 221 no data		
F 222	II,607	
F 223 - F 311 no data		
F 312		M5
F 313 - F 360		
F 361		M55
F 362		M58
F 363		M58
F 364		M57
F 365		M78
F 366		M78
F 367		M78
F 368	II.607	M55
F 369		M50
F 370		M51
F 371		M53
F 372		M53
F 373		M80
F 374	II,606	M83
F 375		M83
F 376		M74
F 377	II,606	M83
F 378		M75
F 379	II,607	
F 380	II,606	M9
F 381	II,606	M83
F 382	II,606	M83
F 383	II,607	M72
F 384	II,607	M75
F 385	II,607	M85

GLASS

G 1	II,356	M62
G 2	II,356	M65
G 3	II,356	M62
G 4	II,356	M44
G 5	II,356	M62
G 6	II,357	M7
G 7	II,357	M7
G 8	II,357	M7
G 9	II,357	M20
G 10	II,357	M49
G 11	II,357	M22
G 12	II,357	M59
G 13	II,357	M58
G 14	II,357	M5
G 15	II,358	M9
G 16	II,358	M9
G 17	II,358	M3
G 18	II,358	M11
G 19	II,358	M38
G 20	II,358	M37
G 21	II,358	M29
G 22	II,358	M55
G 23	II,359	M70
G 24	II,359	M80
G 25	II,359	M37
G 26	II,359	M84
G 27	II,359	M65

ANTLER

H 1	II,474	M22
H 2	II,464	M22
H 3	II,413	M22
H 4	II,437	M22
H 5	II,464	M22
H 6	II,475	M22
H 7	II,449	M23
H 8	II,458	M22
H 9	I,286	M62
H 10	I,287	M22
H 11	I,287	M22
H 12	II,466	M22
H 13	I,287	M22
H 14	I,287	M23
H 15	II,449	M23
H 16	II,478	M22
H 17	II,475	M45
H 18	II,449	M44
H 19	II,465	M24
H 20	II,461	M25
H 21	II,449	M44
H 22	II,464	M44
H 23	I,287	M24
H 24	II,412	M24
H 25	II,478	M24
H 26	II,474	M23
H 27	II,464	M22
H 28	II,449	M25
H 29	II,437	M44
H 30	II,475	M42
H 31	II,475	M42
H 32	I,287	M42
H 33	I,288	M42
H 34	I,288	M44
H 35	II,470	M44
H 36	I,288	M64
H 37	II,458	M46
H 38	II,458	M62
H 39	II,469	M65
H 40	II,475	M43
H 41	II,475	M62
H 42	II,470	M65
H 43	II,470	M62
H 44	II,474	M62
H 45	II,459	M65
H 46	II,470	M65
H 47	II,478	M65
H 48	II,455	M63
H 49	II,475	M63
H 50	II,475	M64
H 51	II,475	M62
H 52	II,475	M64
H 53	II,437	M42
H 54	II,477	M42
H 55	II,478	M62
H 56	II,478	M65
H 57	II,478	M62
H 58	II,471	M65
H 59	II,459	M63
H 60	II,466	M62
H 61	I,288	M63
H 62	I,288	M62
H 63	I,288	M42
H 64	I,289	M62
H 65	I,289	M42
H 66	I,289	M42
H 67	I,289	M63
H 68	I,289	M42
H 69	I,290	M42
H 70	I,290	M62
H 71	I,290	M64
H 72	I,290	M62
H 73	I,291	M43
H 74	II,465	M65
H 75	II,465	M62
H 76	II,449	M90
H 77	II,449	M63
H 78	II,471	M62
H 79	II,455	M62
H 80	II,466	M24
H 81	II,467	M44
H 82	II,474	M64
H 83	II,467	M62
H 84	II,477	M62
H 85	I,291	M64
H 86	II,467	M64
H 87	II,467	M62
H 88	II,449	M62
H 89	II,474	M62
H 90	II,478	M42
H 91	II,469	M2
H 92	II,475	M6
H 93	II,469	M25
H 94	II,478	M48
H 95	II,467	M20
H 96	II,450	M20
H 97	II,450	M20
H 98	II,456	M49
H 99	II,408	M41
H 100	II,467	M49
H 101	I,291	M41
H 102	II,475	M49
H 103	II,475	M50
H 104	II,478	M20
H 105	II,478	M21
H 106	II,459	M21
H 107	I,291	M49
H 108	I,291	M50
H 109	I,292	M49
H 110	II,450	M41
H 111	I,292	M20
H 112	II,459	M25
H 113	II,471	M49
H 114	II,459	M27
H 115	II,474	M49
H 116	II,474	M49
H 117	I,292	M49
H 118	II,474	M49
H 119	II,474	M41
H 120	II,450	M49
H 121	I,292	M49
H 122	II,450	M45
H 123	II,469	M51
H 124	II,457	M49
H 125	II,471	M49
H 126	II,475	M48
H 127	II,474	M49
H 128	II,474	M49
H 129	II,458	M49
H 130	II,469	M45
H 131	II,479	M27
H 132	II,450	M27
H 133	II,469	M27
H 134	II,475	M27
H 135	II,475	M27
H 136	II,464	M27
H 137	II,459	M27
H 138	II,475	M27
H 139	II,450	M27
H 140	II,479	M27
H 141	II,438	M18
H 142	II,474	M27
H 143	II,457	M27
H 144	II,450	M27
H 145	II,497	M27
H 146	I,292	M27
H 147	II,459	M27
H 148	II,470	M27
H 149	II,469	M27
H 150	II,457	M27
H 151	II,459	M27
H 152	II,475	M27
H 153	II,451	M27
H 154	I,292	M27
H 155	II,469	M27
H 156	II,475	M18
H 157	II,479	M18
H 158	II,479	M18
H 159	II,474	M18
H 160	II,451	M18
H 161	II,479	M18
H 162	II,451	M18
H 163	II,469	M70
H 164	II,469	M60
H 165	I,292	M59

H 166	II,475	M59
H 167	II,457	M56
H 168	II,455	M56
H 169	II,476	M55
H 170	I,293	M57
H 171	II,438	M57
H 172	II,472	M5
H 173	II,474	M5
H 174	II,470	M5
H 175	II,459	M5
H 176	II,469	M5
H 177	II,476	M10
H 178	II,451	M10
H 179	I,293	M13
H 180	II,477	M11
H 181	II,464	M9
H 182	II,464	M11
H 183	II,470	M9
H 184	II,472	M9
H 185	I,293	M9
H 186	I,293	M9
H 187	I,293	M9
H 188	II,476	M9
H 189	II,451	M9
H 190	II,472	M9
H 191	II,451	M9
H 192	II,476	M9
H 193	II,451	M9
H 194	I,294	M9
H 195	II,479	M9
H 196	II,476	M9
H 197	II,438	M6
H 198	I,294	M6
H 199	II,464	M9
H 200	II,452	M9
H 201	II,469	M6
H 202	II,461	M6
H 203	II,476	M6
H 204	II,476	M6
H 205	II,476	M6
H 206	II,479	M4
H 207	II,452	M4
H 208	II,438	M4
H 209	II,456	M4
H 210	II,452	M4
H 211	II,429	M4
H 212	II,476	M4
H 213	II,468	M4
H 214	II,472	M5
H 215	II,474	M5
H 216	II,457	M5
H 217	II,457	M5
H 218	I,294	M5
H 219	II,452	M5
H 220	II,458	M5
H 221	II,452	M5
H 222	II,464	M5
H 223	II,474	M5
H 224	II,476	M5
H 225	II,457	M5
H 226	II,452	M4
H 227	II,468	M5
H 228	II,476	M4
H 229	II,477	M4
H 230	II,472	M4
H 231	I,294	M5
H 232	II,459	M5
H 233	II,476	M5
H 234	II,474	M5
H 235	II,472	M5
H 236	II,438	M5
H 237	II,439	M5
H 238	II,439	M3
H 239	II,477	M3
H 240	II,460	M5
H 241	II,460	M5
H 242	II,464	M5
H 243	II,469	M5
H 244	II,474	M1
H 245	II,469	M3
H 246	II,453	M3
H 247	II,434	M4
H 248	II,409	M4
H 249	II,453	M2
H 250	II,453	M2
H 251	II,474	M4
H 252	I,295	M2
H 253	II,474	M2
H 254	II,476	M4
H 255	I,295	M6
H 256	II,453	M6
H 257	II,472	M38
H 258	II,474	M26
H 259	II,479	M28
H 260	II,477	M41
H 261	II,472	M38
H 262	I,295	M37
H 263	I,295	M38
H 264	I,295	M37
H 265	I,295	M37
H 266	II,464	M52
H 267	I,296	M16
H 268	II,476	M16
H 269	II,474	M37
H 270	II,468	M37
H 271	I,296	M35
H 272	I,296	M35
H 273	II,461	M35
H 274	II,456	M33
H 275	II,468	M33
H 276	II,476	M33
H 277	II,476	M30
H 278	II,457	M30
H 279	II,479	
H 280	I,296	
H 281	I,296	
H 282	I,296	
H 283	I,296	M7
H 284	II,453	M57
H 285	II,476	M58
H 286	II,473	M55
H 287	II,453	M78
H 288	II,479	M79
H 289	II,468	M55
H 290	II,460	M78
H 291	I,296	M78
H 292	II,476	M64
H 293	II,474	M78
H 294	I,297	M50
H 295	II,460	M50
H 296	II,479	M53
H 297	II,479	M69
H 298	II,453	M69
H 299	II,453	M69
H 300	II,479	M69
H 301	II,474	M69
H 302	I,297	M68
H 303	II,454	M70
H 304	II,454	M70
H 305	II,468	M70
H 306	I,297	M70
H 307	II,465	M70
H 308	II,479	M70
H 309	I,297	M70
H 310	II,470	M70
H 311	I,297	M70
H 312	I,297	M70
H 313	I,297	M70
H 314	I,297	M70
H 315	II,473	M70
H 316	I,297	M70
H 317	II,479	M71
H 318	II,439	M71
H 319	II,474	M71
H 320	II,460	M71
H 321	II,477	M71
H 322	II,469	M71
H 323	II,473	M71
H 324	I,298	M55
H 325	I,298	M74
H 326	I,298	M74
H 327	I,298	M74
H 328	II,479	M81
H 329	II,454	M71
H 330	II,479	M71
H 331	II,479	M70
H 332	II,479	M72
H 333	II,478	M72
H 334	I,298	M72
H 335	II,479	M53
H 336	I,298	M83
H 337	I,298	M83
H 338	I,299	M67
H 339	II,476	M67
H 340	I,299	M74
H 341	II,454	M74
H 342	I,299	M74
H 343	II,473	M74
H 344	II,439	M74
H 345	II,479	M72
H 346	II,476	M73
H 347	II,479	M72
H 348	II,456	M76
H 349	II,476	M74
H 350	I,299	M76
H 351	II,439	M74
H 352	I,299	M76
H 353	II,479	M76
H 354	II,458	M74
H 355	I,299	M74
H 356	I,299	M74
H 357	II,478	M74
H 358	II,468	M75
H 359	II,454	M73
H 360	II,454	M66
H 361	II,460	M66
H 362	II,440	M66
H 363	II,454	M75
H 364	II,456	M13
H 365	II,474	M26
H 366	II,461	M20
H 367	II,479	
H 368	II,474	
H 369	I,299	
H 370	II,457	M62
H 371	II,479	
H 372	II,454	M9
H 373	II,479	
H 374	II,474	
H 375	II,474	
H 376	II,474	
H 377	II,479	
H 378	II,474	
H 379	II,479	M27
H 380	II,474	M7
H 381	II,456	M7
H 382	II,468	M7
H 383	II,476	M7
H 384	II,474	
H 385	II,474	M9
H 386	II,456	M16
H 387	II,479	M9
H 388	II,479	M16
H 389	II,474	M70
H 390	II,479	M26
H 391	II,469	
H 392	II,469	
H 393	II,479	
H 394	II,479	
H 395	II,458	
H 396	II,468	M20

HAMMERSTONES

HS 1004		M74
HS 1018		M66
HS 1024		M7
HS 1028		M4

IRON

I 1	II,385	M22
I 2	II,380	M46
I 3	II,387	M62
I 4	II,381	M47
I 5	II,391	M25
I 6	II,391	M44
I 7	II,391	M23
I 8	II,389	M23
I 9	II,383	M22
I 10	II,391	M62
I 11	II,385	M64
I 12	II,389	M64
I 13	II,381	M62
I 14	II,391	M63
I 15	II,391	M64
I 16	II,390	M60
I 17	II,383	M42
I 18	II,386	M47
I 19	II,381	M42
I 20	II,381	M62
I 21	II,391	M64
I 22	II,389	M64
I 23	II,390	M62
I 24	II,391	M64
I 25	II,391	M64
I 26	II,391	M64
I 27	II,390	M8
I 28	II,384	M48
I 29	II,391	
I 30	II,384	M48
I 31	II,390	M23
I 32	II,380	M17
I 33	II,384	M41
I 34	II,391	M41
I 35	II,388	M41
I 36	II,390	M26
I 37	II,391	M18
I 38	II,392	M27
I 39	II,390	M18
I 40	II,382	M18
I 41	II,383	M18
I 42	II,381	M18
I 43	II,388	M18
I 44	II,383	M42
I 45	II,382	M42

I 46	II,392	M42
I 47	II,387	M42
I 48	II,382	M61
I 49	II,383	M61
I 50	II,386	M61
I 51	II,387	M61
I 52	II,385	M61
I 53	II,385	M59
I 54	II,386	M60
I 55	II,392	M59
I 56	II,389	M5
I 57	II,392	M5
I 58	II,390	M5
I 59	II,389	M5
I 60	II,384	M5
I 61	II,392	M5
I 62	II,386	M9
I 63	II,383	M9
I 64	II,390	M9
I 65	II,382	M6
I 66	II,389	M4
I 67	II,391	M4
I 68	II,392	M5
I 69	II,392	M4
I 70	II,387	M4
I 71	II,392	M5
I 72	II,390	M4
I 73	II,387	M4
I 74	II,388	M5
I 75	II,383	M4
I 76	II,384	M5
I 77	II,387	M4
I 78	II,390	M5
I 79	II,385	M5
I 80	II,392	M5
I 81	II,387	M5
I 82	II,391	M5
I 83	II,389	M40
I 84	II,388	M15
I 85	II,382	M33
I 86	II,381	M37
I 87	II,382	M30
I 88	II,387	M79
I 89	II,392	M70
I 90	II,380	M70
I 91	II,392	M70
I 92	II,382	M70
I 93	II,387	M71
I 94	II,392	M71
I 95	II,390	M74
I.96	II,386	M76
I 97	II,382	M74
I 98	II,388	M74
I 99	II,382	M74
I 100	II,382	M74
I 101	II,392	M74
I 102	II,388	M74
I 103	II,391	
I 104	II,391	
I 105	II,383	M74
I 106	II,392	M75
I 107	II,388	M75
I 108	II,388	M75
I 109	II,385	
I 110		M73

JET

J 1	I,261	M11

SHALE

K 1	I,262	M64
K 2	I,263	M62
K 3	I,263	M62
K 4	I,263	M64
K 5	I,263	M22
K 6	I,263	M22
K 7	I,263	M18
K 8	I,263	M49
K 9	I,263	M49
K 10	I,264	M20
K 11	I,263	M12
K 12	I,264	M13
K 13	I,263	M12
K 14	I,264	M9
K 15	I,264	M6
K 16	I,264	M5
K 17	I,264	M3
K 18	I,264	M4
K 19	I,264	M4
K 20	I,264	M4
K 21	I,264	M6
K 22	I,264	M15
K 23	I,264	
K 24	I,265	M6
K 25	I,265	M35
K 26	I,265	M30
K 27	I,265	M58
K 28	I,265	M55
K 29	I,265	M70
K 30	I,265	M67
K 31	I,265	M75

LEAD AND TIN

L 1	I,248	M47
L 2	I,248	M47
L 3	I,248	M47
L 4	I,248	M47
L 5	I,249	M47
L 6	I,249	M47
L 7	I,249	M47
L 8	I,249	M47
L 9	I,249	M47
L 10	I,250	M63
L 11	I,250	M44
L 12	I,250	M70
L 13	I,250	M49
L 14	I,250	M7
L 15	I,250	M7
L 16	I,250	M7
L 17	I,250	M22
L 18	I,250	M17
L 19	I,250	M18
L 20	I,251	M18
L 21	I,251	M18
L 22	I,251	M64
L 23	I,251	M11
L 24	I,251	M9
L 25	I,251	M9
L 26	I,251	M6
L 27	I,251	M5
L 28	I,252	M5
L 29	I,252	M4
L 30	I,252	M17
L 31	I,249	M47
L 32	I,252	M36
L 33	I,252	M38
L 34	I,252	M38
L 35	I,252	M33
L 36	I,252	M55
L 37	I,252	M69
L 38	I,252	M71
L 39	I,252	M83
L 40	I,249	M47
L 41	I,249	M47
L 42	I,252	
L 43	I,249	M47
L 44	I,252	
L 45	I,253	
L 46	I,253	
L 47	I,253	
L 48	I,253	
L 49	I,253	M75
L 50	I,253	M7
GLV84		M47
GLV84		M47

HUMAN BONE

M 1	II,673	M44
M 2	II,673	M25
M 3	II,674	M22
M 4	II,674	M22
M 5	II,674	M19
M 6	II,675	M1
M 7	II,675	M46
M 7a	II,675	M48
M 7b	II,675	M48
M 8	II,674	M8
M 9	II,674	M49
M 10	II,674	M49
M 11	II,675	M48
M 12	II,674	M18
M 13	II,674	M18
M 14	II,675	M77
M 15	II,675	M70
M 16	II,675	M69
M 17	II,675	M69
M 18	II,675	M67
M 19	II,675	M67
M 20	II,675	M59
M 21	II,674	M56
M 22	II,674	M57
M 23	II,675	M5
M 24	II,675	M10
M 25	II,674	M9
M 26	II,674	M9
M 27	II,674	M4
M 28	II,674	M4
M 29	II,674	M5
M 29	II,674	M5
M 30	II,674	M38
M 31	II,674	M41
M 32	II,674	M29
M 33	II,674	M37
M 34	II,674	M35
M 35	II,674	M55
M 36	II,674	M70
M 37	II,674	M70
M 38	II,674	M70
M 39	II,674	M71
M 40	II,674	M73

BEAVER BONES

N 1		
N 2		M23
N 3		
N 4		M70
N 5		M6
N 6		M37
N 7		M64
N 8		M75

POTTERY

P 1		
P 2		M47
P 3		M23
P 4		
P 5		M47
P 6	II,530	M4
P 7		
P 8	II,525	
P 9	II,525	
P 10	II,528	M23
P 11		M46
P 12		
P 13		M22
P 14		M44
P 15	II,523	M44
P 16		
P 17		M46
P 18		M21
P 19	II,525	
P 20		
P 21		
P 22	II,525	
P 23		M22
P 24		M62
P 25		M46
P 26	II,524	M64
P 27		
P 28		
P 29		
P 30		M64
P 31	II,524	
P 32	II,524	M64
P 33		
P 34		
P 35		
P 36		
P 37		
P 38		
P 39		
P 40		M20
P 41		M22
P 42	II,525	
P 43	II,526	
P 44	II,530	
P 45	II,526	
P 46		
P 47	II,524	M46
P 48		
P 49	II,528	
P 50		
P 51		
P 52		
P 53	II,530	
P 54		
P 55	II,523	M21
P 56	II,521	M46
P 57	II,533	
P 58		
P 59		
P 60		
P 61	II,533	
P 62		
P 63		M63
P 64 - P 73 no data		
P 74	II,528	
P 75 - P 96 no data		
P 97	II,525	M8
P 98	II,525	M2
P 99		M49
P 100	II,530	M8
P 101	II,526	M49
P 102		M51

P 103		
P 104		M49
P 105	II,526	M49
P 106	II,527	M49
P 107		M49
P 108		M49
P 109		M49
P 110		M48
P 111	II,533	M49
P 112		M48
P 113		
P 114		M48
P 115		M48
P 116		M48
P 117a	II,530	
P 117		M2
P 118		
P 119		
P 120	II,526	
P 121		
P 122	II,528	M48
P 123	II,519	M48
P 124	II,527	
P 125		M45
P 126		M45
P 127	II,528	M49
P 128	II,527	M49
P 129	II,528	M49
P 130		M49
P 131		
P 132		M70
P 133		
P 134		M60
P 135	II,526	
P 136	II,530	
P 137	II,526	
P 138	II,530	M58
P 139	II,526	
P 140		M56
P 141	II,530	
P 142	II,527	M5
P 143	II,529	M5
P 144	II,529	M5
P 145	II,529	M5
P 146	II,529	M5
P 147	II,530	
P 148	II,520	
P 149	II,527	M5
P 150		
P 151		
P 152		
P 153		M13
P 154	II,531	M9
P 155		M11
P 156	II,531	M4
P 157	II,538	M5
P 158	II,531	M3
P 159		M11
P 160		M29
P 161		M16
P 162		M55
P 163		M58
P 164	II,520	
P 165		M55
P 166		M68
P 167		M70
P 168	II,520	
P 169		M71
P 170		M71
P 171	II,521	M70
P 172	II,531	M70

P 173	II,531	M67
P 174		M68
P 175		M68
P 176	II,531	
P 177		M74
P 178		M76
P 179		M75
P 180		M75
P 181	II,533	
P 182	II,533	
P 183	II,532	M44
P 184	II,532	M35
P 185	II,532	M21
P 186	II,532	M21
P 187	II,532	M67
P 188	II,534	M67
P 189	II,534	M18
P 190	II,535	M21
P 191		
P 192	II,523	M30
P 193	II,533	M49
P 194	II,533	M49
P 195		
P 196	II,534	M38
P 197	II,520	
P 198	II,534	M49
P 199	II,531	
P 200	II,535	M18
P 201	II,536	M5
P 202	II,535	M30
P 203	II,523	M2
P 204	II,536	M4
P 205	II,536	
P 206	II,536	M5
P 207	II,537	M18
P 208	II,537	M5
P 209	II,537	M18
P 210	II,537	M18
P 211	II,537	M2
P 212	II,537	M18
P 213	II,537	M5
P 214	II,538	M18
P 215	II,538	M18
P 216	II,538	M5
P 217	II,538	M5
P 218	II,539	M18
P 219	II,539	M18
P 220	II,539	M2
P 221	II,539	M18
P 222	II,539	M6
P 223	II,539	M18
P 224	II,540	M18
P 225	II,541	M18
P 226	II,540	M5
P 227	II,540	M5
P 228	II,541	M18
P 229	II,540	
P 230	II,540	M18
P 231	II,541	M5
P 232	II,540	M5
P 233	II,541	M5
P 234	II,541	M18
P 235	II,541	M6
P 236		
P 237	II,542	M5
P 238	II,542	M5
P 239	II,543	M18
P 240	II,542	M18
P 241	II,542	M18
P 242	II,542	M5
P 243	II,542	M18

P 244	II,542	M18
P 245	II,543	M18
P 246	II,543	
P 247	II,543	M5
P 248	II,543	M5
P 249	II,529	M36
P 250	II,544	M62
P 251	II,544	
P 252	II,544	M18
P 253	II,544	M5
P 254	II,544	M11
P 255	II,544	M9
P 256	II,545	M11
P 257	II,545	M13
P 258	II,545	M11
P 259	II,545	M44
P 260	II,545	M9
P 261	II,545	M9
P 262	II,546	
P 263	II,535	M48
P 264	II,535	M4
P 265	II,536	
P 266	II,546	
P 267	II.546	
P 268	II,546	M30
P 269	II,546	
P 270	II,547	M41
P 271	II,547	
P 272	II,547	M37
P 273	II,547	
P 274	II,547	M38
P 275	II,536	M30
P 276	II,547	M50
P 277	II,548	M56
P 278	II,548	M56
P 279	II,548	M57
P 280	II,548	M57
P 281	II,548	M56
P 282	II,548	M56
P 283	II,548	M56
P 284	II,549	
P 285	II,549	M3
P 286	II,549	
P 287	II,549	M21
P 288	II,549	M69
P 289	II,550	M16
P 290	II,550	M49
P 291	II,550	M38
P 292	II,550	M27
P 293	II,550	M9
P 294	II,550	M49
P 295	II,550	M9
P 296	II,551	
P 297	II,551	
P 298	II,551	M49
P 299	II,551	
P 300	II,551	M21
P 301	II,551	M49
P 302	II,529	M49
P 303	II,551	M42
P 304	II,552	M56
P 305	II,552	M21
P 306		
P 307	II,552	M15
P 308	II,552	M29
P 309	II,552	M22
P 310	II,552	M83
P 311	II,553	M71
P 312	II,553	
P 313	II,530	M46
P 314-P 356 no data		

P 357		M38

QUERNS

Q 1	II,612	M47
Q 2	II,612	M46
Q 3	II,612	M44
Q 4	II,613	M44
Q 5	II,613	M63
Q 6	II,613	M22
Q 7	II,613	M44
Q 8	II,613	M42
Q 9	II,613	M62
Q 10	II,614	M44
Q 11	II,614	M9
Q 12	II,614	M64
Q 13	II,614	M67
Q 14	II,614	M31
Q 15	II,615	M57
Q 16	II,615	M58
Q 17	II,615	M5
Q 18	II,615	M5
Q 19	II,615	M3
Q 20	II,615	M6
Q 21	II,615	M4
Q 22	II,615	M5
Q 23	II,616	
Q 24	II,616	
Q 25	II,616	M6
Q 26	II,616	M5
Q 27	II,616	M5
Q 28	II,616	
Q 29	II,616	M4
Q 30	II,616	M4
Q 31	II,616	M2
Q 32	II,616	M18
Q 33	II,617	M11
Q 34	II,617	M38
Q 35	II,617	M37
Q 36	II,618	M37
Q 37	II,618	M35
Q 38	II,618	M32
Q 39	II,618	M55
Q 40	II,618	M54
Q 41	II,618	M53
Q 42	II,618	M69
Q 43	II,618	M80
Q 44	II,619	M80
Q 45	II,619	M81
Q 46	II,619	M71
Q 47	II,619	M71
Q 48	II,619	M83
Q 49	II,619	M72
Q 50	II,619	M74
Q 51	II,619	M74
Q 52	II,619	M74
Q 53	II,620	M84
Q 54	II,620	M52

STONE

S 1	II,624	M44
S 2	II,590	M24
S 3	II,590	M24
S 4	II,590	M42
S 5	II,595	M42
S 6	II,622	M24
S 7	II,595	M62
S 8	II,595	M9
S 9	II,590	
S 10		
S 11		
S 12	II,590	

S 13	II,624	
S 14	II,624	M43
S 15	II,595	M48
S 16	II,622	M7
S 17	II,595	
S 18	II,606	M6
S 19	II,624	M4
S 20		M4
S 21	II,622	M4
S 22		M5
S 23		
S 24		
S 25		
S 26	II,606	M15
S 27	II,595	M36
S 28		
S 29		
S 30		
S 31	II,622	M58
S 32	II,622	M58
S 33	II,622	M58
S 34	II,595	M64
S 35	II,595	M78
S 36	II,594	M78
S 37	II,594	M78
S 38	II,594	M54
S 39	II,595	M54
S 40		M69
S 41	II,623	M80
S 42	II,595	M74
S 43		M31
S 44		M31
S 45		M81
S 46	II,621	
S 47	II,621	
S 48	II,621	

TUSKS

T 1	II,484	M24
T 2	II,484	M44
T 3	II,484	M48
T 4	II,484	M27
T 5	II,484	M6
T 6	II,484	M4
T 7	II,484	M5
T 8	II,484	M29
T 9	II,484	M37
T 10	II,484	M64
T 11	II,484	M55
T 12	II,484	M70
T 13	II,485	M6
T 14	II,485	M9

SPINDLE WHORLS

W 1	II,597	M22
W 2	II,590	M65
W 3	II,590	M22
W 4	II,587	M46
W 5	II,590	M46
W 6	II,596	M24
W 7	II,587	M24
W 8	II,587	M24
W 9	II,597	M44
W 10	II,587	M42
W 11	II,590	M42
W 12	II,596	M21
W 13	II,590	M46
W 14	II,587	M43
W 15	II,589	M42
W 16	II,590	M45
W 17	II,587	M46
W 18	II,591	M43
W 19	II,597	M64
W 20	II,587	M65
W 21	II,591	M25
W 22	II,587	M42
W 23	II,587	M24
W 24	II,591	M62
W 25	II,591	M65
W 26	II,591	M45
W 27	II,596	M23
W 28	II,591	M62
W 29	II,587	M64
W 30	II,589	M79
W 31	II,591	M62
W 32	II,587	M65
W 33	II,596	M21
W 34	II,591	M9
W 35	II,587	M62
W 36	II,587	M64
W 37	II,591	M62
W 38	II,587	M62
W 39	II,589	M44
W 40	II,589	M62
W 41	II,595	
W 42	II,587	M63
W 43	II,597	M63
W 44	II,560	M62
W 45	II,560	M62
W 46	II,600	M46
W 47	II,600	M46
W 48	II,587	
W 49	II,587	
W 50	II,597	M8
W 51	II,589	M8
W 52	II,587	M7
W 53	II,587	M48
W 54	II,594	M84
W 55	II,600	M26
W 56	II,591	M49
W 57	II,591	
W 58	II,587	
W 59	II,587	
W 60	II,591	
W 61	II,591	
W 62	II,587	
W 63	II,588	M48
W 64	II,596	M49
W 65	II,596	M49
W 66	II,600	M27
W 67	II,600	M42
W 68	II,588	M27
W 69	II,588	M27
W 70	II,591	M27
W 71	II,591	M27
W 72	II,591	M75
W 73	II,599	M18
W 74	II,594	M18
W 75	II,588	M18
W 76	II,592	M18
W 77	II,589	M18
W 78	II,588	M18
W 79	II,589	M18
W 80	II,589	M18
W 81	II,596	M77
W 82	II,588	M42
W 83	II,597	M44
W 84	II,600	M60
W 85	II,597	M58
W 86	II,592	M57
W 87	II,597	M5
W 88	II,588	M5
W 89	II,588	M5
W 90	II,592	M11
W 91	II,594	M9
W 92	II,596	M9
W 93	II,592	M11
W 94	II,588	M9
W 95	II,597	M63
W 96	II,600	M9
W 97	II,597	M9
W 98	II,600	M9
W 99	II,597	M9
W 100	II,592	M9
W 101	II,600	M9
W 102	II,592	M9
W 103	II,597	M9
W 104	II,589	M6
W 105	II,592	M4
W 106	II,589	M4
W 107	II,588	M4
W 108	II,588	M4
W 109	II,589	M4
W 110	II,588	M4
W 111	II,600	M81
W 112	II,588	M5
W 113	II,595	M5
W 114	II,589	M5
W 115	II,588	M5
W 116	II,597	M13
W 117	II,600	M5
W 118	II,589	M5
W 119	II,588	M5
W 120	II,592	M5
W 121	II,597	M5
W 122	II,592	M4
W 123	II,592	M4
W 124	II,596	M4
W 125	II,588	M5
W 126	II,589	M5
W 127	II,592	
W 128	II,597	M18
W 129	II,597	M3
W 130	II,597	M2
W 131	II,596	M4
W 132	II,597	M4
W 133	II,600	M64
W 134	II,598	M18
W 135	II,592	M15
W 136	II,588	M29
W 137	II,588	M38
W 138	II,594	M38
W 139	II,592	M38
W 140	II,592	M38
W 141	II,588	M38
W 142	II,588	M38
W 143	II,588	M38
W 144	II,600	M38
W 145	II,589	M37
W 146	II,598	M37
W 147	II,592	M37
W 148	II,592	M37
W 149	II,594	M37
W 150	II,593	M36
W 151	II,600	M37
W 152	II,593	M16
W 153	II,593	M16
W 154	II,589	M15
W 155	II,593	M16
W 156	II,593	M29
W 157	II,598	M35
W 158	II,599	M35
W 159	II,588	M35
W 160	II,593	M35
W 161	II,588	M36
W 162	II,593	M33
W 163	II,593	M33
W 164	II,596	M30
W 165	II,585	
W 166	II,593	M53
W 167	II,593	M53
W 168	II,588	M69
W 169	II,594	M53
W 170	II,596	M80
W 171	II,598	M70
W 172	II,593	M70
W 173	II,593	M71
W 174	II,589	M71
W 175	II,593	M81
W 176	II,588	M71
W 177	II,594	M74
W 178	II,599	M81
W 179	II,595	M68
W 180	II,594	M68
W 181	II,595	M83
W 182	II,595	M74
W 183	II,593	M76
W 184	II,599	M76
W 185	II,593	M74
W 186	II,588	M74
W 187	II,600	M62
W 188	II,600	
W 189	II,598	M62
W 190	II,595	
W 191	II,594	M12
W 192	II,598	M64
W 193	II,598	
W 194	II,598	
W 195	II,598	
W 196	II,596	
W 197	II,598	
W 198	II,598	M63
W 199	II,598	M63
W 200	II,598	M63
W 201	II,598	M62
W 202	II,598	M62
W 203	II,599	
W 204	II,599	
W 205	II,599	M5
W 206	II,599	
W 207	II,595	
W 208	II,599	
W 209	II,599	
W 210	II,599	
W 211	II,595	
W 212	II,599	
W 213	II,599	
W 214	II,595	M80

WHETSTONES

WS 1100	M81
WS 1101	M71
WS 1102	M69
WS 1103	M76
WS 1104	M69
WS 1105	M69
WS 1107	M75
WS 1108	M70
WS 1109	M70
WS 1110	M68
WS 1111	M71
WS 1112	M69
WS 1113	M70
WS 1114	M69

WS 1115		M70
WS 1118		M69
WS 1120		M71
WS 1121		M74
WS 1122		M75
WS 1123		M84
WS 1124		M75
WS 1125		M71
WS 1127		M69
WS 1128		M53

WOOD

X 1	I,311	M1
X 2	I,312	M56
X 3	I,313	M14
X 4	I,313	M14
X 5	I,314	M61
X 6	I,314	M30
X 7	I,314	M55
X 8	I,314	M4
X 9	I,315	M5
X 10	I,315	M9
X 11	I,316	M59
X 12	I,316	M18
X 13	I,317	M59
X 14	I,317	M5
X 15	I,317	M13
X 16	I,318	M59
X 17	I,319	M30
X 18	I,319	M30
X 19	I,319	M77
X 20	I,320	M59
X 21	I,320	M30
X 22	I,320	M30
X 23	I,321	M30
X 24	I,321	M13
X 25	I,321	M13
X 26	I,322	M61
X 27	I,322	M30
X 28	I,323	M14
X 29	I,323	M71
X 30	I,324	M9
X 31	I,324	M56
X 32	I,324	M56
X 33	I,324	M56
X 34	I,325	M56
X 35	I,325	M55
X 36	I,325	M44
X 37	I,326	M56
X 38	I,326	M44
X 39	I,326	M44
X 40	I,327	M61
X 41	I,327	M67
X 42	I,327	M67
X 43	I,328	M76
X 44	I,328	M74
X 45	I,329	M59
X 46	I,329	M14
X 47	I,329	M60
X 48	I,330	M48
X 49	I,330	M1
X 50	I,330	M68
X 51	I,330	M57
X 52	I,330	M13
X 53	I,331	M2
X 54	I,331	M7
X 55	I,332	M14
X 56	I,333	M14
X 57	I,333	M41
X 58	I,333	
X 59	I,336	M46
X 60	I,336	M51
X 61	I,337	M70
X 62	I,337	M5
X 63	I,337	M57
X 64	I,340	M46
X 65	I,340	M46
X 66	I,340	M8
X 67	I,341	M57
X 68	I,342	M13
X 69	I,342	M30
X 70	I,342	M8
X 71	I,342	
X 72	I,343	M58
X 73	I,343	M66
X 74	I,344	M13
X 75	1,344	M13
X 76	I,344	M85
X 77	I,344	M18
X 78	I,345	M44
X 79	I,345	M9
X 80	I,345	M2
X 81	I,345	M13
X 82	I,345	M13
X 83	I,346	M30
X 84	I,346	M62
X 85	I,347	M61
X 86	I,347	M47
X 87	I,347	M77
X 88	I,347	M8
X 89	I,348	M44
X 90	I,348	M21
X 91	I,348	
X 92	I,348	
X 93	I,349	M7
X 94	I,349	M30
X 95	I,350	
X 96	I,350	M72
X 97	I,351	M44
X 98	I,351	
X 99	I,351	
X 100	I,351	

UNBAKED CLAY

Y 1	II,555	
Y 2	II,555	M50
Y 3	II,555	
Y 4	II,555	
Y 5	II,555	
Y 6	II,556	
Y 7	II,556	
Y 8	II,556	
Y 9	II,556	
Y 10	II,556	
Y 11	II,556	
Y 12	II,556	
Y 13	II,556	
Y 14	II,556	
Y 15	II,556	
Y 16	II,557	
Y 17	II,557	
Y 18	II,557	
Y 19	II,557	
Y 20	II,557	

COINS

Z 1	II,395	M31
Z 2	II,395	M48
Z 3	II,396	M5

Chapter 4

Site Structure: analysis and phasing.

The Glastonbury Lake Village consisted of 90 Mounds most of which were visible as raised areas in the field in 1892; figure 4.1 is a schematic illustration of how Mounds came to exist in the field. Some of Bulleid's Mounds (numbers 10,32,40 and 43) were not recognised as Mounds before being exposed by digging, and 17 other 'Mounds' were not only not recognised on the field surface but turned out to be 'Areas of Clay' when exposed (numbers 19,28,31,34,39,48,50,77,80,82,84-90). All however had some thickness and have subsequently been labelled for pure convenience as Mounds in our descriptions in the Chapters of this book. The point is that not all Mounds were similar, some being very thick and others rather thin. Each Mound consisted of one or more Floors of clay (some merely patches of clay) and may or may not have supported a structure. In this Chapter we aim to present the evidence for site structure, using the relationships and character of each Mound as described in Chapter 3.

Using Bulleid's plans, sections, descriptions and other (unpublished) evidence, we have identified 63 of the 90 Mounds as having potential stratigraphical relationships; thus 27 Mounds are entirely without the possibility of demonstrable relationships with adjacent Mounds. Others have rather tenuous relationships with other Mounds and here the potential for structural analysis is very limited. There are a number of places on the site where the plans show the Mounds touching, or almost touching, or even slightly overlapping, but sometimes the overlap is not made clear as to the sequence of overlap, and some stratigraphical relationships drawn on the plans are not noted in Bulleid's text. Nonetheless, there are potential stratigraphical relationships for 63 Mounds, and as Table 4.1 shows, these produce 14 Mound complexes.

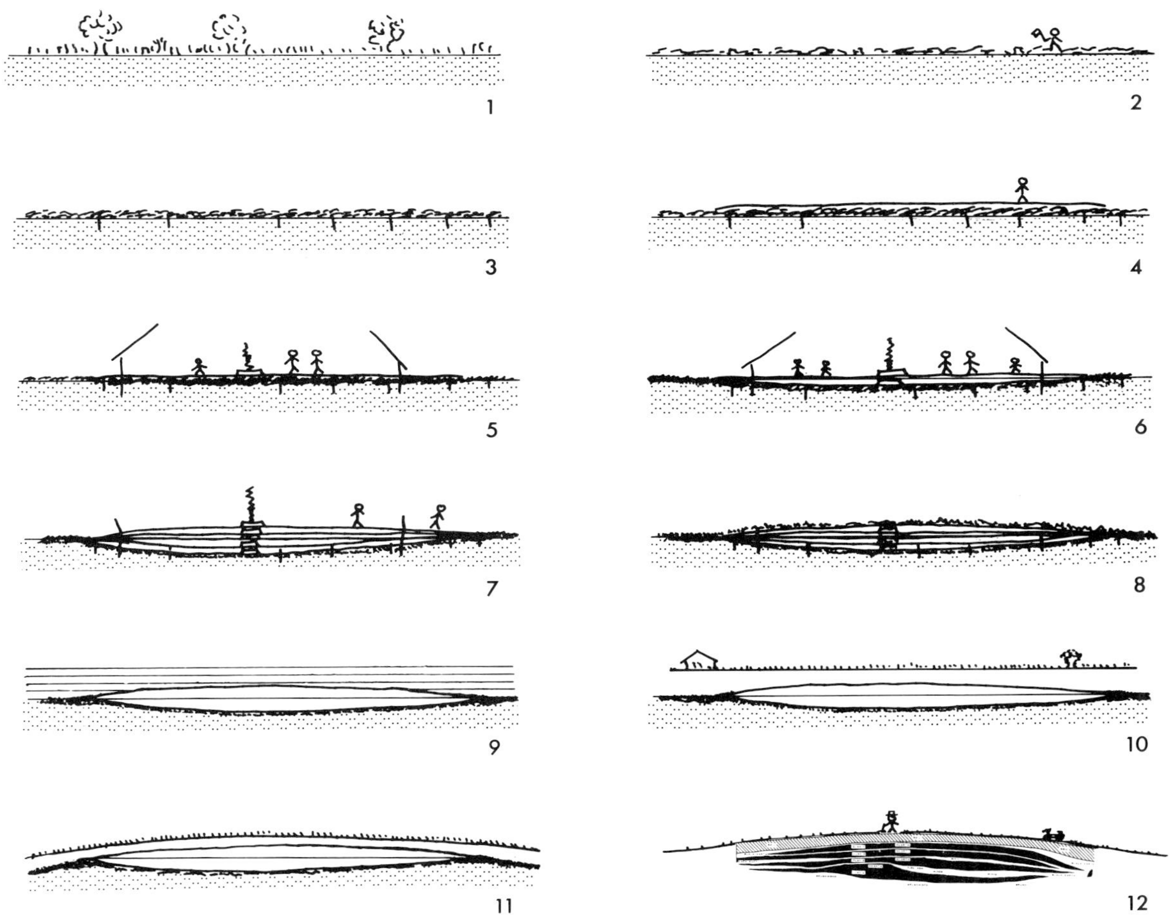

Fig.4.1 The formation of the Mounds, sketch diagrams. 1.Fen carr on peat. 2.Felling of the trees. 3.Timber and brushwood foundation, with posts. 4.First clay Floor. 5.House erected and downward pressure. 6.Sinking of Floor and renewal of Floor. 7.Sinking and various renewals. 8.Abandonment of site and erosion of surfaces. 9.Seasonal flooding and alluvial clays laid down. 10.Medieval pasture on alluvial clays. 11.Shrinkage of peat in recent centuries. 12.Bulleid finds the Mounds in 1892. JMC

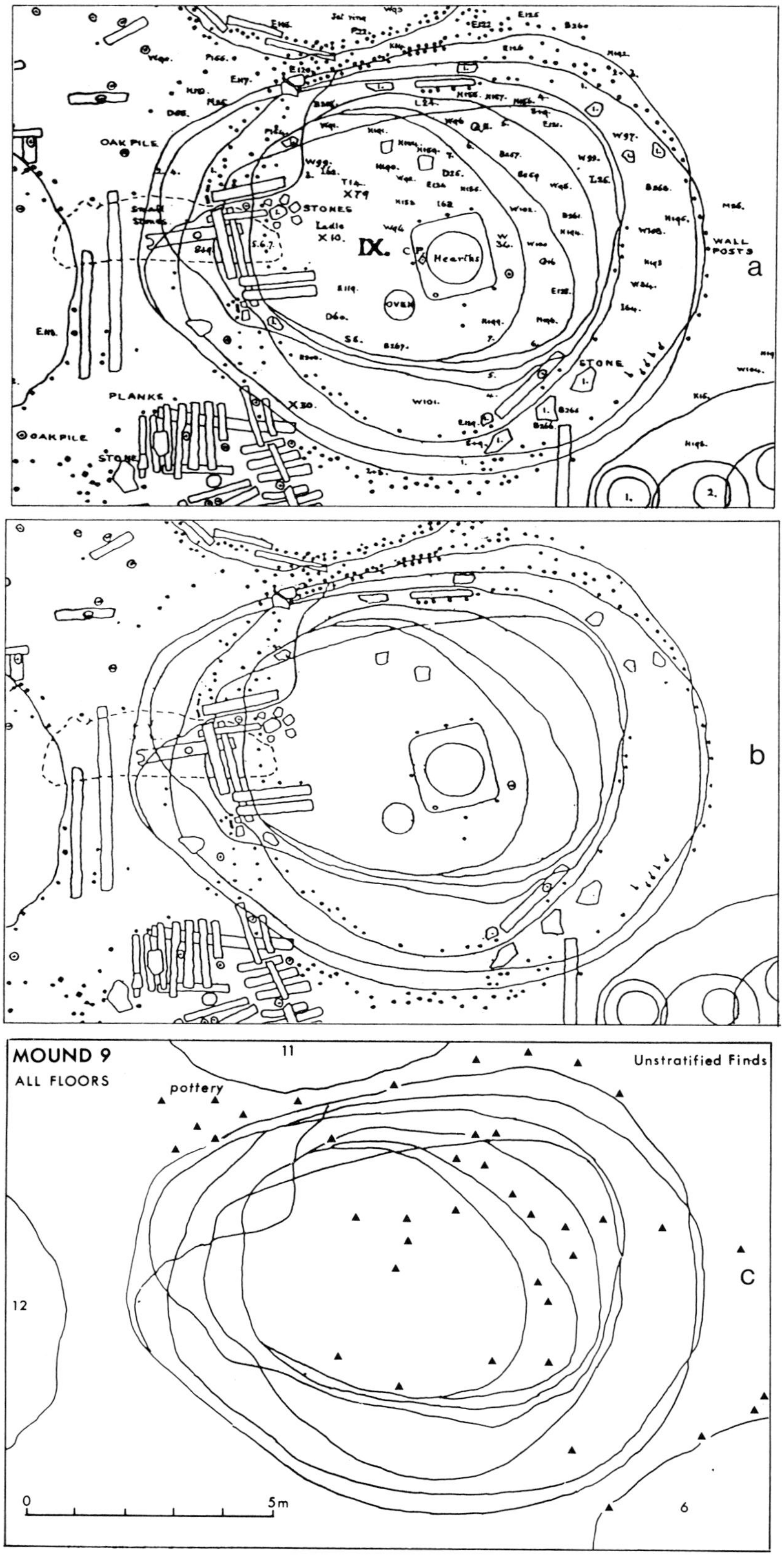

Fig.4.2a Mound 9 dissected. a.Bulleid's published plan. b.His plan with finds and lettering removed. c.Outline of all Floors and unstratified finds.

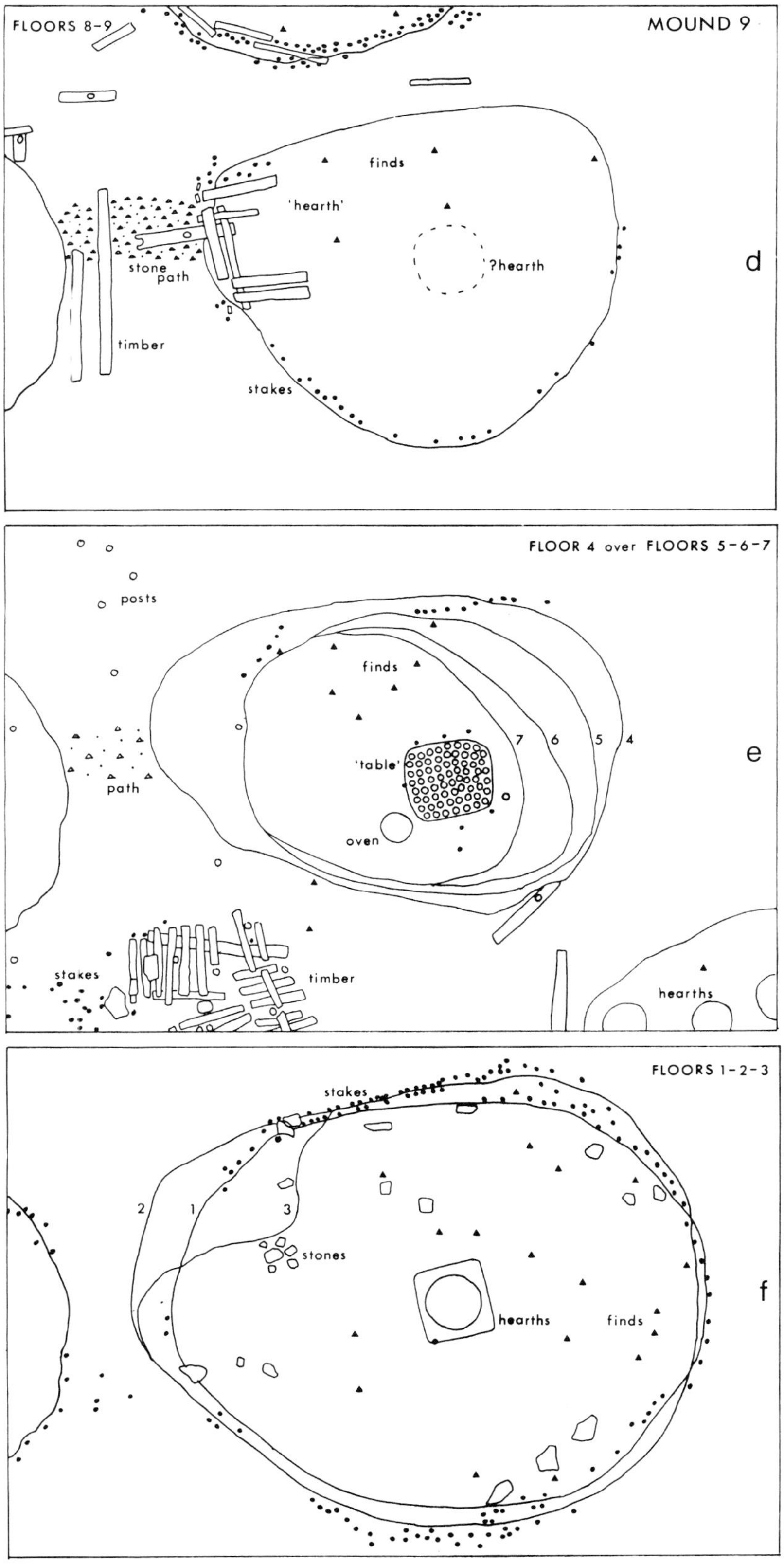

Fig.4.2b d.Floors 8 and 9, associated structural elements and finds. e.Floors 4 - 7 with structures and finds. f.Floors 1 - 3 with structures and finds.

Table 4.1 Mound complexes.

Mounds
1,2,3,4
9,12
17,18
22,23,24
25,44
31,30,32,33,34,29,35,36,14,13,11,15,16,28,27,26,38,41,40
42,43
45,46,49
51,52,53
55,56
58,59,60,61,78
62,63,64,65
69,70,68,83,67,71
72,76,73,84,75,74,66

Some of the relationships are very slender and poorly documented, but a case can be argued for their existence. Others are much more clearly defined as the stratigraphy for each Mound in Chapter 3 sets out. Most valuable is the interfingering of some Floors on some Mounds. There are exactly 250 Floors on the site, including small spreads of clay, and many of these can be put into some sort of stratigraphical position in relation to others.

As an example of the work of analysis that has been carried out for every Mound, figure 4.2a shows M9 with its 9 floors as drawn by Bulleid. He has marked each Floor on the plan so we can extract the lowest Floors 8-9, intermediate Floors 4-5-6-7 and uppermost Floors 1-2-3 (fig.4.2 d-e-f). Using Bulleid's notes it is possible to relate the lines of stakes on his plan to Floors 8-9, and to Floors 1-2-3; these almost certainly represent round houses (see below). The evidence for a built structure for Floors 4-5-6-7 is less certain but two short lines of stakes seem to belong here as well as other structural elements of Floor 4 - a square raised clay 'table', decorated with circles, and with stakes set beside it, as well as an oven set in the Floor (fig.4.2e). The stone path of the earlier floors and the wooden door framing and entry seem clear (fig.4.2d), with a slighter pathway for Floors 4-5-6-7 and nothing similar for the latest structure; a series of well-made hearths are described for Floors 1-2-3 (fig.4.2f). The spread of timber and stake complex to the SW of the Mound is assigned to the Floors 4-5-6-7 period on less secure ground (fig.4.2e). Figure 4.2 also shows parts of the adjacent Mounds with their respective phases of construction. Contemporary with Floors 8-9 of M9 is a stake-built structure on M11 (fig.4.2d); M6 with several hearths is contemporary with Floors 4-5-6-7 of M9 (fig.4.2e). In passing, it will be noted that the Relics from M9 are also plotted on their respective floors; most Relics are unstratified (fig.4.2c). This is but one example of what is possible, or maybe possible.

The structural evidence from the 90 Mounds on the site consists of 14 Mound complexes (Table 4.1), 250 Floors of clay or other material, and 142 potential stratigraphical relationships between Mounds; to this we can add 8 probable relationships where Floors touch one another, and 20 inferred relationships where the texts indicate some specific chronological position for certain Floors. All of these are noted in Chapter 3. These observations and deductions provide us with good, but not excellent, indications of the likely place of many Mound Floors in an overall site structure, and is based upon the 14 matrices developed for the site.

Figure 4.3a-b shows two parts of one of these matrices. They show the relationships drawn for 23 Mounds, by far the largest number of linked Mounds and one that crosses the site from West to East. They are also two of the more difficult matrices. Figure 4.3a shows the clear links between the upper Floors of M11-15-13-14, and between a lower Floor of M14-29-35-36. The relationship between M36 and 33 via M35 on the plan is not clear but inferred, and if real then M32-30-31-34 are also linked. Figure 4.3b is equally mixed in quality, with clear links between certain Floors of M17-18-26-38, M27-28-16 (which gives a probable link with M15 and thus fig.4.3a matrix), M41-40 and probably M42-43. The Floors beneath and above the linking Floors then must fall into relative sequences. This exercise in developing some sort of structure for the site highlights the problems - it concentrates upon the definitions of relationships, their clarity or uncertainty, and it exposes the gaps where we cannot now work out the sequence. For those wishing to repeat the experiment, a look at the plans of the NW of the site will show the extremes of the problem - where do the Floors of M67,68 and 69 actually go (fig.3.2)?

Two useful pieces of additional information have been used in developing the structure. The first is the existence on the plans of lines of stakes from ancient fences or palisades, subsequently flattened as new Floors were laid over them. The second is the line or lines of the real palisade that curve out around some Mounds, as if respecting them, and occasionally are extended and enlarged as if to take account of new Floors or other structural operations. Lines of stakes here and there within the site, or sets of thicker posts, also provide some guidance to relative chronology, although these isolates are mostly without context.

Using all of this information it is possible to suggest, and to demonstrate in some cases, that there are 42 clay Floors (some of them very small patches) that underlie all other Floors, and are therefore Early in the sequence. They are overlain by 58 Floors (some small), thus coming Middle in the sequence. Exactly 100 Floors (a few small) overlie these, and are called Late. At the top are 50 Floors (some small) which are Final. The site is thus phased into four: Early, Middle, Late, Final. It would of course be possible to distinguish more than the four Phases, and perhaps six would have been better, but six would introduce a further precision that we could not demonstrate, and it will be evident that the assignment of a specific Phase to each and every Floor on the site is already introducing a degree of subjectivity. We estimate that our Phasing is perhaps 75% reasonably assured, with the remainder a guess, based on site position, activity layout, Relic distribution and, we hope, common sense. Mounds with no visible stratigraphic relationship to any other Mound are the most difficult, of course, and Mounds with only one Floor give little chance of observed and recorded relationships. There are 25 Mounds with only one Floor, and 27 isolated Mounds; 16 of these Mounds are both single-floored and isolated (M8,10,19,39,48,50,77,80,81,82,85,86,87,88, 89,90). These in particular have been assigned a phase purely on the evidence of adjacent activity and site development theory.

We can now outline in brief the stratigraphical evidence for site development, using the four Phases as markers for various stages in the sequence. The Early Phase is marked by Floors, including small spreads of clay, in the NW and central W of the site, with a few outliers in the central area, and little at the S. Fencing is very slight and the settlement was open. The Middle Phase is an expansion, to central N, central, and S; the E is still an unused area apart from several Floors and the installation of a low bank running N-S. Fencing is now more positive, especially around the W and S, with shorter stretches on N and E. The Late Phase is a further expansion, both infilling voids and extending to the E, with a landing stage built at the E. Fencing now encloses the whole site, with at least six entrances. The Final Phase marks the gradual abandonment of the site, with areas to the NW, central N, central and S much reduced in Floor activity, and extensive Floors laid down in the E. The fencing is strengthened in several places but presumably abandoned to W and N. Fuller description and interpretation of these Phases appear later in this Chapter but it may be of interest to note that our identification of an Early Phase with 5-6 houses

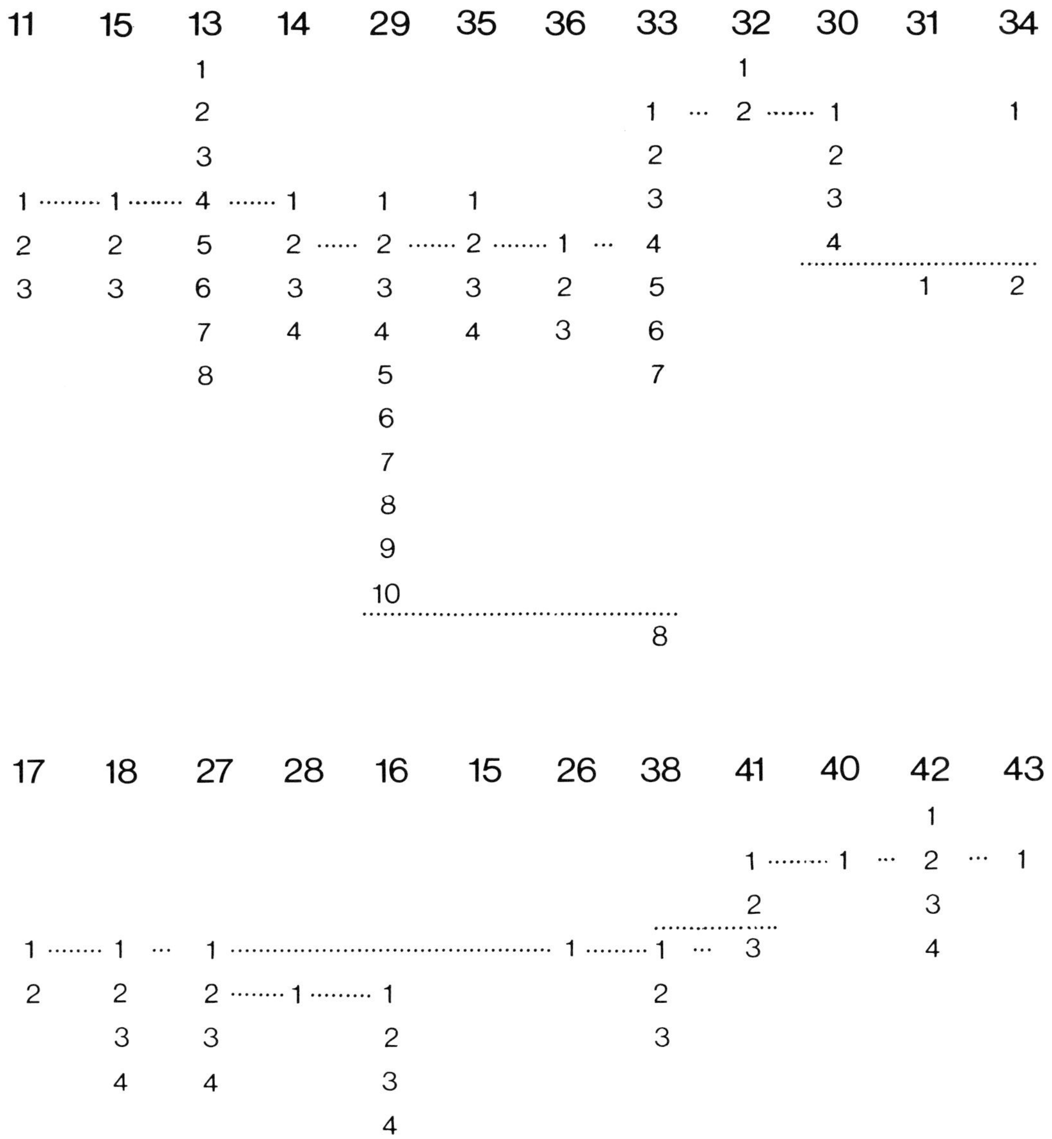

Fig.4.3 Two matrices in the Centre W and Centre of the site showing the relationships of various Floors and stratigraphic positions. Mound 15 may allow the two matrices to link.

is close to Bulleid's suggested earliest occupation of the site, with 4-5 dwellings. He does not identify these first houses, nor does he pursue the idea of a developmental sequence for the site. He and Gray were criticized by some for neglecting this subject: 'unfortunately the excavators have failed to ask, or at least to reveal, how many (huts) were occupied at once' (Grahame Clark 1957,90).

We now turn to the evidence from the Floors and other features and try to interpret their function and appearance.

The foundation.

Bulleid's substructure to the site was recorded by him over the entire mounded area, 8800 sq.m. It consisted of layers or spreads of brushwood and logs (fig.4.4) supplemented by dumps of rush, bracken, peat, rubble and clay, forming an uneven but substantial deposit, growing on or near the site, and were clear-felled at the inception of the settlement (fig.4.1). Bulleid noted that some logs had been roughly dressed into beams, sometimes with mortice holes cut to take stakes, but most of the beams were unstaked, as if the fixing idea had been abandoned. Various scatters of posts were encountered amidst the horizontal wood, some of them helping to hold the brushwood in place, others more probably parts of early structures which will be discussed later.

In many cases Bulleid observed that the horizontal wood, whether logs or brushwood, was flattened, the logs only 25% of their original diameter, the brush 33%; this squashing was caused by the weight of the clay Floors laid upon the base. Brushwood was always seen immediately beneath the Floors, having served its purpose to build up the foundation and provide a drier surface for the Floors. Some of the foundation

Fig.4.4 Excavation by Bulleid of the foundations south of Mound 5. The collapsed fence posts lie beyond the heavy logs and timber.

300-900mm thick, and a dubiously firm and presumably irregular surface for the clay Floors, a cushion rather than a framework. The foundation was strongest on the S and SW of the site. Near the edge it often had rows of logs laid parallel to the yet-to-come fence and sometimes there were rows of logs laid upon one another, N-S succeeded by W-E alignments, which would make a very strong base. Such logs were often 3-4m long alder stems, 150-530mm diameter, but birch, willow, ash and oak were also used. Some of these were woodpiles contained a few Relics, which might indicate slight activity on the immediate site prior to foundation building, hence some dating evidence, or the imperfect nature and small size of the first clay Floor from which or beside which some debris could descend into the woody surface.

The Floors.

As noted above, 250 Floors can be distinguished on the site; some were very small, merely patches of clay, but many were substantial (fig.1.2). Most were roughly circular or oval, 4.0-12.0m in diameter, and 70-500mm thick. They were of a yellow-buff clay believed to come from quarries on the Glastonbury upland about 1km from the site. Bulleid suggests that one Mound had 150 tonnes of clay in its Floors; this must be either a miscalculation or an exceptionally thick Mound. Our calculations are made on the basis of measurements of Floor clay thicknesses and size of Floors for each Mound, and indicate that the 90 Mounds contained 983 cu.m of clay which weigh about 1000 tonnes. Another of Bulleid's estimates give a figure of 1800 tonnes on the site. Whichever is the more accurate, all of this had to be delivered to the site over water or swampy ground from sources about 1000m away. This is no mean task, and we presume that rafts as well as dugouts would be the most economical means of transport. The lowest Floors were often of a blue clay apparently similar in colour to the clay beneath the peat (see Chapter 5), and thus could have been quarried near the site if water was not a problem for deep holes.

The description of the Mounds in Chapter 3 provides indications of the size of all of the identifiable Floors, and of the number of Floors in each Mound. Bulleid gives a list of the number of Mounds with 1,2,3,4,5,7,8,9, and 10 Floors but this disguises the fact that many of the lowest Floors, and some others, are merely patches of clay and not really true Floors suitable for presumed occupation and domestic activity. Some of the patches seem to have been nothing but a small base for a hearth, and some of these were put directly upon the foundation wood, to create an open-air fireplace and nothing else. In other cases, small clay spreads were actually patches, put down to repair an uneven Floor.

It is very important to realize that the Floors are the basis for the stratigraphical sequences on site, as noted earlier in this Chapter, and also provided Bulleid and others with all the evidence for his house identifications and our ideas about open clay spreads. These clay spreads often had hearths built upon them and served as open-air, or windbreak-protected places for eating, meeting and working. Their hearths are in no discernible way different from those of the houses. Therefore when we use the term Floor in our descriptions, this can mean either the floor of a house, or the floor or spread of clay that was unroofed in part or the total. We try to indicate which type of Floor we mean, and often use the term spread for unroofed areas.

The Houses.

According to Bulleid, there were 61 Mounds with distinct remains of "dwellings" (1911,55); later, this figure rose nearer to 70 (1924). It is impossible to accept these totals on the basis of the full report of 1911 and other records. There are, in our view, only 22 Mounds that ever consisted of a structure in Bulleid's sense of a dwelling. He himself noted that 15 Mounds had "little evidence of dwellings", 5 were "doubtful", and 9 had "no signs of occupation"; this last is not the same as evidence of a dwelling and it may be that Bulleid took the presence of artefacts as the presence of dwellings, and for him, dwellings were roofed. But if Bulleid is correct in his statement about 61 dwelling Mounds then he saw but did not write down or draw the evidence for dwellings from about 40 Mounds - this cannot be the case, as he was and is known as a careful observer and recorder. He did state in 1911 that rows of wall posts were seldom found intact, and he recorded many areas of stakes. It is likely that the roundness of some of the Floors led him to presume that they had all formed part of dwellings for which he had good evidence elsewhere on the site.

The classic Glastonbury Lake Village dwelling has been accepted as an Iron Age type of house ever since Bulleid published his first interim report (1894), and his description in the 1911 book is still valid and worth noting here (fig.4.5). In brief, the wall of the round house was of stakes driven through Floor clay into the foundation, the stakes linked by woven rods or panels, and the wall then packed with daub. The stakes were set 150-380mm apart to give a tight and firm weave. Wall panels were not often seen, but collapsed panels on the E of the site were about 2m high, and wall height might have been about the same. The Floors were clay, as noted, renewed or patched from time to time. Bulleid records that 7 dwellings had burnt down, preserving baked clay rubble, clay with impressions of wattle and fingerprints, and charred wall stakes. Charred reed fragments were sometimes encountered, but roofing might also have been rush or heather or straw. Bulleid thought that some of the roofs were held up by central posts which were generally placed near the edge of the hearth, rather a strange relationship; 11 dwellings had these central posts, according to Bulleid, but it is most unlikely that 6 of his 11 ever had any structure at all raised above the Floors. We prefer to see these central posts as marking posts, set in place to show the transporters of the clay where to dump their loads.

According to Bulleid, in only 7 Mounds could an entrance to the dwelling be seen; it consisted of heavy timber posts at either side of the door, in contrast to the roundwood wall stakes. Entrances were 1.4-2.1m wide and their directions were varied. In our view, entrances can be identified for 29 round structures (some being re-buildings on Mounds), and their entrances are as in figure 4.6, mainly W and SW; it may be worth noting that in the Late Phase there are 3 entrances facing E. Bulleid found an oak half-door only 1.1m high, like a saloon-bar swing door; it was only 460mm wide and if paired would not adequately fill any of the entrances to dwellings. Various paved doorways, of lias slabs, some with timber, help define the entrances. All of this evidence is valuable, if puzzling in places, and it has been amplified by a series of experiments designed by Peter Reynolds at the Butser Ancient Farm (Hampshire) to explore the mechanisms of the Glastonbury Lake Village houses. Peter McCrone of the Environment Department, Somerset County Council,

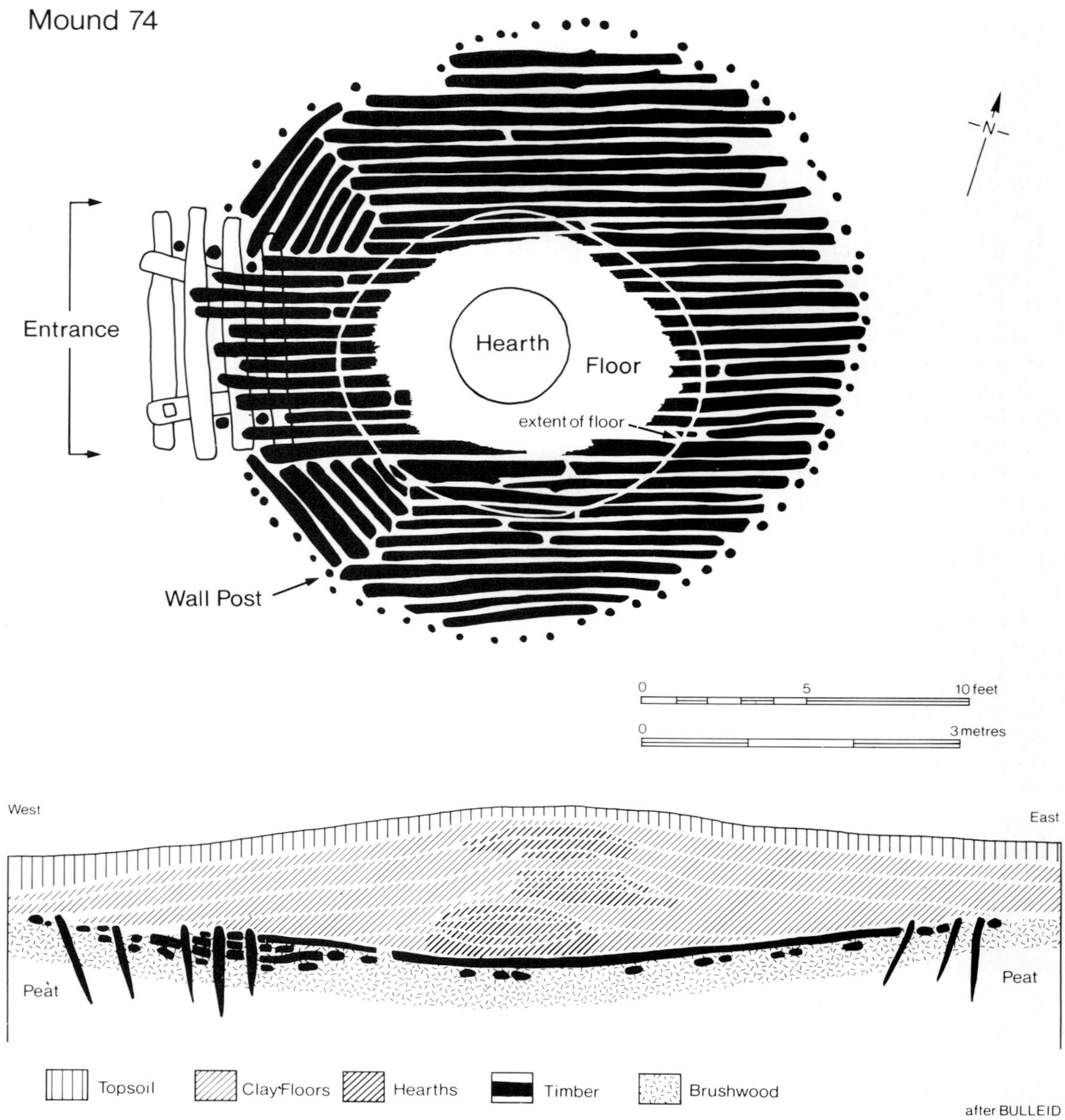

Fig.4.5 Plan and section of Mound 74, one of the classic Lake Village house Mounds. Few of the other Mounds had such clear flooring, wall lines and porch. Drawn by S. Rouillard. (see also fig.2.5)

has constructed two houses also based on Glastonbury houses. Together these experiments point to those elements that Bulleid and Gray did not find on site, and provide useful information on the quality and quantity of materials that went into round houses.

The walls of the experimental houses are best formed by stakes of oak, ash or alder, with oak preferred; these come at the right dimensions (100mm diameter) from 10-15 year coppice. Willow, easily accessible to the Glastonbury builders, is unsuitable for wall stakes unless a sprouting wall is required. The stakes are driven straight into the clay and foundation, without any need for postholes to be dug. The stakes are interwoven with hazel rods, or willow (which will not root being horizontal), perhaps only 4-5 years old (25mm diameter at butt) to ensure flexibility for the tight weave of a very strong wall. The height of the wall is an estimate at 1.5m, and if the average length of the available rods is 3m, the quantity needed for a complete wall is C - D x W ÷ 3 x 60 (where C=circumference, D=Door width, W=Wall height, 60=number of woven rods for 1.5m panel). For a round house 5m diameter this produces a figure of 430m of hazel rods; at 10 usable rods per coppice stool that is 43 clear-fellings. To this is added the required oak stakes, perhaps 60-70 each approaching 2m in length. A house of 8m diameter requires 690m of hazel rods, and 80 stakes. The door posts and lintel will be of squared oak, 100mm sides, cut from 30-50 year-old oak stems.

The daub for the walls is a more complex matter. For a 5m diameter structure about one cu.m (1 tonne) of clay and 2 tonnes of earth and fibre, straw, dung etc will be needed, mixed at about 30% clay, 60%soil, 10% fibre. This will crack least upon drying. The daub for an 8m house might amount to 4-5 cu.m plus straw, dung or other fibre.

The amount of clay required for the floor of a small round house at Glastonbury is likely to be in the order of 3 tonnes, and this would be supplemented by patching and replacement over time. A larger house (8m diameter) might require 8 cu.m of floor clay, plus perhaps 1-2 cu.m for regular repairs. The floors at Glastonbury were put upon a thick wood substructure. A hearth of clay, raised upon the floor, will require .25 tonne of clay, and some Mounds had 5-10 hearths built over time.

The roofing of such a house is very much based upon experimental work at Butser and augmented by comparable information from Somerset. Six rafters descend from the apex of the roof in 2 tripods. The angle of the roof is 45° for straw or reed or heather thatch. For a 5m house, these rafters will be about 3.5m long; others will be a bit shorter to give an eave of about 450mm, the quantity required is about 60m length and diameter about 150mm at butt end. A larger house would require the tripod rafters to be about 7m long, the others only slightly shorter; 35-40 are used for a large house. The rafters can be notched onto the wall stakes, and socketed or drilled into the door lintel. The roofing frame is either interwoven hazel rods, about 540m in total length for a small house, considerably more for a larger house. Or the purlins can be tied to the rafters at intervals. About 1/3 of the way down from the apex, a ring beam will be fixed to hold the rafters apart and give strength overall to the roof; it is an important structural member.

The thatch for a small house will require about 1 tonne of straw from about .5ha of a wheatfield, or .75 tonne of reed from about .25ha reed bed. Looked at from a different view, a larger house needed 1700 bundles of reed (200mm diameter at base) for the roof. Reed can be more easily stepped in than straw, or tied in. The roof will last for 15 years (straw) and 40 years or more (reed).

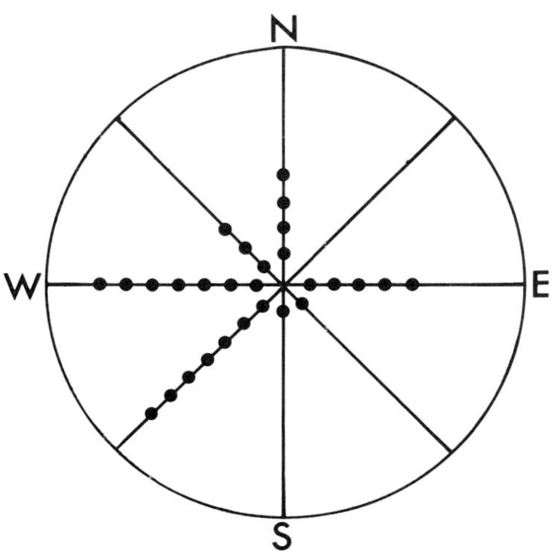

Fig.4.6 Chart to show the direction of house entrances, many to W and SW.

How long would it take the lake villagers to gather materials and construct such houses as these? We do not know as the variables are complex; source of raw materials, its quality, transport, skill and experience of the builders are not easy to determine. We presume they knew exactly what was required, and what to do. Whatever the person/day requirement, it was considerable. One recent experiment took about 700, that is 7 persons for 14 weeks solid work, for one house; but this is no real guide to the labour required at the Iron Age settlement.

An important aspect in this work of analysis and calculation for the Lake Village is the longevity of such structures. Experiments suggest that the survival of the wall and the condition of the thatch are the important elements. We do not know how rapidly the wall stakes might rot, or the daub become fragmented, or the thatch fail, but it is a rough estimate that such a house might have a life of 30-50 or more years if reasonably well sealed and occupied. More is said on this matter later in the Chapter.

Hearths and other internal fittings.

Many Floors on the site held hearths, often placed near the centre of the Floor. Most were of baked clay (over 200 examples), and some were of slabs of lias, or gravel, sandstone, or marl (about 60 in total). They were generally formed by shaping the clay into circular spreads, raised up to a handspan above the Floor level. Some had raised rims and dished interiors, others were markedly convex in section, or more or less flat. Six hearths were rectangular in shape, in Mounds 4(2), 9(2), 67 and 74; those of Mound 9 were particularly large and one was decorated with circles (see fig.2.2).

There were few signs of furniture inside the houses, although some blocks of stone were occasionally noted placed around a hearth, presumably serving as seats. Small spreads of stones here and there may have been paving. Timber flooring was recorded in 8 Mounds (4,13,18,27,65,70,71 and 74); the boards were 150-200mm wide and arranged in rows, sometimes across the Floor and sometimes laid outwards from the central hearth. Details of these appear in the Mound descriptions (Chapter 3) and on Bulleid's plans (fig.3.2 - 3.10). No beds, or divisions into compartments, were recorded.

Sheds, shelters and other structures.

Bulleid noted that "traces of rectangular huts" were found in 5 places on the site. None of the huts survived in any recognisable form, but had been dismantled and the pieces used as foundation timber. He later succumbed to the urgings of John Morland who was of the opinion that the village was established by builders of square or rectangular houses who were replaced by round house builders. This was taken up by E.K.Tratman in 1970, and will be discussed in Chapter 7. However, Tratman demonstrated that, notwithstanding Bulleid's view, some rectangular structure were still in place, represented mostly by beams laid to form squares or rectangles, and sometimes held in place by posts or stakes. In this we concur, and have identified over 10 of these small sheds or barns on the site; Tratman identified more than that. Where we differ from Morland, Bulleid and Tratman is in our opinion that these structures were part of the ordinary development of the site, and did not precede the round house building Phases. Nonetheless, about half of those identified by us are early in the sequence, contemporary with the first occupation Phase (see below).

The Mound descriptions by Bulleid often refer to short curved lines or areas of stakes which he took to represent round house walling, but for some reason found incomplete in the excavations. Some of these are more likely to be complete in themselves and to represent windbreaks or baffles, or well-made shelters without roofs. About 10 of these structures can be extracted from the records, and all are of considerable size, 5-10m in length. There were traces of hurdles on the site and some of these might have been temporary small windbreaks, held upright in beams with holes cut to receive the sails (fig.4.7); a beam under M56 had holes that matched the sail-intervals on hurdles found nearby. These beams are further discussed in Appendix 4.1. The large shelters which we think can be identified were probably made either of a long row of hurdles held by posts, as in M72, or much more substantially by building quarter or half-walls of stakes with woven rods, as in M44 and M71. There would be no difficulty in supporting a light or shallow roof over such structures. Even more substantial was a half-wall built on M62 which was probably wattle and daub, with a heavier roof perhaps of thatch; the framing of such a structure must have been heavy and the excavated evidence shows various posts and stakes that might have been part of the supports.

Scattered over the site were short lines or groups of stakes and posts, the posts often of oak and generally heavier than the hazel, alder and willow stakes. Many of these uprights are not now able to be interpreted as their connections are unknown. We suspect that some of them were marker posts or sight lines, set to help those engaged in structural work for houses, shelters, sheds or fences, or supports for rope lines marking general storage areas for materials of all sorts. Some alignments must represent uprights for wooden fences, probably helping to delineate areas of activity or possession. Some fences, set at angles to one another, N of M34 for example, may have directed animals towards a slaughter area on M34. Angled fences E of M64-65 must have contained a special open area for this complex. Sets of posts not forming lines, such as those S of M81, may have held hurdles or horizontal rails from time to time to make temporary enclosures. With the very great number of posts and stakes recorded in the plans, it is likely, and logical, that there were many small lightweight structures on the site, being repaired, realigned and replaced over time. Most of these cannot

Fig.4.7 Excavation photograph of foundation beam, perforated break and hurdles in the foundation of Mound 56.

be interpreted as shelters, sheds, tent-settings or other structures, but some must have helped in the general activities on the site in controlling animals (or children), storing or hanging materials such as meat or fish or plants (raised above ground) or suspending textiles or mats.

Near the centre of the site (M27,M26,M38), Bulleid noted six posts made of oak or alder; several of their surviving tops were beneath the Floor clays, others had been driven through the lowest Floor of M27. The posts were 1m long and 150-230mm diameter. Around each were 5-7 small stakes forming a ring set only 75mm from each central post. What these represented on site is not known, but they might have been the bases for beehives, for suspending objects, or for decorated poles with human heads (if we are carried away by such ideas). Further comment appears later in this Chapter.

Pathways, stone spreads and dumps.

The 1911 description of Mounds and the site plans show that a few stone paths were built and that here and there various scatters of slabs and pebbles existed. A 20m long path made of sandstone extended N from M4 to M7, and another shorter path linked M9 and M12; other scatters of pebbles and small slabs were more likely to be stances, or to provide drier entry to the site at palisade openings (M21-22). Clay spreads sometimes served the same purpose (see the comments on entrances below), and wooden platforms may have also been used here and there (W of M76, S of M46 etc.). Inside the palisade lines, Bulleid recovered several heavily floored areas of timber and logs and at the extreme SW edge of the site these made in effect a roadway around the end of the site; other smaller platforms of timber were inside the palisade at the SE(M21) and E(M46).

There is a surprising lack of pathways and worn routes through the site; no passages over the peaty soils were noted by Bulleid and Gray except where stones or wood were laid. This could mean that the soils were firm enough over much of the site to permit easy movement, or that the soils were so soft that the whole surface was in a constant state of churning, or that whatever the case the excavators did not notice any such trodden surfaces. We might expect that debris dropped beside a dwelling, or during some activity outside or as the owner walked around the site, would not rest in its original position for long; it would either be retrieved or gradually be pushed underground by the movement of people and animals. Some was apparently picked up or collected and dumped outside the palisade although real middens were never found. The several exits (noted below) at N and E were logical places to take materials out from the settlement, and scatters of debris were recovered outside the palisade, but were either never shaped into thick middens or seasonal waters carried much away and spread the rest thinly over a wide area. Bulleid dug 5 holes well away from the settlement, to S and to N, and found sherds, bones and worked wood in 3 of them (Chapter 2).

Palisade, banks and entrances.

There has always been some uncertainty about the defensive nature of the settlement. Bulleid was categorical in his 1911 report: "With the exception of a short break near the middle of the western border, the Village was surrounded by a continuous line of posts". This is quite clearly not the case as can be seen on the plans. The word palisade itself conjures an impression of defence, fortification and thus potential conflict. We prefer to see the uprights around the site as fencing, although throughout our site and Mound descriptions we use Bulleid's term.

The posts that made up the palisading were mostly of alder, but birch and oak were also used. They were 1.5-4.3m long, 75-230mm diameter, and many had bark still attached. The bases were cut by axe into points or wedges, and they were driven into the soft peat probably with little difficulty. A ladder was found straddling the fallen palisade posts at M14, perhaps used both for pushing in the posts but more likely for work on the roof of the adjacent house. Many of the posts were not vertical but had been squeezed outwards at their tops by the spreads of Floor clay; some posts were broken by this action, as well as by much later slippage of the soil, others were merely slanted outwards. Bulleid thought that the original purpose of the posts was to firm the edge of the foundation wood, to hold back the Floor clays from oozing sideways, and to form a stockade. The variation in angle of posts suggested that repairs and reinforcements were often necessary, thus accounting for 2,3, or even 4 lines of posts in places, although only a single row was often present. The plans show the density of the posts was greatest at the S end of the site as well as on the E at M48, and along the N (M59-60).

A feature not represented in reconstructions of the site is that "coarse wattle-work bound together the upper portions of the palisades; this was seen intact at many places" (1911,51). We should thus envisage the site as held within a woven fence probably less than 1m high - hardly a palisade.

The line of this fence was very irregular, and followed the curving edges of the Floors of the spreads and houses at the edge of the settlement. In some places this shows that the clays were in place before the posts were set up, and some posts were driven through the Floor edges. In other places the sequence is less clear, but the irregular shape of the site and its corresponding "series of curves and semicircles" of the palisade do give the overall impression of a settlement shaping from within and soon thereafter strengthened physically and visibly by a stout fence.

Along part of the W edge there is a gap in the palisade line, between M31 and M76; a patch of clay (M77) was dropped S of M76. The space, about 20m between the Mounds, was filled by a bank of cut reeds and rhizomes forming a coarse peat, packed down to make a wall over 2m wide at the base and about 1m high, held firm by posts driven through the centre line, and capped by clay held back by stakes, which projected sufficiently for a few rods to be woven. In other words, the effect from outside the site would be a solid fence with a low woven top; from inside, the bank provided a convenient walkway along the top linking the centre W with the NW of the site, or a narrow platform for public presentations. However, there is a gap just N of M77, 2m before the outworks of M76 re-assert the palisade. Bulleid did not consider this to be an entrance and the location of his "short break near the middle of the western border" is not made clear (but is likely to be further S, between M30 and M4, see below). There are some posts lying in the M77-76 gap, and maybe it was fenced. It could also have had a hedge grown as a barrier. It may also be that the clean clay of M77 was a dump ready for capping the bank as it was built towards M76, but for some reason it was not completed as the emphasis shifted to the E (the Final Phase, see below).

Bulleid also recorded a low ridge in the field to the E side of the Mounds. The ridge lay NNE-SSW, highest and widest at the N, and was 32m long. When excavated it was identified as a Causeway overlying an Embankment. The Causeway had a clay and rubble base which supported a timber walkway held in place by uprights. In shape the structure was like a hook, with a shorter extension from the N end. Partly beneath it was the Embankment, made of lias blocks and timber, with some hurdles and boarding in its S part; this was probably the first phase of a landing stage, later enlarged by the more elaborate Causeway. The constructional details of the Causeway and Embankment are discussed in Appendix 4.1. From this position it was possible to dock rafts of material and log boats with other cargoes, pinching up the E edge into the fork, or floating around to dock at the strengthened N end or straight W edge. If docking of watercraft was the major purpose of this complex, it is surprising that so little material was recovered by Bulleid in 1893; relics are very sparse in and around this structure.

It is possible to identify earlier fence lines across and through the site, and Bulleid comments on their existence in his 1911 text although he does not expand on them nor develop ideas of site evolution. Several lines are clearly marked on his plans. A line from M60 S under M64, picking up again W of M42 and extending S towards M8, is a major early fence. The palisade at the S of the site was originally set inside the final line, beneath part of M5 and M3. Traces of a very early fence can be detected in the NW of the site, from M83 SE to M65. These will all be noted again later in this Chapter.

Bulleid said very little about entrances to the site; as noted above, he claimed a continuous palisade apart from the W bank which was never interpreted by him as an entry. He makes no comment about how people entered or departed the site. The palisade has a number of gaps and several distinct inward turnings which in effect make funnel entrances to the interior. In the N of the site, between M67 and M61, the palisade lines turn inwards, leaving a gap of 5m with extra palisade posts on the edges. A tree trunk lay partly across this gap, perhaps once serving as a movable barrier. Near the NE corner of the site, the dense palisade ends abruptly with a very sparse line of posts extending outwards along the edge of a tongue of clay (part of M59); 5m across from this is another clay spread and tongue (part of M58) and each must have served as exits and entries for foot traffic; perhaps they led to places of quiet reflection squatting amongst the reeds.

Along the E side of the site there is a wide gap in the palisade between M56 and M48. The dense lines of posts turn inwards, and there is a slender row of posts partway across the gap which again had a tree trunk placed across. Midway along the E side is an extension outwards of the post line, with a timber and log pavement inside; this is probably an original entry from the Causeway, later fenced off. Between M21 and M22 there is another inturned entrance paved in part with stones and 3m wide. A wider entry, also at the ESE, lay between M8 and M20, with M19 just inside and providing a base for traffic; here an earlier palisade line had extended N prior to the site expansion eastwards.

Near the SE end of the site a thin scatter of posts may mark an old entrance which was effectively closed, inside, by a 20m stone path between M4 and M7. There were no significant gaps in the palisade around the S or SW edge of the site but a distinct entry lay N of M14 and the edge of M30. Hurdles had been set up to partly close this gap of 5m so that only 2m were clear of obstruction. The W bank has already been noted, and its only possible gap was at the N end, between M77 (a patch of clean clay) and the palisade S of M76 where the fence was enlarged, extended outwards and the enclosure thus created partly floored by timber and clay. These distinct and possible entrances and exits total 9, of which 5 are very clear (N, NE,E, and two ESE). Closures of these were by tree trunk in two places; others have no visible sign of gates or barriers.

Structural changes on the site

The major elements in the site structure have been outlined above, and these can now be related to the individual Mounds as described in Chapter 3. A very important aspect of this analysis is the demonstration that the site underwent constant change and evolution, sometimes of major significance in the outcome and at other times only minor in impact. Repairs and renewals were always going on, alongside major rebuildings, new constructions and dismantlings or abandonments. The site itself was undergoing expansion for much of its life, new spreads of foundation wood, stone and clay laid down as new areas were selected for occupation and activity. There must have been constant floating and dragging in, dumping and spreading of materials, multitudes of stakes and posts assembled for all manner of functions, both temporary and permanent, and the woodlands and quarries regularly harvested and exploited. Instead of a settlement rigidly organised and structured, with each and every Mound serving one and only one unvaried purpose throughout its life (the basis of one model, see Chapter 7), we believe there was constant movement and change. We can show evidence that 35 Mounds underwent radical transformations over their lives, from a built structure to an open spread or vice versa, or into an entirely new shape on the surface, and this figure excludes 35 changes of shape for clay spreads, and 11 restructurings of buildings. Table 4.2 lists the Mounds that we believe show clear evidence of substantial alteration through their short, or long, lives.

Table 4.2 also points to the large number of major structural changes that took place on the site during the Late Phase; 21 changes are listed, in contrast to only 5 for the Middle Phase and 8 for the Final Phase. Table 4.3 looks at this in another way, and brings in two other aspects.

Table 4.3 shows that no fewer than 81 amendments to the Mounds took place, some only expansion or construction of clay spreads (35 in total), and house rebuilding (11 in total) to go along with the 35 more fundamental changes noted in Table 4.2 as well as here. Both indicate the significant work undertaken in the Late Phase, as well as (Table 4.3) the renewal of 17 clay

Table 4.2 Structural changes in the Mounds by Phase (see Note at base of Table)

Mounds	**Early**	**Middle**	**Late**	**Final**
1-5	4,5	4,5	3,4,5	1,2,3
6-10		9	6,7,8,9,10	9
11-15	13,14,15	11,12,13,14,15	11,12,13,14,15	12,13
16-20	16,18	16,17,18	17,18,20	19,20
21-25		23	21,21,23,24,25	21,22,25
26-30	27,29	25,27,29	26,27,29,30	30
31-35	33,35	33,35	31,32,33,34,35	32,33,34
36-40	36,37	36,37,38	37,38,39	40
41-45		44	41,42,43,44,45	41,42,44,45
46-50		47	46,47,48,49	46,49,50
51-55		51,55	51,52,53,54,55	51,52,53,54
56-60	59	59,60	56,57,58,59,60	56,57,58
61-65		61,62,65	61,62,63,64,65	64,65
66-70		67,68,70	66,67,68,69,70	66,67,68,69,70
71-75	71,73,74,75	71,72,73,74,75	71,72,74	71
76-80	76	76	77,78,79,80	78,79
81-85	83,84	83	81,82,85	
86-90			86,87,88,89,90	
Changes:	-	5	21	8

Note of explanation. The Table lists all Mounds (grouped for convenience into sets of five) and shows in which Phase or Phases their Floors belong, e.g. M4 has Floors dated to Early, Middle and Late Phases. Underlined Mound numbers indicate that there was a substantial structural change in the Mound at the Phase indicated, e.g., M4 was an open spread in Early, a house in Middle (hence change), and an open spread in Late (hence change). Other changes are described further in the text and Table 4.3.

Table 4.3 Remodelling of the Mounds

Phase	*Spread alteration*	*Spread to House*	*Spread to Shelter*	*Shelter to Spread*	*House to Spread*	*House alteration*	*Total*
Early							
Middle	9	2	2	-	2	4	19
Late	9	5	2	4	9	2	31+1*
Final	17	-	-	3	5	5	30
							81

* *Note.* Mound 47 (the Embankment/Causeway) was remodelled in the Late Phase.

spreads in the Final Phase. Palisade remodelling and expansion is not included in either Table. The effect of these analyses is to show the dynamic nature of the site, in no way static or stationary, Most wetland settlements can be nothing but dynamic in the constant requirements for repair as well as any expansions, and maybe dryland settlements were not much less mobile.

We can now turn to the Phase site plans (fig.4.9 - 4.12) which will mostly speak for themselves. However, they represent only what we have taken as the cumulation of all structural activities during an arbitrary period of time. All of the features, round houses, shelters, clay spreads, sheds and fences did not arrive on site at one point of time. What the plans try to show is the totality of the operations at or near the end of the four Phases. Table 4.4 lists these totalities in a more precise way, as some Mounds have, according to the matrices, a number of Floors belonging to one Phase or another. M4, for example, has 3 Floors of the Early, 3 of the Middle, and 1 of the Late Phase. M29 has 8 Early Floors, we think, and M57 has 4 Late Floors, along with other Floors.

The amount of structural activity going on in the four Phases is brought out by this Table and by the four Phase plans. Table 4.5 attempts to refine the data even further, as some open spreads of clay were very substantial, others very small. Equally important is, of course, the unquantifiable nature of pre-existing Floors including those of open spreads and those of houses or shelters. The structures of the Early Phase did not vanish during the Middle Phase. Some were remodelled, like the house of M74, others expanded, like the spread on M73, so any analysis of the Phases should

Table 4.4 Mounds in use, and number of Floors

Phase	*Number of Mounds established/in use*	*Number of Floors, including patches laid down*
Early	19	42
Middle	40	58
Late	71	100
Final	40	50

Table 4.5 Structures

HOUSES

Phase	*Existing unaltered*	*Rebuilt*	*Built*	*Total*
Early	0	0	6	6
Middle	0	4	7	11
Late	0	2	11	13
Final	3?	5	0	8

SPREADS

Phase	*Existing Major*	*Existing Minor*	*New Major*	*New Minor*	*Total*
Early	0	0	6	9	15
Middle	2	1	22	5	30
Late	8	0	31	18	57
Final	18	10	22	8	58

SHELTERS

Phase	*Existing*	*New*	*Total*
Early	0	0	0
Middle	0	3	3
Late	1	5	6
Final	4	0	4

take into account the evidence of the previous Phase where it had not been wholly superseded by a new structure (like M59 where a clay spread was now submerged by a round house).

All of these tables show that there were very major works and structural activities carried on during all the Phases, from a modest base in the Early Phase into an expansionist Middle Phase, re-modelled and substantially augmented in the Late Phase, then somewhat diminished in the Final Phase. The imponderable in this last is the uncertainty about the continued suitability of houses and shelters of the Late Phase into the Final Phase. The plans, which do not reproduce structural events of preceding Phases, suggest that the Final Phase was substantially different from the Late Phase which saw the site at its largest and densest structural activity. We will now look at the four Phases.

Table 4.6 Peripheral structures

Phase	*Mound 47*	*Palisade*	*Total Entrances*
Early	0	slight	open site
Middle	Embankment	major work	2+ open areas
Late	Causeway	extensive work	6
Final	no changes	minor work	5

The Early Phase (6 houses, 15 spreads) (fig.4.9)

From the evidence observed by Bulleid, the earliest settlement on the Glastonbury Lake Village site took place in an area of the fen carr where some substantial trees, of alder and probably willow, were growing (fig.4.8). These were felled and dragged some few metres N to form the foundation wood of an early encampment, in what was to become the NW of the site. Seven spreads of clay were put down here and upon one of these (M74) a small round house was erected. In front of and beside its SW doorway, the clay spreads extended to an area of about 25x15m, with brushwood and other wood between them. Some small windbreaks were erected here and there just outside the doorway to the house. Behind this house were two rectangular sheds. A lightweight fence enclosed all of this complex except for the S part where the fence line curved E into the former area of alder trees. Outside the boundary, to the NE, there were several more sheds and one clay spread, perhaps an assembly dump.

To the S of this small complex was a more densely-clustered grouping of houses and spreads. On the W were three round houses, two of which were probably not exactly contemporary (M29 and M35). The house of M29 had a W entrance from a well-marked clay spread (M33) and may have replaced the house of M35 whose doorway opened to the SSW, onto the wall of

Fig.4.8 Fen carr at Oakhanger, Cheshire. Conditions here are comparable to those at the Lake Village site prior to occupation. Photo courtesy of the University of Lancaster Archaeological Unit

M29 house. These two houses could co-exist but probably are in sequence. Just S of M29 was another house (M14) with a clay spread at its W entrance, and another to the S; this house burnt down soon after construction. A more substantial fence enclosed the W and S parts of this small dwelling complex. Behind the complex were several clay spreads leading E to two small houses (M27 and M18), one of which also burnt down. Probably the M27 house replaced that of M18; they are the same size and so close together that as one burnt, the other would too unless the fire brigade was on hand. The M18 house, probably the earlier, had directly behind it several post-and-stake settings (described already) which might have supported beehives or other raised objects, or have been consecrating elements. There were six of these settings (each with oak post and 5-7 stakes) and six round houses built in this Phase (two of which burnt down). The remainder of the fen carr remained undeveloped although it was probably soon cleared of any substantial wood. Two small dumps of clay were deposited well to the S of the houses (M4,M5), probably on the edge of the carr woodland where water transport of clay and rock effectively came closest to the site. We are pleased to refer to Bulleid's view of 1911: '...it has been conjectured the settlement occupation began with four or five dwellings...'

Units: 4. Population: 50? Generations: 1+?

The Middle Phase (11 houses, 30 spreads, 3 shelters, Embankment) (fig.4.10)

There was a substantial expansion of the settlement in this Phase, both on the existing NW area and in new areas, and the settlement assumed a linear shape, to a great extent enclosed by fences. In the NW, the house at M74 was enlarged and a large shelter constructed on an expanded clay spread of M83. It is important to remember that almost all of these large clay spreads supported and surrounded clay hearths. The spreads, called Floors in many cases, were in effect open areas, firmed by clay, and providing unroofed places and spaces for many activities, from butchering, grinding and cooking to weaving carpentry and metal-working. Just to the W and S of the M74 house several very large spreads were laid down, the 15m spread of M72-76 protected by a set of windbreak shelters. Other clay spreads formed an area about 30x30m and it is possible that two units can be detected, one centered on M74, the other on M83. A strong fence now enclosed this complex on W and N, then ending S where an entry to the site was agreed. To the E of this a new complex was created, a small house just inside the new fence (M61), a huge shelter (which burnt down) on M62 linked by a major spread to a large round house on M65. Various sheds and rectangular enclosures were set up nearby, and the E edge was protected by a short fence. Outside the fence, at the N, was a very small house viewing a tiny patch of clay set well away. The whole unit covered an area 35x15m. To the S of this complex, the site was still open and unbuilt upon over about 20m N-S. The central part of the settlement in this Middle Phase was shaped by expanses of clay, which effectively replaced the houses of Early Phase M29 and M35. The house of M14 was rebuilt (with its entrance still outwards, to the W) and now associated with the wide clay spreads to N, and smaller on the S. The unit area was 30x15m. The two houses of M27 and M18 of the Early Phase were rebuilt and realigned, doorways now to W and to E, with attendant clay spreads, some very large, and this double-house unit was 30x20m. Its E edge was fenced. Beyond the fence, to the E, was a large sheltered area (M44) and a small house of M23 which probably related to the construction of the Embankment. This might have been devised to serve as a landing or loading ramp, for the rafts and logboats bringing clay and stone to the site, but only if access at the S (near M4 or M18) was still unsuitable. The embankment may have begun life as a fishing platform. A damaged logboat was dumped at the N end of the fence, just where a logical channel might have existed to help the arrival of water-borne loads; this area, S of M54 and N of M53, was probably an ingress throughout the Middle and Late Phases.

The settlement was now extended S, with the fence line of the Early Phase partly removed and its direction altered to provide a W edge and S loop for new houses and adjacent spreads. A house at M11 may have had its open stance on M16, M9 faced W, and M4 now had a house built with clay spreads in front of its W entrance. These two or three S units were smaller than the others, with areas 20x10m at most. At this time the settlement was effectively in three parts, NW, NE and a large Central S area of several distinct complexes.

Units: 10. Population: 125? Generations: 2+

The Late Phase (13 houses, 57 spreads, 6 shelters, Causeway) (fig.4.11)

It will be readily seen from the plan of this Phase that expansion continued and was very extensive, both infilling what was already there and outfilling on the E and on the W as well. By the end of this Phase, the settlement was at its peak and some elements of the structures suggest distinct separation of activities; this will be considered further in Chapter 8. The number of Mounds rose from 40 in the Middle Phase to 71, and Floors and spreads laid down almost doubled, to exactly 100. In the earlier Phases, some units, consisting of a house and adjacent clay spread or spreads, have been identified; in the Late phase the same effects are seen but new elements appear.

In the NW of the site, a small house on M70 (which subsequently burnt down) and a large shelter at M71 formed one unit 25x15m, including wide spreads to N. A smaller unit with a house and linked spread (M66 and M74) may have been part of an activity on and around M85 where enclosures and fence lines were erected, maybe to control animals. The palisade was strengthened and extended around the N and W edges of this NW complex. Across the N entrance the houses and shelter were swept away and replaced by huge spreads of clay, from which tongues stretched out beyond the NE entrance which itself was newly-formed. These lobes of clay were probably exits for waste disposal. The large house of M65 was rebuilt and looked out to its wide clay spreads over an area 25x20m. To the NE, a large house was now built (M57), and a smaller one beside with a sheltered area to the W. The area of this unit was 20x15m. The palisade line was extended around this NE sector. A partly blocked entrance between M56 and M49 crossed the original access route to the site interior which was now kept open in part, but various clay spreads (M80 etc.) marked areas for storage or industry. The centre of the settlement, from E to W a distance of about 100m, was now filled by many clay spreads, some shelters and a few houses. On the W, the former locations of Early Phase houses of M29 and M35 were now cleared and new houses erected, side by side, with spreads and sheltered areas adjacent. The units notified are centered on M30, M35, M29 and M13, each with attendant clay spreads, most with hearths as usual. The areas of these units are about 15x10m or a little larger. To the E, similar-sized units can be seen but round houses no longer existed, the replacement being large shelters at M42 and M43 and a small house at M45. Here, a probable entry to the Causeway, now built over the Embankment, was made through the palisade which curved around the E spreads. A small entry through the palisade lay at M21, and a wider entrance at M19. The site was expanded slightly at the S as well. A new house on M3 replaced one on M4 now swept away to become a base for a stone path, possible bank, running S-N to M7 past a small clay spread with several hearths built side-by-side (M6). The palisade enclosed the spreads at M7 and M8, but was not closed off at M3-4; perhaps the stone path or bank substituted for the fence. To the W of this unit was a new large structure on M5 which may have been a focus for metal-working or other high-temperature activity. It was large and set well away from all other spreads and houses. A heavy wooden road was built inside the palisade next to this Mound. To N, another specialised unit was built at M9. Here a previous round or oval house was now reconstructed into an elongated building, with a path linking to M12 and a shed and attendant spread at M10. Inside the long house was a hearth now transformed into a raised square table (fig.2.2) decorated with circles. This might be a focal point for the Late Phase settlement. The palisade of the settlement was now almost complete, with 7 or 8 entrances, most of them on N and E. The interior of the settlement was also infilled and only in the NW sector were several ancient spreads of clay not built over.

Units: 14? Population: 200? Generations: 3+?

The Final Phase (8? houses, 58 spreads, 4 shelters) (fig.4.12)

The plan of this Phase shows considerable differences from that of the Late Phase. Many spaces appear without new structural elements and no new houses were built on previously clear spreads, although 5 houses of the Late Phase were rebuilt or substantially repaired, and 3 others of the Late Phase may have still been in use although this seems unlikely. A clear concentration of new effort took place on the E, as other areas fell into decline. Only 40 Mounds have any sign of new structural activity, and only 50 Floors were laid down, some very small in size; these figures are much reduced from the preceding Phase, 71 to 40 Mounds, 100 to 50 Floors.

At the NW the diminution of occupation continued and although one small house was rebuilt, it was isolated, and the open spreads of clay were mostly very small. Effectively, this sector was abandoned. To its E, the large house of M65 was rebuilt and its adjacent spread renewed. The house at M57 was renewed but its spread reduced in size. At the central W of the site, all houses were replaced by open spreads except those at M29 and M33 which may have continued, but given the length of the Late Phase it seems unlikely that these 2 houses would still be habitable. Farther S a spread on M13 was all that remained and the previous spreads were probably now very unclean and little used. To the S the long house on M5 was now rebuilt into a more normal house with the same entrance W into a small spread, and at the extreme S a renewal of M3 house had 2 new spreads attached, with the palisade now re-aligned outside these 2 areas of M1 and M2.

The major development of the site in this Final Phase was in the central E area where almost every Mound was restructured by large clay spreads, and hearths, which formed a wide open area about 40m diameter, with no houses or shelters, and the palisade opening at M46 now closed off. It is tempting to see this dramatic alteration in the shape and size of the settlement as marking a crucial change in its occupation, from permanent to seasonal. It may be that several units survived, at N and S, and continued the all year settlement, but on the E there were many stances created over time to provide bases for seasonal visits, tent shelters, temporary activities. We will return to this in Chapter 8.

Units: 5. Population: 50+ seasonal. Generations: 1?

The structural life of the settlement.

In drawing this section of the report to a close it is important to reiterate that the 4 Phases as illustrated are but moments in the long life of the settlement. It is highly likely that not all of the structures of any one Phase were in use at one time. Regular and intermittent re-shaping and re-arranging of individual houses, shelters and open spreads must have created an appearance of fluidity to the site. Supplies of building materials were always needed, as Floors subsided or cracked, house walls began to flake or fall, roofing wood and thatch needed strengthening, hurdles required replacement, and palisade posts continued to rot, bend or break. The surfaces of the clay spreads were in constant states of flux, covered by debris deliberately or accidentally dropped, and between the spreads were the dark natural soils seeping through the trampled brushwood layers. If animals were brought to the site alive, they too would cause much movement and mixing of surface deposits. Any periods of drought would cause cracking all over the site, and episodes of flooding of groundwater or by excessive rain would help create slippery and disturbed surfaces at house and shelter entrances, on the open spreads, and probably within the roofed areas as well. All the while, the weight of clay Floors, houses and activities were pressing down into the wooden and peat soil substructure, and squeezing outwards at the edges of the settlement, bending the lines of fence posts outwards. In all this the settlers persisted, and the amount of new material brought to the site was enormous. The amount of clay brought from 1000m away was at least 1000 tonnes. Lias rubble was found even farther away, and special hearth slabs up to 50kg each may have come from sources 10 km away. All came by raft, logboat, mud sled or peat sled, depending on the conditions at the time of need. We think the settlement existed for 200 years, and the annual requirements were very substantial.

The lifespan of the Glastonbury Lake Village is examined elsewhere in this book, but it is relevant here to discuss the chronological implications of the structural elements. We have already indicated that a round house of Glastonbury type built on dry ground might last 50 years. In the conditions on the fen carr site, matters would be different. The worst condition for the survival of wooden posts and stakes is the regular alteration of wetness and dryness, and decay of posts will be focused where buried bases change to exposed upper parts, that is, at the ground surface. Wall posts and stakes would not be likely to survive for more than 10 or 20 years, and their replacements are shown on Bulleid's plans, sometimes as sections of walling totally renewed and sometimes as a more irregular sets of posts propping up or replacing decayed originals. The wall daub of houses would need regular patching, and perhaps after 10-15 years a full-scale renewal. Floor clays were probably patched each year, hearths of clay repaired by clay or stones intermittently. Roof beams if kept dry might last for many years, bindings checked and any movements curtailed. Thatch of reed or straw might last for 35-40 and 10-15 years, respectively. All in all, on a wet site like Glastonbury we might think of a life of 30 years for a round house, before its repairs became so extensive that a new structure was more economical to make. The rebuilding of houses on 8 Mounds (3,9,18,27,57,65,66 and 74) may represent just this, an abandonment of the repair work and a new start. On other Mounds, houses burnt, fell down and were dismantled and not replaced, and there are 17 examples of this (4,5,11, 13,14,18,23,27,29 (twice), 30,35 (twice), 45,56,59,61). Floors and spreads of clay needed replacing too, and over 50 Mounds had more than one Floor or spread in at least one Phase of its life, often two Floors or spreads, sometimes three and occasionally four. This is another indication of the lifespan of some Mounds.

Evidence from the Alpine settlements of the Neolithic and Bronze Age do not support the idea of houses lasting as long as 30 years. By dendrochronological studies of the house posts, it is clear that a substantial rectangular house set on the lake shore (not in the water) would be normally renewed or replaced after only 8 or 10 or 15 years. The reasons for this short life of buildings may be social as well as environmental, but the consistency in early replacement suggests that the damp conditions had severe effects on the house supports and probably on the occupants as well. The same may well have been true at Glastonbury. The life of the settlement on purely structural grounds is likely to have been little more than 200 years. This estimate fits well with the detailed typological dating of the artefacts, and conflicts with the radiocarbon dating; the matter is discussed in Chapter 6.

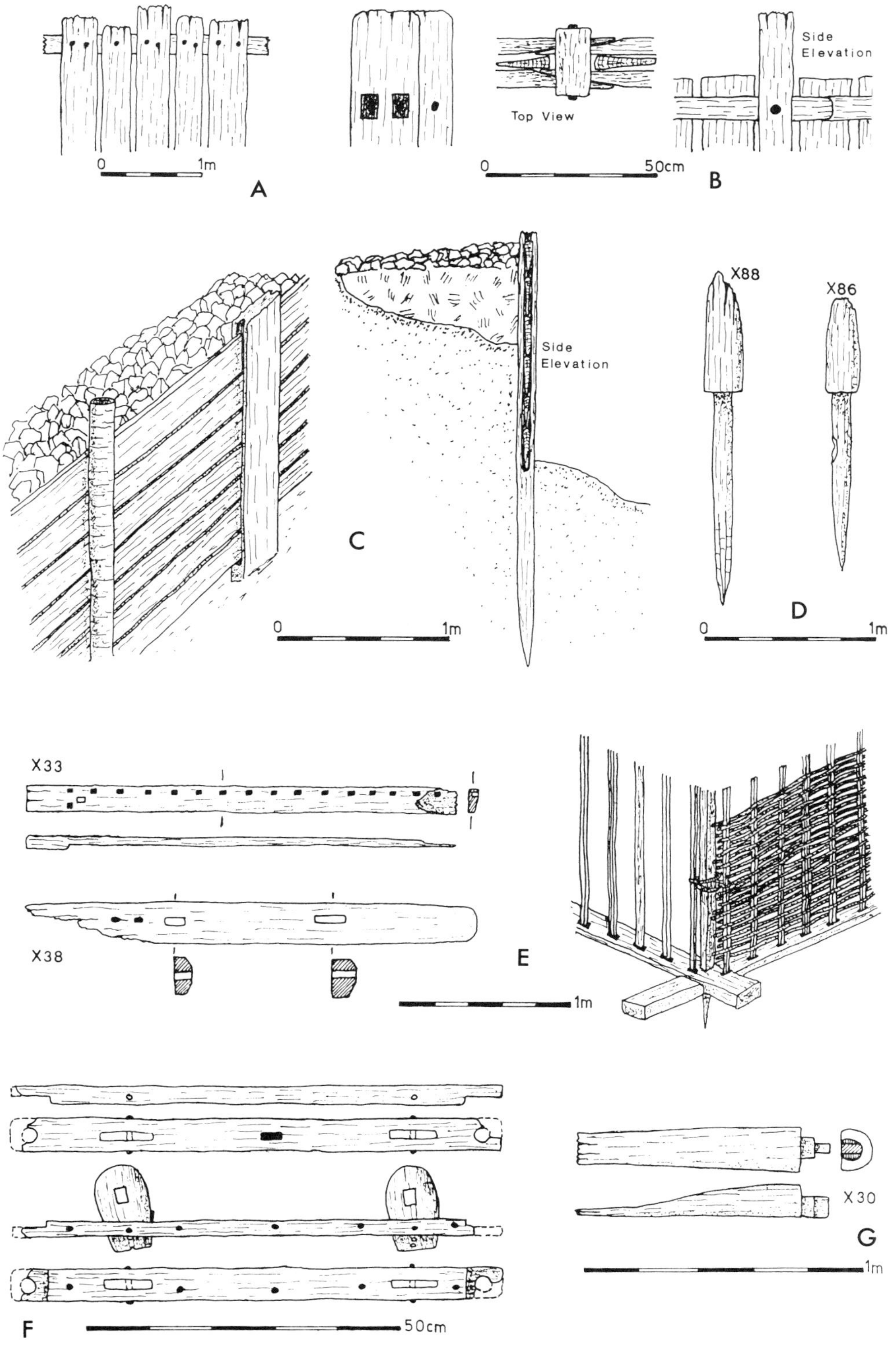

Fig.4.13 Joinery and structural carpentry. Drawn by R. Brunning.

Appendix 4.1 Joinery and structural carpentry

By Richard Brunning

The excavations at Glastonbury Lake Village produced many well made and finely decorated wooden artefacts, but even more importantly the considerable wooden structural assemblage exhibited a variety of joinery techniques, within the revetment of the Causeway and from structural timbers which were reused as foundation material beneath the habitation Mounds. Although the site was excavated at the turn of the century, a detailed record including many precise measurements was kept of the wooden joinery elements. However, very few of the surviving photographs are of any use in verifying this written record.

In this report individual timbers will be referred to using the catalogue numbers from the original excavation report (X 1 to X 100). The references to plates numbered in Roman numerals likewise refer to the photographs and plans of the original 1911 publication.

Revetments. (see fig.3.8 for Bulleid's plan)

Several different types of wooden revetment were discovered in the Causeway and the Embankment which made up M47. The simplest of these occurred at the north end of the Embankment where vertical planks were pegged onto horizontal rails to retain the stone, clay and wood layers which formed the internal structure of the Embankment (fig.4.13A). All that remained of this structure were five of the planks which had collapsed into the peat along with the broken horizontal rail to which they had been attached. From the plan of this feature on Bulleid's plate XXII the planks appear to be cut to a point at one end and to be about 2.1m long. This revetment may have only existed at this one location which is thought to have been a landing stage. Plate XXII, however, appears to indicate that the planks collapsed inwards towards the main body of the Embankment which seems unlikely. Given the lack of further detailed information it is therefore also possible that the structure may originally have been used as an angled ramp down into the water.

The only apparent revetment on the eastern side of the stone Embankment was some wattling but on the south-western edge which faced towards the settlement a complex retaining structure survived. The main elements of this structure were squared oak posts which had two mortice holes cut approximately 250mm below their surviving top ends. The only vertical post measured in its entirety (X 41) was 2.23m in length, 200mm thick and 100mm wide. A post-excavation photograph of this timber exists showing it broken or decayed across the top of the double mortice hole. In each mortice hole two horizontal rails joined each other with a scarf joint that was secured by an oak peg 25mm in diameter which pierced the vertical post transversely (fig.4.13B). The length of the rails apparently varied from 3.25m to 3.35m, and they tapered both in width and thickness towards each end. The number of excavated rails is not mentioned but only two pairs appear on the plan of the area.

This post and rail framework appears to have been used for different types of revetment. Oak boards 180mm to 250mm wide, placed edge to edge, are mentioned as having been driven vertically between the parallel rails to retain the 1.22m deep bottom layer of stones of the Embankment. However the shallow clay layer overlying these stones is also stated as being bordered by wattlework 460mm high, the uprights of which are said to have passed between the rails. A photograph of this latter area contradicts this however as it shows the wattling behind the rails being supported by large roundwork piles driven between the rails. It may be possible that many different types of revetment existed in the area, based on the same basic framework. The contradictions in this evidence suggest that little can be relied upon except the joint between the rails and the upright posts.

The curving Causeway, composed of clay capped by a layer of lias rubble was at least partially retained on its east and west sides by a series of oak boards all of a similar width and thickness (280 x 90mm), the only recorded surviving length being 2.66m. Seven of these upright boards are noted as having grooves along their narrow edges 50mm deep and 50mm wide. In three cases in the SW part of the causeway these grooves received the ends of oak planks which ran horizontally and edge upwards between the uprights over a distance of 2.13m (fig.4.13C). Only a small number of these planks survived *in situ* but in one place a roundwood pile was placed immediately outside the boards to prevent them being pushed out of the grooves in the uprights by the pressure of the clay and stone behind. This pressure may have resulted in similar boards elsewhere in the revetment being lost.

More recent excavations by the Somerset Levels Project in 1984 on the eastern side of the Causeway (Coles et al 1988) confirmed the basic structure recorded by Bulleid but no evidence of planks running horizontally between the uprights was seen, although the edges of one upright were seen to be obliquely faceted from the tip for 1.03m. No horizontal planks were recorded in the original excavations of this area however so their absence should not be used to cast doubt on the existence of the structure as described on the other side of the Causeway.

Measurements of five of the grooves in the upright boards were recorded in the original excavations which show that the grooves on the north edges of the boards were consistently longer than those on the south by 150mm to 230mm and that the grooves survived to a longer length as the uprights progressed northwards. This implies that the revetment was deepening towards its northern end.

Internal structures.

The actual and presumed evidence for round house structures is considered elsewhere in this chapter. Here the foundation wood will be considered. Oak beams with double or triple holes containing vertical posts were found in the substructure of four of the Mounds. This most simple type of joint is frequently encountered in prehistoric sites but more complex carpentry was evidenced by several groups of timbers that had been reused as foundation material for some of the Mounds. The simplest of these reused timbers was a group of seven piles four of which were encountered in Mound substructures and the other three in peat just outside the outer palisade. All these roundwood uprights had a shoulder cut near their top ends below which they tapered to a point, except for two examples which had blunt ends (fig.4.13D). These piles varied in diameter above the shoulder from 180mm to 230mm but six of seven examples had a maximum diameter below the shoulder of 115mm suggesting some standardisation. Several beams reused as foundation material had holes of a similar dimension so it is likely that the shouldered piles were used to peg them down.

Fig.4.14 Bulleid's photograph of some wooden parts of an enigmatic 'frame'.

The total length of these uprights was difficult to determine due to decay, in four cases because the tops had been burnt away. Only one example (X 86) appeared complete, with a length of 570mm above the shoulder implying that the piles did not have any additional structural purposes. Two of the charred piles survived to a greater length above the shoulder (690 and 840mm) however, so the possibility can not be entirely discounted.

Baseplates for wattle walls were also excavated from the foundation material of four Mounds (fig.4.13E). All the seven examples had suffered from decay and none of them survived to their original length, the longest being 2.82m in length. On all examples rectangular mortice holes had been cut between 40mm to 70mm in length, and 25mm to 40mm in width. In four of the baseplates the mortice holes were blind, only penetrating 40mm to 65mm into the top surface. Two of the others may only have appeared to exhibit through mortices due to excessive decay, but the remaining plate (X 96) definitely had fourteen through mortices and only one blind one.

Four baseplates had one surviving end, three of which exhibited simple lap joints to connect with similar baseplates running at right angles. Square through mortices existed at the lap joints slightly offset from the lines of the other holes, and were presumably designed to accommodate the tenons of corner posts. The other holes, spaced from 90mm to 125mm apart, were made to receive the ends of the sails of wattle panel. The rectangular shape of these mortices was necessary because two or three sails were frequently grouped together in the wattling, and in the case of the three wattle panels found next to baseplate X 33 under M56 the sails were made from larger split wood where according to Bulleid "the ends were squared and prepared for fitting mortise-holes". A plaited withy tie attached to one end of one of these panels 460 mm up from the base appeared to be the mechanism by which the hurdles were attached to the corner posts.

The hurdle panels associated with X 33 were 1.98m high but it is uncertain whether the top of this wattle wall stood free or was set into a top plate running between the corner posts. One baseplate (X 38) in addition to the normal blind mortises also exhibited two larger through mortises between which there were no other holes (fig.4.13E). These holes may therefore have been designed for the tenons of large uprights framing a doorway.

Although the evidence is very fragmentary these baseplates probably came from square or rectangular wattle walled structures. These structures would have been fairly sturdy and easy to move and reassemble. The most basic interpretation would be that it was simply fencing to keep animals in or out. The baseplates were not always well finished and the wattling associated with X 33 projected beyond the end uprights of the panels by 100 mm to 120 mm with no signs of trimming or turning back. There was also no sign of any clay daub on the panels. However, the panels were very tightly woven and it is possible that the square structures could have had top plates and a roof which would have provided adequate shelter of an easily assembled kind.

Other more finely made mortised planks and corresponding tenoned pieces were also dismantled. Thirty-seven were discovered underneath M46 and seventeen more were dumped in the peat outside the palisade. Most of the pieces were ash with a small number of oak. The planks normally had lap joints at each end with round through mortises to accommodate the round tenons of some of the uprights. Rectangular mortises also existed on some planks along with the correspondingly shaped tenoned uprights. Small D-shaped boards had rectangular tusk tenons which projected through mortise holes in the planks. Some of these tenons could be pegged in place under the planks while others had several peg holes to allow them to be pegged through the width of the planks at different heights (fig.4.13F and 4.14).

The largest of these planks was only just over a metre in length, and the longest upright component 660mm. Many of the rectangular mortise holes were only 10mm in width and 40mm in length and all the pieces were well finished with some of the D-shaped pieces even bearing burnt decoration. Many of the planks and upright members also had numerous round mortises of both the blind and through varieties for other components of the construction. Bulleid interpreted these artefacts as being part of a weaving apparatus or loom, though this is now considered improbable.

Miscellaneous material.

Several other miscellaneous artefacts found in Mound foundations or in the peat outside the palisades also shed light on joinery and carpentry techniques. A wooden ladder found outside the palisade (X 55) had side pieces of ash with a mortice hole for each rung. The first step survived complete with a tusk tenon at each end projecting through the mortice and pegged on the outside of the ladder to prevent the step slipping out. A large piece of an oak plank (X 91) also had the remains of a tenon at one end with a central peg hole clearly intended for a peg passing through the hypothetical joining mortised timber.

Two wooden artefacts of similar dimensions (X 30 and X 74) displayed evidence for more complex double or stacked tenons (fig.4.13G). Both timbers were incomplete at their top ends. They were D shaped in cross section with a maximum width of 150mm and 90mm. From the complete ends of each piece the timber was cut back to form a tenon of a similar D shape to the main body. Projecting from the centre of these two tenons were two further rectangular tenons. It may be that each tenoned timber was designed to fit into two joining timbers with appropriately shaped mortice holes.

Simple pegged lap joints were evident on two small pieces of wood (X 50 and X 72) found in Mound foundations. They were respectively 175mm and 80mm long, 60mm and 25mm wide, and 45mm and 25mm thick, each having roughly half their thickness cut away over the central third of their lengths to create the lap joint. A single central peg hole pierced each piece and X 50 still retained a peg 20mm in diameter complete at the top end and broken at the bottom. The other block, X 72, was slightly grooved on its short ends and charred on its top surface. Because these pieces were dumped into Mound foundation material it is impossible to determine their exact function but their small size suggest that function was non-structural.

Other non-structural pieces of wood were found in the excavations which demonstrate that the carpenters of the settlement had the ability to undertake very fine and precise joinery. The mortices of the two wheel hubs (X 43 and X 63) and the associated tenons of their surviving spokes are good examples of this, along with the stave built tub (X 3) which was held together with dowels that had a maximum diameter of 5mm. A small block of wood (X 51) 140mm by 80mm by 65 mm, found outside the palisade, had a rectangular tenon projecting from one end and a round blind mortice hole in the face at right angles to this tenon.

Tools.

For evidence of different tools used to make the artefacts described above we have to rely heavily on the observations made by Bulleid. The conversion of timber is rarely recorded but it is likely that they were all split rather than sawn. The only saw found on the site had a blade only 230mm long, but it could have been used for more delicate joinery work. Bulleid noted that only about 20 pieces of wood from the whole site bore the marks of saw cuts and that these only occurred on wood with a diameter of 150mm or less (Bulleid and Gray 1911, 311).

Bulleid frequently records that the planks and beams had been finished with an adze, but it is equally possible, or perhaps more likely, that this work was done with axes. Bulleid made plaster casts of some of the facets which show a blade width of 40-50mm. The mortice holes are recorded as being cut with chisels and gouges, sometimes with both tools apparently being used for different holes on the same timber. Iron gouges and chisels were found during the excavations but it is also possible that axes and simple augers could have been utilised. On some of the 'loom' pieces and on a small hooked artefact (X 6) small holes were also apparently made by boring through the wood with a hot metal rod leaving the outside of the holes black and charred.

Conclusion.

The study of joinery and carpentry techniques from Glastonbury Lake Village is considerably hampered by the limited nature of the surviving records and the inability to study the original timbers. However, the surviving information does show that a large range of joinery techniques were being used including lap and scarf joints and a wide variety of mortice and tenon joints.

Chapter 5

The Environment *by Rupert Housley*

The setting of the settlement and its immediate environs

When Arthur Bulleid and Harold St. George Gray excavated the Iron Age settlement of Glastonbury in eleven field seasons between 1892 and 1907 Bulleid, in particular, made extensive field observations of the sediments that were found, and it is from his notes that we get our first view of the site and its environs.

Bulleid (in Bulleid and Gray 1911,46-49) strongly emphasized the watery surrounding to the site. He thought that the location of the settlement had been chosen because it was an area of peat that was firmer than other parts of the swamp. Surrounding the site he envisaged an expanse of open navigable water. Bulleid noted that in certain places in the village there were the remains of trees - the stools and roots of alder and willow - that had been growing on the site. Because the peat surface between the trees had been uneven, water had filled the depressions, into which had accumulated a stratified layer of leaves of willow and other trees. To Bulleid this 'leafy peat' marked the lower boundary of the cultural deposits. It was on this surface that chips of wood were discovered, almost certainly the debris from wood working as part of the construction of the village. However this leafy peat was only local in its extent, in that it did not form a continuous layer over the whole site; it was not of uniform thickness, nor was it to be found at the same depth below the ground surface. As a layer it became less marked towards the margins of the site and did not extend beyond the perimeter delineated by the wooden palisade.

In contrast to the leafy peat, Bulleid described the deposits outside the village as being of a rushy nature, frequently containing quantities of pond or river weed fibre, and a heterogeneous mass of cultural debris in the superficial deposits near the palisade. He observed that freshwater shells and river weed were more common on the eastern side of the village than on the west, whilst the east and north-east borders produced shells of freshwater mussel and the roots of water-lily. This, together with the extra-ordinary organic preservation conditions, suggested to Bulleid that the immediate environs of the site must have been very wet. The numerous plant remains recovered by Bulleid and Gray were studied by Clement Reid (1917; Reid in Bulleid 1924,67-68). Although we do not know from where within the excavation the remains derive, the list of species does give us some insight into the varied habitats the inhabitants exploited. For example, Reid found plants which favour open water environments (lakes, ponds, slow moving streams and rivers), ones which prefer mires (fen, fen carr, swamps, marshes), others typical of deciduous woodland and scrub, of grassland, of cultivated or disturbed land, as well as some species of cultivars. Some of the plants would have been transported to the site by the inhabitants to be used for various purposes, but others may have actually been growing within the confines of Bulleid and Gray's excavation. Ultimately it is to Bulleid's descriptions that we owe our first view of the site and its environs, and from his picture comes the name by which the site has long been known, the Glastonbury 'Lake' Village.

The next person to study the environment of Glastonbury was Sir Harry Godwin, who in 1946 and 1947 made two borings into the flank of M5 (1955,178). In his borings he found the following sequence:

0-60cm	Grey-brown stiff clay with abundant charcoal fragments.
60-92cm	Mouldered brown peat with abundant wood fragments (cf. *Salix*) and stone of cf. *Crataegus* at 92cm.
92-110cm	Fine detritus mud with occasional wood fragments. Fruits of *Potamogeton* (cf. *natans*) at 99cm, *Nuphar* and *Eleocharis*.
110-400cm	Coarse detritus mud with occasional wood fragments (large wood between 205-225cm, abundant wood 345-350cm and 380-400cm).
400-435cm	Fine detritus mud.
435-	Soft grey-blue clay.

It is important to realise that by putting a borehole through an already excavated Mound, the top of Godwin's sequence would have consisted of backfill from Bulleid and Gray's excavation. It seems likely that the upper 60cm represents backfill, maybe more since it is not certain how deep Bulleid and Gray dug. Godwin (1955,179) emphasized the open-water nature of the sequence, describing the deposit immediately below the village as a 'floating fen carr'. In the pollen diagram from this boring (GLV 1,fig.5.1) the pollen and spores in this deposit were characterised by high quantities of *Alnus*, *Corylus / Myrica*, *Salix*, *Sparganium-Typha*, *Ulmaria (Filipendula)*, and *Filicales*, confirming a fen carr type of environment. To Godwin it appeared as if the village had been 'built as a raft upon the surface of a morass, supported by a multitude of piles and with open water beside it'. Bulleid and Godwin were thus in good agreement.

Although there were two major reinterpretations of the site of Glastonbury between the 1950s and the 1980s, neither Tratman's (1970) or Clarke's (1972) re-examinations involved any palaeoenvironmental investigation. Nor did the limited excavation carried out by Michael Avery in 1968 and 1969. The next relevant

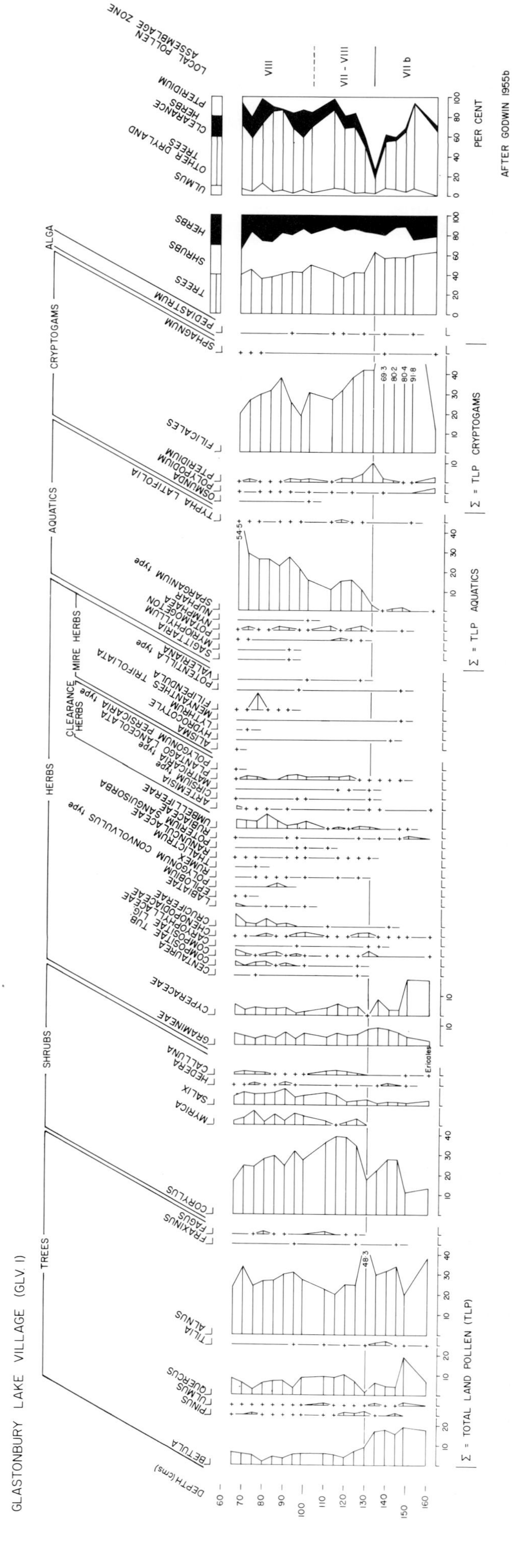

Fig.5.1 Percentage pollen diagram: GLV 1.

study of the village and its environs took place in 1984 when the Somerset Levels Project excavated three small trenches around the margins of the settlement (Coles, Coles and Morgan 1988) in conjunction with the palaeoenvironmental study of the author (Housley 1986, 1988). Of the three trenches which were made, one (SLP 1) proved to be particularly useful in demonstrating the relationship between the leafy peat and the cultural remains inside the palisade, and the open-water deposits beyond.

Located on the margins of the site on the west side, SLP 1 had been selected to investigate the 18m break in the palisade between Mounds 31 and 76. Across this gap Bulleid and Gray (1911,52) had found a bank of black peat of reed stems and roots, about one metre high and over two metres wide, aligned in a NNW-SSE direction. Bi-convex in section, the bank appeared to have been made of placed blocks of peat, with a line of vertical large piles that passed through the centre, and a second line of smaller posts along the outer margin held together by wattle-work. Clarke (1972) termed this gap in the palisade the 'western entrance'. The archaeological results of the 1984 investigations of trench SLP 1 need not concern us here, suffice it to say that at the eastern end of the extension to this trench the following stratigraphic sequence emerged:

0-12cm	Turf and clay topsoil.
12-37cm	Disturbed clay (backfill).
37-39cm	Disturbed clay and peat (backfill).
39-53cm	Disturbed leafy peat (backfill).
53-67cm	Undisturbed leafy wood peat with *Salix* leaves.
67-84cm	Lighter brown *Phragmites* reedswamp peat.
84cm	Base of trench.

The top 53cm represents modern topsoil and Bulleid and Gray's backfill, showing that the eastern end of SLP 1 lay within the margins of the settlement. The sediments in the western end of SLP 1, in contrast, had not been disturbed and thus had been beyond the outer limits of Bulleid and Gray's excavations. The importance of this section is that it shows the relationship between the (removed) cultural deposits, which clearly overlie Bulleid's undisturbed leafy peat, which in turn overlies a deposit of *Phragmites* reedswamp peat the importance of which we will see later. We can be confident that the undisturbed leafy wood peat with *Salix* leaves represents Bulleid's leafy peat, and that both probably equate with Godwin's mouldered brown peat with abundant fragments of *Salix* wood. Thus the stratigraphic sequence within the confines of the settlement can be summarised as having been:

1. A *Phragmites* reed peat accumulated at the base of the sequence.
2. This was succeeded and replaced by alder-willow fen carr, onto which was built:
3. A timber substructure, that supported:
4. Layers and floors of clay, on which:
5. Dwellings were erected. The whole structure being surrounded by:
6. A timber palisade. Outside which on the eastern side was:
7. A 'Causeway' and an 'Embankment'.

As to what deposit, and hence what sort of environment, succeeded the village on abandonment, the answer must be sought outside the confines of Bulleid and Gray's excavations, and it is to the immediate environs of the settlement that we shall now turn. But before we can consider what happened after the village was abandoned, we first need to see what types of vegetation were growing in the immediate environs and to fix where in the stratigraphic column occupation took place. It is here that the significance of the *Phragmites* reedswamp peat beneath the village is realised as will be made clear when we examine the second of the Somerset Levels Project's trenches, SLP 2.

Located approximately 40m north of the northern palisade, trench SLP2 was chosen to provide a long sequence of natural peat, mud and clay deposits away from any cultural debris. In the trench no cultural material was found and the stratigraphic sequence was as follows:

c 5.05-4.70m OD	Turf and yellow-brown stiff clay topsoil.
4.70-4.66m OD	Very dark-brown humified amorphous peaty earth with some dirty clay. Some charcoal flecks.
4.66-4.47m OD	Dark-brown humified fine detritus mud with some *Juncus* and *Typha* sp. fruits and occasional *Chara* oospores towards the base.
4.47-4.46m OD	Dark-brown humified fine detritus mud with many monocotyledon rhizomes and some clay. Fruits of *Potamogeton* cf. *obtusifolius* and *Cladium mariscus*, and some *Chara* oospores.
4.46m OD	Light blue-grey estuarine cum marine clay with many *Phragmites* and monocotyledon rhizomes.
4.46-4.31m OD	Dark-brown humified fine detritus mud with some monocotyledonous rhizomes and occasional *Cladium* rhizome. Fruits of *Ceratophyllum demersum*, *Potamogeton* cf. *obtusifolius*, *Carex* spp., *Nymphaea alba*, *Cladium mariscus*, *Ranunculus* Sect. *Batrachium*, as well as oospores of *Chara*.
4.31-4.11m OD	Dark-brown humified woody to very woody sedge peat with much coarse detrital material. The deposit includes much wood, bark and many leaves,

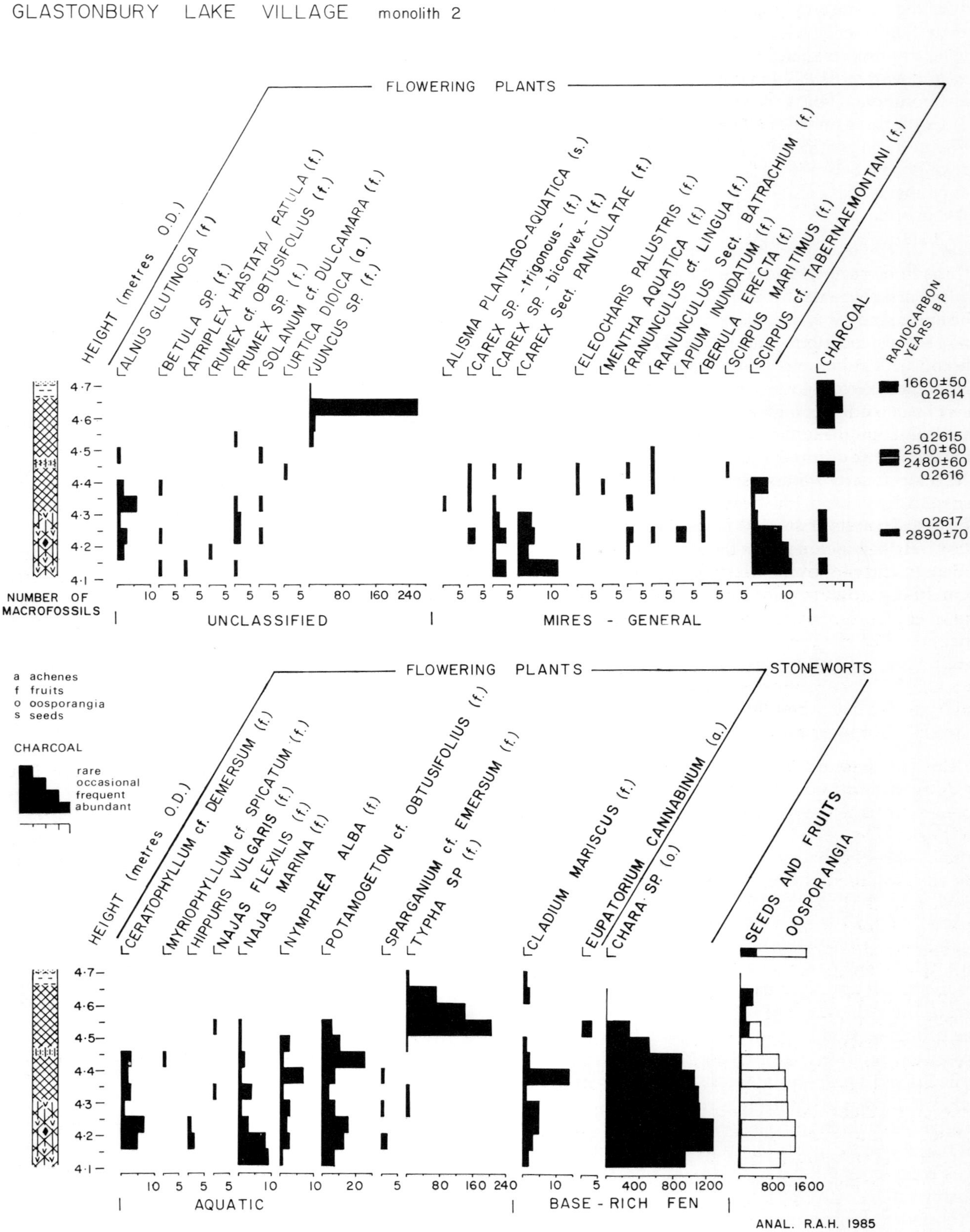

Fig.5.2 Plant macrofossils from the N side of the Lake Village, trench SLP 2.

	as well as some coarse herbaceous rootlet material and the occasional *Cladium* rhizome. Fruits of *Nymphaea alba*, *Carex* spp., *Hydrocharis morsus-ranae*, *Potamogeton* cf. *obtusifolius*, *Ceratophyllum demersum*, *Najas marina*, *Cladium mariscus*, *Polygonum* sp., *Scirpus* cf. *tabernaemontani*, *Chenopodium* sp., *Hippuris vulgaris*, and oospores of *Chara* are present.
Below 4.11m OD	Not sampled

The peat stratigraphy, together with an examination of the plant macrofossils (fig.5.2), provide a good guide to the natural vegetational sequence north of the Lake Village before, during and after occupation. The lowest recorded deposit represents a very wet fen carr. Species like *Potamogeton obtusifolius*, *Hydrocharis morsus-ranae* and *Ceratophyllum demersum* suggest a mesotrophic environment. However, semi-eutrophic and eutrophic conditions probably existed as well in places since *Cladium mariscus* and *Chara* are well represented. High values for the number of macrofossils of *Scirpus tabernaemontani* and *Ceratophyllum demersum* indicate brackish influences in the area. Although there is a detrital element in the deposit, most of the wood was probably growing on or very near to the sampling point since tree trunks were found in the trench during excavation. The majority of the wood was alder, although some willow leaves were also present. The importance of the aquatic elements in this woody deposit indicates that water levels were quite high and the detrital component is far from negligible.

The alder fen carr environment was succeeded by a fine detritus mud with monocotyledon and *Cladium* rhizomes. *Carex* decreases whilst there are minor isolated peaks in *Scirpus* cf. *tabernaemontani* and *Cladium mariscus*. This indicates that the change to a lake mud went via a wet reed-swamp environment. Later some of the aquatics show a slight increase reflecting the wetter conditions. This progression to a wetter environment seems to have started at *c* 2800 BP and culminated at *c* 2500 BP with the deposition of a light blue-grey estuarine clay with the remains of *Phragmites* and other monocotyledon reeds. This represents the extreme southerly penetration of what Godwin (1941, 1943, 1955) termed the 'Romano-British' estuarine clay, although high freshwater levels would have been experienced further inland. This estuarine clay and the abundant *Phragmites* remains correlate with the *Phragmites* layer beneath the village of Glastonbury, thus it is to the layers above this clay that we need to look to find out what the environment was like at the time of occupation.

The deposition of this clay must have had a drastic effect on the depositional environment of the area since many of the species seen earlier disappear. What had been a purely organic depositional environment was replaced by one with a minerogenic component with areas of newly exposed clay adjoining expanses of freshwater lake in which organic lake muds were being deposited. On the clay, *Phragmites* first colonised, to be replaced by *Typha* (which can form dominant communities given the right conditions). South of the clay high water levels persisted, as seen by the continued deposition of a fine organic lake mud. It is probably at this point in the stratigraphic sequence that Glastonbury Lake Village was constructed and occupied, as indicated by the amount of charcoal incorporated in the upper part of the profile.

Towards the top the high lake levels started to drop and the *Typha* dominated stands were succeeded by the growth of *Juncus*. About this time or a little later, the whole drainage regime of the Somerset Levels started to change. The freshwater peats and muds which had characterised the Levels since the end of the Boreal period ceased to be deposited and the organic depositional regime was very slowly replaced by an alluvial silty-clay environment. Although the peat at this point was very mouldered due to shrinkage caused by drainage, a radiocarbon date was obtained of 1660±50 BP (Q-2614). Peat continued to grow after this date in other areas of the Levels, e.g. Godney Moor (V.Straker, pers.comm.) but near the Lake Village the organic sequence stopped. From historical documents it is possible to infer that at least the upper part of this stiff silty-clay represents flood water depositing its suspended load over the Levels during seasonal floods. This process has continued and characterized the Somerset Levels until comparatively recently.

Immediately north of the Lake Village there is thus evidence for high, although possibly falling, shallow freshwater lake levels at the time of occupation. But what of conditions on the other margins of the settlement? Bulleid referred to the deposits beyond the palisade as being of a rushy nature with pond or river weed. The undisturbed deposits at the western end of trench SLP 1 were as follows:

4.87-4.61m OD	Turf and light-brown stiff clay topsoil.
4.61-4.51m OD	Light-brown to darker green-brown clay in a fine detritus mud. Many fragments of charcoal. Fruits of *Typha* sp. present.
4.51-4.43m OD	Dark-brown well humified sedge peat with much fine detrital material. The deposit has a lot of herbaceous rootlet material and a little wood. Fruits of *Potamogeton* cf. *obtusifolius*, *Nymphaea alba*, *Cladium mariscus*, *Hippuris vulgaris*, *Carex* spp., *Ranunculus* Sect. *Batrachium*, *Typha* sp., and oospores of *Chara* present.
4.43-4.31m OD	Dark-brown humified woody to very woody sedge peat with much coarse detrital material. The deposit contains wood, bark, leaves and much coarse herbaceous rootlet material. Fruits of *Potamogeton* cf. *obtusifolius*, *Cerato-*

phyllum demersum, Nymphaea alba, Rumex sp., *Carex* spp., *Chenopodium* sp., *Scirpus* sp. *Najas marina, Cladium mariscus,* and oospores of *Chara* present.

Below 4.31m OD Not sampled.

The plant macrofossil diagram from SLP 1 (fig.5.3) shows the vegetational sequence on the west. The lowest sampled deposit represents a very wet fen carr environment with a number of aquatics like *Ceratophyllum demersum, Potamogeton* cf. *obtusifolius* and *Najas marina* mixed in with birch and alder and a range of fen species. This was succeeded by a wet *Carex* and *Cladium* sedge fen environment with areas of open water indicated by the presence of aquatic plants. Above this, there is a sharp transition to a silty-clay deposit. Except for *Typha* and *Juncus*, most of the taxa seen before disappear. It is possible that the sequence is truncated around 4.51m OD, perhaps by human interference when constructing the Lake Village. Certainly, above 4.51m OD there is a different environment with a silty-clay strata being colonised by *Typha* reeds. It is difficult to be sure where in this sequence the occupation of the Lake Village should be located. The high charcoal values may represent the period of human occupation, or the post-occupational erosion of the site. The alder-willow fen carr deposit in the village (Bulleid's leafy peat) may correspond with the very woody sedge peat at the base of SLP 1. If so it would represent the natural surface on which the Lake Village was constructed and would suggest that, at least at the west margin of the village, the alder-willow fen carr abutted *Carex* and *Cladium* sedge fen.

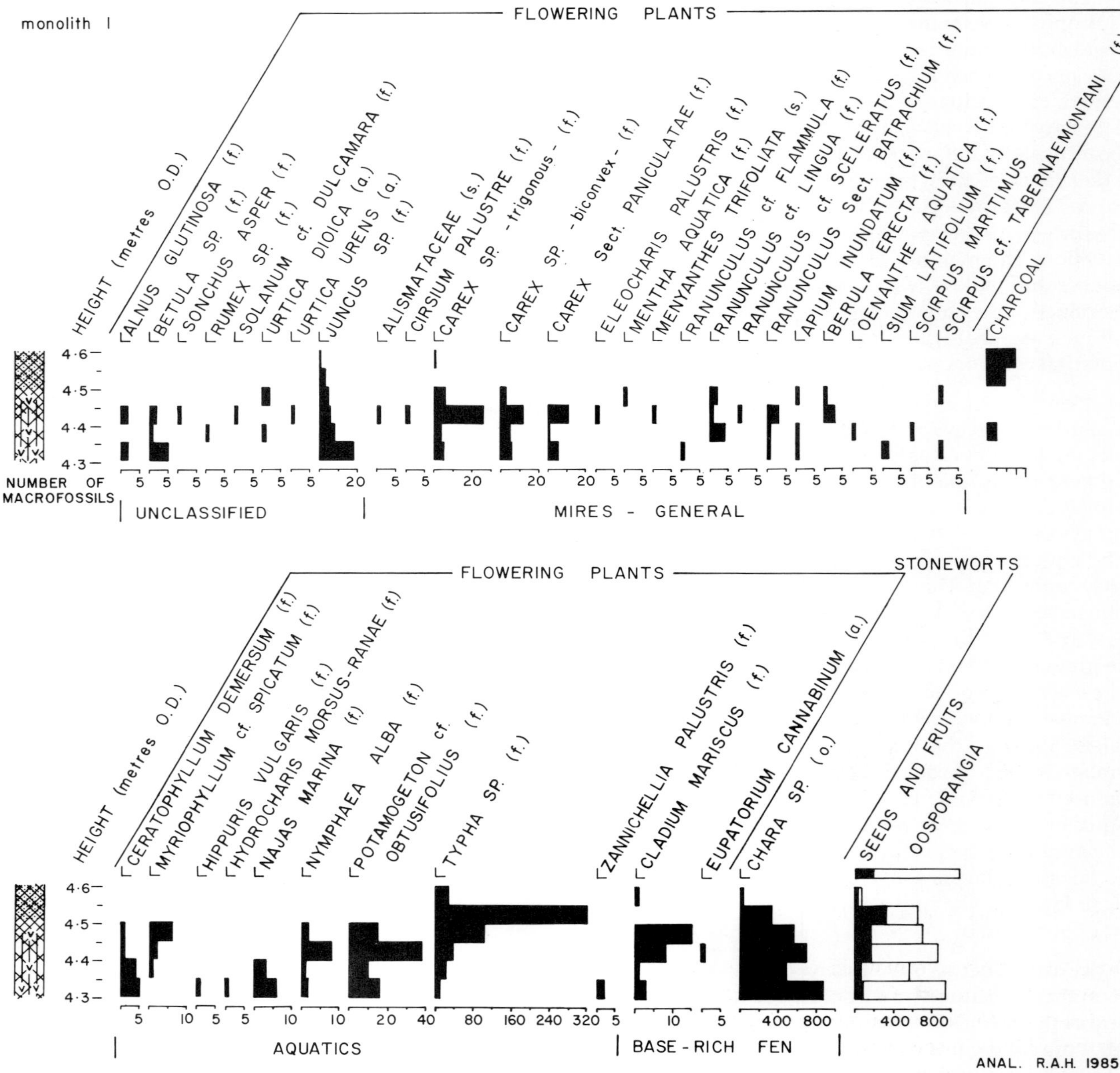

Fig.5.3 Plant macrofossils from the W side of the Lake Village, trench SLP 1.

To the east of the village Bulleid and Gray uncovered two features termed the 'Causeway' and the 'Embankment'. Thought to be a possible landing stage for boats, the third Somerset Levels Project trench, SLP 3, was sited to re-examine them and to investigate the environmental conditions on this side of the village. Because of the presence of backfill, the only secure place where *in situ* samples could be taken was under the Causeway. Two small monoliths were removed, one from directly under the clay structure and one from under the adjacent grey clay with quartzite which adjoined the Causeway. Examination of the plant macrofossils (fig.5.4) from under the actual Causeway revealed a fairly woody *Carex* and *Cladium* sedge fen which seemed to have been getting wetter prior to the dumping of the Causeway clay. It is interesting to note that on the west side of the village the same *Carex* and *Cladium* sedge fen existed. The samples from under the grey clay with quartzite (fig.5.4) showed a less woody detrital deposit with a higher number of aquatics and less *Cladium*. The aim of the builders may have been to locate the Causeway bank on a firmer, more woody, area that abutted a more open, watery one, although it is important to realise that these conditions represent the situation prior to the building of the Causeway, not when it was in use. But assuming the inhabitants sited the structure in an already suitable locality there is no reason, at least as far as the environment is concerned, why boats could not have made use of the Causeway. It is perhaps worth adding that there is no particular reason why this side of the village should have been favoured for such a use over, say, the west margin.

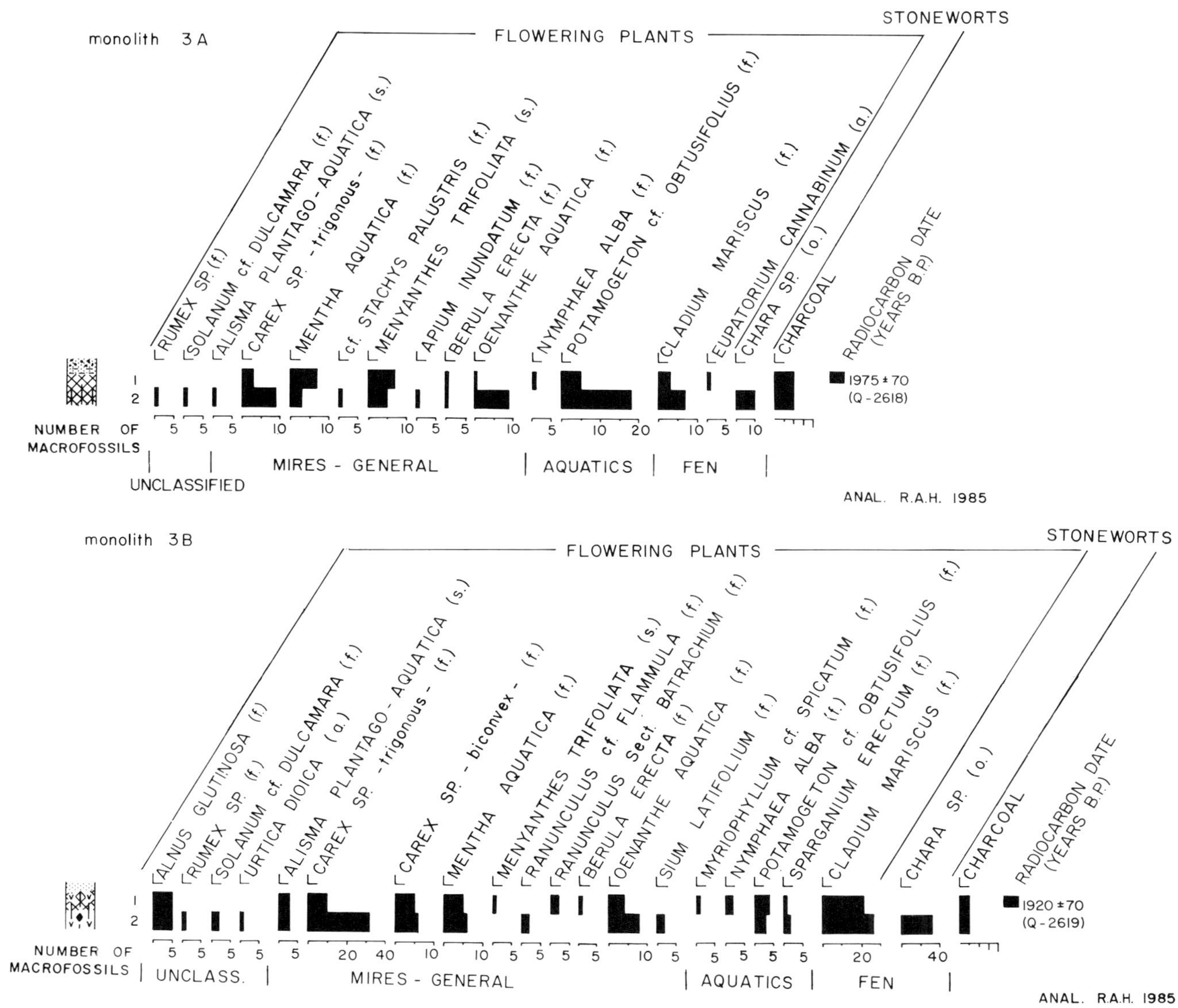

Fig.5.4 Plant macrofossils from beneath the clay and quartzite deposit abutting the Causeway bank (monolith 3A), and from beneath the Causeway bank (monolith 3B).

From the Village to the fen margins.

Looking out from the lake village, there are three areas of higher ground which emerge out of the peat in the distance. These 'islands' (in the sense they would have been surrounded, at least in part, by mire) are, to the SE, the Lias outcrop of Glastonbury where the modern town is situated; to the NW, the Godney ridge; and to the NE, the high ground around Garslade. As the three closest dry land localities to the Lake Village, it is to these areas that the Iron Age inhabitants may have, in part, looked to for their building materials. However, what type of environment separated the site from these uplands?

Godwin (1955) made a limited number of boreholes in the area from Batch Farm across East Waste to the Meare Pool. He found a series of deposits that showed to the west there had been an expanse of raised bog, whereas to the east organic muds and clays predominated. To further elucidate Godwin's findings, in 1983-84 a series of five borehole transacts were positioned across the area centred on the Lake Village (fig.5.5). Although the boreholes penetrated into earlier deposits, as far as the Iron Age is concerned only the top part need concern us, and so most attention will focus on the upper metre and a half.

Godney - Glastonbury.

The first transect, aligned northwest - southeast between the Godney ridge and the Lias outcrop of Glastonbury, consisted of 12 boreholes over a distance of 3km (fig.5.6). As Godwin noted, the stratigraphic sequence can be divided into two, with raised bogs to the south of Godney and detritus muds to the north of Glastonbury. South of Godney the first deposit of relevance is the *Sphagnum-Calluna-Eriophorum* raised bog peat (from *c* 2m OD upward). The development of this ombrogenous bog seems to be due to the onset of wetter, more acidic conditions causing the growth of floating *Sphagnum* mats. Beckett and Hibbert (1979,592-3) showed that for the area between Meare-Westhay and the Polden Hills raised bog growth began around *c* 4650-4000 BP. Based on the radiocarbon date for GV.31, it is clear that raised bog began later in the East Waste, after 3460±50 BP (Q-2462). It is likely that growth of such bogs south of Godney probably resulted from the expansion of already existing raised bog communities to the west or southwest.

It is difficult to know how long raised bog growth continued south of Godney. Often above the *Sphagnum-*

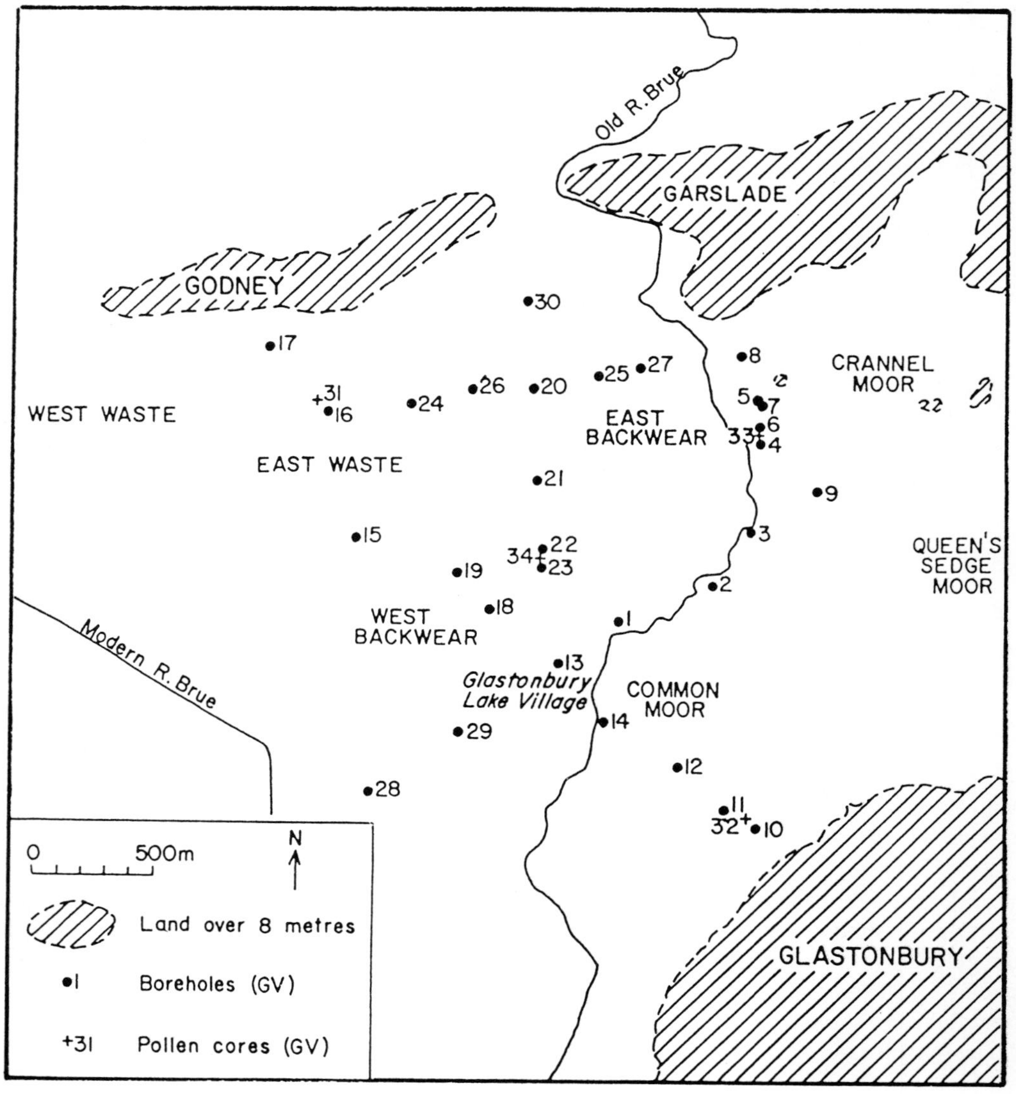

Fig.5.5 Map of the area around Glastonbury Lake Village with sampling stations.

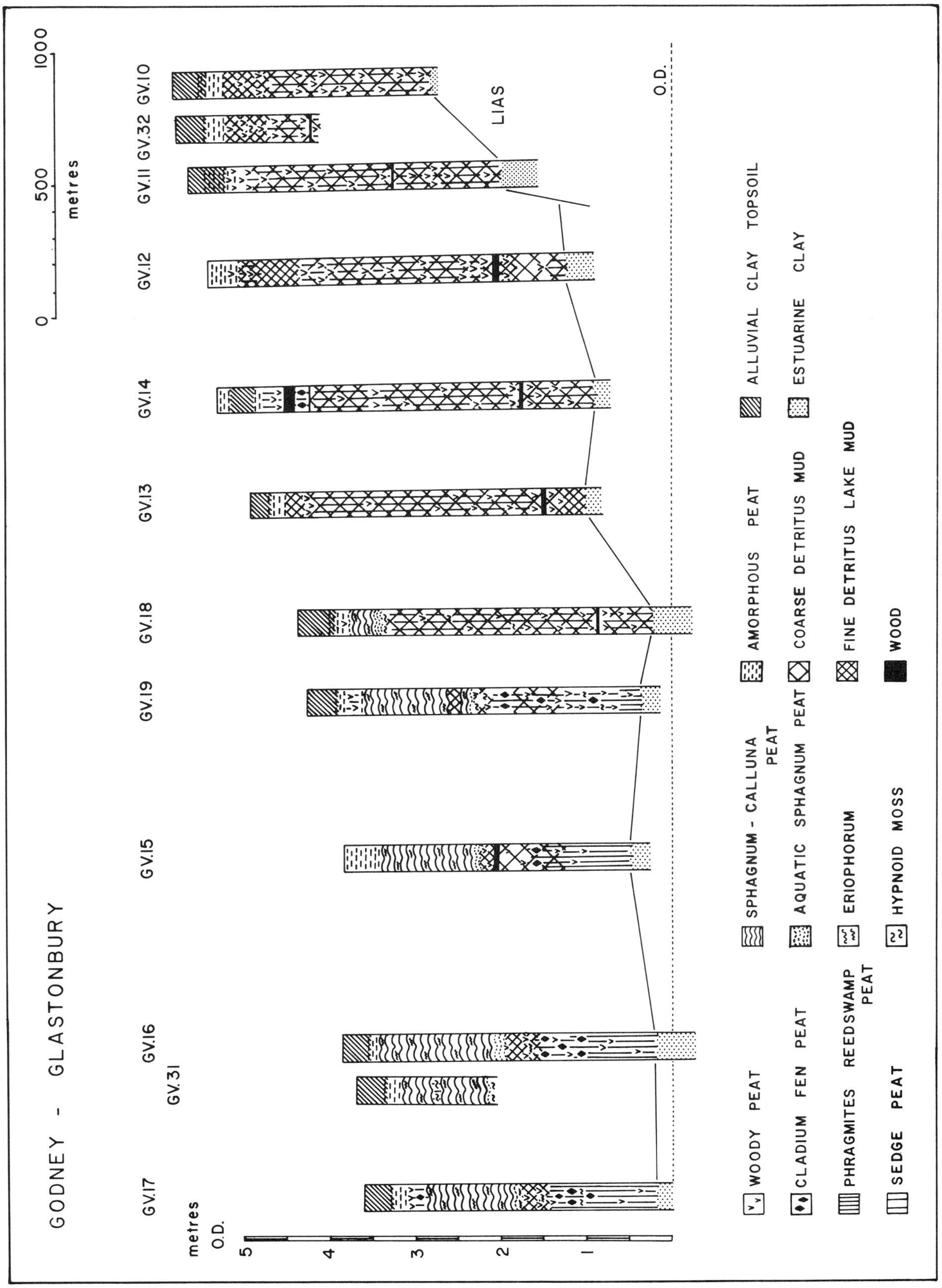

Fig. 5.6 Godney - Glastonbury stratigraphic transect. Key to symbols used in Figs.5.6 - 5.10. Dense stipple in GV.10 and GV. 11: Lias.

Calluna-Eriophorum peat there was a well humified amorphous black earth, sometimes with decayed raised bog elements. In the boreholes marginal to the presumed centre of growth, i.e. GV.17, GV.18 and GV.19, it was noted that overlying the *Sphagnum* bog there was a varied deposit of fragments of wood, monocotyledon rhizomes, sedge rootlets and occasional *Cladium* rhizomes. Such a horizon probably represents flooding of the margins of the bog by eutrophic groundwater. GV.31 was exceptional in that the sediments show a short event within the raised bog sequence where the surface was flooded by base-rich water causing a sedge and hypnoid moss peat to grow. Clapham and Godwin (1948) reported similar horizons in other raised bogs in the Levels. Although short-lived in sedimentary terms, the pollen indicates that high water levels persisted throughout most of the upper profile. In the more central boreholes, GV.15, GV.16 and GV.31, the upper part of the raised bog peat was well mouldered - probably a fairly recent event caused by modern drainage. Originally the upper *Sphagnum* would probably have been less humified than that in the lower profile. At the top of most of the boreholes was a light-brown stiff alluvial clay that forms the modern ground surface.

The SE leg of this transect, across Common Moor, detailed a different picture. For most of the period after *c* 5500-5200 BP, once the basal Boreal clay ceased to be laid down, this area saw the deposition of a range of difficult to characterize sediments, usually coarse detritus muds with monocotyledon rhizomes, some wood, and the fruits of many plants but principally *Alnus glutinosa, Betula, Carex, Potentilla, Rubus, Solanum, Ranunculus* Sect. *Batrachian, Menyanthes trifoliata, Potamogeton, Sparganium,* and *Hippuris vulgaris*. The wood and the fruits of alder and birch indicate a fen carr environment, as do *Potentilla* and *Rubus*. *Carex* suggests fen. *Potamogeton, Sparganium, Hippuris vulgaris* and the *Ranunculus* species favour open-water, confirming the detrital nature of the deposit. The overall impression is of a very wet alder fen carr with many open-water channels and some fringing herbaceous fen vegetation. In places tree swamp probably developed. This wet fen carr persisted for a considerable period of time to judge from the depth of deposit around the Lake Village.

A change occurs towards the top of many of the Common Moor profiles with the deposition of a fine detrital lake mud. This black lake mud had fruits of *Potamogeton* and *Ceratophyllum*, and represents a shift to deeper water conditions. However in places the coarse woody peat persists, indicating that the fen carr managed to survive inundation. It was on such a surface that the Lake Village was built. Radiocarbon results from GV.32 point to a date after 2890±50 BP (Q-2464) for the onset of wetter conditions. Above the fine detritus lake mud is a black very humified amorphous peaty earth which included very mouldered wood. The top of most of the cores was marked by light-brown stiff alluvial clay.

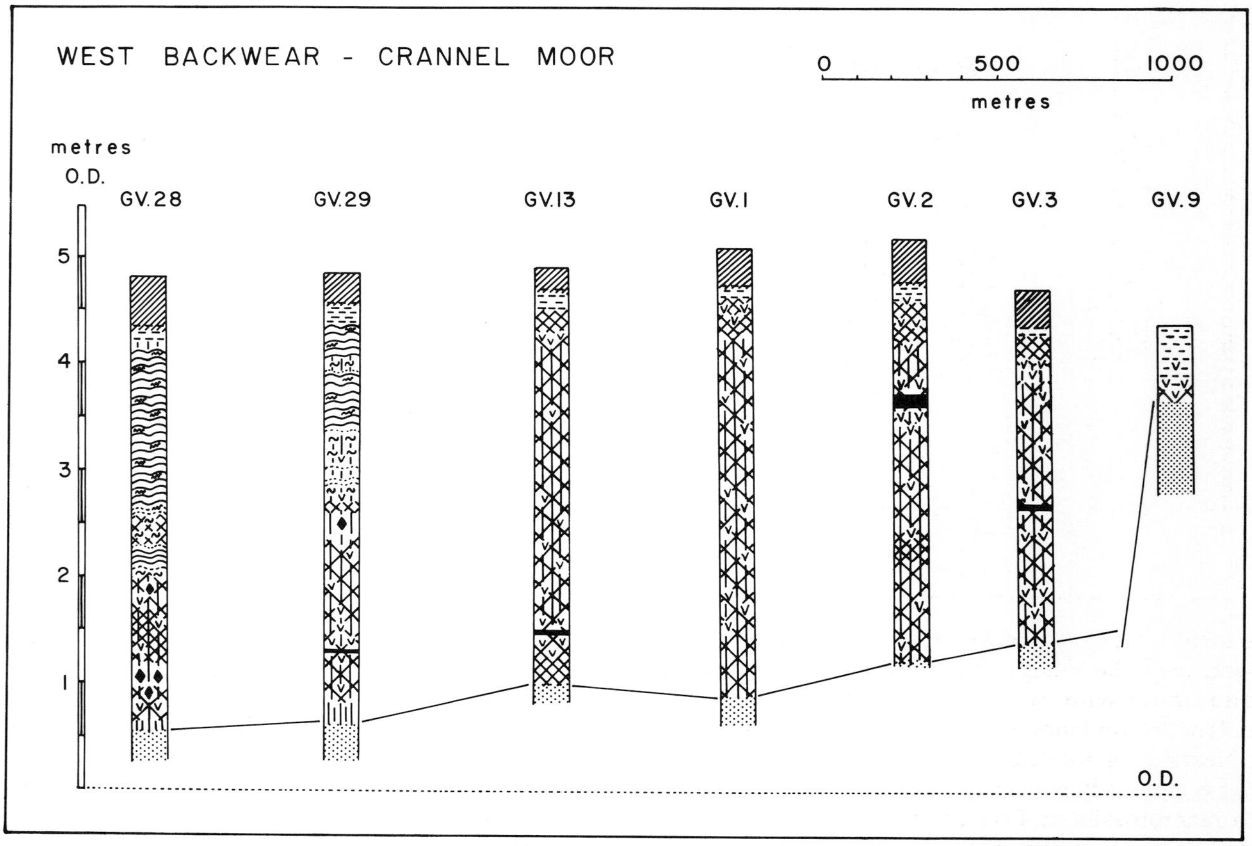

Fig.5.7 West Backwear - Crannel Moor stratigraphic transect. Dense stipple in GV.9: ?Burtle.

West Backwear - Crannel Moor, and West Crannel Moor. The second transect of 7 boreholes ran NE from the modern Brue near Coldharbour Farm to Crannel Moor (fig.5.7). At right angles to the last transect, the stratigraphic sequence closely resembled it, i.e. raised bog to the west and detrital muds to the east. As before, a flooding event was discerned in the upper part of the cores, both in the raised bog sequence (e.g. at *c* 4m OD in GV.29), and as a black lake mud in the detrital sequence (in GV.13, GV.1, GV.2, GV.3). Capping everything was the same light-brown alluvial clay. Borehole GV.9, somewhat unexpectedly, uncovered a buried sand, gravel and clay 'island' which had been hidden beneath a layer of mouldered peat. The presence of such a feature, if it had been above the level of the mire in the Iron Age, would not have gone unnoticed by the inhabitants of Glastonbury, and it may have been used to exploit the fen edge.

The third transect, running north to south across West Crannel Moor adjacent to Upper Crannel Farm, also consisted of 7 boreholes (fig.5.8). The northern boreholes struck the buried sides of a Keuper outcrop which projects out above the peat south of Garslade. In association with the change from fen to lake conditions, alder fen carr was encouraged, most likely on the sides of the Keuper outcrop but also perhaps in the peat-filled basin. Sometime after the deposition of the fine detritus lake mud at GV.33 there was a phase of reed-swamp development with fruits of *Scirpus* cf. *tabernaemontani* and *Cladium mariscus*, and *Chara* oospores. This coincided with high values of *Sparganium* type pollen and the spores of *Typha latifolia*. Above this reed-swamp phase the organic sequence becomes very humified, before being capped by the light-brown alluvial clay.

Batch Farm (East Backwear).
The two Batch Farm transects (figs.5.9 and 5.10), one running NS from just south of the Godney-Garslade 'gap' to close to the Lake Village, and one going WE from East Waste to Crannel Moor, cross the area known as East Backwear to the north of the Lake Village. Together they detail the sedimentary changes associated with the deposition of Godwin's Romano-British marine clay. In many of the cores in this area, the organic sediments have been heavily compressed and deformed due to the large overburden of clay.

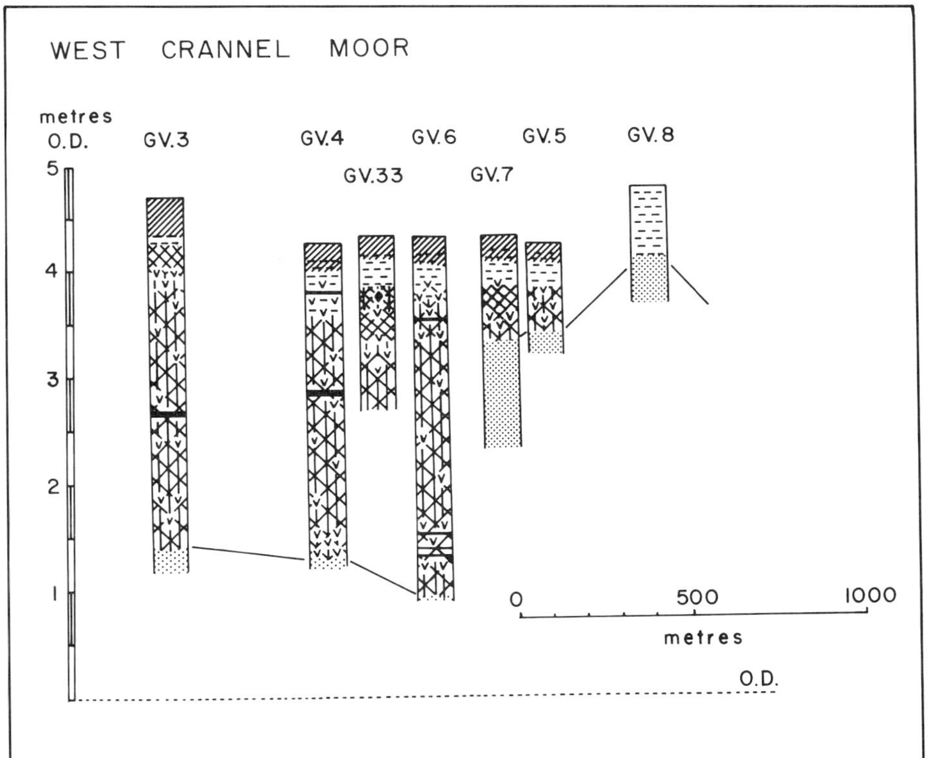

Fig.5.8 West Crannel Moor stratigraphic transect. Dense stipple in GV.5, GV.7 and GV.8: Keuper.

The sedimentary sequence closely resembles that around the Lake Village and on Common Moor, i.e. detritus muds with varying amounts of wood, occasional rootlets and monocotyledon rhizomes dominating. Near the top the coarse detritus muds give way to either very woody peat or to a fine detritus lake mud with macrofossils of *Ceratophyllum demersum* and *Potamogeton*. The pollen from GV.33 records high values of alder from the lake muds suggesting that in as-

Most of the early deposits, i.e. the basal estuarine-marine clay, the *Phragmites* reedswamp and the *Cladium* fen peat need not concern us. The first relevant deposit is the fine detritus lake mud which immediately precedes the upper unit of blue-grey estuarine clay. The position of this mud shows how deeper water conditions were caused by a rising groundwater table in the perimarine zone ahead of the marine incursion. The lake mud grades into dirty clay with *Phragmites* and

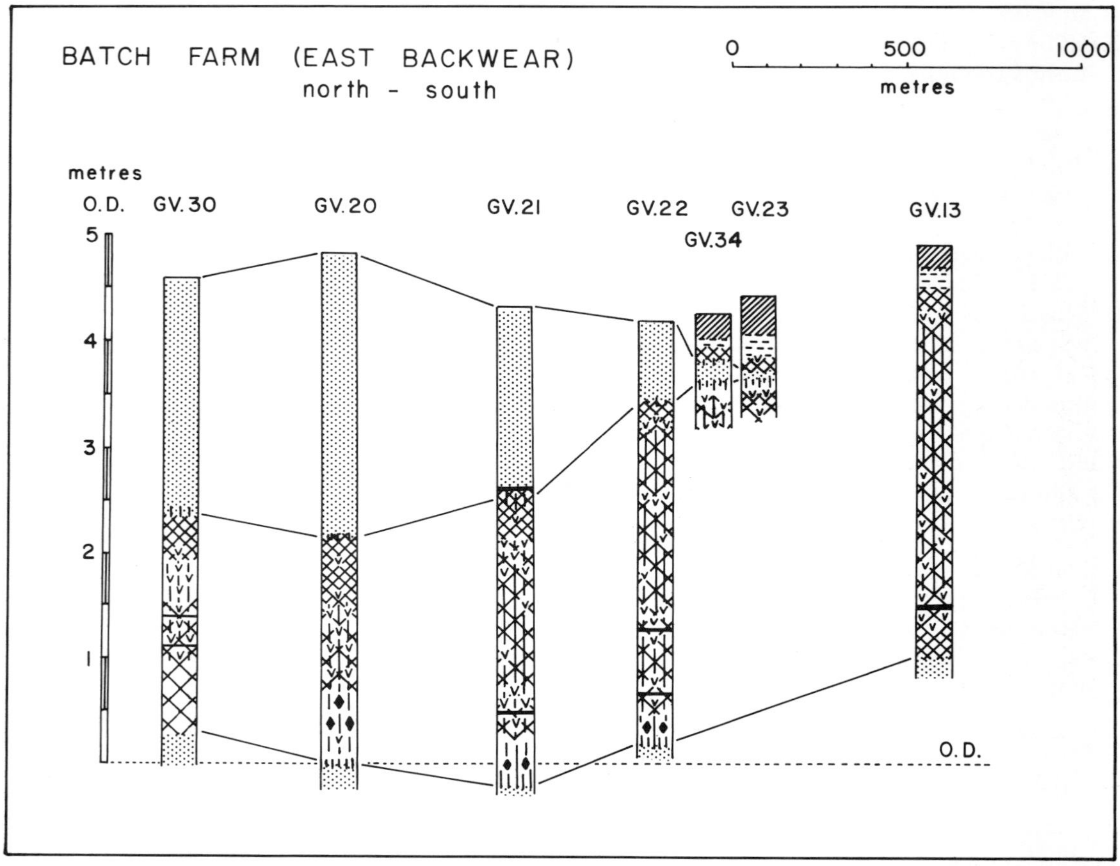

Fig.5.9 Batch Farm (East Backwear) stratigraphic transect, N - S.

monocotyledon rhizomes that marks a very short reedswamp phase before minerogenic deposition commenced. Macfadyen in Godwin (1955,185-190) examined the upper blue-grey clay for foraminifera, diatoms and other microfauna and concluded that it contained two components: an indigenous fauna of brackish water far removed from sea water, and a derived estuarine (almost marine) fauna. Pollen from GV.34 shows the persistent presence of *Chenopodiaceae* throughout reinforcing the saline message of the microfauna.

In many boreholes above the clay there are no more deposits. However in GV.23 and GV.34 further organic deposits occurred. In these boreholes the high water levels continued for a period after the clay ceased deposition. Because of humification it is difficult to characterize the succeeding deposits, however the pollen from GV.34 would suggest that as the high freshwater lake levels started to decline, there was a brief reedswamp phase (high Gramineae: *Phragmites*?), followed by sedge fen (high Cyperaceae) before alluviation commenced. Possibly alluvial clay may have overlapped some of the blue-grey estuarine clay, but if so then soil formation has destroyed any field evidence for this.

GV.24 is slightly different to many other boreholes in this area. At around 3m OD developed a *Sphagnum-Calluna* peat, probably the result of easterly encroachment of raised bog from East Waste. However the oligotrophic conditions could not be maintained. The rising ground water levels caused the *Sphagnum-Calluna* peat to cease, to be replaced by a *Carex* sedge fen peat via an aquatic *Sphagnum* phase. This development with higher ground water conditions continued producing a monocotyledon reedswamp, and culminating in the deposition of a thin band of dirty blue-grey estuarine clay. What happened after the clay is uncertain, because of poor preservation in the upper sediments, however a sequence as GV.23 and GV.34 above the clay is likely.

The final piece of evidence for conditions in the wetlands comes from differences in the proportion of wetland taxa in the two pollen diagrams sited near the centre of the mire, Godwin's GLV 1 (fig.5.1), under M5 of the Lake Village, and Long Run: GV.34 (fig.5.11), on the margins of the Romano-British clay to the north. The points of relevance are the higher amount of alder in the GLV 1 diagram, implying greater local development of alder carr in the vicinity of the village (Bulleid's leafy peat layer on which the substructure of the settlement rested). Secondly, the higher percentage of *Sparganium* type pollen at GLV 1 indicates more open-water around the village. Thirdly, the higher percentages of Gramineae and Cyperaceae pollen at Long Run suggests water levels were lower such that stands of reed and sedge predominated. It is likely that once the sea had regressed, the recently deposited blue-grey clay was colonised by *Phragmites* and other reedswamp grasses and, in areas where the water depth was shallower, by sedges.

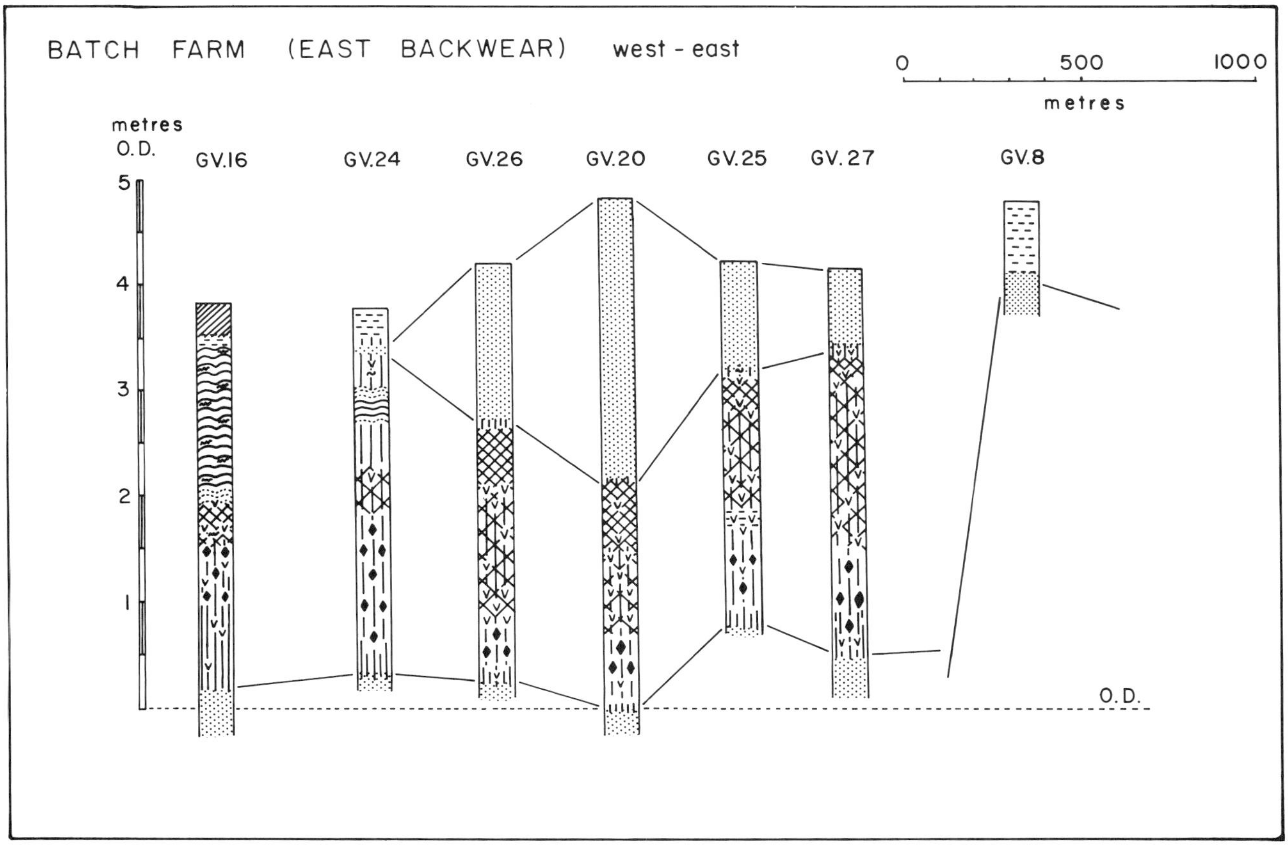

Fig.5.10 Batch Farm (East Backwear) stratigraphic transect, W - E. Dense stipple in GV.8: Keuper.

As the summary map (fig. 5.12) shows, it is possible to divide the area around Glastonbury Lake Village into four regions which have a broadly similar history of environmental development reflecting the influence of local topography and drainage conditions.

East Waste has a sedimentary sequence which is closest to that in the well-studied Shapwick and Meare Heath areas, with a succession from basal estuarine clay, to a *Phragmites* reedswamp, to a *Cladium* fen peat. Above this it differs from the latter in having a woody detritus mud phase before the growth of raised bog. A probable flooding horizon with sedge and hypnoid peat occurs in some profiles, only to revert back to raised bog later. Most of the raised bog is capped by alluvium.

On Common Moor and Crannel Moor the surface of the basal estuarine clay and the Lias margins was rapidly colonised by alder and willow fen carr with associated sedge fen communities. This produced a long series of detritus muds, sedge and wood peats in the lower part of the profiles. Once established, the environment remained remarkably stable for over two millennia, suggesting sedimentation kept pace with rising ground water. Increasingly wetter conditions in the first millennium BC saw the deposition of a fine detrital lake mud. Later, as lake levels fell, sedge and wood peats grew signifying a reversion to fen and fen carr. However this was soon stopped by silting as alluviation took over.

The West Backwear area has a complex sedimentational and vegetational history, to some extent resembling East Waste but with many differences particularly in the lower profiles. It is best seen as transitional between the fen and fen carr region to the east and the reedswamp and raised bog area to the west. Above the basal estuarine clay developed *Phragmites* and monocotyledon reedswamp which was succeeded by fen carr. The length of this fen carr phase varies geographically (longer in east than west). *Cladium* sedge fen followed in the western area, to be replaced by a rootlet mud - perhaps a channel deposit. Eventually after a further fen phase *Sphagnum -Calluna* raised bog grew. But conditions for ombrogenous bog growth were interrupted by a period of detritus mud deposition before raised bog development resumed. A flooding horizon occurred in the upper part of the bog sequence before the surface was covered by alluvium.

Batch Farm and East Backwear initially followed a hydroseral sequence of basal estuarine clay, reedswamp and sedge fen, paralleling the Shapwick and East Waste areas. The hydrosere continued with fen carr, but was interrupted by wetter conditions represented by a fine detrital lake mud. The rise in the water table was a precursor to the deposition of a thick belt of estuarine clay caused by marine incursion of the area. In many places the estuarine clay is the uppermost deposit with the modern soil developed on its surface, however on the margins subsequent organic deposition shows a period

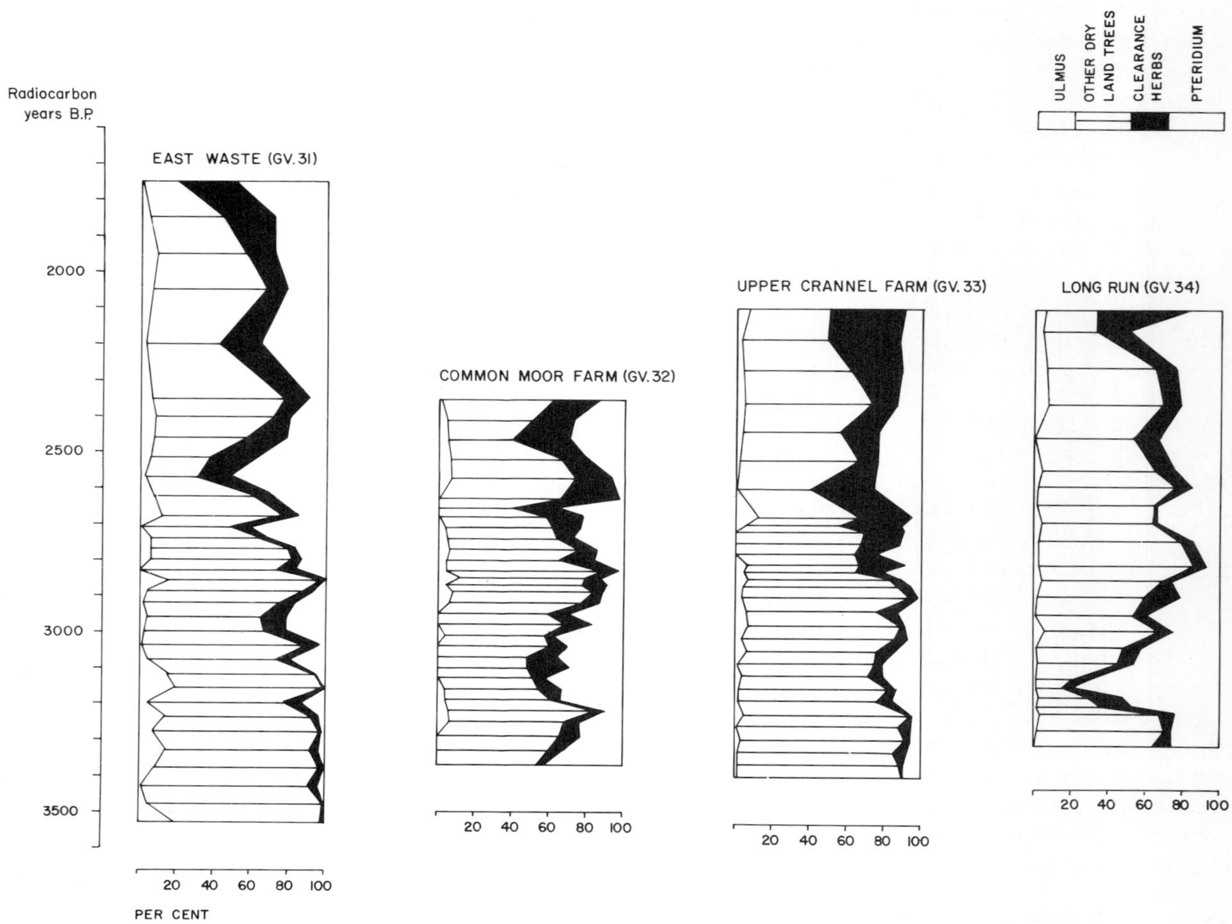

Fig.5.11 Summary diagram of selected taxa from 4 pollen sites around Glastonbury.

of continued high water levels before a succession through reedswamp to sedge fen. This was halted by alluvial silting and soil formation.

The Environment on the Uplands.

There is almost no direct environmental evidence for what conditions were like on the upland areas of Godney, Garslade and Glastonbury. Indirect evidence comes in the form of pollen produced by the vegetation growing on these uplands that has carried into the surrounding mires and been preserved. By examining localities adjacent to the uplands, a picture can be assembled of the plant communities that grew on these dry areas.

Although Godwin's (1955,178-80) GLV 1 pollen diagram from the Lake Village is well placed to provide a picture of the regional pollen rain, a single diagram in the centre of the basin is insufficient to discern local vegetational differences. But in conjunction with three other diagrams (East Waste: GV.31, Common Moor Farm: GV.32, Upper Crannel Farm: GV.33) that show conditions on the dry uplands, and one (Long Run: GV.34) associated with the estuarine-marine clay to the north, it is possible to distinguish the vegetational developments of the different areas.

In the first millennium BC, at the same time as the trend towards a wetter environment in the peatlands was happening, there were changes in the woodland cover of the dry margins. The relative effect of clearance activity on differing areas around the Lake Village can be gauged from the summary diagram of selected taxa (fig.5.11). One of the sites, Long Run, like Godwin's GLV 1, has a more regional pollen influx than the three marginal pollen sites, and not surprisingly the summary plots from both are similar. The most striking feature is the large decrease in dry land trees and corresponding increase in spores of *Pteridium* in the lower half of both profiles. This feature seems to have been of regional significance since it is found on the Meare Heath and the Abbot's Way diagram (Beckett and Hibbert 1979), where it is linked with a decline in *Ulmus*. It is much less apparent in the cores from the margin of the basin, implying that clearance was not taking place on the dry lands of Glastonbury, Godney and Garslade, but rather elsewhere. Higher up the Long Run and GLV 1 profiles there are a series of clearance and regeneration episodes, although no consistent pattern can be discerned. The top of Long Run probably dates to *c* 2100 BP and coincides with a large expansion in clearance herbs and a reduction in dry woodland cover. An approximate age estimate for the top of GLV 1 would be around *c* 2350 BP.

Turning to the three marginal sites, the East Waste summary diagram shows that before *c* 2850 BP inroads into the dry land forest on the Godney ridge were relatively minor - each clearance phase being followed by woodland regeneration. After *c* 2850 BP cycles of clearance and regeneration continue, but the clearances become more extensive and of longer duration. By *c* 2600 BP the influx of clearance herbs had become consistently greater, implying Iron Age activities were demanding more extensive inroads into the woods along the ridge. In the late Iron Age we probably should imagine the emergence of a more open landscape on Godney, with major tree loss having taken place by around *c* 1750 BP.

The Common Moor Farm summary diagram (fig.5.11) contrasts with East Waste in that, at the base, forest clearance seems to have been more extensive on Glastonbury than on Godney. This implies more Bronze Age activity was taking place on Glastonbury and may reflect greater ease of access to that area, since the Glastonbury would have been a promontory, whereas Godney would have been an island surrounded by mire. It appears that the Common Moor diagram shows greater emphasis on clearing larger areas and with less subsequent regeneration. From *c* 2650 BP through into the Iron Age clearance increased on the upland of Glastonbury. However it is not possible to say what the state of woodland cover was when the Lake Village was occupied since the later Iron Age is not covered by this diagram.

The Upper Crannel Farm summary diagram (fig.5.11) shows an intermediate picture between that of East Waste and Common Moor Farm. In the Bronze Age the woodland cover around Garslade may have been heavier than on Glastonbury but lighter than on Godney. Before *c* 2850 BP clearances were relatively restricted, with woodland regeneration between phases of activity. After *c* 2850 BP there is greater evidence for human impact as dry land trees decline and clearance herbs increase. By *c* 2100-2200 BP the proportion of clearance herbs at Upper Crannel Farm had reached 40%, and linked to a persistent record of cereal type pollen showing that late Iron Age arable agriculture was well underway nearby.

The Environmental Context of Glastonbury.

It may seem obvious, but it is worth emphasizing that the site was built and occupied when the environment was wet. Glastonbury was not a dryland site which subsequently became flooded and drowned. The alder-willow fen carr would have been firmer than the surrounding deposits, but it still required the building of strong foundations. To say Glastonbury was a lake settlement is true in one sense, depending on what type of lake is envisaged. Unlike some of the Alpine lake villages, it was not situated on the edge of a large deep steep-sided lake. The depositional regime was mostly organic with peats and muds rather than minerogenic with clays and silts. Nutrient conditions in the water probably varied, ranging from oligotrophic close to the raised bogs to the west, to mesotrophic and eutrophic conditions closer to the settlement. Water depths were probably mostly shallow except for a few deeper channels. Water flow would have been slow to almost negligible. The presence of reeds, rushes, sedges, and trees such as alder and willow would suggest that a more accurate description of the surrounding environment would be a tree swamp or fen carr, and that the settlement was a swamp village rather than a lake village. However the presence of open shallow (relative to deep lakes but deeper and more open than in earlier periods) freshwater round the site itself is attested by the occurrence of fine detrital lake mud with floating leaved aquatic plant remains at the top of many of the cores around the settlement. In essence the picture that emerges is of a giant crannog (giant in the sense that most crannogs had no more than one or two houses) built on a pre-existing clump of cleared alder and willow fen carr surrounded by an area of shallow openwater lake with attendant stands of reedswamp, sedge fen and fen carr. But to envisage the area around the Lake Village as a uniform environment is almost certainly wrong. By the Iron Age the diversity of environment in the Brue valley was probably very high, in part due to the actions of humans but in part due to sea-level changes and the amount of time the environment had had to develop differing ecological niches. It is therefore probably better to see it as a varied mosaic of different plant communities, each needing differing water depths, nutrient conditions, types of rooting strata, flow tolerances and of differing potential exploitative value to man.

To some extent the water conditions near the site can be inferred from the species of fish which Bulleid and Gray recovered, although it is possible that the 'catch' could have been brought to site from some distance away. The presence of perch, which dislikes opaque muddy conditions, implies that the water had little silt or clay sediment load. The change to alluvial deposition was thus not yet important in the Levels. The presence of shad may be significant, with its preference for estuarine environments. Godwin thought the estuarine clay was Romano-British in age - based on the discovery of third century AD archaeological finds within it - however the radiocarbon dates indicate otherwise. In fact the Romano-British clay, deposited north of the Village between *c* 2850-2500 BP, should be correlated with Godwin's first flooding horizon. The remains of shad cannot therefore be associated with this event. However it is possible that the final phase of Glastonbury coincided with Godwin's second flooding horizon dated to *c* 2060-1900 BP at Meare Heath (Beckett and Hibbert 1979). This second horizon may be due to sea-level changes, although this cannot be so well demonstrated as for the first. But if the second horizon was also due to marine incursion then estuarine conditions may well have existed in the Iron Age only a few miles to the north of the Lake Village, perhaps (based on Godwin's Drakes Drove profile) north of Panborough-Bleadney in the upper Axe Valley.

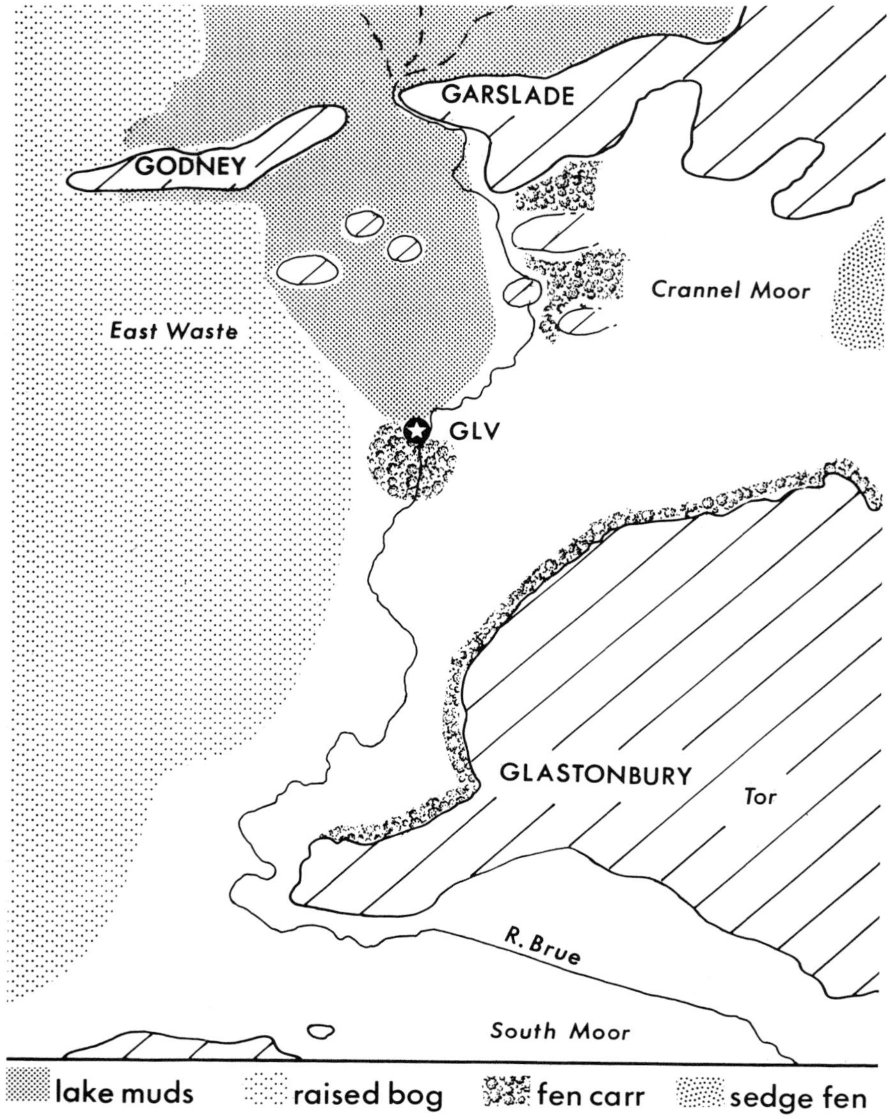

Fig.5.12 Map of the area around the Lake Village with the approximate extent of raised bog, estuarine lake muds, fen carr and sedge fen in the later first millenium B.C. The unshaded area is the Glastonbury swamp. The hatched area is upland over 8m O.D. except small islands which are lower. The line of the river is its medieval course; in the Iron Age it was probably more diffuse. JMC

An attempt will now be made to pull together all the strands of evidence to present an integrated picture of the environment around the Iron Age settlement at the time the site was occupied. If one had been able to look out from Glastonbury during the time of occupation, to the west one would have seen ombrogenous raised bog blocking the drainage of what is today the central Brue valley. To the north and out to the far west (well beyond the raised bogs) would be expanses of estuarine-marine clay colonised by *Typha* and Cyperaceae sedge fen, whilst in the then lower Brue (today the Axe valley) the sea continued to deposit the same blue-grey estuarine clay. In the eastern part of the Brue valley, around the Lake Village, expanses of reedswamp, sedge fen, fen carr and shallow water lake plant communities predominated. On the dry upland margins the forests had begun to be extensively cleared - a process that ultimately would lead to the decisive change in character of the landscape as organic-rich marsh and mire gave way to water meadows and alluvial grassland. The Iron Age settlement would have been sited on a clump of alder-willow fen carr whilst *Carex* and *Cladium* sedge fen circled the palisade. Surrounding both would be a shallow open freshwater lake. In one sense Glastonbury could be described as a true lake village, although one might perhaps more accurately describe it as a mire or swamp settlement. The wetter conditions may have in part been due to the onset of climatic deterioration in the latter half of the first millennium BC, however the more important factor would seem to have been a rise in relative sea-level. Although the estuarine-marine clay had long ceased to be deposited on the doorstep by the time the Iron Age inhabitants arrived to clear the alder fen carr and build their settlement, the regressive cycle may well have been temporarily reversed if the second flooding horizon in the raised bogs is any indication, although this reversal - if it occurred - did not bring the sea back to the edge of the village as in earlier centuries. The proximity of the sea cannot be totally dismissed though as shown by the bones of the white-tailed sea eagle, the cormorant and the puffin that Bulleid and Gray uncovered in the settlement.

Chapter 6.

The Material Culture and On-site Activity.

6.1 INTRODUCTION

An exceptional amount of artefactual material was excavated at the Glastonbury Lake Village. The small find reports in Bulleid and Gray's Volumes 1 and 2 provide detailed catalogues of much of this archive. Resources were not available to enable a comprehensive re-examination of this material in the light of modern research, nor would such a course of action have equated with our primary aims. However, some categories of artefact, such as the evidence for metalworking, received minimal attention from Bulleid and Gray, and to help broaden our understanding of the settlement and its on-site activities a number of specialist reports on this and other aspects considered to be of particular significance were prepared and appear below. The opportunity was also taken to incorporate some of the results of other research undertaken on the artefacts in recent years. The result is, perhaps, that the Chapter is unbalanced in its treatment of the evidence but no apology is made for this and readers are referred back to the original publications for more information on the finds.

Wherever possible and appropriate the following sections attempt to pinpoint specific areas of activity in

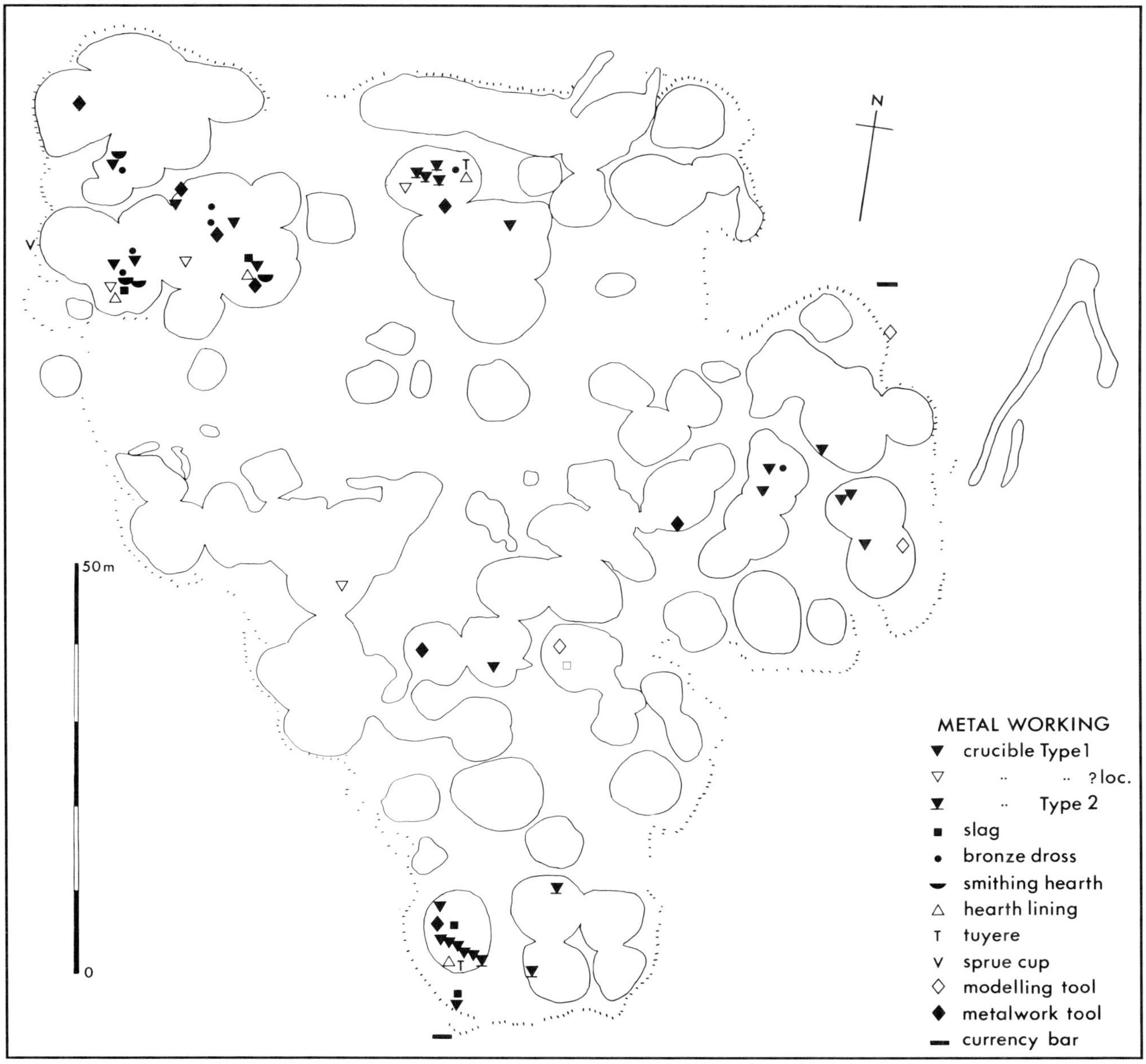

Fig.6.1 Distribution of metalworking debris and artefacts. SCM and JMC

terms of location and Phase. For much of the material this potential is severely limited by the excavators' recording; 68% of the artefacts either derive from areas outside the Mounds or come from within a Mound but lack contextual data. Both categories are effectively unstratified and can only provide hints as to their significance.

6.2 FERROUS AND NON-FERROUS METALWORKING

By Catherine Mortimer and David Starley

Evidence from the settlement included debris from both ferrous and non-ferrous metalworking. The exact nature of this activity is not made clear in the original publication of the site where the term 'smelting' is applied to any high temperature process involving metals. In this report **smelting** is used in its more specific current usage to indicate the primary production of a metal from its ore, **smithing** refers to the hot workings of metal, whilst **melting** indicates heating prior to casting of (in this instance, non-ferrous) objects. Similarly, Bulleid and Gray use the term 'furnace' for any structure in which high temperature metal processing appears to have been carried out. This report will follow the current convention in which a **furnace** is an enclosed structure for the smelting of metal ores and a **hearth** is a much more open structure without specific purpose, unless further qualified, for instance as a **smithing hearth** for the hot working of iron. The fired clay structures described in the original report would therefore be termed hearths. In the absence of samples from these hearths, which could be checked for any vitrification resulting from temperatures in excess of those expected in domestic hearths, metalworking activities in them can only be identified from any closely associated metalworking debris.

The surviving 'slag' totals 6kg, a relatively small amount for any but very short term ironworking activity. The stored material appears to match the descriptions given in the report although the slag was quantified there only in the most general terms, such as 'some fragments'. It seems reasonable to assume that the retained assemblage has survived fairly complete, however, the effectiveness and commitment of the excavators in recovering slag is not known. Contextual descriptions are, at best, to Mound number and Floor level but more commonly only to Mound number. Approximately one third of the slag lacked all provenance data. The assemblage is reported to have included unfinished items of iron, but no specifically metalworking tools have survived to be listed in the report.

It is not known whether the recorded non-ferrous metalworking debris is representative of the total assemblage at the site. It seems likely that most ceramic material would have been retained, since pottery has long held an important place in archaeological studies. However, it is curious that most of the crucible fragments are relatively large and it is probable that further small pieces were overlooked during excavation. Bulleid and Gray clearly recognised the importance of the crucible finds and devoted some effort to considering their significance, although there was little comparative material known at the time. No moulds were recovered or recognised at the site. Mould fragments may not have survived because they are not as highly-fired as crucibles. Fragments from 25 'crucibles' (the term includes pieces unlikely to have been used in metalworking, see below) and 4 pieces of metalworking dross were examined. The metal content of 17 lead, tin and lead-tin objects was also determined; these included two bars, a piece thought to be ore and an amorphous piece, all of which may have some relation to metalworking.

Table 6.1: Summary of slags and ferrous metalworking debris

Context	*Weight (gm)*	*Interpretation/comments*
Between M4 & M5	467	vitrified hearth lining
M5	1123	vitrified hearth lining
M5	5	fuel ash slag
M5	51	cinder
M5	49	ironworking slag
M5 W	108	ironworking slag
M5 W	13	ironworking slag
M5 W	84	vitrified hearth lining
M62 Floor 2	2200	tuyère block (D 30)
M67 S of	84	vitrified hearth lining
M71	265	smithing hearth bottom 85x85x40mm
M75, base of	224	dense ironworking slag
M75, base of	117	fragment of smithing hearth bottom
M75, base of	30	fuel ash slag
M75, base of	68	vitrified hearth lining
M75, base of	80	ironworking slag
M75, base of	28	cinder
M76	220	smithing hearth bottom 105x80x40mm cindery
M76	357	smithing hearth bottom 105x80x50mm
M76	295	vitrified hearth lining
M76	115	fuel ash slag
M76	84	fragment of smithing hearth bottom
M76 Floor 3	1	fuel ash slag
M76 Floor 2	383	ironworking slag
M76 Floor 2	36	vitrified hearth lining
Unstrat	235	smithing hearth bottom 95x80x35mm very cindery
Unstrat	184	smithing hearth bottom 100x80x35mm very cindery
Unstrat	228	smithing hearth bottom 100x85x35mm very cindery
Unstrat	741	ironworking slag
Unstrat	203	fragments of tuyère block
Unstrat	543	vitrified hearth lining
Unstrat	147	cinder
Unstrat	50	dense ironworking slag
Unstrat	7	fuel ash slag

Slags and ferrous metalworking debris. (DS)

All available slag was examined visually, classified to type and weighed separately.

Table 6.2: Slag weight totals

slag type	*kg*
smithing hearth bottoms	1.69
dense ironworking slag	0.27
undiagnostic ironworking slag	1.37
tuyère block	2.42
vitrified hearth/furnace lining	2.70
cinder	0.23
fuel ash slag	0.16
total	8.85

The most diagnostic debris was that classified as **smithing hearth bottoms**. These slag blocks are recognisable by their characteristic plano-convex form, having a rough underside and a smoother, vitrified upper surface often hollowed as a result of downwards pressure from the air blast of the tuyère. Hearth bottoms are normally largely fayalitic (iron silicate) in composition, resulting from high temperature reactions between the iron, iron scale and silica from either the sand used as flux or from the hearth lining during the smithing *i.e.* hot working of iron. The Glastonbury smithing hearth bottoms were unusual in being poorly consolidated, being easily broken apart by hand. Qualitative X-ray fluorescence (XRF) analysis showed unusually high levels of calcium, phosphorus and sulphur. The enhanced contents of these elements might be explained by the use of peat as a fuel during ironsmithing; analyses have shown peat to have higher levels of these elements than charcoal (Percy 1861,76; Tylecote 1986,224). The weight and dimensions of these six smithing hearth bottoms are also very small in comparison with those of any other period.

Table 6.3: Smithing hearth bottom dimensions

	range	mean	std. dev.
weight (gm)	180-360	250	50
length (mm)	85-105	100	10
width (mm)	80-85	80	2
depth (mm)	35-50	40	5

The contrast between the crumbly smithing hearth bottoms and the **dense iron working slags** suggests that the latter may derive from a different process. Similar material is known to be produced during iron smelting, i.e. the primary production of metallic iron from its ores. However, the limited quantities of this category and lack of supporting evidence would strongly imply that iron smelting was not being carried out in the settlement.

Another major component of the assemblage was that initially classified as **undiagnostic ironworking slag** because it could not be attributed to either smithing or smelting on morphological grounds. This material was, however, sufficiently similar to the 'crumbly' hearth bottoms to suggest that its origin was also ironsmithing.

The largest category by weight in the assemblage was that identified as **tuyère block**, the remains of removable fired clay nozzles for the inlet of air into a furnace or hearth. Item D 30 consisted of a largely complete tuyère block, the furnace end of which had been reconstructed with plaster of paris preventing examination of any heat/slag modified structure. Three further fragments of tuyère block (two of which could be fitted together), from an unstratified context showed moderate vitrification on the surface. It was not possible to determine the high temperature process from which these derived. A further tuyère block (D 78) was also found at the site but has not survived for examination.

Another large component of the assemblage was the **vitrified hearth/furnace lining** which may derive from structures used for iron smelting, ironsmithing or other high temperature process and is therefore not diagnostic. The material forms as a result of high temperature reactions between the clay lining of the hearth/furnace and the alkali fuel ashes or fayalitic slag. A compositional gradient from unmodified clay on one surface to an irregular cindery material on the other may be evident. An associated material, classed as **cinder**, comprises only the lighter portion of this, a porous, hard and brittle slag formed as a result of high temperature reactions between the alkali fuel ashes and either fragments of clay which had spalled away from the hearth/furnace lining or another source of silica, such as the sand used as flux during smithing.

Much smaller amounts of material were classified as **fuel ash slag**, a very lightweight, light coloured (grey-brown), highly porous material which results from the reaction between alkaline fuel ash and silicates from soil, sand or clay at elevated temperatures. The reaction is shared by many pyrotechnological processes and the slag is not diagnostic.

The largest number of diagnostic ferrous metalworking finds came from M5, M75 and M76, comprising 49% of the extant sample by weight (86% when only stratified material is considered). The number of finds is insufficient to suggest any difference in assemblage type between these three Mounds. Vitrified hearth lining, fuel ash slag and cinder were also found mainly in these Mounds, where stratified.

The metalworking assemblage from Glastonbury Lake Village, although small in size, contained a variety of ironworking debris. The only fully diagnostic slags were those associated with ironsmithing, i.e. hot working of iron, and it is likely that most of the undiagnostic slags also derive from smithing rather than smelting activities. The only possible evidence for iron smelting was a few uncharacteristically well-consolidated 'dense ironworking slags'. The surviving assemblage from Glastonbury is insufficient to support suggestions that ironsmithing and particularly iron smelting were important activities on the site, which would have produced much larger quantities of metalworking debris.

Non-ferrous metalwork and metalworking debris. (CM)

Three types of fired pottery which had been classified as metalworking **crucibles** by the excavators were examined. Although a representative sample remains for investigation, several of these finds now cannot be located. Metalwork from the site was not examined.

The most obvious metalworking crucible debris consists of fragments from vessels which are triangular in plan (**type 1** in Table 6.4). Nine examples of these crucibles came from in and near M5, where a tuyère (D 78) and other high temperature debris were also discovered (see above). Findspots for the other type 1 crucibles were scattered across the settlement, with two examples being found in M76, two in M24, two in M74 and five other individual finds from various Mounds. The fabric of these crucibles is generally rather friable, except at the edges of some examples, where vitrification has taken place.

The second most common form of fired pottery is the thumb pot (**type 2** in Table 6.4), of which six provenanced examples are known, three from M62 and three from other Mounds. These are of various sizes, some very small (e.g. C 14, 20mm high) and others rather taller (e.g. C 9, 44mm high). These pieces are not heavily vitrified but they are, at least in part, reduced fired (some are oxidised fired at the base).

There are also three examples of a square-sided vessel form (**type 3**), which may also have been used for high-temperature purposes. Two of these were found in M62, as was an unusual small pot (C 12), possibly with a handle, which may have been used in high-temperature work. These pieces are not highly vitrified but are instead oxidised fired; this suggests that these examples are unlikely to have been used in metal melting procedures.

The association of the tuyère D 30 with the thumb pots C 9 to C 11 may be significant. Conversely, the lack of association between type 1 and type 2 crucible forms may also have some significance. Type 1 and 2 crucibles are typical of those found in other Iron Age contexts (Tylecote 1985,96-100) but parallels for the type 3 vessel form are not known.

All available fragments were submitted to surface XRF analysis in an attempt to identify types of metalworking that were carried out at the site. Analysis was concentrated on areas with evidence of vitrification or metal deposits. Many of the analyses did not demonstrate substantial evidence for non-ferrous metalworking activities; this may be due to surface loss during deposition, to washing after discovery or to metalworking processes which leave little trace on the available surfaces. Where pieces are oxidised fired, it is unlikely that metal melting was carried out.

Table 6.4: Analyses of crucibles

Number	Context	Type	Elements
C 1	M22	1	Cu Sn
C 2	M23	3	-
C 3?	M44	1?	Cu Sn (Pb)
C 4	M24	1	Cu Sn
C 5	M45	1	Cu (Pb)
C 7	M24	1	Sn Cu Pb (Zn)
C 8	M62 Floor 2	3	(Cu)
C 9	M62 Floor 2	2	-
C 12	M62 Floor 2	handle	-
C 13	M62 Floor 2	3	(Cu)
C 14	M64	2 small	(Cu)
C 15	M5 SW of	1?	Cu Pb (Sn)
C 16	M4 Floor 1	2?	Zn
C 17	M5 Floor 2	1	Cu Pb Zn (Sn)
C 18	M5 Floor 5	1	Zn
C 19	M5 Floor 5	1	Cu
C 20	M5 Floor 5	1	-
C 21	M5 Floor 5	1	Cu Zn (Pb)
C 25	M71 Floor 2	1	Zn (Cu)
C 26	M76 Floor 2	1	-
C 27	M76 Floor 2	1	Cu Pb (Sn)
C 29	M74 Floor 4	1	Cu Pb (Zn)
C 34	M29	1	**Cu Sn** Pb
D 49	M?	2 large	Zn (Cu) (Pb)
D 57	M5	2 small	(Cu)

Codes for Table 6.4:
Elements: Cu = copper, Sn = tin, Pb = lead, Zn = zinc.

Iron was detected in all samples analysed and is therefore not noted separately.

All peaks were relatively weak except those in **bold**, which are strong and those in brackets which are very small.

Type 1 (triangular) crucibles show the clearest evidence for copper-alloy working at the site. Analysis showed that many of the fragments have traces of copper, tin, lead and zinc on their surfaces in varying proportions; iron is normally present in clays and therefore in crucibles. The proportions of the elements detected are unlikely to be helpful in establishing the exact type of metal used. Zinc is a volatile element (it 'boils off' on heating) and a glass-forming element, so small amounts of zinc are often present, even amongst bronze working debris; copper alloys containing significant amounts of zinc are unlikely to be found at this period.

The type 2 (thumb-pot) and type 3 (square-sided) vessels show very low levels of non-ferrous metal concentration on the surfaces available for analysis (inside surfaces could not be analysed). Some of the metals detected may be present because of contamination in the burial environment. It is possible that a different type of metalworking - at lower temperatures - was carried out in these vessels or that they were not used. The oxidised-fired examples are unlikely to have been used in metal melting.

The non-ferrous metalworking carried out on the site

is most likely to have been copper-alloy melting and casting. Bronzes (copper-tin alloys) are the copper alloy most likely to have been used.

Four pieces of amorphous non-ferrous **dross** were examined and analysed using XRF. A further eight fragments were recorded at the site but were not submitted for analysis.

Table 6.5: Analysis of non-ferrous dross

Numbers	Context	Elements/comments
E 36	M62	**Sn** (Pb)
E 172	M5 NW of	**Cu** Sn (Pb)
E 253	M74 Floor 5	**Cu Sn** Pb
E 268	M75 Floor 3	**Cu**

Zinc was not detected in any of the pieces. Iron was detected in all cases, as a contaminant from the soil.

Such metal droplets are often found at non-ferrous metalworking sites, indicating the spillage of small amounts of metal during casting. Analysis of the four extant pieces confirm that bronzeworking took place in or around M5, M74 and M75. The distribution of the recorded dross fragments conforms with the general pattern of crucible distribution. There are slight indications of correlation between dross composition and ceramic form/use; M62 produced a piece of tin-rich dross together with type 2 and type 3 fragments, M5 and M74 both produced a piece of copper and tin-rich dross and type 1 crucibles. This could be taken to strengthen the argument that the different 'crucible' forms were used for different processes, but the data are by no means conclusive.

Recycling may have been employed, ensuring that most scrap metal was recovered and reused.

Many **lead, tin and lead-tin objects** were recovered from the site. A selection was submitted for analysis. The original excavation report successfully identified the alloy type in most cases. Some compositional patterning can be detected amongst these objects. The five 'sinkers' are made of lead, with traces of copper occasionally detected. Apart from the sinkers there are three objects made out of pure lead, or lead with only traces of tin or copper (a spindle whorl, a roll and a ring) and a fragment labelled as 'ore'. The 'ore' is unlikely to have been galena, since it did not have the characteristic cubic form, but may have been the product of a metal refining process. L 33, L 34 and L 27 may have similar derivation. None occur in Mounds with indications of working metal of low melting point. L 38 from M71 Floor 2, on the other hand, is galena. Three objects are made out of tin, or tin with only small amounts of lead or copper (two bars - including the 'sceptre', see below - and a spindle whorl). Four objects have substantial amounts of both lead and tin present (two spindle whorls, a lump/dribble and a bar). The 'sceptre' (L 50) is confirmed as being a tin bar with leaded bronze terminals. It is not possible to determine

Table 6.6: Extant lead, tin and lead-tin alloy objects

Number	Context	Object	XRF/comment
L 2	M47	Sinker	**Pb** (Cu)
L 3	M47	Sinker	**Pb**
L 11	M44	Bar	**Pb Sn**
L 13	M49 N of	Whorl	**Sn** (Pb) (Cu)
L 15	M7	Ring	**Pb**
L 20	M18 Floor 4	Whorl	**Pb Sn** (Cu)
L 23	M11 Floor 2	Lump/ dribble?	**SnPb** (Cu)
L 26	M6	Pendant	**Sn**(Cu)
L 29	M4 Floor 1	Whorl	**Pb Sn**
L 31	M47	Sinker	**Pb**
L 39	M83 Floor 1	Whorl	**Pb**
L 40	M47	Sinker	**Pb**
L 43	M47	Sinker	**Pb**
L 46	M?	Roll/weight	**Pb**
L 48	M?	Ore	**Pb**
L 49	M75 Floor 4	Bar	**Sn** (Pb)
L 50	M7 NW of	Bar/sceptre (on main body)	**Sn** (Pb)
		(at end)	**Cu Sn** Pb(Zn)

Iron was present in all samples, although at a lower level than in the copper-alloy dross.

the precise composition of the bronze, without further sampling; the heavy corrosion in this area suggests that sampling would have to be very destructive indeed. The surface analysis did not reveal any gold, which had been detected during the earlier investigations, nor is there any visual evidence for gilding. (see p. 206)

The four spindle whorls are made of three different types of metal. This could suggest that tin and lead were not clearly differentiated at this time, both having low melting temperatures and being malleable at room temperature; however, the five sinkers are all made of lead. The lump of lead 'ore' (L 48) and the tin-lead lump/dribble (L 23) with a 'melted' appearance suggest that lead may have been exploited and tin-lead alloys may have been worked at the site, although none of the analytic evidence from crucible fragments confirms all this. Unusual characteristics of ore fragments (visual appearance and weight) may have caused L 48 to be retained out of curiosity, rather than for use and L 23 may be an accidentally-melted object, since tin-lead alloys melt at low temperatures, which are found in a domestic fire. None of the findspots for the lead, tin and lead-tin objects has any significant correlation with findspots for non-ferrous metalworking debris.

The non-ferrous metalworking evidence is sufficient to suggest that copper alloys were melted and cast at the site. Three types of fired pottery were identified, two of which were likely to have been crucibles and the third possibly for another type of high-temperature industry. The two different types of crucible may have been used for different processes.

- Ancient Monuments Laboratory Report 53/93

Metalworking summary. (SCM)

Evidence for copper alloy and iron working was found for the Early, Middle and Late Phases with the Middle Phase apparently seeing the height of the activity. Metalworking was primarily focussed upon M5 in the south and M76 and, to a lesser extent, M75 in the north west. There was some very minor activity in the east (fig.6.1). The surviving data shows copper alloy and ironworking to have occurred on the same Floor in some instances; poor recording probably conceals other instances. Floor 5 of M5 (Middle Phase) may have been for copper alloy working only although slag, vitrified hearth lining and fuel ash slag demonstrate that iron working also took place at an indeterminate level within the Mound. M76 produced evidence for both copper alloy and iron working on Floors 3 and 2 (Early and Middle Phases). The presence of copper alloy 'dross and fragments' may also indicate some activity on the latest Floor. Small quantities of ash were found on Floor 2 whilst Floor 3 was covered with fire ash and slag reaching a depth of 170mm in places. Floor 3 was therefore presumably the site of the greatest metalworking activity. Unfortunately the three smithing hearth bottoms from M76 have no Floor attribution. There is some evidence for copper alloy working on Floor 4 of M75 (Early Phase), a crucible and small amounts of slag, but ironworking occurred on this site prior to the laying down of the Floor.

A crucible, charcoal and fused copper alloy in the SW quadrant of Floor 2, M71 (Late Phase) suggests copper alloy working there as does the presence of a crucible and dross on Floor 4 of M74 (Middle Phase). There is a broad scatter of crucible finds from Mounds 3, 4, 16, 22, 24, 29, 44, 64 and 73 but none provided other evidence and are therefore most unlikely to have been metalworking sites. In this context it is regrettable that the three smithing hearth bottoms and tuyère block fragments newly recognised during the recent processing of the metalworking debris (see above) have no provenance.

Floor 2 of M62 (Middle Phase) was probably used for metalworking but the nature of the activity is more problematical. This Floor produced the main concentration of type 2 (thumb nail) crucibles, two square-sided vessels of type 3, a tuyère and probable fragments from a metalworker's hearth. XRF analysis of the type 2 crucibles was inconclusive (see above) but the presence of the other material lends support to the suggestion of lower temperature metalworking. M62 also produced the fragment of dross, E 36, now identified as tin rather than copper alloy.

All four of the main metalworking sites (M5, M75, M76 and M62) were located on clay spreads rather than within buildings. Only M62 had evidence for any kind of contemporary superstructure; this comprised a shelter or substantial windbreak on the east and north sides. Quantities of ash, baked daub and charcoal and charred wall-posts show that this structure burnt down.

Metalworking took place for only a limited period in the history of each Mound and recorded artefacts show that different activities usually occurred on preceding and succeeding Floors. In this sense M76 was unusual, as metalworking appears to have taken place throughout most, if not the whole period, of its use.

Few other types of metalworking-related artefact were found. There were no metalworkers' tools such as heavy hammers and tongs which would certainly have been required for the processes represented. There are no moulds or mould fragments amongst the clay and stone artefacts. S 1 from M44 was identified by Bulleid and Gray (1917,624) as a possible mould but this can now be discounted (F. Roe pers. comm.). The absence of moulds has led to the suggestion that casting took place away from the settlement and that the crucibles and tuyères were simply on site being looked after, rather than used, by the smiths (Howard 1983,384-385). This argument was further supported by the presumed danger of undertaking such work inside timber buildings, something which we know not to have been the case. More plausible is the likelihood that the excavators did not recognise mould fragments among the assemblage, in which case they would probably not have been retained. Only very modest amounts of baked clay were preserved. Some weight is given to the probability of on-site casting by the presence of a possible sprue cup, D 50, found outside the palisade to the E of M72.

Bulleid and Gray and, more recently, Vanessa Fell (1990,339-363) identified a number of iron tools for the cold-working of metal. X-radiography of the miscellaneous unidentified pieces of iron would probably reveal more. The seven definite or probable files and one small hammerhead derive from contexts across the site. The pieces consist of:

Files:
- I 3 from M62
- I 47 from M42 Floor 1
- I 81 from below M5
- I 84 from M15
- I 98 from M74
- I 102 from M74 Floor 3

Possible file:
- I 107 from M75 Floor 2

Hammerhead:
- I 90 from below M70

The hammerhead, which retains carbonized traces of its wooden handle, is only 58mm in length and must accordingly have been used for a relatively light industrial or craft purpose, not necessarily metalworking. Similarly, it should not be forgotten that files were also used for working other materials such as antler and bone.

Fell (1990,231) identified a range of other artefacts possibly, though by no means certainly, used in connection with metalworking: three copper alloy tools (E 75, E 109, E 140), antler mallets and the bone and antler modelling tools referred to below. The various fragments of sheet bronze and dome-headed rivets may be testimony to the working of sheet bronze on-site. Rivets, in particular, occur widely across the site, but rarely in circumstances indicative of the working metal. The main exception is M5 Floor 2 where two rivet heads were found along with a crucible (C 17), punch (E 140) and antler hammer (H 236). Bulleid and Gray were of the opinion that the rivetted sheet metal repairs carried out on bowl E 19 were probable evidence for on-site working.

Three bone and antler tools, B 148, B 205 and H 3 have been identified as possible modelling tools for shaping the wax during the mould-making process (Wainwright 1979,141). The argument is based on their close resemblance to four bone implements from pit 209 at Gussage All Saints believed to have been used for this purpose. There is no direct association between these objects and the working of metal at Glastonbury Lake Village but mould-making need not have taken place at the same location as casting.

Two iron currency bars were found, one N of M48 and the other S of M5. Widely accepted as being ingots normally destined to be forged into tools, they are clearly a part of the metalworking process. In the absence of evidence for iron smelting it is probable that the source of iron for smithing was currency bars and/or scrap. Both surviving currency bars, however, were found outside the palisade and lacked any recorded associations. It is difficult to conceive of them having simply been lost, even less likely thrown away. Hingley (1990,101) draws attention to the widespread occurrence of currency bars found, both singly and in hoards, in association with Iron Age defences and settlement perimeters and has proposed that they represent ritual deposits. The Lake Village currency bars were included in Hingley's argument and it is possible that this may account for their location. Whether it is significant or not is unknown but both were found in fairly close proximity to human skull fragments, M 7a and M 7b in the case of Z 2 and M 23 in the case of Z 3.

Whetstones were found widely across the site although recording by Mound seems only to have begun on any scale with the arrival of Gray. The surviving stonework produced 54 whetstones to which can be added a number of multi-purpose tools (see 6.9 below), very few provenanced to a Floor. Whetstones could have been used for finishing off newly made objects of metal or re-sharpening existing ones. The provenanced whetstones bear no proven relation to the sites of metal-working.

Hilary Howard (1983,373-384) examined examples of crucibles type 1, 2 and 3 microscopically. From a technological point of view the Glastonbury Lake Village refractory material is unusual in that a high proportion was fired to a vitrification temperature. Clement Reid (Bulleid and Gray 1917,300) considered the origin of the raw materials used in the making of the crucibles and suggested the fire clay or gannister beds of Bristol coalfields. Howard took samples from the Nettlebridge and Blackers Hill areas in an attempt to source the clay. Whilst no precise match was found in the limited number of samples taken, the indications are that the Coal Measure clays were the probable source of the type 1 triangular crucibles, some 20km NE of Glastonbury Lake Village.

An unusually large number of lead and tin objects was found. In the case of lead this is almost certainly a reflection of the proximity of the site to the ore source on Mendip, though it must be said that Iron Age exploitation of Mendip lead still remains to be conclusively, archaeologically or scientifically, proven. Bulleid and Gray published the results of 15 metal identifications of lead and tin artefacts by Dr. Gladstone based upon their specific gravities (1911,245-247). Recent analyses, listed above, show the situation to have been more complex than Gladstone appreciated in that mixing of lead and tin was occurring. Four objects described as tin by Gladstone, when analysed by XRF, proved to be of both metals (L 11, L 20, L 23 and L 29). Other examples may exist among those pieces not re-examined. There was, nevertheless, an unusually large amount of tin present, which has no local source. Of particular note is the 'sceptre' L 50.

Overall the evidence clearly demonstrates the smithing of iron, melting and, presumably, casting of copper alloy, the probable melting of metal of low melting point and the coldworking of metal. The quantity of the surviving evidence shows, however, that all were done at a relatively modest level, almost certainly catering for no more than the needs of the settlement's inhabitants. This situation is paralleled on other non-hillfort Iron Age sites in southern Britain.

6.3 BONE AND ANTLER WORKING

By Tina Tuohy

The 1911 and 1917 volumes on the Lake Village gave descriptions backed up by drawings and photographs of much of the worked antler and bone. The aim of this report is to supplement the original by looking at some of the objects in detail with regard to manufacture and use.

396 specimens of worked antler were given find numbers; of these 81 were combs. The majority of antler is of red deer (*Cervus elaphus*) with a small amount of roe deer (*Capreolus capreolus*). Antler differs from bone in that it is solid throughout. There is an outer layer of compact bone and an inner 'spongy trabecular matrix' (Clutton Brock 1981) which gives it a strong and resilient character.

It is difficult to estimate how much of the antler found at Glastonbury was shed and how much was the result of hunting, as in many cases the surviving pieces were sawn off the beam and have neither burr nor frontal. However, a number of finished objects, for example some of the hammers, and waste burrs clearly derived from shed antler. The relatively small number of deer bones found on the site may indicate that shed antler was the main source of supply. In many cases only tines are left but from larger pieces the number of points in the crown indicates that antlers came mainly from animals five years old or under.

Shed antler does not last long once dropped. It is vulnerable to decay and can be eaten by animals, even by the deer themselves on occasion. It is therefore necessary to observe the deer closely during the shedding season to enable the antler to be collected almost as soon as it is shed while it is still fresh and in good condition.

Roe deer antler is also found at Glastonbury though in smaller quantities. Only the bucks have antlers and the Lake Village antlers come from both shed and dead animals. Again the antler came mainly from younger animals between their first and third year. In some cases the complete antler is used so that the number of points can be counted and the age assessed.

465 bone objects were given small find numbers of which 8 were combs. Predominant species used were ox, horse and sheep. Absence of epiphyses shows many of the bones came from young animals. A description and list of the types of bone used can be found in the Bulleid and Gray report. Many of the bones show butchery marks and it can be assumed that the bone tools were made from left-over waste. This also suggests that where some bones are thought to have been hollowed-out for use, these may simply have had their marrow removed for food and some tibiae noted as gouges could have been used for this purpose.

Methods of working.

As a preliminary to bone and antler working it has been suggested that soaking in water would be necessary. Fresh antler is supposed to be more malleable, but by the time it was collected and brought back to site and maybe stored, even for a short time, it would already have been fairly dry and hard. Macgregor suggests that boiling might also have been used and quotes experiments where antler is shaved first after 48 hours soak-

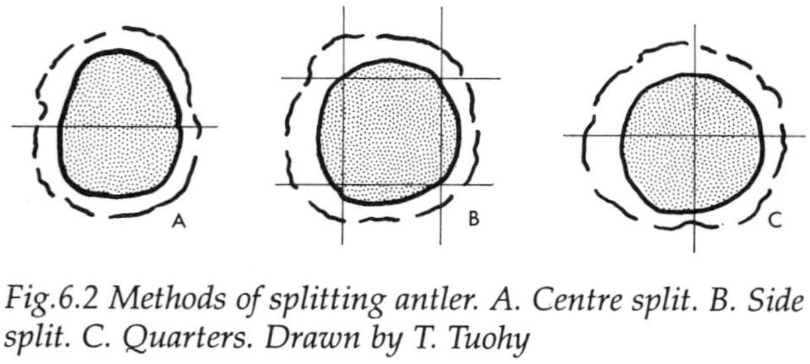

Fig.6.2 Methods of splitting antler. A. Centre split. B. Side split. C. Quarters. Drawn by T. Tuohy

ing and then again after an additional boiling in water for 15 minutes (Macgregor 1985,64-65). The antler appears to be considerably easier to work after the second treatment. It may be then that the antler was first sawn into usable chunks when dry and then boiled prior to more elaborate work or decoration. Antler and bone found at Glastonbury bear manufacture marks from various tools of which the saw and knife appear to be the most common. Drills were also used as well as gouges and awls and in some cases chisels. There is evidence of shaping by rasp or file, and polishing possibly achieved by sand and leather (pers. comm. Dr Linda Hurcombe).

132 tines were found at Glastonbury of which 34 were cheek pieces, 19 were knife handles, 24 were assorted worked pieces such as toggles, ferrules etc. and 55 were waste or unused pieces. All were sawn off. It appears that the antler was mostly used in the round with holes gouged into it or slits cut to hold knife blades. Antler can also be split, at Glastonbury the types of split used in figure 6.2 were the most common. The majority of the combs, for instance, are a straight cut (fig.6.2A) but in some cases a thinner piece from the side of the antler is used (fig.6.2B), for example H 36, a comb blank.

Saw marks are evident on both antler and bone. The smaller pieces are usually cut straight through and broken off at the end leaving a jagged edge, for example H 130, H 131, H 92, H 102 and B 297. On the larger pieces of antler, such as the burr and beam, two or three separate cuts were made with the saw before severance was achieved. H 180 (Bulleid and Gray 1917, Plate LXVII) is a sawn off antler burr 80x66mm in size with saw cuts from three different directions; one cut goes across for 24mm, another cut comes from the other side for 24mm leaving a triangular piece still attached and a third cut is put in from the outside to enable the cancellous tissue to be broken off. It appears that the first two cuts stopped when the saw could go no further and then the third had to be made to enable the job to be finished. The need to make several saw cuts is doubtless a reflection of the limited of efficiency of the saw blade. H 98 (Bulleid and Gray 1917, Plate LXVI) is a curved beam of antler with the bez and brow cut off. At the lower end there is a longitudinal slit 95mm long. The cut is irregular as if the worker was using a small saw that had to be inserted more than once to finish the cut. The saws found at Glastonbury all have narrow blades, I 53: 28mm, I 11: 20.3mm and I 52: maximum of 24mm.

Except in cases where the brow tine was used as a handle (H 344 and H 53), hammers were made using the burr end of the beam and severing the brow and occasionally the bez tine, such as H 29, leaving a usable chunk. A shaft hole was then put through the beam directly above the burr. Marks on the inside of some of these holes look like saw marks and it may be that the holes were initially roughly chiselled out and then a small saw put through to smooth out the facets before inserting the shaft. The holes themselves tend to be larger at one end than the other. H 208 has a hole 23x14mm at one end and 20x15mm at the other. H 237 measures 24x16 and 31x15mm.

In the bone pieces termed notched and perforated tibiae

and made from the tibiae of ox or horse it can be seen that two cuts have been made with the saw each approximately 2mm wide and then joined to make one broad notch or slot between 4-6mm wide. B 381 has a notch in the proximal end from two cuts, one 2mm and the other 3mm wide. The intervening piece between these cuts has been chipped out to make a notch 6mm wide. B 299 has been sawn off at the distal end. Two cuts 2mm wide were made at either side but a third was still needed to sever the piece completely.

Knives were used on the larger objects for shaping and decoration and for complete manufacture of smaller items such as needles. The square bone point B 131 appears to have been shaped with a knife, the cuts are crude. In many cases where bone and antler has been hollowed out it is likely that the work was started with an awl or gouge and then finished with a pointed knife. Antler cheek pieces made from sawn off tines are frequently shaped and flattened down on one side, for example H 96, H 97, H 178 and H 284. B 62, not illustrated by Bulleid and Gray, is a rib cut by knife and saw along one edge to produce a series of coarse teeth.

Drill holes appear in a large number of objects both in antler and bone. In many cases it seems that holes were started with drills and then enlarged with other implements such as gouges or knives. It was thought by Bulleid and Gray that bow drills were used and they suggest some examples of decorated ribs as having been part of these tools (B 25). Drill holes usually measure on average 3-5mm. In some cases two holes have been drilled next to each other and then joined to make one oval hole.

Rasps and files were mostly used for shaping, as on antler cheek pieces such as H 299. Evidence for this type of abrasion also exists on combs. Antler ring H 95, probably made from a hollowed out piece of beam, bears rasp marks from its original shaping.

Uses.

In most cases the uses of the objects seem fairly straight forward and have been fully discussed in the 1911 and 1917 books. Some objects, however, seem to have served more than one function, including hammers, long bones with notches, the metacarpals and metatarsals of sheep and antler cheek pieces.

Hammers.

All hammers show very heavy use and battering at either end and also on the sides. In H 237 the battering on one side is so severe that a hole has worn right through to the shaft. In H 208 wear has cracked the head from end to end. On this hammer scratches and marks on the side suggest that when it became useless as a hammer it was used partly as a small anvil but also as a practice pad for ring-and-dot decoration. Three examples of ring-and-dot exist on one side and three attempts at circles that were not successful. H 197 has heavy wear on the ends and also pit marks and cuts on the sides that suggest secondary use as an anvil.

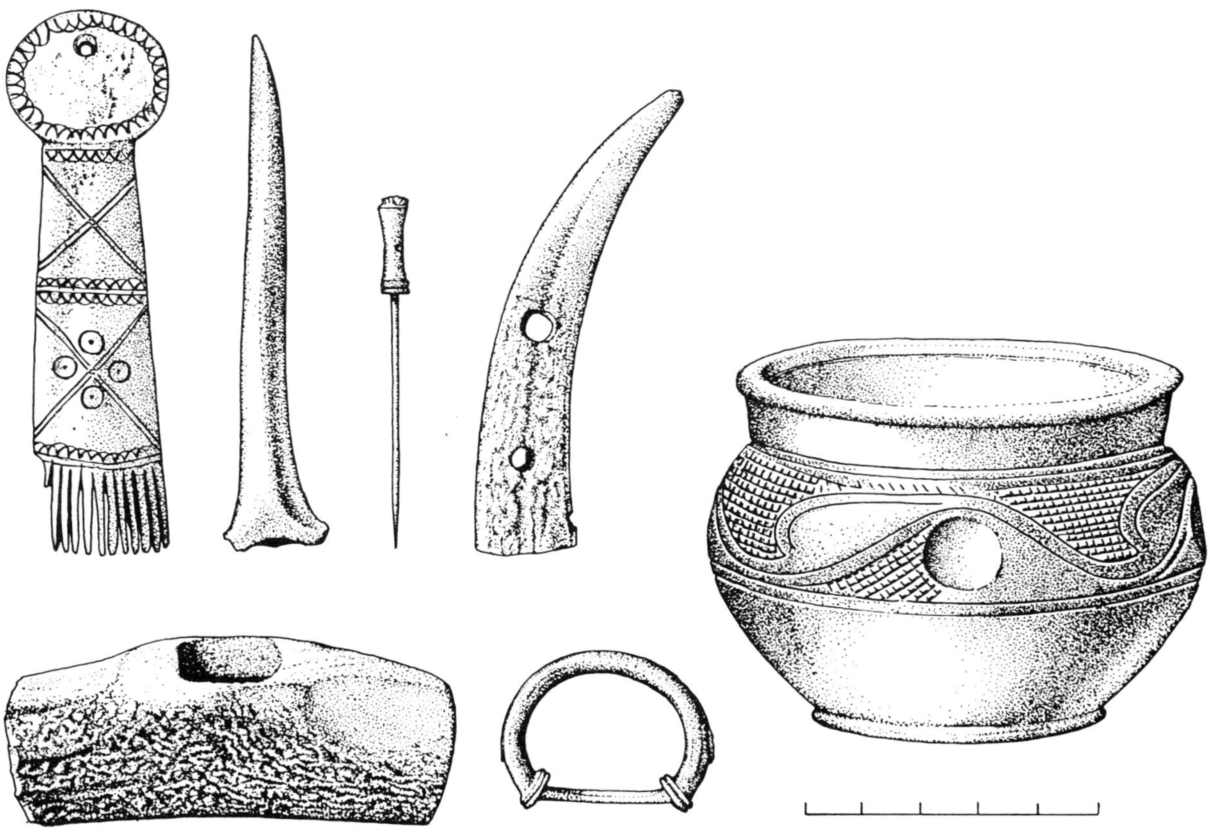

Fig.6.3 Bone and antler tools, pottery and other objects. Drawn by M. Rouillard. Scale in cm.

Thirteen antler hammers were found. They span the duration of the settlement showing no apparent change in form or use.

Antler cheek pieces (fig.6.3).

Some (H 341, 77mm; H 21, 84mm; and H 110, 93mm) seem far too small to be part of even a pony's bridle. The possibility of traction by smaller animals, such as goats or dogs, using bridles with leather bits, must also be ruled out as these animals are worked using a shoulder harness and are led by halters or leads. It is possible that iron bits were used for riding and leather ones with cheek pieces for traction or smaller ponies. The cut and design of several cheek pieces do appear to be in matching pairs, where one side is flattened and the other decorated so that these could indeed have been in use as some kind of bridle wear if one assumes that the flattened side is adjacent to the cheek of the horse and the decorated side facing outwards e.g. H 96, H97, H122 and H 18. Although categorised together cheek pieces may well have served more than one function but convincing alternative explanations have yet to emerge.

Out of 31 cheek pieces listed, 19 have been assigned to Mounds and specific Floors. They span the Early to Final Phases.

Miscellaneous pieces of sawn antler.

Evidence from Glastonbury shows antler to have been in use throughout all periods of occupation. Blocks and lengths of sawn antler and sawn off tines are noted by Bulleid and Gray and in most cases simply given Mound numbers but no Floors. Exceptions to this include some pieces of worked antler which show particular saw or knife marks and some that are classed as knife handles but which are more likely to have been part of an antler worker's working stock. Most of these seem to come from the Middle to Final period. It is difficult to identify any development in manufacturing techniques and it would appear that they remained little changed over the 200 years of the settlement's existence.

Knife handles.

Study of knife handles was more rewarding as five examples were noted in one Mound, (M5), all with Floor numbers denoting different Phases. All five either had slits or gouge holes for the insertion of tangs. One, H 220, had part of the tang remaining. This suggests that this form of hafting was common to all Phases from Early to Late. Tines showing evidence for rivets appear from the Middle to Final Phases e.g. H 354, H 129 and H 320.

Notched and perforated tibiae.

As mentioned above these are usually made from the tibiae of ox or horse. They can have one (B 177), two (B 382) or three (B 2) notches made by saw cuts 4-6mm wide. Sometimes this is achieved by two cuts joined together, see above. There can be up to eight (B 217), but more often five holes (B 198) drilled in the wider proximal end. These are not necessarily opposite one another. Bulleid and Gray suggested they were implements for cleaning sinews but evidence of wear or polishing would be expected if this was their function. In several cases these bones have broken off at the notch showing that they were vulnerable to breakage and therefore must have been under pressure. Similar objects were found at Meare but are very rare elsewhere. It seems that whatever their use it was something concentrated at Glastonbury and Meare.

Attempts to assign these tools to Phases was disappointing. The Excavation report states that they are "found in 21 Mounds" or "12 have only one in each", without stipulating which Mounds they are. All that can be said is that whatever their use, these tools were in existence throughout the duration of occupation on the site.

Metacarpals and metatarsals of sheep.

152 of these objects were found representing one third of the bone numbered objects. They are quite common on Iron Age sites and it is generally agreed that they were used in some manner in the production of cloth, possibly as bobbins. Prior to the Glastonbury excavation this idea was put forward by Pitt-Rivers. Both he and Bulleid and Gray saw them as the bobbin for a boat shuttle. Although this type of shuttle was in use in the 19th century upright looms, it can hardly have been used in the Iron Age on warp-weighted looms as the shuttle requires a wooden bar along which to run. After study of all these bones I can find no evidence of the transverse striations one would expect with yarn wrapped tightly round these bones if used as bobbins, although marks like this have been found at Danebury (Sellwood 1984,389-392). They are often polished and frequently have wear marks in the form of longitudinal scratches, in most cases 2 or 3 and in some more. These objects occur in unusually large numbers at Glastonbury Lake Village. There is a number of variations in form which were described by Bulleid and Gray as types A-F and by Sellwood as Class 1-5 (1984,389). These variations may reflect different functions. Some light may have been shed on the question of use by an association with other classes of object had more of them been ascribed to a Floor at the Lake Village. Seventy-five were attributed to Mounds but only 13 were actually assigned to Floors. They occurred widely across the site and come from all Phases.

Weaving combs (fig.6.3).

Eighty-nine combs were found at Glastonbury of which 81 were antler and 8 were of bone. Of those with their butts still intact 33 have perforations; two have two perforations, one at the butt and the other in the centre (H 13 and H 73). The combs are the most highly decorated of the antler and bone objects found and display a high degree of expertise in their manufacture. They are of interest also because they show examples of the comb-making process from blanks to the finished comb, through effects of wear during use up to examples of combs discarded as being no longer effective. They also exhibit a number of decorative techniques.

The combs have an average length of 141mm and are normally dentated at one end with an average width at the teeth of 30mm. Four are double ended with teeth at both ends (H 32, H 34, H 194 and H 218). The length of the teeth varies considerably and an average cannot be estimated as so many are broken or have been worn down during use. Surviving butts can be plain, rounded or square and decoration consists of lines, ring and dot or a combination of both (fig.6.4). In two cases, H 231 and H 255, crossed diagonal lines are infilled and H 352 has an infill of crossed lines at the butt. On the particularly fine H 69 interlinked circles provide edge decoration around the butt and handle.

Manufacture.

Combs are normally made from the beam of the antler and as far as possible the straighter pieces are chosen. Comb blanks, that is pieces of antler made for combs but before the teeth are cut, show that the antler, at least as far as Glastonbury is concerned, is usually split down the centre (H 85 and H 185) or taken from the side of larger pieces (H 36). Cutting could have been done with a saw, but if so, the back of the comb, in particular the areas of bony tissue, must have been well-smoothed as no saw marks are left. An alternative method mentioned by Ambrosiani (1979,110-113) and McGregor (1985,57) is to split the antler longitudinally with a sharpened tine driven into the cancellous core in much the same way as a log can be split using wedges. The outlines of the required strip are first marked out by deep grooves. Macgregor quotes a recent find from Hedeby where a beam section of antler was found with a tine embedded in it. It is unclear how precise this method would be and whether blanks such as H 36, cut from the very outside of a piece of beam,

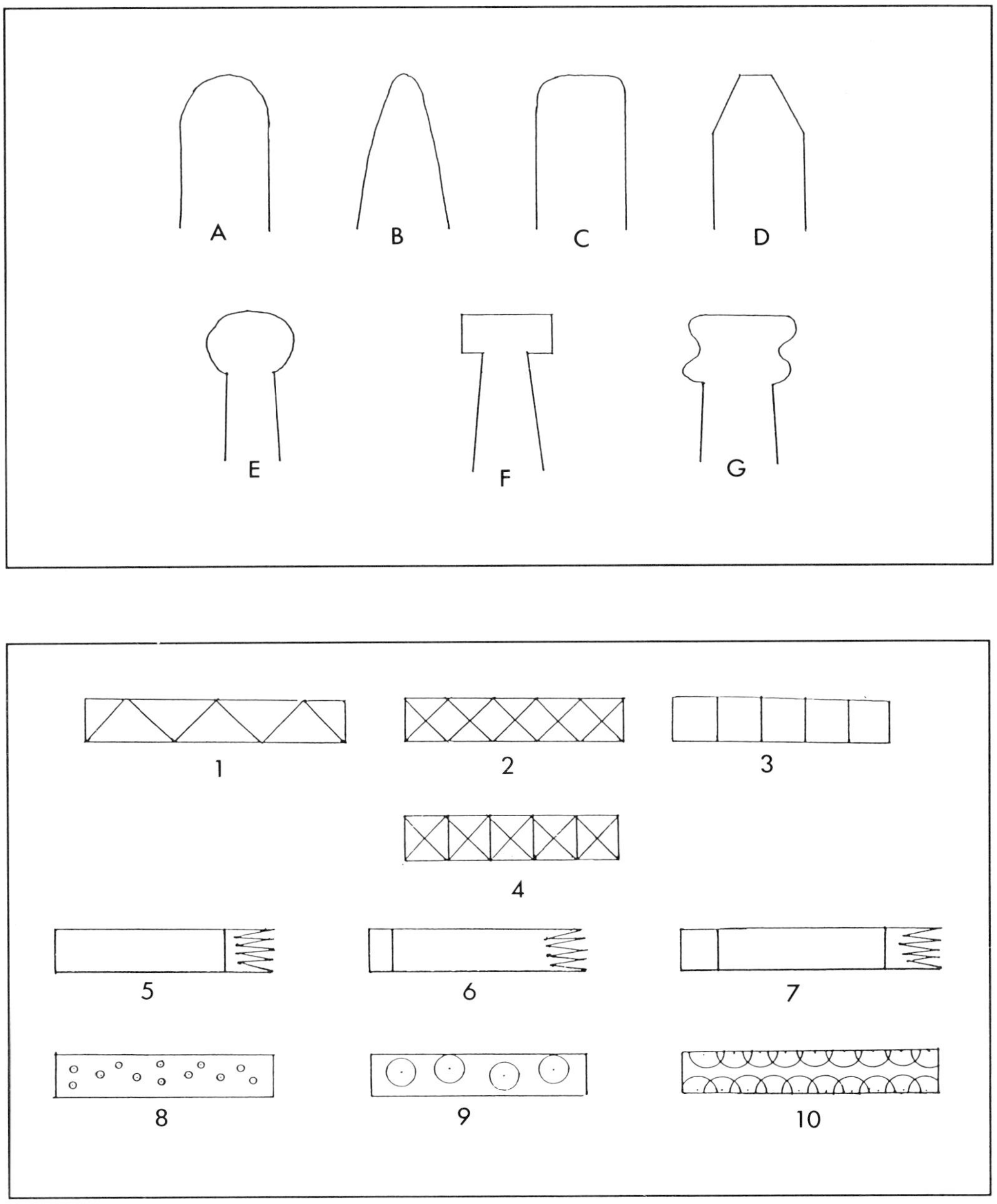

Fig.6.4 Weaving combs: butt shapes and decoration.

could have been produced in this way.

Once the blank was formed the teeth appear to have been cut initially with a saw, such as H 342 and H 325, where the teeth are seen as still squared off and then shaped and finished with a knife when all saw marks disappear. Although it does not occur among the Glastonbury combs there are combs from other sites where cuts can be seen on the teeth where the knife has slipped during manufacture. In the case of double-ended combs the shape and number of teeth can vary. H 218 has 12 teeth at one end and 15 the other. H 34 has 7 teeth one end and 11 the other. In this case there is a considerable difference in the width of the teeth. Butts are shaped with a knife and then polished smooth with a rasp or file (H 108 and H 198), and buffed up with sand and leather. Experiments have shown that it is easier to form the blank in dry antler but that further working was easier after soaking for 48 hours. After this, holes through the butt could be made quite easily with an awl and finished with a knife.

There is no direct evidence of manufacture, such as blanks or combs with half finished teeth in the Early or Middle Phases. One blank comes from the Final Phase (H 185) and two more from Mounds spanning Late to Final Phases (H 85 and H 36). Two half finished combs (H 186 and H 342) come from the Late Phase and one from the Final Phase (H 186). Re-cuts, that is where teeth have been re-cut into the decoration to prolong the life of the comb, exist in all Phases, e.g. H 337 (Early), H 267 (Middle) and H 10 (Final).

Decoration.

The number of decorated combs (fig.6.4) noticeably exceeds those without decoration. The former occur in all Phases. Of the 81 combs only 8 have no decoration at all and two of these are in the process of manufacture.

Linear decoration was almost certainly done with a knife. Cuts made this way in the comb show a V-shaped section, e.g. H 356. Some are very finely incised e.g. H 13, H 179 and H 68. Double lines at Glastonbury vary in spacing and are far from regular e.g. H 67 and H 101. Ring-and-dot decoration was common in the Iron Age and is so symmetrical that some kind of implement with a centre bit must have been used. The form of this tool is the subject of some controversy, no implements have as yet been found. Some kind of scribing tool was probably used at Glastonbury Lake Village for all examples of ring-and-dot except for comb B 362 where the design appears to have been deeply impressed into the bone with some kind of large punch rather than inscribed. MacGregor, in discussing punches, refers to Schoknecht (1977) as suggesting that this type of work can be applied to antler and bone after soaking has softened the material (MacGregor 1985,71).

Ring-and-dot was used either on its own (e.g. H 117 and H 355) or in conjunction with incised linear decoration (e.g. H 10, H 69 and H 267). Both ring-and-dot and linear decoration occur from the Early to Final Phases.

In all cases of decoration I would suggest that the antler would have had to be softened as attempts to incise dry material with a knife creates little more than an imprecise scratching. The deeper cuts seem almost to have dented the surface like a skin so that it rises slightly on either side of the cut. It may well be that this only occurred when decoration was applied following soaking and/or boiling.

Uses of combs.

Bulleid and Gray made a well-argued case for the use of combs in weaving which needs no repetition. I have also discussed this (Tuohy 1990). Since then I have studied upwards of 700 combs in the British Isles and would add the following. In a large number of combs heavy wear occurs on the inside of the outer teeth of the comb, eventually resulting in their breaking off from the inside outwards. This is not the type of wear that would occur if they had been used in the manufacture of a large piece of cloth when wear would occur on the outer side of the tooth as well as the inside. In all, I have found wear on the outer side in less than 10 combs, none of them from Glastonbury. There are, however, Glastonbury examples of wear on the inside of the outer teeth (H 108, H 313) and there are 21 examples of combs with the outer teeth broken. I would therefore suggest that they were used for making braids, ribbons or narrow strips of material for which there would have been a great demand, such as halters for animals, straps for bags, belts, even slings (Ryder 1993,316-318). This would account both for the wear marks under the teeth and on the inside of the outer teeth only. The only other equipment required for the making of these items would be a heddle bar and 3 flat pieces of wood for shed sticks. The warp can be attached to anything, a fence, post or even the big toe as done by women in Peru to this day. Combs could have been used in the production of ornamental weaves. Iron Age fabric with an ornamental border with some embroidery was found in a burial at Burton Fleming (Stead 1991).

Combs are traditionally associated with weaving through their connection with spindle whorls and loom weights but the majority of the latter come from the Early to Middle Phases when there are few combs and the rest come from the Late Phase and none at all from the Final Phase. Either this bears out that these combs were not in use with warp weighted looms, as I suggest, or else there were different types of loom in use on the site that have not been recognised as such.

Combs derive from all Phases: Early (5), Middle (6), Late (23), Final (18). It appears that there was a marked increase in the use of combs in the Late and Final Phases.

Butts are illustrated in figure 6.4. Butt C is the most common, numbering 16, with or without perforations, and exists in all Phases. Butt E is in use only in the Early and Middle and Butt F in the Late and Final

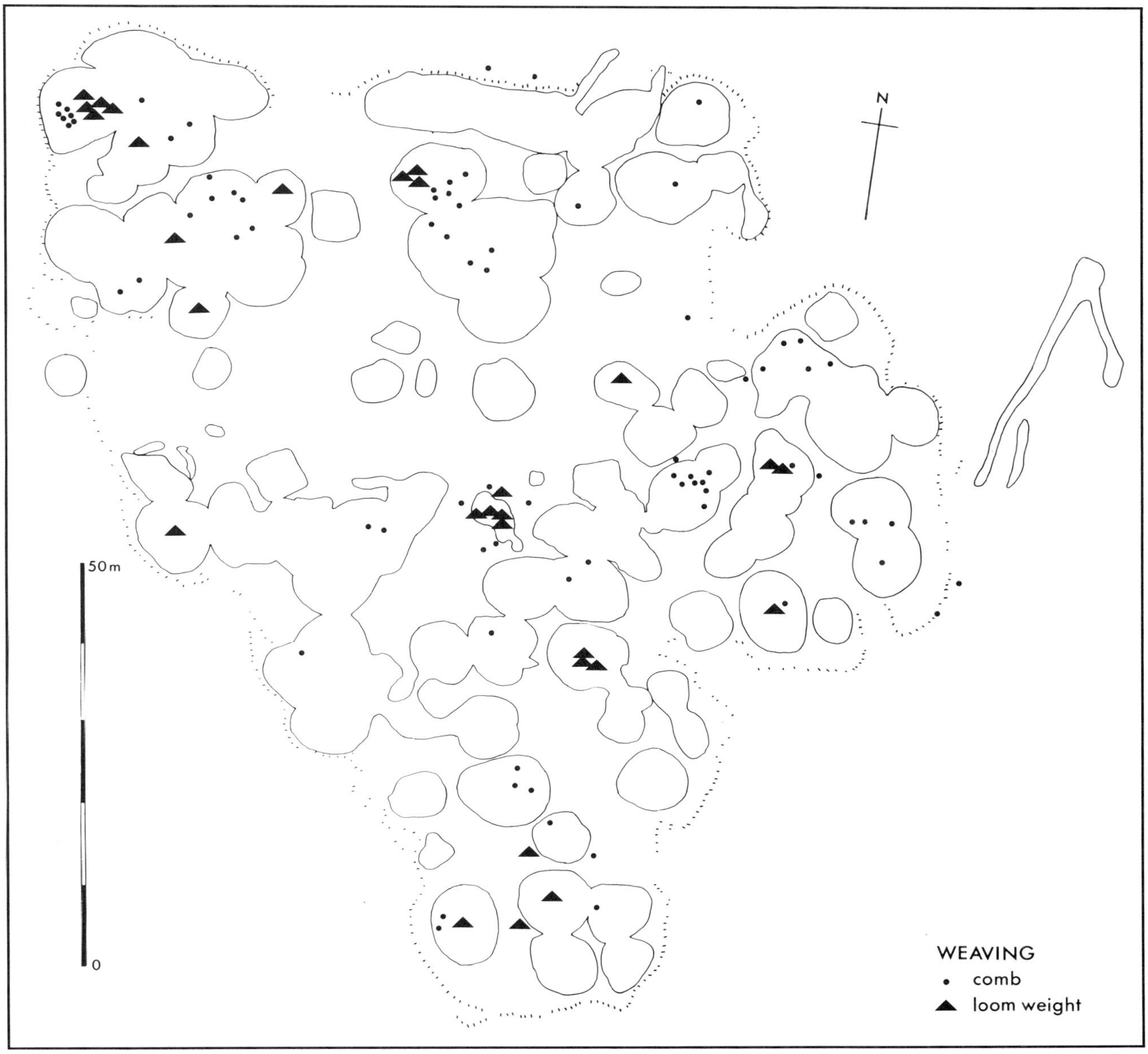

Fig.6.5 Distribution of weaving combs and loom weights. JMC

Phases. Of interest are combs with Butt F: H 170, Middle Phase, and H 66, H 369, H 101 in the Final Phase with H 109 in Late-Final Phase. Combs with these Butts were common at Danebury and H 170 is indeed very similar and dating would correspond with Cunliffe's Late Phase when the most combs were found, 48 in all. But the combs in the Final Phase at Glastonbury continued on after use at Danebury had stopped.

In general, worked bone and antler seems to be fairly well distributed among the Mounds. Nowhere is there a Mound such as M38 at Meare Village West that can reasonably be assumed to have been the site of an antler worker. This Mound contained 49 pieces of antler of which 8 were finished articles, including knife handles, cheek pieces and pottery stamps and the rest was waste. This is what one might expect to find in an antler workshop. It would seem therefore on present evidence that although the manufacture of weaving combs shows a high degree of expertise, suggesting specialist craftsmen, most bone and antler working at Glastonbury was domestic rather than industrial.

6.4 TEXTILE MANUFACTURE

Of all industrial and craft activities on the Lake Village site, in terms of surviving equipment, the various stages in the production of woollen cloth and braids were both the most prolific and widespread. They took place throughout the existence of the settlement. The distribution plots (figs.6.5 and 6.6) show categories of find undoubtedly associated with the activity, such as spindle whorls, as well as others whose precise function is unclear but which were almost certainly involved in some as yet uncertain manner. The latter include the perforated metatarsals and metacarpals of sheep and goat which traditionally are termed bobbins and the sheep and goat tibiae sliced transversely at one end to

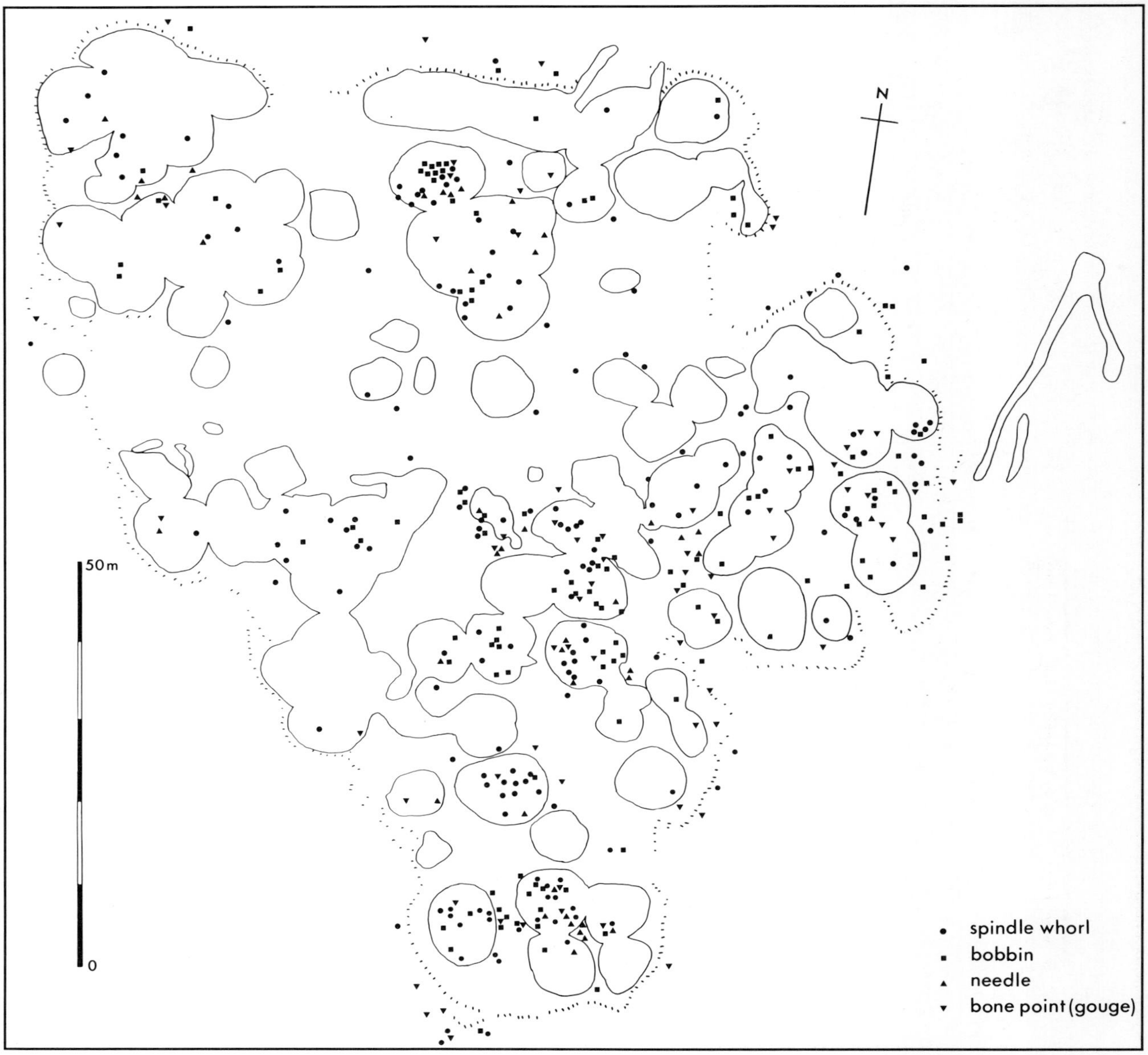

Fig.6.6 Distribution of spindle whorls, bobbins, needles and bone points. JMC

produce a point and which are normally, wrongly, called gouges; here they are less specifically referred to as point (gouge). Gray classified the bobbins and points (gouges) into a series of types on the basis of the variations of form which may reflect functional differences, but for present purposes they are grouped together. There does seem to be an association between both bobbins and points with other spinning and weaving equipment at Glastonbury and a general consensus elsewhere that there is a link. It has, for example, been suggested that some of the points may have served as pin beaters in the weaving process and that others may have been used in hide dressing (Sellwood 1984,387).

Scope for assessing the chronological pattern for spinning and weaving and for a detailed analysis of artefact type associations is severely limited by the generally low level of context recording. What does emerge is that there is a large number of spindle whorls compared with loom weights, 195:45+. This either reflects greater importance of spinning than weaving or that more people were involved. This imbalance between whorls and weights is one that has been noted elsewhere for settlement sites as opposed to hillforts where the loom weights tend to occur relatively in much larger numbers (Sellwood 1984,438-439).

The baked clay loom weights are primarily triangular in shape. A minimum of 45 weights and fragments were recorded, a sum that infers the presence of only a small number of warp weighted looms. Although largely lacking contexts the distribution plot of loom weights does show particular concentrations in M37, M62 and M70. M70 produced the largest number with 10 found below the clay Floors, probably on 'Floor 3' of the Middle Phase which had no identifiable clay Floor but did have a series of hearths and ash and charcoal spreads.

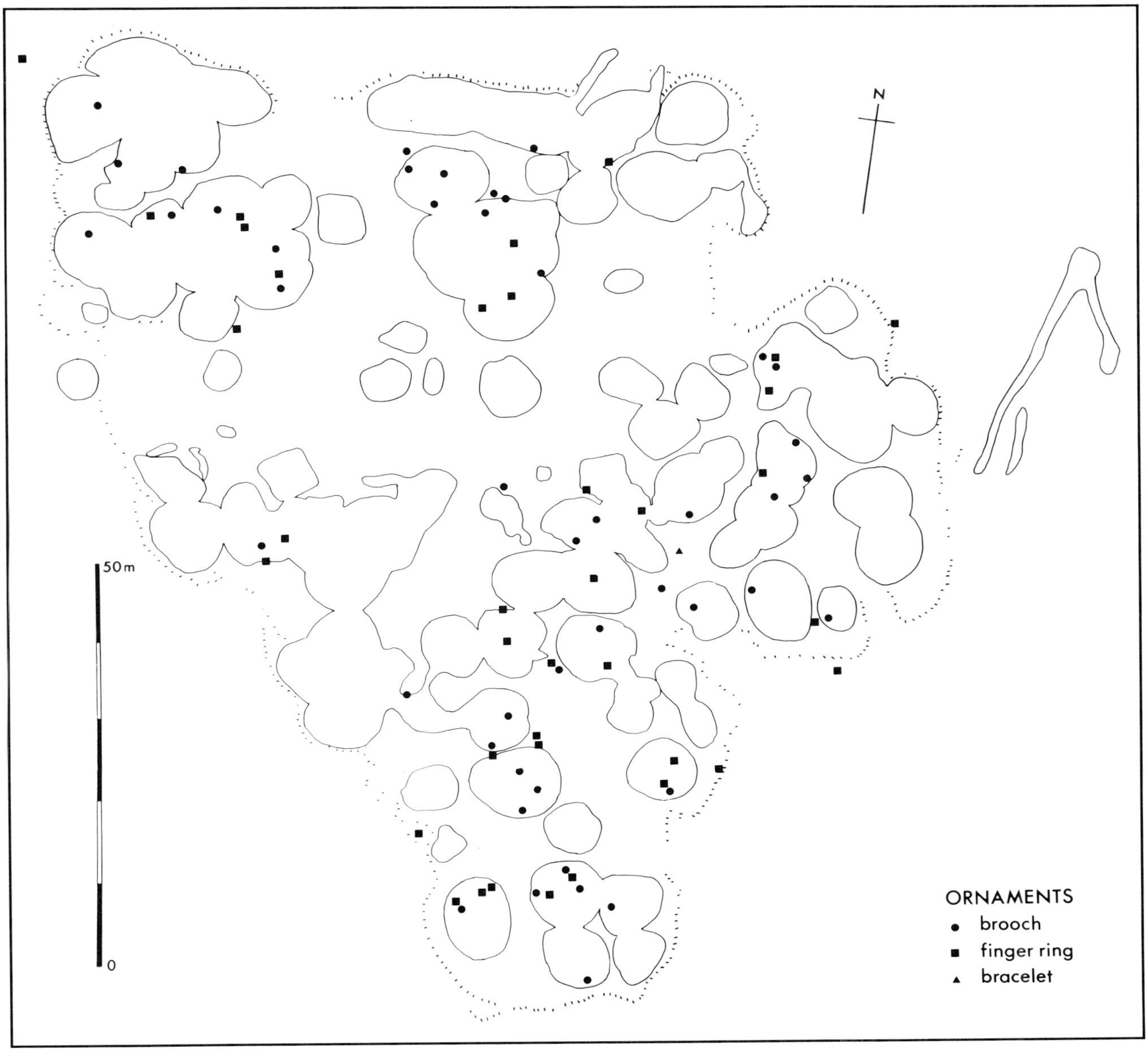

Fig.6.7 Distribution of brooches, rings and bracelets. SCM and JMC

Nine were found in M37 of which "several" were from Middle Phase Floor 3 which was a clay spread. M37 and the immediate vicinity produced a concentration of other wool-working tools: combs, whorls, bobbins, points (gouges) and needles. The loom weights from M62 have no context and do not necessarily come from the same Floor. Again this Mound appears to be especially important from the spinning and weaving point of view with its concentration of a wide variety of equipment. All that can really be said about the activity is that it is unlikely to have occurred on Floor 2 which was dedicated to metalworking. A further group of "several" loom weights came from Floor 2 of M18, the site of a building in the Middle Phase.

The weights would have been used with a warp weighted loom. No identifiable pieces of such looms were found amongst the worked wood. The only wooden artefacts believed by Bulleid to have been connected with textile production were X 65 and X 69. These consisted of 63 pieces of framework "presumably parts of looms or appliances for making textile fabric" and were found mainly near M8 and M46. The size of the frames and spacing of the holes make it most unlikely that Bulleid's identification is correct; another function such as skin stretching should be sought for the pieces.

Weaving combs, no longer believed to have been used in connection with the warp weighted loom, occur in two particular concentrations: Floor 1 of M42 where six were found, and below the clay Floors of M70 from where seven combs and fragments came. The latter deposit also yielded weights and spindle whorls and is the only known circumstance in which combs occurred in some kind of association with loom weights.

Spindle whorls occur across the site, presumably a reflection of the fact that spinning was an activity that

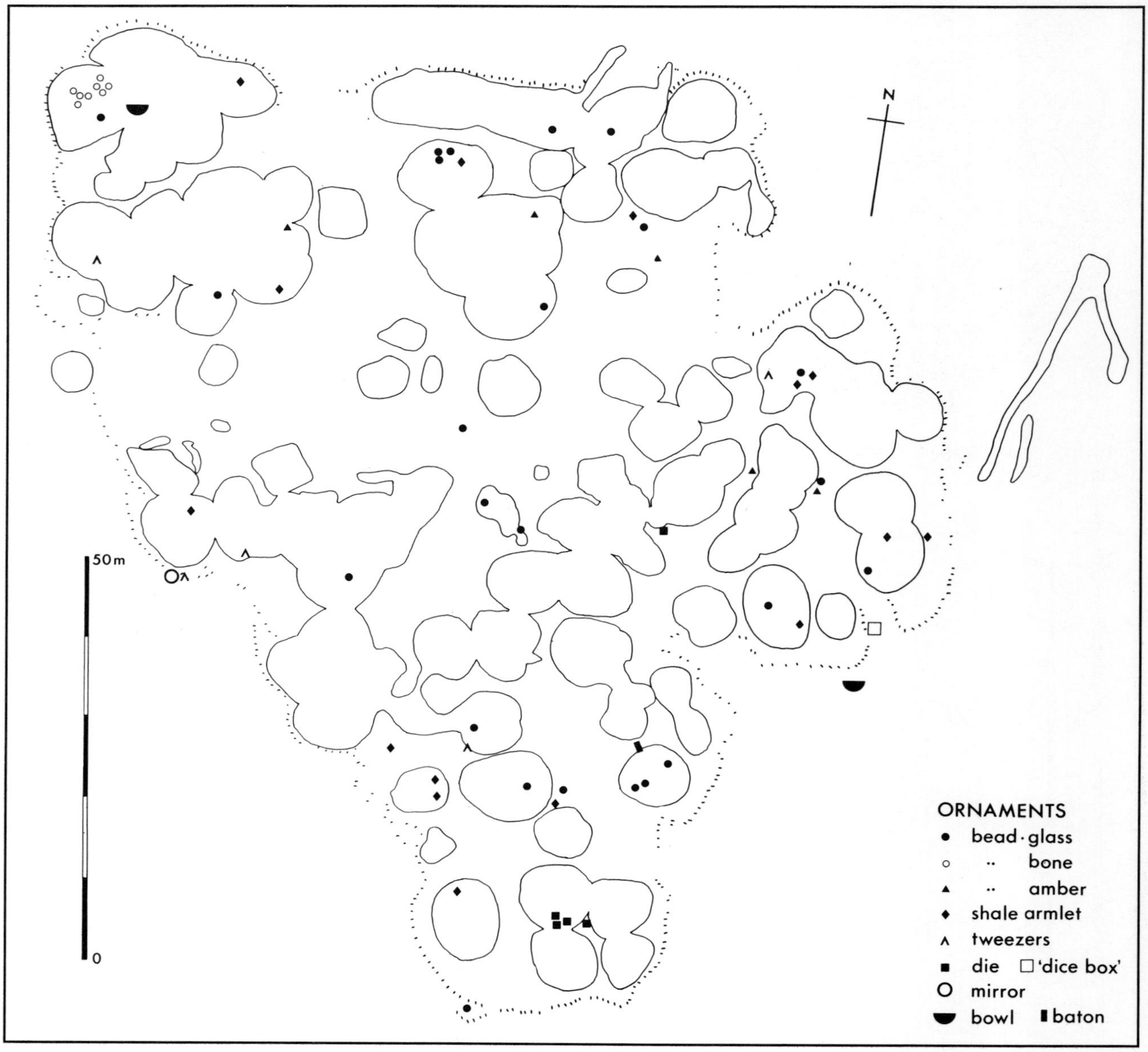

Fig.6.8 Distribution of ornaments, various materials. SCM and JMC

need not have been confined to a specific location, indeed could potentially have taken place more or less anywhere. This is emphasised by the fact that whorls are found in many contexts in association with a diverse range of other artefact types. A number of concentrations of spindle whorls did occur including Floor 1 of M4, Late Phase (6), Floor 4 of M18, Early Phase (6) and Floor 2 of M38, Middle Phase (4). One of the latter spindle whorls was unfinished and this, added to a number of other similar finds, suggests that the relatively simple business of making whorls took place on site.

Bobbins and points also occur across the site. The notable concentrations of bobbins came from Mounds 16, 18, 27 and particularly 62.

6.5 PERSONAL EQUIPMENT

A wide range of personal and decorative items of copper alloy, iron, antler, bone and glass (figs.6.7, 6.8 and 6.9) was excavated emphasising the strongly domestic nature of the artefact assemblage. This material includes brooches, armlets, finger rings, beads and a number of clearly personal items such as the mirror. Some, notably brooches (55), finger/toe rings (35) and glass beads (25) occurred in unusually large numbers. The brooches have been considered in two recent works, Hull and Hawkes 1987 and Olivier 1991.

These categories of artefact are sparse in the Early Phase perhaps reflecting pre-occupation with other matters or a relatively impoverished society in terms of its ability to indulge in personal display or, once again, are a result of the excavator's recording. In actual fact when the distribution is compared with the phasing the lack

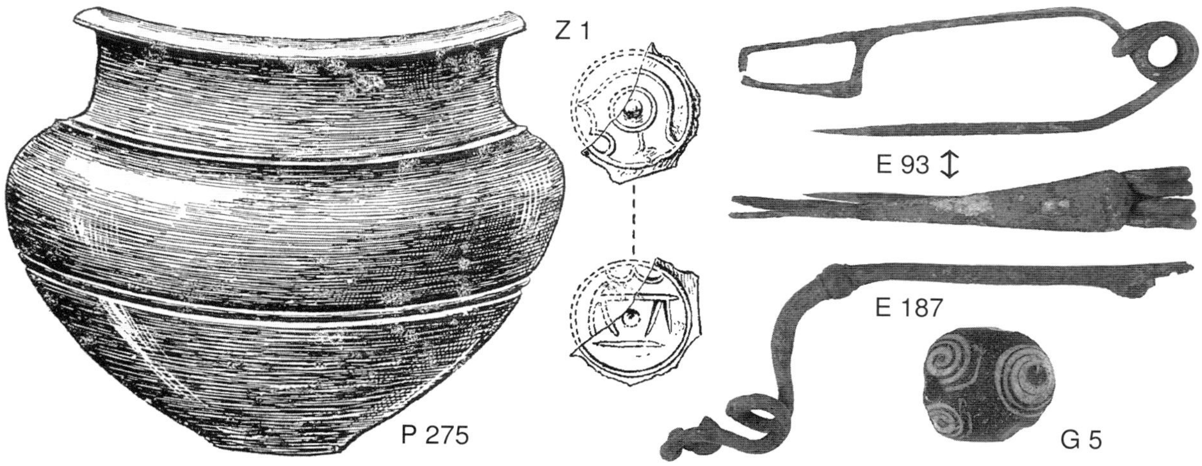

Fig.6.9 Some of the objects important for the dating of the settlement. Scale 1:1 except for P 275 which is 1:2. Photo L.Bostock.

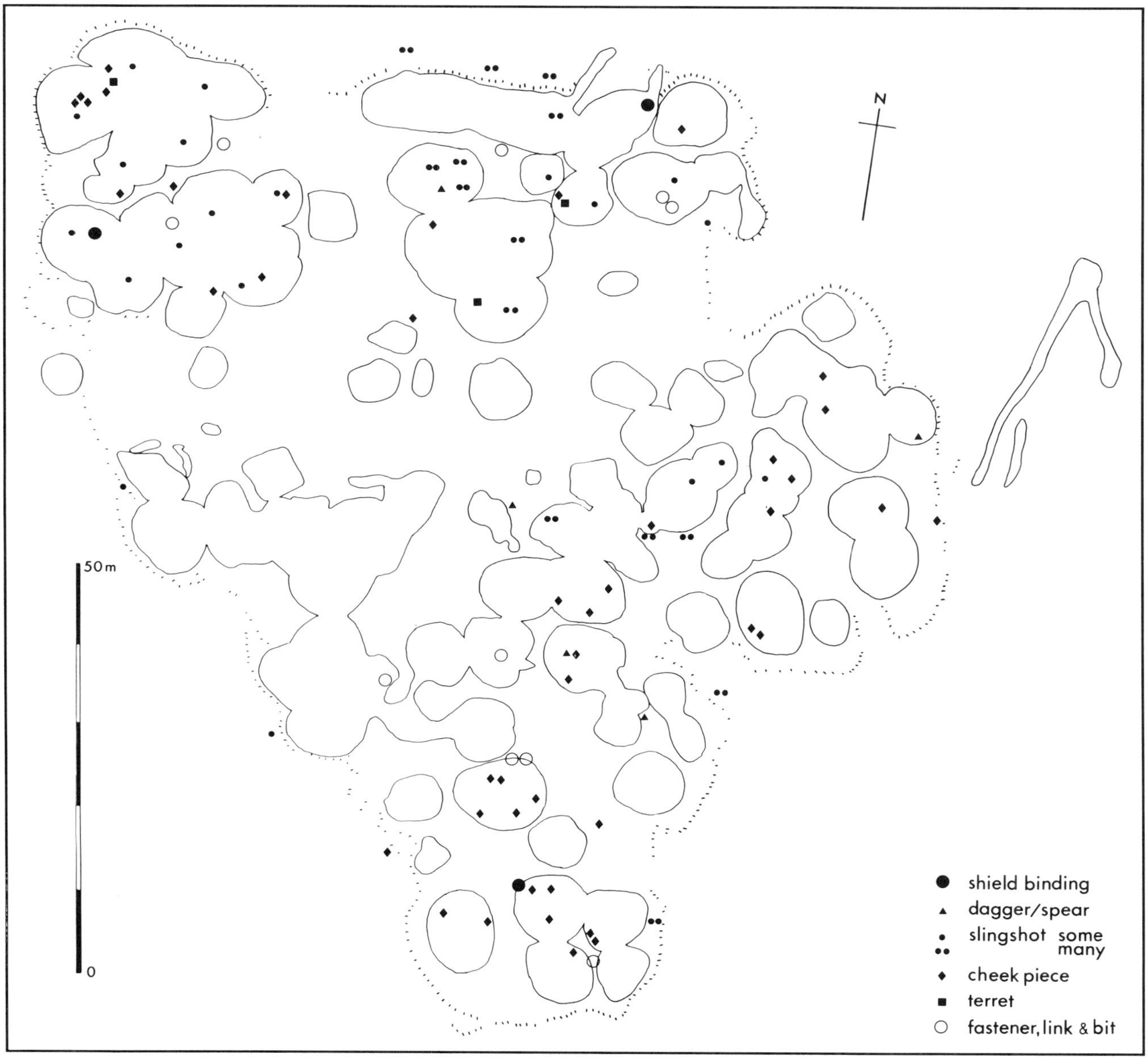

Fig.6.10 Distribution of weapons and harness equipment. SCM and JMC

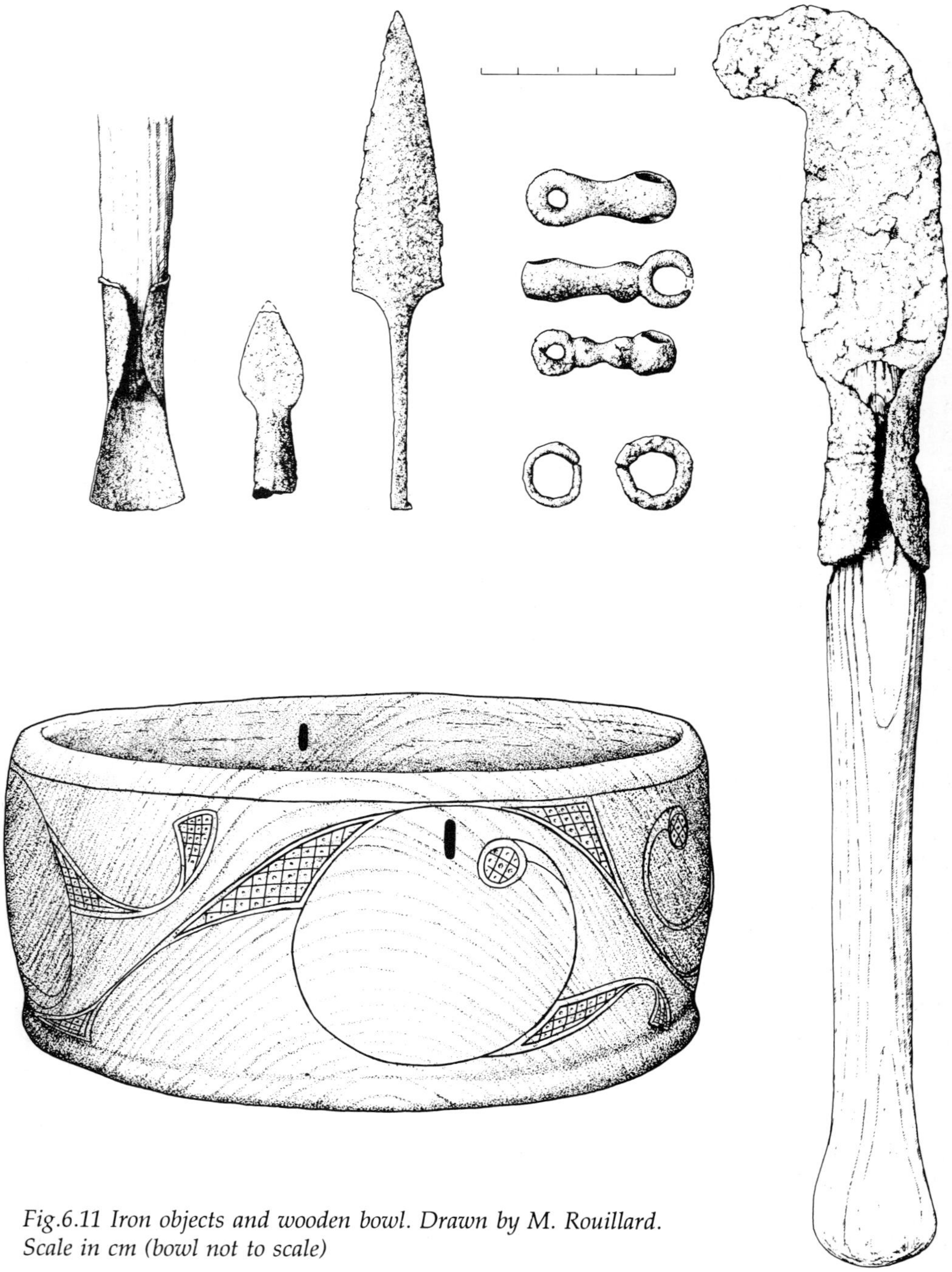

Fig.6.11 Iron objects and wooden bowl. Drawn by M. Rouillard. Scale in cm (bowl not to scale)

of material from the Early Phase does appear real. The only two objects certainly, and indeed likely to be, from the Early Phase are fibula E 244 from Floor 5 of M74 and finger ring E 272 from Floor 4 of M75.

Subsequent phases show a general scatter across the site with few notable concentrations. The main concentrations are Mounds 4, 5, 7, 9, 49 and 62. Of these Middle Phase M7 appears to have produced the largest number of pieces attributable to a Phase though it is not known whether they are from Floor 1 or 2. M62 contained the largest single total but none was related to a Floor. The finds have a slight preponderance for the sites of buildings, but only slight. It may be that an absence of this category of material is significant. The main blanks in the distribution occur mainly around the northern, eastern and western edges of the settlement as well as the central area.

Whilst "glass bead necklaces can be considered as relatively prosperous" (Henderson 1991,108) and unusually large numbers of artefacts of a personal and display nature were found, notably brooches and glass beads, they did not include amongst their numbers anything that could be construed as indicating somebody of outstanding wealth or status. Perhaps the single most impressive item is the sheet bronze 'Glastonbury Bowl'. Whilst of very fine workmanship the bowl is, nevertheless, relatively modest in terms of the Iron Age metalworker's capabilities.

Weaponry.

Dawkins made much of the settlement having been terminated by massacre. His view was based upon the skulls which bore sword cuts. So far as the material culture is concerned the only overt weaponry consists of two daggers, I 2 and I 32, recently identified scabbard binding fragments from hide-shaped shields, I 66, E 107 and E 247, (Stead 1991b) and three spearheads I 20, I 42 and I 86 (fig.6.11). In an attempt to investigate the possibilities further, objects potentially associated with a warrior element or which might have been used for defence purposes were plotted (fig.6.10); besides the pieces already mentioned these included terrets, cheek pieces, button and loop fasteners, belt links, bridle pieces and sling shot. This review of the evidence produced no clear pattern of associations or distributions. Hundreds of pieces of sling shot, mainly of baked and unbaked clay, were found. Most occurred singly although some concentrations, usually spread over an area rather than tightly grouped, were found. Two possible small hoards were discovered between the E edge of M2 and the palisade and outside the palisade E of M8. The main concentration of sling shot appears to have been in and around the Mounds in the centre north of the site and outside the palisade to the north of this area. The low level of recording of sling shot makes the significance of their quantity and distribution difficult to discern. Bulleid and Gray (1917,565), however, were clearly of the opinion that hunting and fowling rather than warfare or defence lay behind their presence.

Cheek pieces were found in unusually large numbers. Outlying concentrations of these objects do occur but the primary distribution is in the southern area. In spite of their numbers there is only one recorded instance of a cheek piece having been found in the same context as another in the categories plotted on figure 6.10, a terret on Floor 1 of M78. The implication is that cheek pieces were for civilian rather than military use. Variation in form also suggests that they may have had more than one function. The fasteners, links and horse bits were too few in number to yield a pattern in their own right but when compared with the other categories on the plot show no association and again were not necessarily part of the kit of war.

The impression therefore is of a population little involved in fighting and not facing a significant threat from people outside.

6.6 A RECONSIDERATION OF THE GLASS: SOME ARCHAEOLOGICAL AND TECHNOLOGICAL ASPECTS

By Julian Henderson

Although the excavations at Glastonbury Lake Village produced only 27 glass or vitreous artefacts the chronological and technological information that can be gained from their study is significant. The beads have largely been illustrated already (Bulleid and Gray 1917, Plate LIX) and since this publication they have also been carefully considered by the late Margaret Guido (1978) who placed them in a broader geographical/regional context.

Glastonbury Lake Village is actually very close to the very important site for glass-working, Meare Lake Village. Meare is generally considered to be earlier in date for most of its use than Glastonbury Lake Village and has produced unparalleled evidence in Europe for the manufacture of glass beads. Although Glastonbury Lake Village has produced evidence for other high temperature industries, glass-working is not amongst them. However, by combining studies of bead typology and chemical analysis it has been possible to relate the glasses found there to specific production spheres, more than can be said for the products from many other high temperature industries.

The beads and their production techniques.

The types of beads from Glastonbury Lake Village are quite limited in range. Out of the 25 beads from the site only one is of a distinctive early Iron Age type and found in its largest concentration at Meare Lake Village; the rest are either of late Iron Age or of undiagnostic types.

Colourless with opaque yellow chevrons (fig.6.12a).

This is a barrel-shaped transparent colourless bead with opaque yellow chevrons applied to the outside (Guido 1978,81-84, class 11). Evidence for the manufacture of this bead type includes bead mould fragments from Meare Lake Village (Henderson 1980, 1981, 1987a). This evidence from Meare is of European significance since there is nothing else to compare with it. It is likely that the colourless matrix of the bead was made in a mould so as to regularise the shape of the bead; the chevrons were also probably applied with the aid of a mould, or at least moulded into position. Unlike spirally-decorated beads from Meare, where a mould seems almost certainly to have been used in order to achieve the very close proximity of the arms of the spirals on the bead surface (Henderson 1987a), the application of chevrons did not need such careful control. Indeed there is quite a wide variation in the quality of the chevron-decorated beads made, only some of which would have required the careful positioning of the chevrons by using a mould.

Cobalt blue horned beads with opaque white spirals (fig.6.12b).

The manufacture of this type of bead (Guido 1978, class 6, the Oldbury type) needed a high degree of control. While the basic shape of the deep cobalt blue body of the bead could have been poured into an open mould, the opaque white spirals were probably applied to the bead surfaces in one of two ways. The first way would have been to re-heat the bead and pull out horns from the bead surface with tweezers, or, if even spacing was required their formation would have been part of the original moulding process. The opaque white spirals would have been trailed around the horns. The point at which the opaque white rod was applied to the bead's surface, trailed on and then pulled off can usually be seen clearly. Although a supply of thin opaque white rods would have been necessary none have been found on Iron Age European sites. The total number of complete beads or fragments of beads of this type from Glastonbury is five, the largest number from any Iron Age site in Britain.

Whirl-decorated (ring) beads (fig.6.12c).

These beads fall into Guido's (1978) Class 7a. They are not very common in Britain during the Iron Age, and occur far more frequently in European oppida. They are most common along with monochrome ring beads and armlets in German oppida (Haevernick 1960, Kunkel 1961, Henderson 1987b), in central European oppida (Venclova 1990) and on a range of Dutch sites (Peddemors 1975). The technique which was probably used for their manufacture was described by the medieval monk Theophilus Presbiter perhaps writing in the 12th century (trans. Dodwell 1961). A gob of glass was first gathered on a tapering wooden stake with a wooden 'wrist guard'. The hot glass was whirled around the stake so that its diameter increased with each revolution of the rod. Translucent monochrome ring beads were produced in this way, but frequently the whirl and ray decorated beads found in Europe are decorated with opaque white or yellow glass. Some examples of the beads appear to have been made in a remarkably complex way with an initial ring of glass being added to by the addition of an outer layer of glass to double its thickness. The cross-section of the beads produced this way are always D-shaped with one of the angles of the D being more rounded off than the other. This can probably be explained by the wider end of the hole through the bead being tighter against the rod around which it was made than the narrower end, making the profile more squared off at the wider end of the bead. Another feature of the cross-section is that opaque glass is sometimes found in the middle of the bead. This appears to show that either an initial bead was decorated and then more glass added on its outside or that the bead itself was built up rather carelessly with both translucent and opaque glass. Adding opaque glass to the body of a translucent glass bead to increase its volume would be a technologically strange thing to do.

The opaque glass is often found in circumferential streaks around the face of the bead's hole, where it has been smeared during the twirling motion during bead production. Opaque decorative glass was evidently also sufficiently fluid to have been thrown outwards from the edge of the hole across the surface of the bead due to centrifugal force during the swirling decoration.

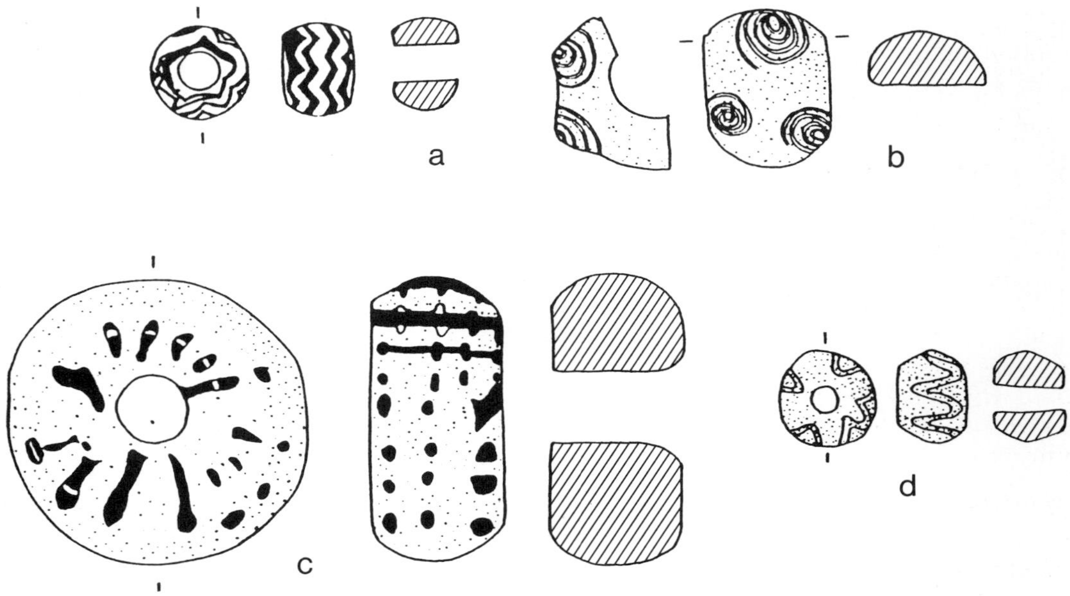

Fig.6.12 The key glass bead types: a. Meare Class 11 (colourless with opaque yellow chevrons); b. Class 6, Oldbury type (cobalt blue with applied opaque white spirals); c. Class 7, a ray bead of typical ring bead form combining opaque and translucent glass; d. zig-zag decorated bead with blue matrix and opaque white decoration. (Note. The illustrated beads do not come from Glastonbury Lake Village)

Whirl (and ray) beads are generally classified as ring beads (the German 'Ringperlen') and were probably manufactured in Continental oppida after the 2nd century B.C. There does not appear to be any evidence for their production on smaller scale settlements. It is therefore no coincidence that other examples have been found at Hengistbury Head, Dorset (Henderson 1987b) which certainly formed part of the oppida trade/exchange network during the late Iron Age. Lumps of unworked purple glass were also found there, a colour which was often used to make such beads as well as technologically related armlets.

Zig-zag decorated bead (fig.6.12d).

A single example of this bead type comes from Glastonbury. It is translucent blue with opaque white zig-zag decoration applied circumferentially. The type was manufactured in the early Iron Age probably somewhere in Europe, but cannot be considered diagnostic in terms of its form. A monograph dealing with the form and composition of this bead type has been published (Haevernick 1983). The study shows that the bead type is found across a wide area of central, southern and western Europe during the Iron Age. In Britain the largest concentration has been found at Wetwang Slack in Humberside (Dent 1982) dating to contexts as early as the 5th century B.C. In spite of the undiagnostic form and decoration, the chemical analysis of the opaque white glass can provide an approximate means of dating the bead type (see below).

Undecorated globular and annular beads.

Six annular beads (Guido's 1978, group 6) in translucent purple, blue and green glass were chemically analysed. Translucent purple is an unusual glass colour in non-oppida contexts. A single turquoise globular glass bead (Guido's 1978, group 7) and a translucent globular cobalt blue bead were analysed. Four beads or fragments of beads from Glastonbury are undecorated ring beads (two of which were analysed) also manufactured in the environment of the oppida system. Four other translucent annular beads and one globular bead were found at Glastonbury but not analysed. G 19 is a large translucent green bead which may have been used as a pin head and still contains an iron tube which possibly formed the end of the pin.

Chemical analyses of the beads.

The beads analysed were a class 11 chevron-decorated type (fig.6.12a), five Oldbury type beads (fig.6.12b), two whirl-decorated beads (fig.6.12c) one zig-zag decorated bead (fig.6.12d), six monochrome annular beads and two globular beads.

The technique of analysis.

The technique used was energy-dispersive X-ray fluorescence spectroscopy. The beads were prepared for analysis by polishing a flat or nearly flat face on one side of the bead with a foam-backed emery disc so as to produce a surface which was free of weathering. The prepared area of the bead (matrix or decoration) was positioned centrally under the X-ray beam and a collimated X-ray beam used for the analysis (*c.* 2mm in diameter on the sample surface). The X-ray tube was operated at 30kV and 29.9nA. The intensities for each X-ray peak were quantified by using the fundamental parameters technique with ESF and Corning glass standards. Where there was interference between X-ray peaks gaussian peaks were stripped out using a program called Simulstrip. Nevertheless, the technique did not cater particularly efficiently with the interference between aluminium K alpha and silicon K alpha peaks, for example, with the effect that the results for aluminium are sometimes rather higher than would be expected for glass of the type. Translucent soda-lime-silica glasses for the Iron Age and Roman periods tend to contain *c.* 2.5% aluminia; the results for analyses 1, 3, 10 and 23 are higher. Results were converted to oxides by stoichiometry. Full analytical conditions are published elsewhere (Henderson and Warren 1981).

The principal glass components.

The compositional results for the analysis of Glastonbury glass beads are given in Table 6.7. All the glasses analysed are of a soda-lime-silica or lead oxide-soda-lime-silica composition and are consistent with other Iron Age glass beads from Europe. The probable source for the soda (Na_2O) is a mineral such as natron, a sodium sesquicarbonate (Turner 1956, Henderson 1985). The silica (SiO_2) source used was probably sand and the calcium oxide (CaO) used was probably introduced as a shell impurity in the sand. Apart from the glasses which contained high levels of lead oxide or tin associated with coloration the range of chemical compositions in the translucent glasses are: 14.2%-20.8% soda (Na_2O), 66.3%-73.6% silica (SiO_2) and 3.9%-8.0% calcium oxide (CaO). These ranges fall well within those for so-called 'Roman' glasses, though it is too simplistic to assume that the Roman world had a completely dominating effect on the late Iron Age glass industry (see below), and in any case glass of this general composition was in use since the 8th century B.C. in Europe.

The colorants used.

The glasses can be divided according to whether they are opaque or translucent.

i. Opaque glass. The opaque yellow glass colour used for the decoration of the Meare class 11 chevron-decorated bead is due to lead antimonate crystals, and this is why it contains 18.07% lead oxide and 0.8% antimony (expressed as antimony trioxide in Table 6.7) as complex lead antimonate crystals. This is a typical opacifier found in ancient glass from *c.* 6th century B.C. which is added to but not replaced by yellow lead stannate in *c.* 2nd century B.C.

Indeed the opaque yellow glass used for the decoration of G 21 with a translucent brown matrix is opacified with lead stannate crystals. The opaque white glass used for the whirl decorated surface of G 14 is opacified with tin oxide crystals. Neither of these tin-based opacifiers was used before the 2nd century B.C.

Opaque white glass was also used for the decoration of the Oldbury type beads, also late Iron Age types. The important difference in the compositions of the two opaque white glasses analysed (when compared to whirl-decorated beads) is that calcium antimonate crystals were used for the Oldbury bead decoration instead of tin oxide. The specialised used of antimony instead of tin-based opacifiers would appear to be the result of regionalised production of glass in the Iron Age and certainly has chronological significance (see below). It is especially interesting that contemporary but typo-

Table 6.7 X-ray fluorescence analysis of glass from Glastonbury Lake Village (Bead type: C = Guido's class; Gu = Guido's group)

Analysis no.	1	2	3	4	5	6	7	8	9	10	11	12	13	14	15	16	17	18	19	20	21	22	23	24
Bead type	C6	C6	C6	C6	C6	C6	C6	C7	C7	C7	C7	C11	C11	Gu5	Gu5	C6	Gu6	Gu6	Gu6	Gu6	Gu6	Gu6	Gu7	Gu7
Find no.	G 1	G 1	G 9	G 9	G 11	G 11	G 12	G 14	G 14	G 21	G 21	G 22	G 22	G 18	G 18	G 5	G 6	G 7	G 10	G 19	G 25	G 24	G 2	G 8
Colour	white	blue	white	blue	white	blue	blue	white	purple	yellow	brown	yellow	none	blue	blue	white	blue	purple	blue	green	'black'	green	blue	turquoise
Matrix/Dec.	D	M	D	M	D	M	M	D	M	D	M	D	M	D	M	D	M	M	M	M	M	M	M	M
Na_2O	14.3	19.2	9.9	15.9	15.7	19.0	15.4	11.9	20.1	3.7	20.8	13.3	14.4	19.2	19.6	20.0	18.2	14.2	20.8	18.7	19.2	16.0	16.3	18.7
MgO	2.1	0.9	0.4	0.5	0.3	0.7	0.9	0.3	0.8	0.5	0.6	0.7	0.3	1.9	0.7	0.8	0.7	0.9	0.7	0.8	0.7	0.9	0.4	0.9
Al_2O_3	6.9	2.9	8.7	3.3	4.1	3.2	2.3	3.8	1.9	7.1	2.3	2.5	3.1	1.4	2.6	2.6	1.0	2.4	2.8	1.0	1.4	1.8	5.3	2.4
SiO_2	68.2	68.8	70.9	71.7	69.7	69.0	72.4	70.8	67.4	44.3	70.5	58.9	73.6	66.2	68.1	69.9	72.1	72.9	67.3	72.1	61.3	66.3	68.7	67.6
K_2O	0.78	0.63	2.0	1.4	1.2	2.1	0.8	0.9	0.6	1.0	0.4	0.4	1.0	0.06	1.4	0.9	0.3	0.9	0.6	0.02	3.1	1.2	0.9	0.4
CaO	4.5	5.8	3.7	5.3	6.8	3.9	5.4	6.4	6.2	3.7	4.4	3.5	5.7	5.4	4.9	5.34	5.9	6.7	5.9	6.4	6.2	8.0	4.9	7.2
SnO_2	ND	ND	ND	ND	ND	ND	ND	3.6	ND	7.0	ND	ND	ND	ND	0.3	ND	ND	ND	ND	ND	ND	ND	ND	ND
Sb_2O_3	1.1	ND	1.7	ND	0.8	ND	ND	ND	ND	ND	0.3	0.8	1.1	0.4	ND	ND	ND	ND	ND	0.8	ND	ND	ND	ND
TiO_2	ND	0.03	0.14	0.1	0.9	0.03	0.13	ND	0.07	-	0.04	-	ND	0.06	0.04	ND	ND	0.08	0.08	0.4	0.18	0.08	0.13	0.06
MnO	0.02	0.67	0.1	0.53	ND	0.26	1.07	1.31	2.33	0.27	ND	ND	ND	3.33	1.06	0.02	ND	1.43	0.59	ND	3.77	1.91	0.75	0.28
Fe_2O_3	1.47	0.81	0.9	0.66	0.75	0.74	1.08	0.31	0.34	1.27	0.46	1.77	0.25	0.78	0.64	0.29	1.17	0.39	0.84	0.26	0.45	0.54	1.24	0.4
CoO	ND	0.13	ND	0.08	ND	0.11	0.17	ND	ND	ND	ND	ND	ND	0.06	0.05	ND	0.08	ND	0.04	ND	ND	ND	0.12	ND
Cu_2O/CuO	0.06	0.13	0.01	0.09	ND	0.11	0.14	ND	ND	0.02	ND	0.01	ND	0.12	0.19	0.01	0.18	ND	0.07	ND	0.01	ND	0.39	1.67
PbO	0.02	0.02	2.49	ND	0.06	ND	ND	0.32	ND	30.92	ND	18.07	0.18	ND	0.55	0.01	ND	ND	0.03	ND	0.01	3.24	0.32	0.26

logically distinct beads have different compositions and appear to reflect the existence of different production spheres.

In addition to the calcium antimonate used to opacify the decorative glass of the Oldbury bead types they can be characterised further. The relatively high levels of manganese oxide in the white glass is typical of the 2nd century and later (Henderson 1986) and analyses so far have found that these levels of manganese oxide are not found in opaque white glass produced earlier than the 2nd century B.C. In this the opaque white glass compositions have a chronological significance for the beads. The reason why there is a sudden change in the glass compositions in the 2nd century B.C. probably relates, in a narrow sense, to the change in base glass compositions - a shift in the use of an antimony decolorant in the base glass to the use of manganese instead. The matrix of the chevron-decorated bead from Glastonbury is decolorised with antimony trioxide (Table 6.7, analysis 13) because the bead dates to the earlier Iron Age. In producing opaque white glasses the decolorant (antimony or manganese oxides) has probably been added to 'clean' a pale green glass.

Interestingly this change in the base glass composition is also found in the white glass used for the decoration of zig-zag decorated beads.

ii. Translucent colours. Translucent glass colours are due to the presence of brightly coloured metal oxides of mineral origin dissolved in the glass. Only very small amounts of the colorants are necessary and their addition to colourless or pale green glass would have been closely controlled by using a small quantity of coloured frit or highly coloured fragment of glass. Alternatively bead production centres may have used imported ingots or fragments of highly coloured glass which were then worked into beads as evidently occurred in the late Iron Age (Henderson 1987b).

The blue glasses from Glastonbury are coloured by cobalt oxide, all accompanied by relatively high levels of manganese oxide, so it would appear that a manganese-rich source of cobalt had been used at some point in the production process. The translucent purple glass contains relatively high manganese oxide levels and no detected cobalt; Table 6.7, analysis 21 includes 3.77% manganese oxide which is apparently excessive producing a very deep translucent purple 'black' glass. The single translucent brown glass analysed (Table 6.7, analysis 11) appears to be coloured by iron oxide (with no manganese detected). A single translucent green glass bead analysed (Table 6.7, analysis 20) also contains iron but no detected manganese; the reason why different colours are produced in the brown and green beads, where iron acts as a colorant, is due to the atmosphere within the furnace being predominantly oxidising for the green glass and reducing for the brown glass (Henderson 1985).

The translucent turquoise bead is coloured by cupric oxide dissolved in the glass. Although at one time it was considered necessary for lead oxide to be present in a soda-lime-silica glass for a turquoise colour to develop (Biek and Bayley 1979), this analysis with a low lead level (Table 6.7, analysis 24) amongst others indicates that this is not always the case.

The single example of a transparent colourless glass analysed forms the matrix of the 'Meare' chevron-decorated bead. The bead has been decolorised with antimony trioxide (and the yellow glass used in its decoration opacified with lead antimonate) showing that antimony was used for two different functions on the same artefact (Henderson and Warren 1981). Antimony trioxide was replaced by manganese oxide as the principle decolorant in Iron Age European glass in the 2nd century B.C., the former being a more effective decolorant producing a 'water colourless' glass.

Chronological and archaeological significance of the beads.

The glass from Glastonbury Lake Village constitutes the third largest collection of beads from a single Iron Age site in Britain after Meare Lake Village, Somerset (Henderson 1987a) and Wetwang Slack, Humberside (Dent 1982 and Henderson 1987c). The importance of the beads from Glastonbury is that most of the diagnostic decorated bead types (Guido's Classes 6 and 7 and ring beads of group 6) are of second century and later date. Out of the three late Iron Age types one type, the blue bead with bosses and white spirals, is thought to have been produced somewhere in north-western Europe, but not necessarily within the oppida system. On the other hand the other types decorated with whirl decoration and the undecorated ring beads are typical of the products from Continental oppida. The raw materials used for the whirl-decorated bead type incorporate tin as an opacifier which is thought to be a product of Celtic innovation in glass production, to the extent that the classical Late Hellenistic and Early Roman worlds can no longer be seen as the only and obvious influence on the development of Iron Age glass technology.

On this occasion it is possible to relate the radical socio-economic changes that befell Europe in the 2nd century B.C. and the emergence of oppida and their trade network with the introduction of new glass raw materials. This suggests that the supply and source of glass raw materials changed in the 2nd century B.C. and that presumably the entire organisation behind the production of glass as a specialised industry also changed (Henderson 1991,135). Industrial organisation certainly became more centralised in the late Iron Age.

Chemical analysis of the Oldbury type bead reveals a separate and equally interesting situation. The beads appear to be a product of an industry at the periphery of the oppida system in Europe using different opacifiers and therefore presumably not linked to or produced in the oppida system.

Glastonbury Lake Village is unusual in having a mixture of beads, both those typical of oppida and non-oppida systems. Indeed for the late Iron Age this is significant in that it suggests that it was a site of exchange or trade which possibly lay at the fringe of both oppida and non-oppida systems, with Hengistbury Head forming a northern edge of the Continental oppida system proper (Cunliffe 1978,1987) where lumps of (imported) raw glass were found which can be paralleled in other European oppida. In an earlier phase of the Iron Age Meare Lake Village can also be seen as lying at the interface of two tribal territories and perhaps offering political neutrality to the artisans who worked glass and other materials and for exchange.

Quite distinct in its composition is the glass used for the manufacture of the colourless barrel shaped ('Meare') bead decorated with opaque yellow chevrons. This would have been made in a period before the 2nd century B.C. and the diagnostic compositions of its colourless and opaque yellow glass shows that discrete and diagnostic raw materials were used in its production which can be easily distinguished from late Iron Age glass. Meare is a unique site in a European setting producing some very unusual and distinctive evidence for the manufacture of glass beads there (Henderson 1980, 1981, 1987a). The only example of a Meare type glass bead from Glastonbury probably indicates that it remained in circulation for between 100-200 years after Meare Lake Village went out of use.

Although there is evidence for the use of new raw materials for the production of opaque glass during the European late Iron Age to produce distinctive Iron Age glass bead types, however, evidence for fritting, the first stage in glass production where the primary raw materials are partially fused together, is lacking. Since no proven evidence for fritting has been found in the Roman world either, where considerably larger volumes of glass were used, we cannot discount the possibility that glass was made from primary raw materials in Iron Age Europe during the late Iron Age and possibly the earlier Iron Age.

Figure 6.8 shows that the glass beads occurred widely across the site. They were found in contexts dating from at least the Middle Phase through to the Final Phase.

6.7 SHALE (fig.6.8)

Bulleid and Gray were reticent about committing themselves as to whether shale working had taken place on site. On-site working of shale probably did occur but at a very low level of output. A single Calkin (1953) type B lathe core (K 4) and four unfinished shale rings (K 1, K 3, K 21, K 22) are the sole evidence. The waste core attests to the use of the lathe for turning shale on the site whilst the rings were all handcut and awaiting finishing. The roughouts may have been produced from a block of shale on site or, equally well, they may have been imported in that state from elsewhere for finishing at Glastonbury Lake Village; either way they demonstrate on-site working. Apart from the core there is no record of any other waste material or debris derived from shale working, something that would have been present in quantity had the activity taken place on any scale, nor were any raw blocks of shale found or tools that could be identifiably associated with shale working. The worked flint was specifically examined from the latter viewpoint. We are left with no indication of where this small-scale activity occurred. The objects listed above derive from a variety of disparate contexts. K 1 and K 4 came from some indeterminate position within M64, K 3 was found in M62, K 21 SE of M6 and K 22 in M15. The limited evidence for shale working balanced against the relatively large number of finished items, particularly armlets, argues for the importation in finished state of at least a proportion of the pieces. Repairs attempted on armlet K 30 imply that such objects were not readily available.

With a single exception all shale, finished, unfinished and waste, related to rings of various forms, predominantly armlets. The exception is K 27 a rim fragment from a lathe-turned bead-rimmed bowl.

K 9, K 11 and K 13 are fragments from a single armlet and provide a rare example for the on-site movement of material. K 9 was found within M49 whilst K 11 and K 13 are from M12 Floor 1 on the other side of the site. Based upon our proposed phasing of the settlement K 9 should derive from Floor 1 or 2, the Final Phase. It is regrettable that the context of this piece was not recorded, as a rare opportunity to use artefactual material to assist in the phasing has been lost. However, M12 Floor 1 is Final Phase, and M49 has only Late and Final Phase Floors.

6.8 FLINT AND CHERT

Bulleid clearly regarded flint as being of minimal interest during the first period of the excavations, hence few pieces found during this time have a provenance. The only comment that Gray was able to make about the earlier finds was that "more flakes and scrapers were found in Mound V than in any other dwelling". The recording of worked flints was much improved in the period 1904-1907 and it is these that were published in the 1917 report. Recorded flint occurs overwhelmingly in the NW and NE of the site with a more minor occurrence in the area of Mounds 80, 81, 82 and 90; this coincides precisely with the areas excavated in 1904-1907 (see fig.2.4). The haphazard approach to the recording is well-illustrated in Appendix 3.1.

Report

By Julian Richards

The assemblage examined totalled 444 pieces of chipped stone out of a total of 520 reported as having been found by the excavators. The material was individually tabulated and a copy of this data is held by the Somerset County Museums Service. The levels of retrieval and recording mean that the questions that can be asked of the assemblage are limited.

Raw material is primarily flint (93% of the material from Mounds, 95% of the overall assemblage). Both gravel and chalk flint were identified by cortex. The remainder of the worked stone is chert, both of a coarse grainy nature, but , more commonly, of a fine grey type. The proportions of the different stones utilised may be a factor of both recognition and selectivity.

Only general comments can be made with any confidence about technology with such a mixed assemblage. Both blade and flake industries are present, represented both by cores and products. The size of the cores, predominantly small, shows considerable effort involved in husbanding the raw material and maximising production potential. The relative absence of larger and cruder cores may, however, be a reflection of selectivity on the part of the excavators.

Identifiable and individually diagnostic pieces date from the Mesolithic to the earlier Bronze Age. Blades, blade cores and a single microlith of geometric form derive from activity at the earlier part of this range. A leaf-shaped arrowhead and fragments of ground flint tools, including one axe fragment, indicate earlier Neolithic activity. The majority of the scrapers, knives and piercers can be ascribed to the remainder of the Neolithic and the earlier part of the Bronze Age. The assemblage also includes two Group VII (Graig Lwyd) stone axe heads.

The problems of identifying the lithic industries of the metal ages are well known and there is nothing in this assemblage which could be confidently identified as a product of the period of the later Iron Age. Gray's assertion that flint working took place on site cannot therefore be sustained.

Comment

(By SCM and JMC)

This conclusion leaves unanswered the question of how the flint reached the site. In spite of the woefully inadequate recording it is very apparent that flint occurred across the site and was not concentrated in a specific area. Just six pieces are ascribed to a Floor, therefore nothing can be ascertained from their contexts of discovery other than that these Floors range from the Early to Final Phases. Some of the more distinguished items such as the leaf-shaped arrowhead and the stone axes may have been picked up on dry land and brought back as souvenirs, or for some other purpose, but this can hardly explain the great bulk of the finds. Clay for the Floors was quarried on dry land and it may be that in the process of extraction they inadvertently destroyed the site of an early settlement bringing back quantities of flintwork within the clay. This explanation is unsatisfactory. Debris from an earlier settlement located on the site of their clay source would have lain primarily in the top soil or upon the surface of the clay and as such lay above the solid clay in which they were interested. Whilst in such circumstances some flint may have become incorporated with the clay to be transported to the Lake Village site it is very difficult to accept that this can be the explanation for such a widespread distribution of flint over the site brought in over a period of time spanning the settlement's existence.

It is important to emphasise that there was no occupation on the Lake Village site prior to the Iron Age settlement so that all 500-plus flints are a part of that occupation. The early disinterest in flint must inevitably mean that the extant pieces represent but a part, possibly a small part, of the actual assemblage; the remainder probably rests in backfill or dumps. It is clear that some of the flints exhibit earlier technology or typology and as such are unquestionably not products of the Iron Age. A large majority, however, are undiagnostic flakes or lumps, lacking any identifiable or recognisable characteristics. They are opportunistic pieces gathered, flaked, used and discarded at random by Iron Age people who placed no real value on flint as a raw material except for occasional edges or points. That we can distinguish no Iron Age technology cannot mean that there was no Iron Age use of the material.

A similar problem exists in relation to the nearby sites of Meare Village East and Meare Village West. Both were located on virgin sites but produced substantial, highly dispersed quantities of worked flint. 1974 pieces of worked flint were found, 505 and 1469 respectively, in secure Iron Age contexts. Excavations on Mound 19 at Meare Village East in 1982 produced a total of 53 flints, a good indicator of the failure of Bulleid and Gray to save or even notice flintwork in their excavations. This figure, if Mound 19 was a typical sample, implies that a total of many thousands of flints should have been retrieved from the three sites. As with Glastonbury Lake Village both Meare assemblages included typologically diagnostic early Neolithic and late Neolithic-early Bronze Age forms (Orme et al 1983,61-63; Coles 1987,78-81; Gray and Cotton 1966,360-370; Smith 1981,65)

A fully satisfactory explanation for the presence and also the use of the Glastonbury Lake Village flintwork remains to be found but the problem is shared with Meare Villages East and West.

6.9 STONE

By Fiona Roe

A total of 510 pieces of stone were examined, and in addition two thin sections were made. Querns and quern fragments account for 19 of the pieces and the remaining items were nearly all waterworn pebbles, although not all of these appeared to have been utilised. The main sources for this worked stone were relatively few (Table 6.8), and all needs for lithic materials could be met relatively locally, the longest journey to obtain stone being around 25km from the site.

There were three main source areas: 1. Beach pebbles

for various uses were collected from the Severn shore, along part of Bridgwater Bay; 2. other small pebbles could be collected from the Burtle Beds somewhat nearer to the site; 3. the quern materials and a few other miscellaneous pieces came from the Mendip area.

The Severn Shore.

A source for the worked pebbles along the Severn shore near Steart was suggested in the original report (Bulleid and Gray 1917,621), and it was thought that they might derive from Carboniferous sandstones. Recent work now enables further explanation of why this particular source was favoured. There are 272 examples of worked beach pebbles, all elongated in shape and often fairly flat. Many of these pebbles were used for two or more purposes (Table 6.9). I have assumed the probable main utilisation, sometimes an arbitrary distinction, and also the subsidiary uses. It is clear that a great many of the pebbles were used as polishers.

There are storm beaches along part of the Severn shore in Somerset, and today a shingle ridge some 7 metres above O.D. can be found north of Stolford, extending eastward towards Fenning Island (Whittaker and Green 1983,84). The coastline of the Severn has changed over the centuries, but in this particular area there is some evidence for stability, in the form of buried shingle from earlier beaches (Kidson and Heyworth 1976,218 and fig.4).

Fieldwork on Catsford Common (ST 238457) has demonstrated that the pebble bank is a mixed deposit. There is a high proportion of Lias pebbles, and these were not collected by the Glastonbury people. There is also an abundance of sandstone pebbles of similar sizes and shapes, colours and textures to those seen on the pebbles from the site. The pebbles on the storm beaches have been described as deriving from Pleistocene gravel outcrops (Whittaker and Green 1983,84), and there are known deposits of Head which contain pebbles of Devonian sandstone from the Quantocks (Whittaker and Green 1983,86; Edmonds & Williams 1985,51). Fieldwork in the Quantocks has provided further confirmation that the sandstone beach pebbles could have originated in the Devonian Hangman Grit from the northern part of the Quantocks, while thin sections made from two of the worked pebbles also seem to suggest a Devonian source. This then explains how the Glastonbury worked pebbles come to be made of sandstone from the Quantocks, rather than from the Mendips, which might otherwise have appeared to be the more local and obvious source. The distance from source to site is 24km.

Uses.

<u>Polishers</u>. The most frequent use for beach pebbles was as polishers, and many of them show traces of this kind of utilisation (Table 6.9), though for a number of pebbles it was thought to have been a subsidiary use. These pebbles tend to be rather flat and have a gloss on one or usually both flat surfaces. The finer-grained varieties of the Hangman Grit were selected, and these tend to be grey-brown or buff, grey-mauve, -pink or -purple, the colours of the excavated examples now being more muted than those of the freshly ground present day beach pebbles. Only five polishers are of different materials, four from smaller quartzite pebbles and one from black chert, and all these were probably obtained from the Burtle Beds.

The polishers were frequently used for one or more activities (Table 6.9). They often have some battering at the ends, but were also used among other things as whetstones, grinding stones and point sharpeners, and are unusual in comparison with other Iron Age assemblages of worked stone. There were a number of polishers at South Cadbury (Roe forthcoming), and there is evidence for similar artefacts from Meare (Gray and Cotton 1966,372-2), and also some pebble burnishers at Cadbury Congresbury (Rahtz et al 1992,214,224 and fig.77). Polished pebbles have been noted from other Iron Age sites, but in very small numbers only.

The actual purpose of these polishers remains enigmatic. Two of them show traces of red ochre, two pieces of which were also recorded, but preparation of colouring material may not have been the primary use. A possibility is use as burnishers for pottery, but it is not thought that pottery was being made on the site. Another suggestion is that they were used for the preparation of leather. This idea was also put forward for highly polished quartz pebbles from Marshfield, Avon, which were thought to have been slickstones (Barford 1985,230). Slickstones were curriers' tools, used for preparing leather once the tanning process had been completed (Thompson 1983,147).

<u>Whetstones</u>. Altogether some 71 pebbles were considered to have been used for whetting, 54 of them with whetting as the main use. Most of them are elongated in shape, though some are flat pieces with worked edges. A number were also used as polishers, and sharpening grooves occur on 7 examples. They are on the whole smaller than the polishers. Some have been worn to an uneven shape. None, however, has been worn down to a small butt, as sometimes seen on other sites, probably because of the abundance of suitable whetstone material. There are two perforated examples (WS 10 and S 46), both illustrated in the original report.

All but three of the whetstones are made from Hangman Grit beach pebbles, finer-grained, predominantly grey varieties having been selected. Three whetstones are made of slate, also likely to be Devonian, and from the same beach source, having again probably originated in the Quantocks. One whetstone, (also with a bevelled end) was thin sectioned (R 269). The rock was shown to be a siltstone with a grain size averaging 0.06mm, containing angular quartz grains, and also mudstone pellets. Such pellets are a feature of certain beds in the Hangman Grits (Hallam 1934,438).

At the time of writing other whetstones made from

Hangman Grit beach pebbles have not been recorded, although further examples from this prolific source could be expected.

Grinding stones. There are 27 worked pebbles with bevelled ends which appear to have been used for grinding purposes, most of them as the main utilisation of the pebble. These are quite varied in shape and size. Some are relatively short and thick, with worn facets that are quite roughly ground, while others are more long and slender, and the facets may be more smoothly worked if used as a polisher and point sharpener. Pebbles with the end worn flat may belong in the same category. There are 7 further examples of these, all occurring as subsidiary uses on other artefacts.

As with the other pebble artefacts, the grinding stones were made predominantly from Hangman Grit, though there is one example each of quartzite and black chert, again probably from the Burtle Beds. One grinding stone was thin sectioned (R 268), and proved to be made from a fine-grained sandstone, with a grain size of about 0.1mm, consisting of angular quartz and altered feldspar, with smaller amounts of calcite, rock fragments, zircon, tourmaline and a little mica. In general this can be compared with a description of thin sections made from the Hangman Grit (Edmonds and Williams 1985,6), though an exact comparison cannot be undertaken without a more extensive thin sectioning programme.

The grinding stones were often used for subsidiary purposes, such as polishing or whetting (Table 6.9), though the exact way in which the bevelled ends were being utilised is uncertain. There are some similar tools from Meare (Coles 1987, fig 3.63).

Pebbles with used ends. There are many pebbles with traces of battering at the ends, in most cases occurring as a secondary or combined use. About half have also been used as polishers. The battering is too slight to merit the description of hammerstone or pounder, a term used here for spherical implements with indications of more robust use, as described below. The pebbles with used ends are usually elongated, either flat or rounded, and all but one are made from Hangman Grit, the exception being a smaller quartzite pebble from the Burtle Beds. This seems to be a type of implement specific to Glastonbury Lake Village, and probably relates to the ready availability of pebbles for tools.

Pebbles with nicked edges. Another feature that may be found on the beach pebbles is nicked sides. Some are pebbles that have been used in a way that suggests point sharpening, sometimes for quite small items such as needles. All these artefacts are made from Hangman Grit.

Point sharpeners. Point sharpening could also produce a longitudinal groove, either along the flat surface of a pebble, or along the edge. There are 11 examples, all made out of Hangman Grit pebbles, and all have been used for other main purposes. Such point sharpeners, though never common, occur regularly on other Iron Age sites, including Meare (Coles 1987,150 and fig.3.63 S20).

Rubbers. There are a number of small rubbers, not all of which may have been used with saddle querns, on account of their size. They can be contrasted with a larger saddle quern rubber of distinctive bun shape. These small rubbers are more varied in shape than the other worked pebbles, and include flat, waterworn pebbles, split halves of more spherical pebbles and small rectangular blocks. Ancillary uses are not very common (Table 6.8). Most of these 25 rubbers appear to be made from coarser-grained varieties of the Hangman Grit, but some of the pieces may have been acquired in the Mendips.

Unworked. Altogether 98 imported pebbles appear to be unworked, though some may have been used for purposes which have left no trace. They were in any case probably brought to the site with the intention of utilisation, though some may subsequently have proved to be unsuitably shaped, while others, with quartz veins, may have been collected for curiosity value. The large number of apparently unused pebbles simply demonstrates the ease of procurement.

The Somerset Levels.

Smaller pebbles from the Glastonbury Lake Village excavations were used as slingstones, and these consist of a different range of materials, mainly flint and quartz, contrasting with the pebbles from the Severn shore both in size and types of stone. These smaller pebbles are likely to have been obtained from the Burtle Beds. The Somerset Levels are not, by nature, an area where good exposure of lithic materials might be expected, but the Burtle Beds stand out as small, low lying islands formed of quartz sand and comminuted shell (Bulleid and Jackson 1938), and they also contain gravel deposits which include pebbles of Chalk flint, quartz and various sandstones. The main outcrop lies around Burtle Hill, about 10km from the site (Green and Welch 1965,112), but there are other localities nearer to the Lake Village. Here were sources for pebbles of a suitable size for slingstones, and occasionally for larger pebble artefacts.

Uses.

Slingstones. There are 63 small pebbles which appear to have been slingstones. The majority are smaller than the slingstones usually seen from Iron Age sites, with an average weight of 27gm. Most of the Lake Village stones weigh less than 25gm. and have a maximum diameter of less than 36mm. Only 24 of the slingstones are larger than this, and the omission was made good with numerous clay slingstones (Bulleid and Gray 1917,624). The larger stone shot weigh between 30gm. and 120gm. and have maximum diameters of between 39mm and 62mm. There was probably some variation in the quarry for which these slingstones were selected, from small birds to larger game.

Table 6.8. Materials used for worked stone.

Severn Shore

		Hangman Grit	Devonian slate
Polishers	135	135	-
Whetstones	54	51	3
Grinding stones	20	20	-
Used ends	27	27	-
Nicked edges	4	4	-
Small rubbers	25	25	-
Unworked	-	98	-
Total	265		

Somerset Levels

		flint	quartzite	black chert	vein quartz	lias	misc. sandstone	igneous	shelly limestone Burtle Beds?	Wedmore stone?	Old Red Sandstone (O.R.S.) misc.
Slingstones	63	36	12	5	4	1	4	1	-	-	-
Pebble tools	8	1	5	2	-	-	-	-	-	-	-
Counters	8	2	-	-	-	2	-	-	-	-	4
Cylinder	1	-	-	-	-	-	-	-	1	-	-
Working surfaces	2	-	-	-	-	-	-	-	-	2	-
Total	82										

The Mendips

		O.R.S. misc.	O.R.S. Beacon Hill	Harptree Beds	Triassic sandstone	red ochre
Saddle querns	6	6	-	-	-	-
Rotary querns	5	2	1	2	-	-
Quern fragments	8	7	-	1	-	-
Smoothers	25	25	-	-	-	-
Hammerstones	6	6	-	-	-	-
Weights	6	6	-	-	-	-
Anvil	1	1	-	-	-	-
Palette	1	1	-	-	-	-
Ball	1	-	-	-	1	-
Colouring material	2	-	-	-	-	2
Total	61					

Table 6.9. Combined uses for beach pebbles. (Totals for main use in bold)

	Polishers	Whetstones	Grinding stones	Flat ends	Used ends	Nicked sides	Sharpeners	Small rubbers
Polishers	**139**	23	10	6	31	8	7	-
Whetstones	23	**54**	10	2	12	5	7	1
Grinding stones	10	10	**22**	1	5	1	3	-
Flat ends	6	2	1	**-**	-	3	1	-
Used ends	31	12	5	-	**28**	7	1	4
Nicked edges	8	5	1	3	7	**4**	1	2
Sharpeners	7	7	3	1	1	1	**-**	-
Small rubbers	-	1	-	-	4	2	-	**25**

The majority of the slingstones (57%) are pebbles of Chalk flint, and there are others of materials including quartzite, vein quartz and black chert. Flint and quartz have been quoted as being particularly common in the Burtle Beds (Bulleid and Jackson 1938,194).

At Meare, by contrast with the Glastonbury Lake Village, there were large numbers of stone slingstones, and very few clay ones (Gray and Cotton 1966,377). One explanation may be that the available exposures of gravel in the Burtle Beds were exploited during the Meare occupations, leaving a scarcity of suitable small pebbles in the area. The few larger slingstones at Glastonbury have an average weight of 56gm.

Other pebble tools. A few of the polishers and other implements were made from pebbles collected from the Burtle Beds (Table 6.8). There are only eight examples, since pebbles large enough must have been scarce. Quartzite was the most versatile material, being used for polishers and tools with bevelled and battered ends. One polisher and one grinder were made from black chert, and there is one flint hammerstone.

Counters. The original reports for both Meare and Glastonbury recorded many counters or small discs (Bulleid and Gray 1917,623; Gray and Cotton 1966,279), but only eight have been examined for the present report. Two proved to be small, flat flint pebbles from the Burtle Beds; four are local Old Red Sandstone, and two are made from Blue Lias, another local material, which could have come from the Polden Hills. The Lias was, however, barely used at the site.

Cylinder. An enigmatic object (S 1), originally of approximately cylindrical shape, is made of a soft, very shelly limestone, perhaps an indurated shelly deposit from the Burtle Beds. It has circular burnt marks on the flat surfaces, and part of a groove round the curved edge.

Working surfaces. Two large slabs could have been working surfaces for domestic jobs such as kneading bread, or preparing other kinds of food. One measures 380x380x85mm, the other 400x370x70mm, and both are made of friable, light coloured [calcareous?] sandstone, which may have been obtained from the Isle of Wedmore, about 15km to the north west.

The Mendips.

The main lithic resource in the Mendips, as far as Iron Age communities were concerned, was the Old Red Sandstone, which was of importance because of its suitability for querns, an essential item of equipment. There are five separate areas of Old Red Sandstone in the Mendips (Duff et al 1985), and it seems probable that more than one source would have been in use. A conglomerate was obtained from Beacon Hill, about 3km north west of Shepton Mallet (Green and Welch 1965,13) and was used mainly for rotary querns. Micaceous Old Red Sandstone, which splits readily into slabs, was more suitable for saddle querns. This and other less micaceous, but sometimes feldspathic sandstone are from unknown sources in the Mendips. The nearest outcrop to Glastonbury would have been just north of Wells, about 10km from the site.

Another rotary quern material came from the east end of the Mendips, a hard silicified sandstone with fossil casts from the Harptree Beds (Green and Welch 1965,109). Further materials from the Mendip area such as Triassic sandstone and haematite were used for the odd item only, and are described individually below.

Uses.

Querns. The Glastonbury Lake Village excavations produced eighteen saddle and thirty-eight rotary querns (fig.8.2), which were described in the original report, together with geological identifications (Bulleid and Gray 1917,608). Forty of the querns were reported on as being made from Old Red Sandstone and thirteen from silicified sandstone. A number of these querns are now lost, and only eleven of the more complete examples have been examined for this report, together with eight fragments. These included five saddle querns of Old Red Sandstone, one of which (Q 15) appears to have been made from a cobble or small boulder, suggesting surface collections of loose material. There is also half a bun-shaped rubber of Old Red Sandstone (Q 31). There are five surviving rotary querns. Three are made from Old Red Sandstone, one of them (Q 15) a conglomerate likely to have come from Beacon Hill. There are also seven querns or rubber fragments of Old Red Sandstone.

Two lower rotary querns (Q 1 & Q 8) and also a fragment (Q 51) are made from silicified sandstone which contains casts of Jurassic fossils. In the original report it was suggested that this material came from a liassic shore deposit near Croscombe (Bulleid and Gray 1917,612), but a day of fieldwork in the area yielded nothing that could be compared with the querns, while a thin section (R 259) of a sandstone from a Rhaetic shoreline deposit near Crapnell Farm (Green and Welch 1965,84) also produced a negative result. However, fieldwork around Oakhill, about 6 km north east of Shepton Mallet, located a similar stone from the Harptree Beds, so boulders lying on the surface may have supplied the material for querns. The lower stone of a rotary (Q 8) has an uneven under-surface suggestive of just such a weathered boulder. The hard silicified stone, combined with cavities left by fossils, would probably have been very suitable for the grinding of corn, in the same way that the vesicular nature of Niedermendig lava lent itself to milling and grinding.

The querns from Meare were also from Mendip Old Red Sandstone, including likely pieces from Beacon Hill (Gray and Cotton 1966,385), and there was also a rotary fragment (Q 98) of the silicified sandstone.

Smoothers. Flat slabs with a smooth working surface can be distinguished as another tool type, likely to have been used differently from the pebble polishers and perhaps also the small rubbers. They are on the whole larger than the rubbers, but are still of a size convenient to hold in the hand. There are 25 such slabs, and their purpose is unknown. They could have been used on saddle querns with a fairly flat working surface, though other uses need not be discounted. They are all made from Old Red Sandstone, which is sometimes micaceous, and in shades mainly of pink, with buff and grey, contrasting with the shades of grey-mauve and grey-purple found with the worked pebbles.

Hammerstones. Mendip Old Red Sandstone was also used for hammerstones or pounders. There are six of these, mostly approximating to a spherical shape, and also one large flint pebble with battered ends (HS 31). In addition three of the weights described below show traces of use as hammerstones.

Weights. There are six shaped objects which are considered to be weights. These approximate to a cubic shape, but with all the edges rounded, and, like the hammerstones, they appear to be made from Mendip Old Red Sandstone.

Anvil. A large boulder of Old Red Sandstone has a battered surface as if it had been used as an anvil.

Miscellaneous worked stone. A stone palette is an unusual item, without known parallels in Iron Age contexts. It is made from a rectangular block of fine-grained, purplish-red sandstone, probably Mendip Old Red Sandstone again. It has a concave upper working surface with a gloss in the centre and also traces of polish on the flat underside and one of the sides.

A small stone ball is made from Triassic sandstone which could have been obtained from the southern margin of the Mendips. It may link with small balls of clay reported from both Meare and Glastonbury (Coles 1987,62 and fig.3.9, D21).

Two pieces of red ochre can be linked with traces of similar material on the edges of a polisher, and on the flat surfaces of a polisher/grinding stone. The colouring matter could also have come from the Mendips (Green and Welch 1965,165).

There is little evidence that sources other than the Severn shore, the Burtle Beds and the Mendips were exploited in any consistent way.

Discussion.

Bulleid was ahead of his time in describing the worked stone from his Glastonbury excavations, and in obtaining geological identifications for the materials used. He was, however, unable to compare the assemblage with material from other sites. The Glastonbury stone is unusual on two counts; first, for the large number of utilised pebbles, and secondly because everything was obtained from within a radius of 24km and often from considerably nearer. Good local supplies of stone meant that there was no need for long distance trade in quern or whetstone materials. Even the silicified sandstone of the Harptree Beds came from only about 15km away.

Supplies of good quality beach pebbles seem to have been a feature of Iron Age economy, particularly in Somerset. At Meare 751 whetstones were recorded (Gray and Cotton 1966,376), and these must surely also have been worked pebbles from Bridgwater Bay.

Spindle whorls were not examined as part of the above work but we are grateful to Dennis Parsons for comments. Of the finished and incomplete spindle whorls approximately 51% were made from stone probably derived from the Severn shore, whilst 44% were of Lias either from a source very local to the site or from the Severn coast. There is a single whorl of Ham Stone (W 163). Amongst the spindle whorls are four fossils, three ammonites (W 6, W 124 and W 131) and an ichthyosaur vertebra (W 144). The vertebra had very clearly been perforated whilst the ammonites had had their centres pushed out. W 144 derives from the Lias. W 6 and W 124 respectively have been identified as *Hildoceras* cf. *bifrons* and *Dactylioceras*, species uncertain. Both are characteristic of the Middle-Upper Lias Junction Bed, the nearest location of which is in the Ilminster region some 30km S of the Lake Village. W 131 is of the genus *Arieticeras*, species uncertain, and probably comes from the Middle Lias Marlstone Rock Bed. The latter underlies the Junction Bed at Ilminster but also occurs much more widely.

6.10 WOODEN ARTEFACTS

Besides the very extensive wooden structural and foundation remains, wooden artefacts were also found. At first sight it may appear that there were surprisingly few such objects in an environment so clearly conducive to the preservation of wood. It should be remembered, however, that there would have been a constant need for fuel, well-illustrated by the large number of hearths, and most broken or superfluous pieces of wood and basketry would have gone on to the fire. The majority of objects that survived to be excavated came from either outside the palisade or were incorporated with other wood in the Floor foundations. The foundations of M30 were particularly prolific yielding various wheel parts and handles. Just three pieces were found on Floors, a position where they would have been less well protected from the normal processes of decay; these are X 8, a ladle, from M4 Floor 6 (Early Phase) and two unidentified objects X 30 from M9 Floor 4 and X 79 from M9 Floor 6, both Middle Phase.

Earwood (1988 and 1993) has recently re-examined the wooden artefacts and shed further light on their nature and method of manufacture. Regrettably only a relatively small proportion of the total number of objects found is available for examination; as stated in Chapter 1, many pieces, particularly the larger items, were reburied on site in an attempt to preserve them. The range of objects found was wide and related to both domestic and economic/craft use: containers, ladles, baskets, a variety of handles, mallets, part of a logboat, wheel hubs and spokes (fig.6.13), a ladder, an anvil-like object (fig.6.14) and possible traps (X 36 and X 71).

Most common were containers and handles. The former totalled at least 16 and included stave built, lathe turned, hand carved and bent wood types (fig.6.15). It is in the containers that the full sophistication of their woodworking capabilities can be seen. The care taken in their making is reflected in the fact that some containers of all types are decorated with incised and sometimes burnt decoration some of which bears a close similarity to that which appears on the pottery. Baskets were used although only parts of two, X 64 and X 90, were identified. A number of bungs or stoppers, X 47, X 48 and X 73, suggests the use of bottle-like containers. Slotted, tapered and socketed handles of various sizes and forms were found. Some retained the tool for which they were made- a saw, billhook, sickle and gouge. Others were probably for tools such as awls and knives.

The excavators were erratic about identifying wood species used for the artefacts. From those that were identified the clear preference was for oak followed by ash. This contrasts with the timber used for the foun-

Fig.6.13 A selection of wooden artefacts. Length of ladle at top left is 215mm.

Fig.6.14 Wooden anvil.

dations where alder was predominant followed by oak, ash, willow and birch.

The finds from the site included tools that were, or may have been, for woodworking. All were for lighter work and as such could have been used in the making of artefacts as well as finishing off structural timberwork. They include:

Adzes: I 77(M4), I 70 and I 73(M4 Floor 2), I 50 and I 51 (SW of M61), I 88(M79 Floor 3) and I 93 (under M71).

Gouges: I 54(under M60), I 62(M9 Floor 7) and I 96(M76 Floor 2).

Spoon augur: I 18(M47).

Wooden mallets: X 27(SE of M30) and X 42(N of M67 outside the palisade).

Draw knife: I 4(SE of M47).

Saws: I 1(E of M22 outside the palisade), I 11(M64 Floor 3), I 52(N of M61 outside the palisade) and I 53(N of M59 outside the palisade). Saws apparently played a minor part in woodworking (see Appendix 4.1).

Some of the 12 iron knives could also have been used for woodworking amongst many other things. Bulleid certainly records the use of knives in the working of smaller objects.

No attempt is being made in the present work to seek external parallels for the Glastonbury Lake Village artefacts but mention must be made of a find at Porz Lind, in the Rhineland, which bears a remarkable similarity

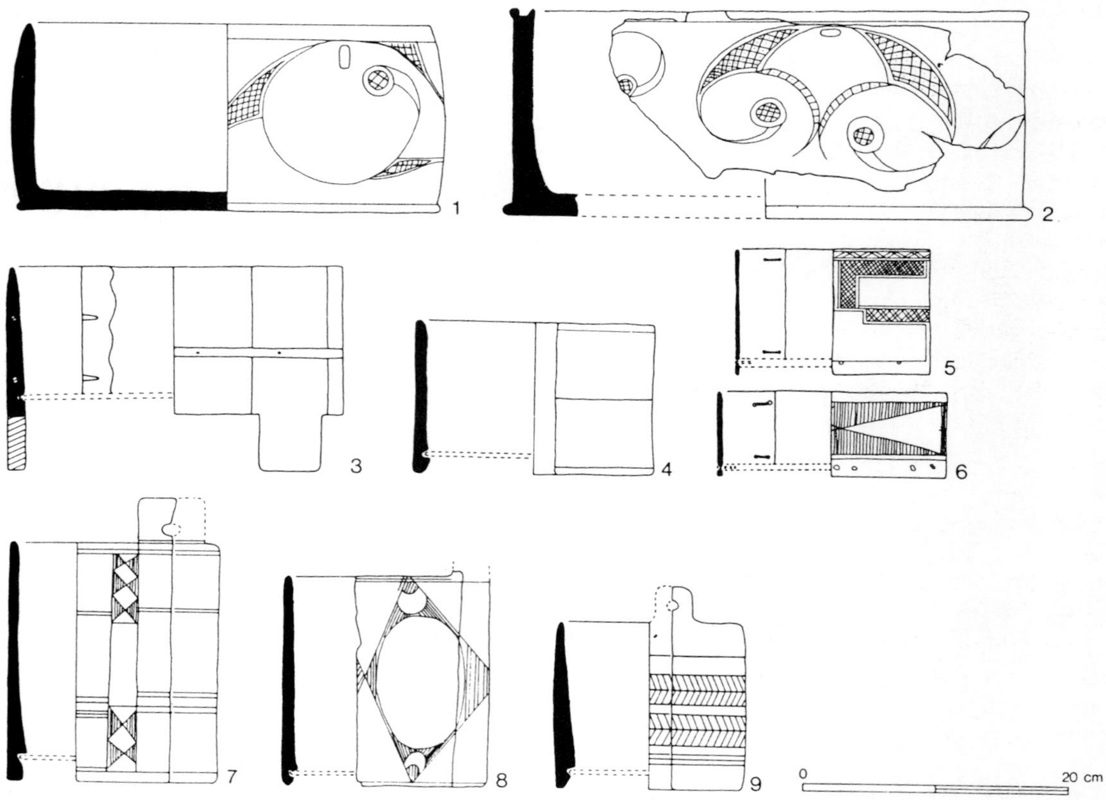

Fig.6.15 Decorated wooden containers. Drawn by C. Earwood.

to the decorated bent wood box X 17 (fig.6.15,6). Porz Lind was an island settlement from which material was deposited in a marsh down slope. Interestingly the Porz Lind find has been dated by dendrochronology to 120-50BC which conforms precisely with Glastonbury Lake Village (Hans Eckhart Joachim pers. comm.).

6.11 POTTERY

A substantial quantity of pottery was excavated, several tonnes according to Bulleid. Detailed examination and analysis of this archive has never been undertaken and lay outside the remit of the current work. Scope for such an exercise would be severely limited by the constraints of poor recording and only a macro approach would be possible (see Chapter 2). Little was allocated to a specific Floor and uncertainty exists as to whether the pottery comes from the actual Mound specified on the box or somewhere in its vicinity. Bulleid only gave a find number to the larger pieces of decorated pottery and the more complete coarse ware vessels (see fig.2.6).

Bulleid was especially interested in the pottery and visited many museums in a search for parallels. His analysis of the pottery from 52 Mounds identified a total of over 5200 vessels. His approach was to categorise the pottery according to distinctive features, decoration, lugs, perforation etc. A comparison of decorated and undecorated pottery was done for the 10 most prolific Mounds (M5, 6, 9, 18, 35, 37, 38, 42, 48 and 69) which produced a ratio of 1:7 respectively. Notes made by Bulleid during this analysis survive in the Somerset Record Office.

Bulleid was interested in trying to establish the source of the pottery and concluded that manufacture, including the decorated vessels, took place on or near the site. No kilns were identified within the settlement, nor were quantities of wasters found, indicating that pottery making did not take place on the Lake Village site. The only identified waster, P 352, from an unknown location has two cracks running vertically from the rim which clearly occurred during firing. J. Allen Howe F.G.S. was provided with a typical sample of the Glastonbury pottery and undertook an examination of the inclusions within the fabric; this lent support to Bulleid's view that they were almost certainly locally made.

Since Bulleid's work on the pottery little more has been done on the collection. The exceptions are H. Howard's work on the crucibles already referred to and the petrological study of the rock inclusions of Glastonbury ware (fig.1.8) carried out by Peacock (1969) which involved the thin sectioning of 58 sherds from the Lake Village. The results of this work are well known. Pottery from 5 of the 6 Groups identified by Peacock were found amongst the Glastonbury sample and, of these, Groups 2 and 3 with a Mendip origin predominated. A particularly close match for the sandstone inclusions of Group 3 was found in the outcrops of Beacon Hill, near Shepton Mallet. This is worth noting, although it was not fully confirmed by Peacock, as this area has already been identified as the probable source of stone used for the manufacture of a proportion of the Lake Village querns. Peacock only looked at decorated pottery of typical Glastonbury ware type but more recent work at Meare Village East (Rouillard 1987) has shown that Groups 3,4 and 5 included undecorated pottery.

Amongst the Glastonbury Lake Village pottery is a number of published and unpublished cordoned bowls. Although few in number Bulleid recognised them as being distinctive and numbered them XX in his summary of pottery forms (1917, Plate LXXVI). Examination of these sherds by Val Rigby has identified them as imports: P 275 from M30 (Bulleid and Gray 1917, Plate LXXX) is a wheel-thrown Armorican import of a type found in central southern Britain but with a particular concentration at Hengistbury Head. It belongs to Freestone and Rigby's Group 9 (1982) and dates from circa 120 B.C. to before Caesar's conquest of Gaul. P 228 from M18 (Bulleid and Gray 1917, Plate LXXXIII) is a cordoned jar with a black bitumen-like coating. Such a carbon coating is common in northern France through to Armorica. This type was not found in the Hengistbury Head assemblage indicating another point of entry into southern Britain. It is of similar date to P 275. Unnumbered cordoned bowl sherds of Freestone and Rigby's vesicular fabric 8 (1982) were found in M12 and from between M51 and M53. The source of these bowls is uncertain but they are probably imports. Again their date is as P 275. Part of a fourth cordoned bowl was found in M23, this time of an unclassified sandy fabric. Another potential import, P 190 from M21 (Bulleid and Gray 1917, Plate LXXX), cannot be traced.

Whilst small in number these five, possibly six, vessels are important in bringing Glastonbury Lake Village within the group of sites in southern Britain receiving such imports. They were found across the central area of the Lake Village but being so few in number and lacking all contextual data little can be said about their on-site significance. Meare Village East produced no such imports whilst the Meare Village West assemblage included an Armorican wheel-turned graphite-coated bowl, P 90, and the base of another possibly imported bowl, P 87.

Among the many thousands of unnumbered sherds are a few that appear to exhibit traces of some paint-like substance (J. Bayley pers. comm.). Painted wares of the late Iron Age are rare in Britain but are well documented in continental western Europe (Société Archéologique Champenoise 1991).

Mention must be made of the small amount of Romano-British pottery found. P 166 and P 175 were discovered in M68, P 132 outside the palisade to the west of M69 plus, apparently, some unnumbered and untraced sherds from M69 itself and an unnumbered bowl sherd was found in or near M16. Bulleid, fortunately, recorded the fact that the pottery from M68 and M69 came from a higher level than the Iron Age finds and as such was clearly a later arrival and nothing to do with the period of occupation of the settlement. The pottery dates to the 2nd-3rd century A.D. (M. Langdon pers comm).

6.12 HUMAN REMAINS

By Geraldine Barber, Rebecca Wiggins and Juliet Rogers

Bulleid and Gray prefixed the human remains find numbers by the letter M; to avoid confusion Mound is spelt in full in this section rather than abbreviated to M as elsewhere in this book; thus M 13 (bone) from Mound 18.

Adult Remains.

Skulls with evidence of injury.

For each individual the sex and age were estimated where possible (Brothwell 1981). Each skull and mandible was measured using standard osteological landmarks (Brothwell, 1981) and any cranial or mandibular non-metric traits were noted (Brothwell, 1981). The presence of any pathology was recorded, described and where possible an explanation or diagnosis given.

M 6. A complete skull and complete but broken mandible in excellent condition were available for examination. From the shape and size of the skull it was concluded that it was from an adult male.

The mandible and maxilla were complete, with spaces for 30 teeth (the lower left and right third molars being missing or unerupted) two of which were lost post-mortem. No evidence for caries or ante-mortem tooth loss was present. The degree of tooth wear is that of an adult aged between 33-45 years.

The skull was 189mm in length (glabella to posterior point on occipital) and 140mm (biparietal breadth at right angles to mid saggital plane). No cranial non-metric traits were present, except for an extrasutural (Wormian) bone around the lambda. This is of no special significance and occurs in approximately 70% of Iron Age/Romano-British individuals.

The skull had at least four cut marks on it. The first and largest was a cut from the right frontal bone 116mm long to the right parietal. The cut is through the entire table of the skull, fracturing the right parietal in several places. There is no evidence for healing either endocranially or ectocranially.

A second slice was present to the back of the head. The cut is 81mm long and is from just to the right of the saggital suture across the middle left parietal. The cut is through the width of the table and there is no evidence of healing.

A third cut was found to the back of the head. The cut is through the entire table of the skull, communicating with the second cut leaving a partially severed roundel of bone in the left parietal.

A fourth cut was found on the right of the occipital a third of the way down from the lambda. The cut glances off the skull, cutting through to the diploe, but not the entire table. Again, there is no evidence of any healing or bone reaction.

The shape, size and appearance of the four cut marks are consistent with blows from a sword or other sharp object and are not due to post-mortem or excavation damage. As there is no evidence for healing or any bone reaction it is concluded that these injuries occurred just before or at the time of death.

M 8. A complete skull with no mandible (the fragment of mandible labelled M 5 was said to be from this individual in the original report, but it does not appear to be so, although it is too small a piece to be conclusive) was submitted for study. The shape and size of the skull is that of an adult male.

The maxilla was present with sockets for 15 teeth (the upper left third molar was missing or unerupted) of which 11 were lost post-mortem. There is no evidence for caries or ante-mortem tooth loss. From the degree of tooth wear it is calculated that this individual was aged between 25-35 years.

The skull measures 185mm long and 139mm wide and has no cranial non-metric traits.

This skull had a number of cut marks present. The first was a cut at the base of the skull of roughly rectangular shape between the vomer and the pharyngeal tubercle and the left foramen ovale and right carotid canal. There is no evidence for healing or bone reaction, but it is impossible to tell if this cut occurred at or just before the time of death, or if it is post-mortem interference. Associated with this cut is a slice from the back of the head to the front, shearing the left mastoid and left zygomatic arch.

The second injury was a glancing cut on the left parietal which removed a 53mm by 9mm piece of bone. The cut just breaks through the table at one point. There is no evidence of healing.

A third cut removed a piece of bone 21mm by 6mm on the left parietal at the junction with the frontal suture midway down the parietal. The cut did not break through the table and there is a slight bone reaction, which indicates that this injury occurred a while before death and is not contemporary with the other injuries present on this skull.

A fourth cut was found on the right occipital and parietal across the lamboid suture, 41mm in length. There is no bone removed, table cutting or evidence for healing.

The outside surface of the skull was smooth except for two areas of fine pitting over the frontal bone, and also over the posterior of the left and right parietals. The pitting may be due to some sort of scalp infection, possibly even from the earlier wound (see third cut) but this is not certain.

At least two of the cut marks are consistent with a sword or other sharp object and happened at or just before

the point of death. The other cuts may also have occurred at this point, but there is not enough information to conclude this.

M 15. The skull had no associated mandible. The shape and size of the skull is that of an adult male.

The maxilla was present with tooth spaces for 16 teeth, 10 of which were present. The 6 missing teeth had all been lost post-mortem, and there was no evidence for caries, abscesses or ante-mortem loss. From the state of wear of the present teeth it is concluded that this individual was between 17-25 years old at the time of death.

The skull is 187mm long and 143mm wide, of normal shape and size. There is no evidence for any cranial non-metric traits except for the presence of a right parietal foramina, which is present in most skulls and is of no known significance.

There is one cut mark which is at the posterior of the left zygomatic arch, with no evidence of healing. This mark may be due to a cut from a sword or other sharp object, but in this case, post-mortem damage cannot be ruled out.

There is also a small circular lump approx 20mm in diameter, two thirds of the way down the saggital suture. This does not seem to be of any significance.

There is inconclusive evidence of pathology on this skull, and as such no cause of death can be given.

M 19. A complete skull with associated mandible. The shape and size of the skull, 181mm long and 139mm wide, is that of an adult female.

The mandible and maxilla had 32 tooth spaces present, of which 14 teeth were present. The other teeth were lost post-mortem as there is no evidence for ante-mortem loss. There is no evidence for caries, abscesses or any other dental abnormalities.

The skull has an extrasutural (Wormian) bone at the lambda, which is not of any significance (see previous comments).

The skull has a slight indentation to the left of the midline of the frontal bone which is a healed past lesion (differential diagnoses: from either old healed injury or sebaceous cyst) with no evidence of infection.

A large cut mark caused by a sharp object such as a sword was present on the back of the left parietal, 90mm long, causing a curved fracture round to the right parietal (172mm long in total). There is no evidence for healing leading to the conclusion that this injury happened just before or at the time of death.

Disarticulated and charred human remains.

It is difficult to obtain much information from isolated animal or human bones, and what can be gained depends entirely on which fragment of bone is recovered. From unburnt disarticulated bones the species, age, sex, stature and notes of any bony pathologies present are the maximum of information that can be gained. Charred material is more difficult as burning distorts the shape and size of the fragment, making measurements of any kind impossible. Often only the type of bone species present is all that can be identified.

For this assemblage, the bones were identified using a reference collection. Where the material was charred, this is mentioned. The human material has been aged where possible using Brothwell (1981). Where immature animal bones were present these were aged using the criteria of Silver (1969).

M 1. 72 Fragments of unidentifiable human skull and longbones

M 2. 1 human ?right humerus shaft fragment

M 5. 8 human mandible fragments from an adult aged ?25-35. None of the teeth showed any signs of caries, abscesses or dental abnormalities. One of the teeth, the lower left third molar, is not present. (see comments on skull M8)

M 7/7A/7B. 3 fragments of adult human skull, one right and one left parietal and one occipital. These are all from one person

M 9. 1 human parietal fragment

M 11. This consisted of both animal and human remains. The charred animal bone comprised:

1 left distal humerus fragment from an adult cow(*Bos taurus*)
1 left proximal femur from a ?cow (*Bos taurus*) under 42 months old
1 right distal humerus from a pig (*Sus domesticus*)
8 skull fragments from a cow (*Bos taurus*)
4 fragments of a pelvis of sheep/goat (*Ovis aries/Capra hircus*)
2 mandible fragments from a cow
1 mandible fragment from a pig
1 scapula fragment from a large mammal
1 sheep/goat scapula fragment
1 sheep/goat cervical vertebrae fragment
7 medium mammal rib fragments
2 large mammal rib fragments
3 carpals from a cow including one right astragalus
1 sheep/goat atlas (first cervical vertebrae)
1 left medial phalange of a pig
1 right sheep/goat ulna
1 left proximal radius of sheep/goat
5 small mammal ribs
1 ?frog longbone fragment
101 fragments of unidentifiable bone

The charred human material (all fragments) consisted of:

55 skull
136 longbone
1 right ulna
1 left ulna
2 scapula
8 tibia

2 humeral head
1 phalange for first metatarsal
2 first metatarsal
3 thoracic vertebrae
1 proximal phalange
1 medial phalange
1 medial cuneiform
1 intermediate cuneiform
3 pelvis
1 right femur without femoral head
1 radius head
1 vertebral body
1 distal femur
1 cervical vertebrae
1 left clavicle
1 metacarpal head
7 ribs
1 proximal tibia
1 talus
1 right fourth metacarpal
120 unidentifiable human bone fragments
3 fragments of mandible. Thirteen sockets with all teeth lost post-mortem. The socket for the lower right second incisor is rotated.

All these fragments could have come from the same person. In addition, there is a left tibia fragment from a young infant (?foetal).

M 12. 1 human left tibia shaft fragment. Dawkins stated that the bone had been gnawed by a dog, there is no evidence for this.

M 13. Charred and ranging in colour from white to dark grey. The following fragments of human bone were identified:

88 small and medium fragments of left and right parietal (MNI=1), the largest of which measures 75mm by 61mm

1 fragment of a femoral head of an adult ?female, but shrunk

1 fragment of unidentifiable longbone

Animal bone was present: 1 carpal from a cow

M 20. 1 human clavicle shaft fragment with gnawing at both ends. This could have happened at any time between the original deposition and excavation and is not necessarily significant. The gnawing of this bone may have been by any one of a number of species, including fox and cat and not only dog as stated by Dawkins.

M 23. 1 human right temporal bone from an adult ?female

M 26. The material was charred to a black colour, and consisted solely of human material. The following fragments were identified:

21 skull fragments

6 mandibular and maxillary fragments

44 tooth fragments

These fragments are from the same individual, an adult aged between 33-45 years. None of the teeth showed any evidence of caries. The presence of a non-metric trait, a metopic suture in the frontal bone was also noted. This is not thought to be of any significance. No pathology was visible on any of these fragments.

M 27. 60 human adult skull fragments

2 human infant/foetal vertebral bodies

1 human infant/foetal thoracic vertebrae fragments

1 human infant/foetal longbone fragment

M 29. A fragment of a left human mandible with 3 teeth present (1st and 3rd molars). The mandible was from an adult aged between 17-25 years old. No pathology was noted.

M 30. 35 human skull fragments (including parietal and temporal)

M 31. 1 human lower left first molar fragment from an adult aged 25-35 years

M 32. 1 human upper first molar from an adult aged between 25-35 years

M 35. 2 human parietal fragments

M 40. 14 fragments of adult right parietal from one individual. There was no evidence of any pathology.

The Subadults.

Ten subadult inhumations were found at the site of Glastonbury Lake Village. None of the individuals was complete: the average amount of bone preserved was 40%, and only seven individuals could be assigned to the neonatal age group with confidence. Three of the individuals could not be aged so accurately, due to their state of preservation; however, they were placed tentatively in or near the neonatal category. The methods of assigning ages to the skeleton will be discussed below.

Ageing.
The age of the skeletons was determined by using standard subadult techniques. These were:

1. dental development
2. epiphyseal fusion
3. long bone length
4. length of the basioccipital and ilium

Dental development is considered the most accurate method of ageing subadult skeletal material, as it is believed to be under less environmental control than is skeletal development (Demirjian 1986). This appears to be particularly true of tooth root closure and crown development, with eruption times and sequences being slightly more variable. It is therefore important to examine every aspect of each tooth in the dentition. Schour and Massler (1940) are the standard used most widely for modern and ancient skeletal material, and were used in this report.

Epihyseal fusion is regarded as a somewhat less accurate method of ageing subadults than the dentition; but, while the times at which these fusions occur tend to be variable, sometimes within a two year span, their sequence appears rigidly controlled. Therefore, this is an important aspect of subadult ageing, particularly in infant and foetal skeletons, in which many skull fusions occur in a relatively short space of time. Gray's Anatomy (1980) was used for estimating the occurrence of epiphyseal fusion.

Long bone length is probably the most variable, and therefore least accurate, method of ageing subadult skeletons. The theory relies on the concept that all children are of a uniform average bone length at each stage of biological development, that can be related to calendar years. There are many exceptions to this rule; the variation in bone length is often too great to have any significance to biological or calendar age. However, Maresh's (1955) radiological study of long bone length provides us with a standard of approximate long bone lengths for age from a large sample size. This can then be used as a guide to compare long bone lengths to other ageing methods. The size of the ilium should not exceed 40mm length and 36mm breadth prior to birth. The basisoccipitalis is equal in length and breadth (before birth the length is greater) at birth (Fazekas and Kosa 1978). All individuals were aged using as many of the techniques as the preservation of the skeletons allowed. The cases in which it was not possible to age with confidence (M 16, 17 and 39) were not as well preserved as the other individuals. M 16 was considered to be a neonate or 9½ lunar months old. M 39 had a long bone length greater than its fusion stage, placing it between 7½ months in utero and birth. M 17 was placed between birth and three months of age. All the other skeletons were placed in the neonatal category.

Pathology.
There was no evidence of pathological lesions on any of the subadult skeletons.

Conclusion.
The Glastonbury Lake Village subadult burials were comprised of ten individuals in or close to the neonatal age category. The state of preservation was in general reasonable, although all lower legs and feet were missing, and there were some fragmentation and worn bone surfaces. There was no evidence of any pathology associated with any of the skeletons.

The following human remains could not be traced and have therefore not undergone re-examination: M 3, M 4, M 10, M 14, M 17, M 18, M 24, M 34, M 36.

Discussion (SCM)

Human bone occurred in all contexts: outside the palisade, in the timber foundations, below clay spreads, in the peat and black earth and directly associated with clay spreads and the Floors of houses. The distribution coincides with the general spread of debris across the site, including the gap in activity in the centre (fig.8.10).

Dawkins (1917,675-8) claimed that the distribution of single bones and the presence of injuries on four of the skulls, probably inflicted with a sword, was sufficient evidence for the settlement having been brought to a violent end "....it may be concluded that the Lake-village was stormed and that the inhabitants were massacred, some being decapitated and the heads carried on spears, before they were thrown into the morass outside the palisades." Bulleid, correctly, did not concur with this view but nevertheless allowed Dawkins to have his say. Few of the human remains can be ascribed to a phase but there are sufficient to show that there was no single event responsible for their distribution.

Early Phase:

M 13 from Floor 4 of Mound 18 (house)

M 34 found on Floor 4 of Mound 35 (house)

Middle Phase:

M 12 found on Floor 2 of Mound 18 (clay spread)

M 36-38 from 'Floor 3' of Mound 70 (no identifiable surface)

Late Phase:

M 22 on surface of Floor 4 of Mound 57 (house)

M 39 on Floor 2 of Mound 71 (clay spread)

Lack of detailed recording makes for difficulties in the interpretation of the human remains. The more complete of the remains may well represent burials and these are very largely composed of neonatals and probable neonatals. Of the sub-adult burials one (M 16 and M 17) was found outside the palisade to the north of Mound 49, three (M 25, M 28 and M 33) were found between Mounds and four were directly associated with Floors, two (M 37 and M 38) from 'Floor 3' of Mound 70 in close association with the first hearth from where a fragment of humerus was also found, one (M 39) from Floor 2 of Mound 71 and one (M 22) from close to the NW edge of the hearth on Floor 4 of Mound 57.

Two reasonably complete adult remains were found; both had undergone charring. M 26 which lay with its head orientated to the north west was found in brushwood immediately to the east of Mound 9. The bones were in poor condition at the time of discovery with only the skull, two femora, tibiae and fibulae surviving. Regrettably they are now reduced to skull, mandible and tooth fragments. The long bones were described as in 'apposition' when excavated. M 11 from outside the palisade NW of Mound 48 comprised the most fully representative range of bones amongst the adult remains. Nothing is known of the circumstances of deposition except that they were scattered over "a few square feet" (Bulleid and Gray 1917,489)

None of these burials, neonatal or adult, is recorded as having come from a specific context such as a grave. Archaeological data is absent except for those associated with a Floor when they are described simply as having been 'on' or 'on the surface of' the Floor. With one exception none is known to have had associated objects. The exception is M 11 where the recent re-examination revealed that the charred assemblage included a significant proportion of animal bone. Amongst the species represented were cow, pig, sheep/goat and possibly frog. Animal offerings found in association with cremations is a well known feature of the European late Iron Age (Meniel 1993). Cremated animal bone has, for example, recently been provisionally identified in about 25% of the samples of cremated material in the late Iron Age cemetery at Westhampnett, Sussex, where the animal remains were usually those of chicken or pig (Fitzpatrick 1994).

M 13 from Floor 4 of Mound 18 comprised mainly skull fragments plus an adult femoral head, possibly female, and a long bone fragment, all charred. Floor 4 had two levels. Quantities of fire ash, baked clay rubble and charred wood, including wall posts, show that the building associated with the first level suffered a major fire. No mention is made of M 13 in the description of Mound 18 hence its relationship to the burnt debris and the possibility that the charring of M 13 occurred in the conflagration, rather than intentionally, remains undetermined. Indeed M 13 may even have been a casualty of the fire. Except for I 39 and W 76 all artefacts known to come from Floor 4 lay within 2 metres of M 13 but, again, the absence of an attribution to a level means that it is impossible to establish whether these objects derived from the same Floor as the skeletal remains. The survival of a tin spindle whorl in an unmelted state would indicate that this object at least came from the second level of Floor 4.

Individual skulls, complete and fragmentary, form the largest category within the numbered human assemblage, some 40%. This figure excludes individual finds of mandibles and teeth which have been included with the miscellaneous bones in the distribution plot (fig.8.10). The distribution of skulls and fragments shows a preponderance towards the edge of the settlement. Four complete and particularly well-preserved skulls were found (M 6, M 8, M 15, M 19). M 15 and M 19 were found outside the palisade to the NW, M 6 was found outside the palisade to the SE whilst M 8 was found to the NW of Mound 8 just inside the palisade. All had suffered, or probably suffered in the case of M 15, injury inflicted with a sharp object such as a sword at or around the time of death. None of the fragmentary skull remains bore similar evidence though the proportion surviving and the condition might well militate against this. As part of his massacre theory Dawkins stated that M 8, M 15 and M 19 all had evidence for decapitation. Decapitation invariably involves the severing of the cervical vertebrae, the cervical vertebra, however, is absent in each case. None of the cut marks present is in a position appropriate for decapitation or attempted decapitation; they are more consistent with fighting wounds. Dawkins further went on to say that M 8 and M 19 had, after decapitation, been stuck on to spears. M 8 has a large rectangular cut mark on the base of the skull which would be consistent with an object of some kind being put through the base of the skull. Two small nicks on the inside of the foramen magnum of M 19 are far less conclusive. I am grateful to Geraldine Barber for this information.

B 59 is a disc of human skull 70mm in diameter, which has a central perforation and is well smoothed. Found to the NW of Mound 64 this object may have served as an amulet although the absence of signs of wear around the hole from a cord or thong leaves open the possibility that it was a spindle whorl.

The predominance of skulls amongst human bone assemblages from occupation sites has been noted elsewhere. At All Cannings Cross, for example, (Cunnington 1923,40-41) 32 fragments of human skull, representing perhaps 12 individuals, were found in various contexts across the site and of these 4 had been deliberately cut to shape and one pierced for suspension. Similarly at Danebury (Cunliffe 1984,454-455) and Gussage All Saints (Wainwright 1979,24) skull fragments occur more frequently amongst the individual bones than any other part of the skeleton and in a variety of contexts. These examples show that the phenomenon was not confined to one type of site only. They appear to show a particular interest in the human head and its selection for some kind of special treatment. Cunliffe (1991,507) suggests that the presence of skulls and other individual human bones are a reflection of complex rites and beliefs and that disposal of the dead was primarily by excarnation with certain bones being brought back into the domestic situation. The Glastonbury Lake Village assemblage looked at in its entirety may represent up to 25 individuals of which 10 are infants. Disposal of the dead therefore clearly took place off-site. Bulleid and Gray offered a reward to anyone who discovered an Iron Age cemetery, anywhere in the area, but no-one ever claimed the prize.

6.13 DATE OF THE SETTLEMENT

The question of date and duration of the settlement was first dealt with by Dr Robert Munro in his Introductory Chapter in the 1911 book in a section entitled Chronological Range of the Occupation of the Village (1911,29-35). In a somewhat protracted review of the evidence derived from the artefacts his conclusion was that "the range of the occupancy of the Glastonbury Lake Village should be, at least provisionally, restricted to a period of 150 years, extending from 100 B.C. to 50 A.D." The evidence for the latter date, to his mind easier to sustain, was based primarily upon the virtual absence of Romano-British material. A settlement occupied later than the mid-1st century AD would inevitably have yielded greater quantities of such material. A date for the beginning of the occupation was more problematical and his views rested on the absence of anything identifiably earlier than the 1st century BC and the lack of any apparent typological development within the various categories of artefact between those found on the highest and lowest Floors.

When Bulleid came to write *The Lake Villages of Somerset*, he was less specific in giving absolute dates and simply said that the foundation of the settlement was later than that for the nearby site at Meare West for which a date of *c* 250 BC was given. The terminal date for Glastonbury Lake Village was "before the Roman colonization of Britain had taken place, or at any rate before Roman civilisation had made itself felt so far west as Somerset." The issue was not elaborated upon further.

Subsequent researchers have addressed the question of dating. Tratman's proposed timespan for the site was from *c* 250-200 BC through to abandonment in *c* AD 50 (Tratman 1970,164-166). Clarke in his reinterpretation gave the settlement a duration of about 100 years within the period *c* 150±50 BC to 50±50 BC. Without being specific, Clarke said that his dating was artefact based and involved taking "the latest find stratified in the earliest floors, and the latest find stratified within the latest floors" (Clarke 1972,829). Somewhat inexplicably he goes on to state that this dating is "crudely confirmed by pollen analysis, by the four or five feet of peat which accumulated during the occupation of the settlement, and by independent chains of assumptions involving the numbers of superimposed hearths and floors, the frequency of houses and granary rebuilding, and the sample numbers of surviving fibulae, querns, spindle whorls, potsherds and food debris". Further comment appears in Chapter 7.

Recently attempts have been made to place the dating of Glastonbury Lake Village on a more scientific footing. Following the 1984 excavations samples were taken from two planks for tree-ring dating (Morgan 1988,61-62). The hope was that these, allied to other recently taken samples from Meare East and Meare West, would extend the already established short tree-ring chronology for Meare West and, ultimately, provide absolute dating for all three sites. Unfortunately, little progress was made. All the later Meare samples came from small well-worked pieces of wood and no match was found with the existing 53 year chronology. In spite of both Glastonbury samples having a tree-ring series of around 100 years no match was found here either. Comparison with chronologies established elsewhere also failed to produce any convincing results. During the course of the present work the situation was reviewed but remains unchanged (J.Hillam pers.comm.). Had an absolute date been possible for the Glastonbury Lake Village series, the absence of outer sapwood due to the heavily worked condition of the pieces from which the samples were removed would, in any case, have only provided a *terminus post quem*. Dendrochronology undoubtedly has a contribution to make to the dating of Glastonbury Lake Village. This will remain unfulfilled, however, until the opportunity arises to take a series of samples from unworked sections of wood which remain on site and a local tree-ring chronology has been confirmed.

Problems in the calibration of radiocarbon dates for the Iron Age are well known (summarised in Cunliffe 1991, 591-2). Nevertheless an attempt to apply radiocarbon dating to Glastonbury Lake Village was considered justified. Two dates already existed for the Causeway (Coles et al 1988, 81) and it was hoped, depending where they fell upon the calibration curve, that an additional series of dates would provide a reasonable indication of the absolute dates for the duration of the settlement. A second reason for acquiring further dates was that they could provide a check on the proposed phasing of the site described in Chapter 4.

In order to fulfil the latter aim a rigorous review of material suitable for sampling was undertaken. Choice was limited to only bone and antler. This was advantageous in that both bone and antler are short-lived in terms of their C14 uptake - bone ceased at the time of death of the animal and antler when shed by the deer or at death. Pieces that could reasonably be considered to be stratified were identified for each Phase. Bulleid and Gray saved little unworked material, options were therefore confined to worked bone and antler. As far as possible the pieces selected for sampling were off-cuts or waste, to avoid distortion by the heirloom effect or a long period of usage. As only worked pieces were available for sampling, sample size had to be kept to a minimum. Accelerator dating was clearly most appropriate. A successful application was submitted for SERC funding for 15 dates by the Oxford Radiocarbon Accelerator Unit. Unfortunately, some of the antler samples proved unsuitable and the number of dates was reduced to nine thereby making the spread of dates by Phase less balanced than was wished. As far as could be ascertained from the records and visual inspection none of the objects sampled had been subject to treatment, such as conservation work, which might have caused contamination and a distortion of the resultant date. A certain amount of repair work using glue had been carried out but areas affected were carefully avoided during sampling. Had the samples been contaminated the result would probably have been a less consistent series of dates than Table 6.10 shows.

In spite of the extremely low standard deviations the calibrated age ranges are unfortunately very wide, up to 362 years, because of the existence of two radiocarbon plateaux. The quality of the samples and results are such that there is a very strong argument that the absolute dates lie within that span for each sample (R. Housley pers. comm.). Figure 6.16 presents the results in graphic form and includes radiocarbon dates from other Iron Age sites in the vicinity. The latter produce a far more consistent result which, in the case of the Meare dates, is reasonably in line with the artefact typology.

So far as the relative chronology of these dates is concerned one anomaly is instantly apparent; the date for H 357 from Floor 3 of M74 is significantly earlier than that for B 406 derived from the "black earth" below the

Mound. There is no overlap between their calibrated dates. With the exception for the dates for M1 and below M74 the range of calibrated dates for each sample is such that they can be said to conform with the phasing but in reality are so wide in range that they cannot be used as confirmation of the phasing with any confidence.

The radiocarbon dates give an earlier date for the settlement than expected. The calibrated dates give a potential maximum time span of 792BC to AD145 or a minimum span of 472-8BC. The structural and artefactual evidence do not support either possibility.

The site was extremely rich in artefacts. All are unequivocally of Iron Age date (fig.6.9) except for some imported earlier lithic material, a small amount of Romano-British pottery, a probable modern glass bead and sherds of a 14th century jug. Whilst typological dating is insufficiently precise to serve as a means of phasing the site or dating the phases when worked out on the basis of stratigraphical data, viewed as a whole the artefact assemblage can be used to determine the probable duration of the settlement. The evidence is consistently for an occupancy during the first two centuries BC, in other words later than the calibrated radiocarbon dates. In summary the artefact-based dating evidence is as follows:

Pottery. Data contained within the pottery assemblage remains largely untapped. Two comments can be made in the present context. Firstly, Glastonbury ware occurs throughout the period of occupation. Production may have begun by the 4th century BC but certainly continued into the 1st century BC. Secondly, and of more value, are the imports and probable imports of cordoned vessels referred to in section 6.11 which can be confidently dated to the period *c* 120 to mid-1st century BC (Val Rigby pers. comm.). None of the latter material has precise contextual information but the Mounds from which the sherds came span the Early to Final Phases; all have a Late or Final Phase within them:

M12 Late to Final Phase
M18 Early to Late Phase
M21 Late to Final Phase
M23 Middle to Final Phase
M30 Late to Final Phase

All are located within the southern half of the site. It may also be significant that no Durotrigian pottery was found on the site.

Metalwork. Mainly of copper alloy the material can be dated with varying degrees of precision:

The single potin coin (Z 1), found to the south-east of M31, falls in Van Arsdell's (1989,88) Cantian class D or E. It dates from the late 2nd to 1st century BC.

Two iron currency bars were found immediately outside the palisade, one to the north of M48 (Z 2) and one to the south of M5 (Z 3). Though they cannot be precisely dated they are certainly a feature of the 1st century BC and, probably, also the 2nd century BC (Hingley 1990, 111).

Three Wild class 1 button-and-loop fasteners were found (E 151, E 159, E 174). Wild (1970) dated the type to the late Iron Age-Early Roman period. An example closely comparable to E 159 with a plain, solid double-boss head was found at Hengistbury Head in a late Iron Age 2 context of 50 BC to AD 50 (Cunliffe 1987,153).

The three terret rings conform with a 2nd-1st century BC date (Val Rigby pers. comm.). Moulds for casting terrets closely similar to E 8 and E 192 were found in a 1st century BC context in Pit 209 at Gussage All Saints (Wainwright 1979,136 and 133; Foster 1980).

Two links from three-piece bridle bits, both numbered I 12 although from different bits, are of a form with a

Table 6.10. Radiocarbon dates by Phase.

	Find no.	Mound	Years BP	Calibrated date
Early Phase				
OXA-4744	B 198	M27 Floor 4	2230±45	392-197BC
OXA-4745	B 217	M18 Floor 4	2350±45	541-366BC
OXA-4746	B 406	under M74	2190±45	384-164BC
OXA-4747	B 407	M75 Floor 3	2485±50	792-472BC
Middle Phase				
OXA-4748	B 326	M38 Floor 3	2345±45	540-363BC
OXA-4749	H 357	M74 Floor 3	2475±45	785-468BC
Late Phase				
OXA-4750	B 398	M71 Floor 2	2180±45	379-157BC
OXA-4751	H 215	M5 Floor 2	2180±45	379-157BC
Final Phase				
OXA-4752	H 244	M1	2465±45	769-460BC
Causeway				
Q-2618		M47, peat below	1975±70	168BC-AD143
Q-2619		M47, peat below	1920±70	94BC-AD236

Full details of the radiocarbon dates are given in Appendix 6.1.

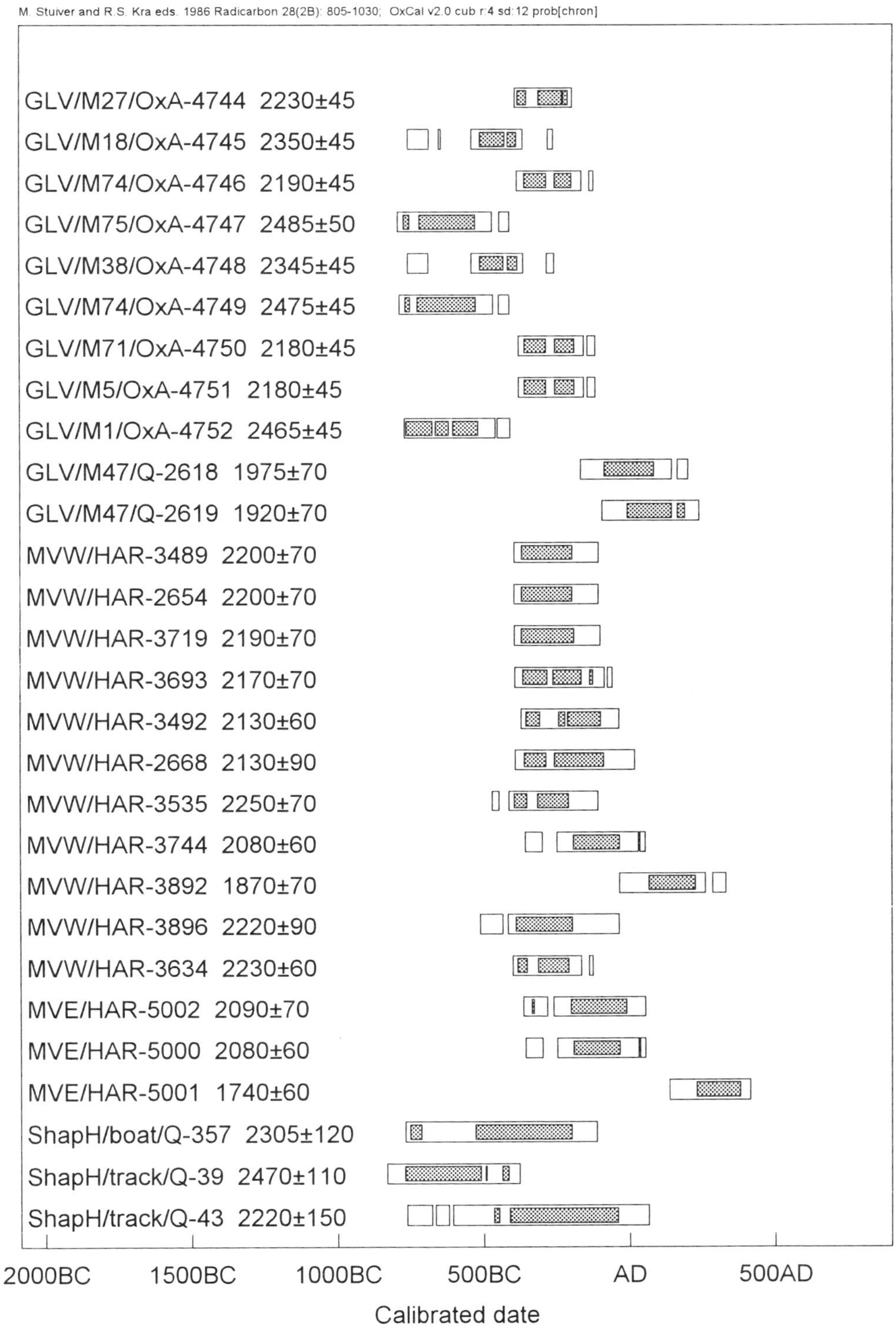

Fig.6.16 Plot of the calibrated radiocarbon ages from Glastonbury Lake Village (GLV/...) with Mound numbers (../ M27..) and Laboratory Codes (OxA = Oxford Accelerator; HAR = Harwell; Q = Cambridge). The other radiocarbon results are from Meare Village West (MVW/..), Meare Village East (MVE/..), the Shapwick Heath logboat (ShapH/boat/..) and the Shapwick Heath trackway (ShapH/track/..). Calibration was done using OXCAL computer program of Ramsey and Hedges (forthcoming) and the bi-decadel calibration curves of Stuiver and Pearson (1986) and Pearson and Stuiver (1986). The individual calendrical age ranges are listed in Table 6.13. The symbols are as follows: shaded bars, one sigma age ranges; unshaded bars, two sigma age ranges.

western distribution and classed as the 'Llyn Cerrig Bach' type. An example was found amongst other items of scrap in pit 209 at Gussage All Saints (Wainwright 1979,129), 1st century BC.

Brooches provide some of the most useful dating evidence, especially for a terminal date. Glastonbury Lake Village produced an unusually large assemblage of brooches and fragments, 55 including the 10 penannular brooches. There are two La Tène II type fibulae (E 173 and E 57) which are 2nd century BC in date and unlikely to be much later than 100BC. Both are of Hull and Hawkes (1987) type 3b. The remaining brooches, which include a rare British example of a true Nauheim type, are all likely to be 1st BC in date. The latest brooch is probably Aylesford type E187 and is pre-Augustan in date (Val Rigby pers comm). Uncertainty surrounds the provenance of this brooch, Gray ascribes it to M30 with a question mark (Bulleid and Gray 1911,202).

The brooch assemblage is large in comparison with most other sites and of a fairly tight date range. Noticeably absent from the group is the Colchester type. The earliest Colchesters are late Augustan in date. The form certainly occurs in the area of Glastonbury Lake Village with examples from Camerton (4) (Jackson 1990,41), Ham Hill (2), Polden Hill hoard (Brailsford 1975,229), Kingsdown Camp, Mells (Gray 1930,fig.5, 610) South Cadbury (9) (Olivier in Barrett forthcoming) and Maiden Castle (Wheeler 1943,fig.83). Absence of the Colchester type brooch at Glastonbury and also from amongst the extensive brooch series at Meare West and Meare East, along with clear evidence at all three sites for external contacts, provides a strong argument for all having been deserted before the end of the 1st century BC.

Glass. Twenty-five glass beads and a probable pin head were found. Except for the single Meare type (G 22) of 3rd century BC date, all are attributable to the last two centuries BC (see section 6.6).

Other evidence. Wooden and shale objects attest the use of lathes, a tool believed to have been introduced in the 1st century BC. Whilst on the subject of wooden artefacts, reference should be made back to section 6.10 and the decorated container from Porz Lind which has a close similarity to the bent wood box X 17 and which has been dated to 120-50 BC.

With the exception of the Meare-type bead nothing among the assemblage stands out as being unquestionably pre-2nd century BC.

We conclude that the Glastonbury Lake Village was established in about 250 BC and continued until approximately 50 BC. The initial date of 250BC allows for a period when the settlement was established, and little material culture was deposited. Such a time range fits the artefactual evidence and the structural evidence, and is internally consistent. It does not fit the series of radiocarbon dates which remain an unsolved puzzle (to us) at this time. Within the proposed time range for the site the structural evidence, based upon units of occupation, renewing of Floors and reshaping of Mounds, longevity of houses and clay spreads on a wet soil, suggests that 8 generations (each of about 25 years) may be an appropriate level to serve as a basis for chronology; the artefacts do not disagree with this. Doubtless future refinements in radiocarbon dating and, above all, the acquisition of samples for dendrochronological analysis will permit critical assessments of this proposed settlement chronology.

The calibrated age ranges are listed on the following page.

Dating postscript.

The dating evidence from the site has been reviewed by Colin Haselgrove, with reference to the brooches. He argues for a slightly later dating of the Village, with Middle and Late Phases (the major occupation) dating from the mid second century BC (no earlier than 180BC) to the mid first century BC, and final desertion occuring perhaps a generation later, in about 20BC. On this basis, our Early Phase would commence early in the second century BC. This refinement in dating evidence is welcome. The structural phases remain as postulated but the occupation might now be slightly more compact — 170 years in total rather than 200 years. The issue of dating can only be resolved, ultimately, by dendrochronological analysis of surviving timbers on the site.

Reference. C Haselgrove, Iron Age brooch deposition and chronology, in A. Gwilt and C. Haselgrove (eds) *Reconstructing Iron Age Societies* (1997) 51-72

Table 6.11. Comparison of radiocarbon and artefact dates where both could be applied to the same Mound produces results ranging from potentially close to highly improbable:

M5	
Floor 2 (Late Phase)	
E 142 La Tène III brooch:	1st century BC
H 215 calibrated radiocarbon date:	379-157 BC
M18	
Floor 4 (Early Phase)	
B 217 calibrated radiocarbon date:	541-366 BC
Floor 1 (Late Phase)	
E 93 Nauheim brooch:	*c.*100-50 BC
M38	
Floor 3 (Middle Phase)	
B 326 calibrated radiocarbon date:	540-363 BC
Floor 2 (Middle Phase)	
E 168 La Tène III brooch:	1st century BC
M71	
Floor 2 (Late Phase)	
B 398b calibrated radiocarbon date:	379-157 BC
Floor 1 (Final Phase)	
E 239 La Tène III brooch:	1st century BC
M74	
below Mound	
B 406 calibrated radiocarbon date:	384-164 BC
Floor 5 (Early Phase)	
E 244 La Tène III brooch:	1st century BC
Floor 3 (Middle Phase)	
H 357 calibrated radiocarbon date:	785-468 BC
M75	
Floor 3 (Early Phase)	
B 407 calibrated radiocarbon date:	792-472 BC
Floor 2 (Middle Phase)	
E 57 La Tène II brooch:	2nd century BC

Appendix 6.1

Calibrated age ranges in calendar years (cal AD/BC) for the radiocarbon determinations in figure 6.16. The 68.2% confidence intervals are the one sigma calendrical age ranges and the 95.4% the two; sigma being the error term (standard deviation) which follows the mean value and ± on an uncalibrated radiocarbon measurement. Because some of the ranges are interrupted, probability factors are given for each. For dates with only one range the probability equals 1.00.

Where there are more than one range the higher the probability factor the greater the chance that the true age lies within the particular interval. For determinations with interrupted ranges the sum of the probabilities comes to 1.00. Taking OxA-4752 as an example, one could say with 95.4% confidence that there is a 91% probability that the true age of the sample lies in the period 769-460 cal BC and a 9% probability that it falls within the range 452-411 cal BC.

DATE GLV/M27/OxA-4744 : 2230±45BP			
68.2% confidence	382BC (0.24) 353BC	310BC (0.64) 231BC	226BC (0.11) 211BC
95.4% confidence	392BC (1.00) 197BC		
DATE GLV/M18/OxA-4745 : 2350±45BP			
68.2% confidence	512BC (0.62) 429BC	416BC (0.38) 387BC	
95.4% confidence	758BC (0.13) 687BC	652BC (0.00) 645BC	541BC (0.85) 366BC
	278BC (0.01) 262BC		
DATE GLV/M74/OxA-4746 : 2190±45BP			
68.2% confidence	360BC (0.56) 285BC	256BC (0.44) 198BC	
95.4% confidence	384BC (0.98) 164BC	136BC (0.02) 124BC	
DATE GLV/M75/OxA-4747 : 2485±50BP			
68.2% confidence	771BC (0.09) 752BC	717BC (0.91) 528BC	
95.4% confidence	792BC (0.94) 472BC	445BC (0.06) 412BC	
DATE GLV/M38/OxA-4748 : 2345±45BP			
68.2% confidence	511BC (0.56) 431BC	416BC (0.44) 384BC	
95.4% confidence	758BC (0.11) 688BC	540BC (0.86) 363BC	282BC (0.02) 258BC
DATE GLV/M74/OxA-4749 : 2475±45BP			
68.2% confidence	766BC (0.08) 750BC	725BC (0.92) 526BC	
95.4% confidence	785BC (0.93) 468BC	447BC (0.07) 421BC	
DATE GLV/M71/OxA-4750 : 2180±45BP			
68.2% confidence	360BC (0.54) 286BC	255BC (0.46) 190BC	
95.4% confidence	379BC (0.95) 157BC	144BC (0.05) 118BC	
DATE GLV/M5/OxA-4751 : 2180±45BP			
68.2% confidence	360BC (0.54) 286BC	255BC (0.46) 190BC	
95.4% confidence	379BC (0.95) 157BC	144BC (0.05) 118BC	
DATE GLV/M1/OxA-4752 : 2465±45BP			
68.2% confidence	764BC (0.40) 676BC	664BC (0.20) 620BC	605BC (0.39) 519BC
95.4% confidence	769BC (0.91) 460BC	452BC (0.09) 411BC	
DATE GLV/M47/Q-2618 : 1975±70BP			
68.2% confidence	86BC (1.00) 82AD		
95.4% confidence	168BC (0.97) 143AD	164AD (0.03) 200AD	
DATE GLV/M47/Q-2619 : 1920±70BP			
68.2% confidence	8BC (0.92) 143AD	165AD (0.08) 188AD	
95.4% confidence	94BC (1.00) 236AD		

Chapter 7

Early reconsiderations and provisional models

Since the publications by Bulleid and Gray in 1911 and 1917, the Glastonbury Lake Village has figured in most textbooks of British prehistory, usually with only the most general of discussions. The lake village idea, the clustering together of 60 roundhouses or so, the abundance of material culture in the form of artefacts, and the fastness of the site stuck in an environment more water than land - all these visions were part of our ideas of late Celtic society. A few comments appeared here and there, mildly critical of the lack of phasing of the site by Bulleid and Gray, but enthusiastically accepting the animal bones, plants and finds in various economic and cultural studies (e.g. Clark 1952 and 1957).

The Lake Village remained without serious analysis until 1970 when E.K.Tratman, a scientist from Bristol, presented a Reconsideration which we will discuss below. He was followed soon after by D.L.Clarke, an archaeologist from Cambridge, who produced a Provisional Model in 1972. Both studies were widely read, particularly Clarke's, and his model scheme is often summarised and reproduced in textbooks and general studies. A few archaeologists began to criticize Clarke's model in the 1980s (e.g.Coles and Coles 1986; Moberg 1981) and in 1987 J.Barrett concluded that Clarke had been naive in accepting Bulleid and Gray's account without acknowledging "the historical context of the excavation, the nature of the record or the form of the publication" (Barrett 1987,421). Nonetheless the model persists (e.g.Sharer & Ashmore 1993,137;Renfrew & Bahn 1991,36;Rahtz 1993,24) although it is interesting that every one of these authors comments that doubts exist about its reliability. We will demonstrate that unreliability below, in an effort (probably unsuccessful) to eliminate Clarke's model for good, while at the same time applauding its conception.

TRATMAN'S RECONSIDERATION.

In his 1970 paper, Tratman attempted to dissect Bulleid and Gray's records, using the plans and Mound descriptions. He produced a site plan in which he not only phased the site but identified many elements that he thought were the first to be put in place. For Tratman, each Mound existed in only one phase and we have already shown in Chapters 3 and 4 that many are of several episodes, so Tratman's Mound sequence is at best incomplete and at worst wrong; we think the latter (see Table 7.1). If his early Mound phasing is correct, the whole site was occupied, at S,W,NW,N,NE,E and SE right from the start. If we ignore the stratigraphical evidence laboriously assembled in Chapter 3, he could be right of course.

Much more important was Tratman's extraction from the record of a number of square or rectangular structures, and many posts, that he thought pre-dated all the clay Floors and round houses. The components in this earliest occupation were "oak piles, oak beams, other pieces of oak from buildings and hurdles with oak uprights. The buildings are here referred to as square houses" (Tratman 1970,144). Bulleid had already made a similar comment in a footnote (1911,60): "It appears that rectangular and round dwellings were not co-existent at Glastonbury....the site was first occupied by people who built square dwellings, followed by a tribe of round hut builders". Bulleid believed that all the oak timber buildings had been dismantled, but Tratman could show that some of the beams were still pinned in place, and of course many heavy posts were still stuck vertically in the peat. Examples of the *in situ* settings are as follows: SW of M29, possibly NW of M16, between M61 and M60, N of M75, SE of M65 (figs.3.2-3.10). Several of these have horizontal beams with posts through holes, others are entirely of post arrangements. Tratman believed that these represented parts of houses raised on piles a metre or so above the wet ground; this matter is discussed later in the Chapter.

Table 7.1 Alternative phasing: an example

Mound	Tratman	Clarke	Coles & Minnitt
11	3	1	M & L
55	2	3	M & L
57	1	4	L & F
58	3	4	L & F
59	4	4	E & M & L
62	1	3 & 4	M & L
63	2	4	L
64	3	3 & 4	L & F
65	2	3 & 4	M & L & F
78	4	3	L & F

The question is whether these structural fragments represent an earliest occupation, or merely form part of an early settlement which also included clay importation, Floor-laying and round house construction. It is our opinion that the latter interpretation is correct (insofar as anything can be judged correct on this site). There were many heavy beams as well as logs in the foundation of the settlement, beneath the clay, with brushwood piled above often pegged down to hold it roughly in place prior to the clay dumps on top. Where the ground was particularly soft and wet, the foundation was sometimes made of layers of timber as well as logs, and these seem to be foundation rather than a building element. Most of Tratman's square houses are not in fact beneath Mound clays so are not stratigraphically early, and we see them as sheds or other structures associated with round houses and open spreads across the site (Chapter 4). Seven are assigned to our

Early Phase, and others are later in the sequence. We agree with Clarke who identifies some of these settings as granaries and storerooms, but on occasion he too has misread the evidence for the shape and stratigraphical position of particular settings (Coles & Coles 1986,168). H.Gent extracted three of the settings of horizontal beams, pegged down, and one setting of posts, from Bulleid's plans and showed that grain or legumes had been found beside or near them (Gent 1983). This kind of evidence is examined in Chapter 8. Tratman's other post scatters must represent the remnants of fences, barriers, supports, markers and tether posts which were found all over the settlement, mostly not covered by clay Floors. There is no reason to extract them from the site plan and presume they underlie everything else.

However Tratman's contribution to the continuing dialogue about the Lake Village is still valuable. He was the first to pick-up on John Morland's opinion about the existence of square structures, and to demonstrate that Bulleid's (late) acceptance of the idea was based on good evidence. He thus introduced the idea of variance of structure in the Lake Village, and also the concept of its evolution over time. In these ways he was the forerunner of D.L.Clarke who soon expanded these ideas in new and imaginative ways.

CLARKE'S PROVISIONAL MODEL.

Clarke began his analysis of the Glastonbury Lake Village with the comment: "No archaeological study can be better than the reliability of observations upon which it is based" (1972,803). He emphasised the experimental nature of the analysis, introducing "a set of experimental models and the manipulative capacity of the computer"; there is no evidence that a computer was actually used in the handling of the data, but the concept was good. Clarke went on to outline the site: "a settlement built on adjoining artificial mounds or crannogs .... set on a raised bog and alluvium promontory...., with 'an embanked stockade'," gates providing land access in dry weather for carts....", and so on. Already we can see that 5 misreadings of the evidence have occurred:

not on artificial mounds,

not a raised bog,

not an alluvium promontory,

not an embanked stockade,

no land access.

A set of specific analyses was then introduced: 1. vertical spatial relationships, 2. horizontal spatial relationships, 3. structural relationships, and 4. artefact relationships. These analyses which were not published (and we think do not survive as working papers) led to the identification of 1. "five interlinked settlement clusters on five crannogs", in four phases of development; 2. settlement development on a piecemeal and individual basis but nonetheless with a "culturally accepted building format"; 3. eleven elements that could define "repeated structural categories with a distinctive polythetic signature"; and 4. "artefact concentrations and residuals" across the site structures. Clarke stressed that the artefact analysis was only in a preliminary stage. He then went on to present a site assessment and a structural model in which he identified "seven polythetic categories of construction...internally subdivided by the intersection of their sets with differing sets of artefact association patterns and the structure's location relative to other structures". This was the famous "modular unit - the social and architectural building block of which the settlement is a multiple", a unit reproduced *ad infinitum* in many books (e.g. Coles & Coles 1986) and doubtless inspiring, perhaps confusing, multitudes of students.

The modular unit was the key to the Village gate, it seemed. Every Mound and structure had its place in the system, in shape, size, location and performance. The artefacts found on, in or beside each structure were consistent in pattern, fortifying the identity. In this way the settlement conformed to a Celtic purpose, "several patrilocal extended families of non-noble freemen farmers, united by kinship ties, and a system of allegiance through a headman, supported by a range of dependents or clients", bound together in their "demanding but rewarding marshland home".

Clarke produced an interesting set of Phase plans, four in number, with the settlement originating in the ultimate centre of the site (M30 across to M42 and S to M11), expanding E, and S, then N both NW and NE. Again he noted that the scheme was tentative. In the four Phases, he identified many houses: Phase I 12 houses, Phase II 15 houses, Phase III 21 houses, Phase IV 15 houses; that is 63 houses in all, representing 23 Mounds. (In our scheme, we identify less than 40 houses, on 22 Mounds). Clarke identified six modular units on site, one of them a "mega-unit" centered on M42, which he saw as the residence of the headman, if the settlement had such a person, and also as the focal point of the village right from the beginning. (In Chapters 3 and 4 we indicate our view that M42 was not in existence until our Late Phase, and that it never had a house but only a windbreak or shelter.) In the later sections of his paper, Clarke proceeded to talk of the social, economic and political relationships of the inhabitants of the Lake Village one to another (the most famous, or notorious, comment here being the "within settlement exchange of women between the extended family units", and written in the early 1970s at that) and to the regional world of the late Iron Age. Clarke's paper was criticised by J.Barrett in 1987 (discussed below), and Barrett concluded that Clarke had ignored many of the fundamental problems of the archaeological evidence; he had acknowledged their existence, to be sure, but had proceeded to dismiss them as irrelevant to his investigations.

Our criticism of Clarke's stimulating and provocative paper should not be taken as outright dismissal of his ideas. It was right, in 1972, to propose new approaches to old evidence. It was also right to be forceful in the delivery of the new ideas. What has taken place since the appearance of the Provisional Model is that the tentative conclusions have been accepted while the theory behind them has been passed by. Clarke's model approach was in itself the achievement; that the evidence did not, could not, fit the model should not matter if it was taken only as a demonstration of the possibilities. Unfortunately, the possibilities on the chosen site became the probabilities and then the certainties, and the evidence was rarely questioned. The Model entered into the traditional literature and belief of Iron Age societies with few able to resist its attractions (one who did resist was B.W.Cunliffe who makes no mention of the Model in his 1991 book on the British Iron Age).

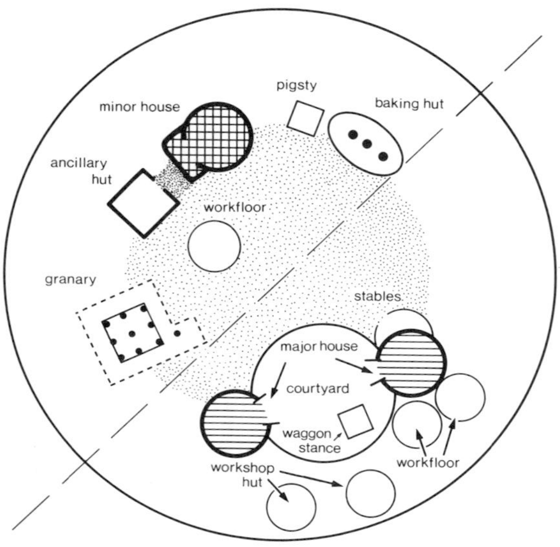

Fig.7.1 Clarke's modular unit, in theory. Nothing on the site fits this scheme.

In the following section of this Chapter we will present some of the evidence that reflects upon Clarke's Provisional Model (fig.7.1). We begin with several general comments. There is no evidence that Clarke ever visited the Glastonbury Lake Village, or inspected at first hand the material culture that resided in the museum in Glastonbury. Most of the finds were inaccessible to all but the most fervent and persistent. The various notebooks, papers and the Black Book of Relics were not available, some being lost, in the late 1960s. The environmental record of the Somerset Levels was, however, available through the work of Harry Godwin in the Botany School, Cambridge (200m from Peterhouse where Clarke worked); there is clear evidence that Clarke did not pursue this avenue (see below). It is our view that he both misread and misunderstood Bulleid and Gray's accounts in the 1911 and 1917 books, ignored Godwin's work of 1941 and 1955, and did not comprehend what an archaeological excavation involved, particularly one that was on a wet site.

In Chapter 4 we have tried to demonstrate that the Lake Village was in constant change, expanding, repairing, restructuring, and that there were 81 alterations to structures or spreads of clay along with the 90 events that established the presence of activity on the locations that eventually became Mounds. These 81 changes are documented in Bulleid's plans and texts. Clarke presented only 5 changes in his developmental sequence. As one example, M11 for Clarke was a round house from the beginning to the end of the settlement. Yet the evidence is clear - a round house was built there at first and was then swept away and the house Floor covered by a clay spread that flowed W into M13, 14 and 15 with a house now put over the M13 Floor. We think thereafter M11 was abandoned. We have already referred to M42, the hub of Clarke's Model; this was never a house, we think, nor were there houses on another 6 of his house Mounds. Conversely we have 9 Mounds with houses that are not considered by Clarke to represent house locations. We agree on 15 house Mounds, so it seems we are at least talking about the same kind of evidence (and the same site, we think, although it sometimes seems arguable).

The phasing of the settlement has already been mentioned, and Clarke's four Phases (I-IV) do not in any real way match our four Phases (e.g. Table 7.1). There are very severe stratigraphical problems for Clarke's phasing in some areas of the site. M3 and M4 are an example. Here the base of M3 overlies the top of M4 as Bulleid states in his text: "The three floors of Mound III overlapped Floor i of Mound IV" (1911,68). Yet Clarke places M3 in his Phase III and IV, and M4 in his Phases II, III, and IV; Phase IV for M4 is not possible. Mounds 22, 23 and 24 have the same problem, as do M83 and M71, and also M45, M46 and M49; these and other Mound complexes do have stratigraphy, sometimes obscurely presented by Bulleid, but it seems perverse to ignore or misread those Mounds that exhibit some chronological order.

One of the problems in making these critical remarks is that Clarke does not distinguish which Floors on the various Mounds belong to any one of his four Phases. A Mound may have from one to 10 Floors and each has its own identity and structure. The schematic plans of the four Phases in his paper are a little difficult to read and identify the Mounds depicted, and the Floors are impossible to separate into his phases, but it is just possible to disentangle his plans and distinguish Mounds. From this, we can recreate Clarke's phasing for the site, Mound by Mound, and see how it relates to our scheme. In brief, we agree on 14 Mounds, which means we disagree on 76. That may not be serious if we are more or less totally wrong in our analysis, but it does seem strange to find that Clarke has 16 Mounds where the ratio of Floors to Phases is unbalanced. We might think it normal to deduce that a Mound with, say, 6 Floors might represent 2 or 3 Phases. Clarke has six Mounds where a single Floor is taken to represent 3 of his Phases, two Mounds with a single Floor representing all his 4 phases, and four Mounds where 3 or 4 Floors represent only one Phase; he also has four

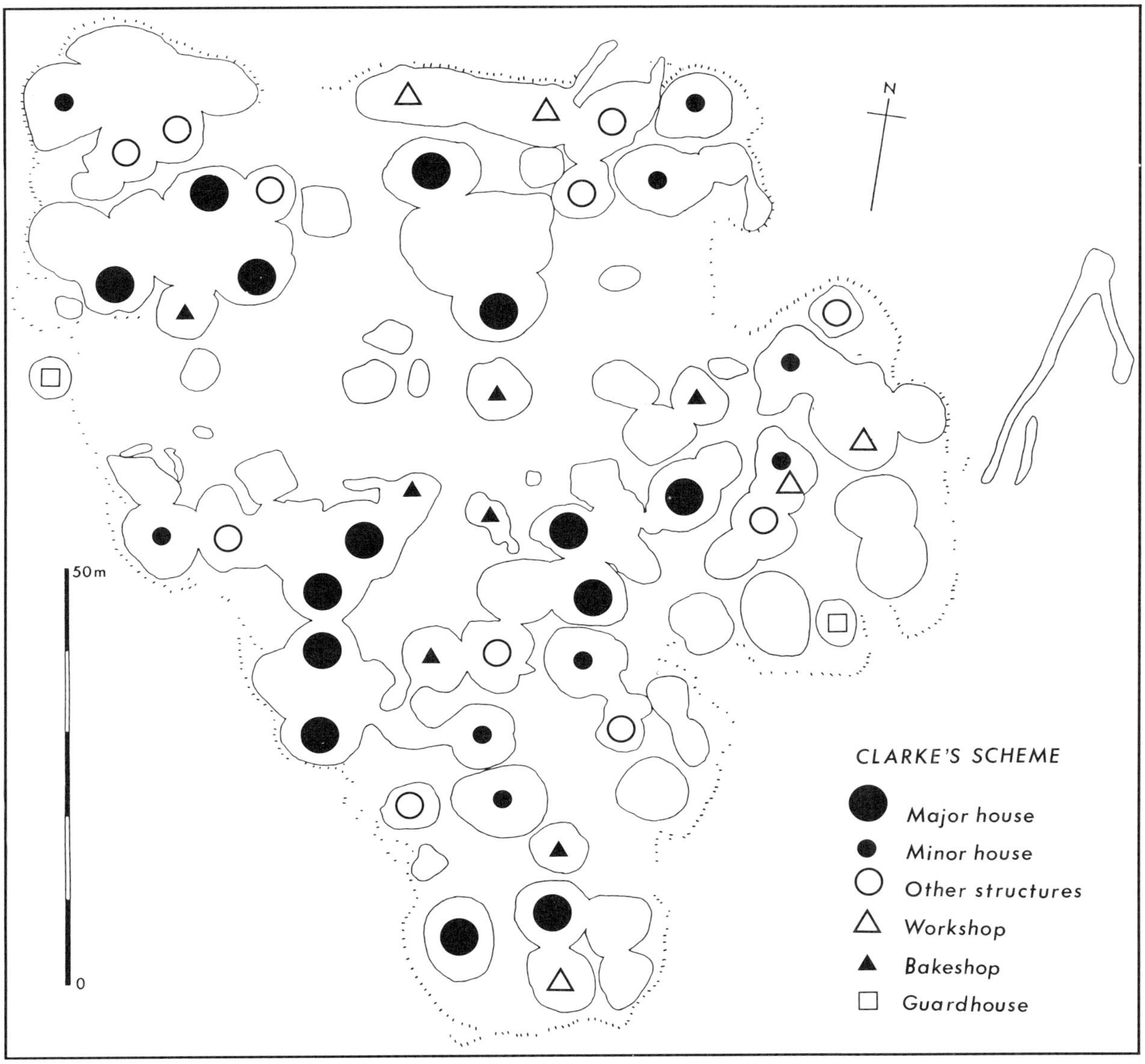

Fig.7.2 Clarke's scheme for the Lake Village. This plan reflects his written lists of Mounds and his identifications, although there is some confusion between his Mound listing and his plans of the site. Areas without symbols represent his Working spaces, clay patches and other open spreads. The Other Structures include Ancilliary and Annexe buildings. JMC

Mounds where 2 Floors represent either all 4 Phases (3 examples) or only 1 Phase (1 example). This all seems peculiar to us.

When we come from these general assessments on to the more detailed elements of Clarke's modular unit, we encounter serious difficulties. We will only comment on a few of the more obvious, as we move through his structures (fig.7.2). Clarke's descriptions will begin each section, followed by our comments.

Ia Major house pairs.

These were substantially built houses, renewed successively, and occupied over a long time. They had heavy timber foundations, clay Floors, hearths, wattle and daub walls, central roof support, stone slab doorways, porches and timber flooring. The objects found were numerous and varied: harness, weapons, ornaments, tools. Activities associated with the houses included workshops for smithing, carpentry, textile production, food preparation, and stonework. Clarke selected 13 Mounds for this class of structure, 12 of them in pairs on the site with a common yard (and other elements noted below). The Mounds and pairings were M4 and M5, M13 and M14, M29 and M35, M27 and M38, M62 and M65, M74 and M76; and M42 was the central dwelling.

Comment. Of these 13 Mounds, we think houses did not exist on three of them, and out of a potential 42 units of occupation (7 Mounds in all 4 Clarke Phases, 2 Mounds for 3 Phases, 4 Mounds for 2 Phases) we think 35 are justified. But houses existed during only 16 units of occupation out of the claimed 42, as the other units of occupation took place on non-house Floors. None of Clarke's major houses had stone slab entrances, only

2 out of 13 had porches, and 8 of 13 had some form of timber flooring. All in all, the percentage is not impressive. So what went wrong here? Basically it is the same as for the other classes - it was easy to find one or two classic structures, clear house wall posts, multiple Floors and hearths, abundant artefacts, and then to ease the requirements for inclusion. The pairing of major houses is a case in point. M62 and M65 are large round clay Floors, with spreads of clay between (M63 and M64); a Clarke house existed on M65 and a substantial shelter, not a house, on M62. The complex looks neat and organised. So perhaps did M29 and M35, with a yard to the W, and M14 and M13 although here the yard is less clear. M4 and M5 have no shared yard at all. Our phasing for these Mounds does not support Clarke's contention about pairing of houses. For example M14 had a house in our Early and Middle Phases, its matching M13 a house only in the Late Phase; replacement rather than pairing seems a more logical idea. The M4 house was not contemporary with the house on M5, and here replacement and not pairing is likely.

Another of Clarke's defining features for major houses was the variety and abundance of small finds. The Mounds chosen do have finds of most categories, but the variation in quantity is great. M62 had 165 objects, M5 almost 100; but M14 has only 7 artefacts recorded, M29 has only 6, M13 has only 10. It is difficult to see M13 and M14 as one of Clarke's units with only 17 artefacts between them. But the artefacts from all these major houses are varied and reasonably abundant in the overall site. The claim that these Mounds contained "the highest ratio of discarded fine wares to undecorated pottery" must have been a wishful thought; there is no way Clarke could have made such a deduction. As it is, 8 of the 13 Mounds have rather little in the way of pottery overall (fig.2.6).

Ib. Minor houses.

There were nine of these houses in the Village, according to Clarke. They closely resembled the Major houses, but were somewhat smaller in size, had no porch, but had a wind baffle entrance. Each of these houses served one of the major house pairs, and were set about twice as far away from them as were the Major houses to one another. The Mounds with these Minor houses were M9, M11, M18, M49, M57, M70, M55, M30 and M44. The activities represented in, on or around them were less extensive, with no male-orientated debris such as crucibles, iron tools and weapons. Female-orientated work was dominantly represented, grinding food, weaving and leather work included, and an "overwhelming proportion" of female trinkets and other gear were present. The abundant pottery has a high percentage of undecorated wares. Some human remains got incorporated in the deposits, "in many cases very young children". In other words, this is where the ladies lived and where they worked for their menfolk, and where the babies got buried.

Comment. Of the proposed 9 houses, only 6 actually existed, and one shelter. Two houses were larger than normal, and two were smaller than normal. Several were not in existence when the Major houses were, so the menfolk must have been disappointed when calling for their food; in fact, only M18 had a house in the Early Phase, to satisfy 3 sets of Major houses. The artefacts found ranged in number from 11 to 86, with weaving and spinning tools, some bone tools, a few querns, many ornaments, some harness-gear, a bit of metalworking slag. Pottery was not uniformly represented, nor was it in much abundance; 4 of the Minor house Mounds had either little or only some pottery, 4 had much pottery (fig.2.6). Mound 9 was included in the Minor house category; we think this Mound had a large house, converted into a long house which served as some sort of centre for the settlement in our Late Phase, which was then rebuilt into a very large house in the Final Phase. It had much weaving and spinning equipment, ornaments, harness gear, tools, querns and flints, pottery and bone and antler tools, and more artefacts including pottery than every other Mound on site except three, therefore exceeding the tally from 10 Major houses. It was ridiculous to exclude M9 from Clarke's Major unit, but he had no choice as M5, the other contender to go with M4, was equally large and "rich" and also had much crucible and furnace debris and thus "male" in character.

IIa. Ancillary huts.

There was an ancillary hut for each unit on the site with a path or patch of clay leading to a Minor house. These huts were light structures, of hurdles tied to posts, with roofing held by a central post, and a hearth. The Mounds with these huts were M83, M16, M25, M78, M12, M32, M48, M58 and M17, with one Phase of M34 and M38. No 'male'-associated artefacts were found, only impoverished versions of the female Minor houses adjacent. There were many flint scrapers but artefacts in general were scarce. Clarke thought these huts were female-orientated, and were perhaps milking parlours, food stores or huts for housing cows, ewes or goats which were on site all year.

Comment. We think M83 was more substantial than this, with 4 Floors and a strong part-roofed shelter in our Middle Phase; M58 was a very large clay spread laid down at the NE exit. The others were rather nondescript both in shape and artefacts and most had 2-3 Floors. Flints were numerous (relatively speaking - there were 17) in M83, only 2-5 in M78,M48 and M58, and none at all in the other six Mounds. M16 had some weaving tools. It is difficult to come up with a category for all these Mounds and it will be the trend of activities on more than single Mounds that allow us to advance our model (Chapter 8).

Before moving on to other classes, we should point out that, in our opinion, there were 8 other substantial houses on the site (M3, M23, M45, M56, M59, M61, M66 and M83) that do not figure in Clarke's lists of houses;

instead they are classed as 5 workshop huts (small and neat), one annexe hut (lean to), one ancillary hut (light hurdle-walled) or one work Floor (open). Clarke seems to have misread Bulleid's descriptions for several of these structures, although his workshop huts were reasonably substantial structures.

IIb. Workshop huts.

These were small neat circular huts, roofed, and positioned near the pair of Major houses; they were the focus of groups of working Floors adjacent. Clarke identified these huts as M75 (with open Floor M73), M45 (with M46), M59 (with M79), M23, M3 (with M1), M61, M60 and M44. The huts had debris from metalwork, stonework, bone and antler work, and whetstones, flints and iron tools were also found. Female-orientated querns and trinkets were absent or scarce. Various of the huts had woodworking debris nearby. They were focal points for major house industries.

Comment. There are some problems here, as usual. We think that dwelling houses existed at M45, M59, M23, M3, M61 and a substantial shelter on M44. Not all were of the same Phase of course, and M75 had 5 Floors, the others had 2-3 Floors and M59 had 4 Floors. The debris of activities is very mixed on these Mounds. Slag and crucibles were absent on three of the listed Mounds, and only M75 and M44 have much of substance in metalworking debris. M5, not a workshop hut but a Major house, has a very large amount of furnace and crucible debris. Spinning and weaving operations are inferred for M75, M45, M23. and M44, not in Clarke's list of preferred activities. Querns on M44 and M46 are also at variance with his model, as are the heaps of beans, barley and wheat on M60, and "female trinkets" on M59 and M75.

IIc. Courtyards.

These were "enclosed open spaces", or irregular clay spreads with little substructure and, at most, a light roof held up by scattered posts (an unlikely structural feature, we think). Each pair of Major houses had a courtyard adjacent, and house entrances could open on to the yard. Hearths were built on the yard, generally at one end of the spread rather than in the centre. Courtyards were proposed for M1-M2, M28, M33, M40-M41-M26 complex, M63-M64, and M73. The amount of debris deposited was "average" with male orientated equipment dominant, and horse and waggon gear. Clarke suggested that many hunting and sheep dogs stayed in the courtyards, and that middens built up alongside threshing Floors and outside workshops.

Comment. These Mounds are not as uniform in size, character or artefacts as the model suggests. Some are large, several are rather small. Hearths are more or less central in 5 of the 6 spreads; M33 had 7 Floors, the others only 1-3 Floors. The artefacts were very mixed, and weaving and spinning tools were found on 5 of the spreads, much pottery including decorated wares on 4, personal ornaments such as brooches and finger rings also on 4 spreads, querns on 2, and "male-orientated" gear hardly at all; cheek piece fragments and bits of chain occurred on 4 spreads. Nonetheless, the position of these spreads appears to link them with some of the houses we think existed (Chapters 4 and 8).

IId. Baking huts.

Clarke identified 7 baking huts, one for each unit, set slightly apart from the main houses. Here grain was ground, food prepared and cooked. The clay Floors were irregular and had "a longitudinal array of hearths and ovens". There was a light roof to protect the females at work, "gossiping pleasurably in the comfort of this warm and dry micro-environment". The Mounds identified as bake huts were M37, M51, M15, M6, M84, M80, M36. The artefacts associated included much pottery, including the highest percentage of undecorated to decorated wares on the entire site. Also common were beads and other trinkets, whorls, flints, querns and bones of fur-bearing animals.

Comment. There are several problems here. The model required a bake hut for each unit, so M6 (with only one Floor) had to serve through 3 of Clarke's Phases (although this is further noted below), while M51 with five Floors served the same purpose. The longitudinal array of hearths and ovens which provided the cosiness for the women existed only in one place on the site, M6; here there were 3 hearths side by side, replacing the original hearths which were built on the single clay Floor and found to be unsatisfactory. All the other "bake hut" Mounds had hearths, but they were all built on top of one another; M37 had 7 hearths in a stratigraphic pile, M51 had 5, M15 had 7, M84 ended up with none on its top Floor, M80 had only ever one, M36 had 2 but its top Floor had no hearth. Clarke got his model bake hut from M6, and how he succumbed to the evidence of the other Mounds is unclear. The artefacts from these Mounds are, in a way, irrelevant as the structural evidence is so much in conflict with the model. The ratio of decorated to undecorated pottery is not known, nor could it be in 1972. There were many Relics from M37 and M6; M37 had a set of loom weights and weaving tools, perhaps not usually seen in a bake hut.

IIe. Guard huts.

Two Mounds were interpreted as guard huts by Clarke, to oversee the entrances on the W and on the SE. He did not consider that other entrances existed (see Chapter 4). M21 and M77 had, for him, small circular structures, lightly built, where the site guards sat and watched overnight, playing with dice and otherwise leaving little of their debris behind. M21 was on the left flank of the entrance, which was protected by a wicket gate hung on heavy posts. A hard standing for vehicles was laid inside the gate. M77 was on the right of a probable W gate, involving a W road that ran alongside the palisade. The artefacts recovered included the famous "dice box and dice at the eastern gate", and "fragments of impaled skulls with sword cuts".

Comment. This scenario, attractive as it is, seems most unlikely. There were at least six entrances through the palisade. There was no W road at all, and probably no W entrance. M77 had no structure at all, and was merely a dump of clay devoid of any artefacts and with no occupation (black earth) traces whatever. Clarke said M77 was used during two of his Phases. M21 had three Floors, only one with a hearth, and no certain structure to it; it was merely a patch at first, then more clay

Fig.7.3 Gambling with dice. Forestier's drawing of 1911.

was spread. There is no trace of the heavy posts, nor for a swing gate. The M21 Floor yielded a brooch and a whorl, and decorated pottery, perhaps unlikely to be guards' equipment. The bone box, said to be a dice box, was found outside the palisade near M21, but the nearest die was off the edge of M42, some 20m away, and others were at M4 50m away (fig.7.3). The question of impaled skulls is more difficult (see Chapter 6), but none was noted by Bulleid near M21; one was near M77. So we are left with an imaginative and attractive suggestion for which there is no proof, and no evidence whatsoever. A pity.

IIf. Annexe huts.

These were simple lean-to structures attached to major houses (Ia) but with separate entrances, and they had horse bones buried in the Floor or nearby, but otherwise very few artefacts were associated. Clarke identified two annexe huts, M43 and M66.

Comment. M43 was an open spread, attached to M42, each with a hearth, and both had a sheltering wall on the NW in our Late Phase. M66, on the other hand, was a small round house with a hearth rebuilt three times, and a wide variety of artefacts although the quantity was small: pottery, flints, loom weight, cheekpiece, awl, hammer, and slingstone. There seems little reason to single these two Mounds out as a separate type of structure. There are other Mounds that may well have served as adjuncts to larger Mounds or Mounds with houses (Chapters 4 and 8). Clarke does not list any other annexe huts, but his plan shows M4 as an annexe; this was a substantial house in our Late and Final Phases.

III. Work Floors.

Clarke identified 12 work Floors on the site. These were irregular areas of clay and timber, with no heavy foundation, small hearths, no walls, and were mostly unprotected. They were positioned around the edge of the settlement and were attached to one or other of the major wealthy units through proximity to minor houses or workshop huts. Activity on these Floors was intensive, with both male and female complexes: metalwork, spinning, weaving, grinding, bone and antler work. They also served as dumps for raw materials such as antler caches. The Mounds selected for these workshops were M7, M20, M22, M24, M46, M53, M54, M56, M67, M68, M69 and M72.

Comment. These Mounds represent a variety of shapes and sizes. All but one have a hearth, and we think that M72 was a major shelter in the Middle Phase, and M56 was a round house in the Late Phase. Clarke is again illogical in Phasing these work Floors which, if activity was intense, should have been renewed on occasion; some of his work Floors existed, for him, in more Phases than they had Floors (M22, M24, M46, M53); M20 had 5 Floors and M46 had 2 Floors and each had a life in three of Clarke's Phases. Other spreads of clay could as well have been selected as these for working Floors, which we think were widely spread across the site. The artefacts are varied in both quantity and identity. Many were found in some Mounds (e.g. M7, M22, M24, M69) and only a few in other Mounds (e.g. M54, M67, M68). Personal ornaments in M7 were numerous and outside Clarke's criteria, and a child's skeleton was found under M56 (which we think was a house). Otherwise the debris includes tools for weaving, spinning, metalwork, bone and antler work.

IV. Clay patches.

There were 17 clay patches in Clarke's scheme. These were rather difficult to identify on his plans but he provides a list: M8, M10, M19, M31, M34, M39, M50, M52, M72(probably M82 in fact), M79, M81, M85, M86, M87, M88, M89, M90. These were scattered around the other compounds, some merely patches or repairs, some paved as stances or approaches to other structures. Few artefacts were associated.

Comment. There are only minor difficulties here. M31 has only one Floor, as do most of these Mounds, but Clarke includes it in all of his four Phases. M34 has two Floors but for Clarke it only existed in one of his Phases. M19 has one Floor, for three Phases, as has M10 and M50. This seems illogical. We think M34 was a well-built shelter or pen, as was M85. M8 was a very large spread 12m long, more than a clay patch, and M19 was large too. The objects associated were generally few in number. M8 had pottery and ashwood frame, possibly for skin or embroidery work. M31 had a quern and a heap of beans. M19 had bobbins, brooch fragments and various bone and metal pieces. All in all, Clarke's clay patches are mostly just that but some seem to be rather more than a simple dump of clay. M77 (Clarke's guard hut) is a classic clay patch and nothing more.

V. Granaries or storehouses.

Clarke says there are or were traces of at least 25 footings for granaries or storehouses, presumably raised above the ground. Only one existed for each unit at any one time. These were about 3x4m with "sugarloaf piles" driven through morticed plates and enclosed within a fenced area about 5m square with a "stepped" perimeter (whatever that is). Various wooden fragments on the site persuaded him to identify these granaries as hurdle-walled rooms supported on piles about 1m above the ground and entered by ladder. They held barley and wheat and Clarke considered a capacity of 10 tonnes was possible; this seems over large, and problems might arise for the piles stuck in the soft peats. J.Barrett comments thus: "If this had once been true no such arrangement is either recorded or allowed for by the excavators" (1987,418). No lists or positions for these structures were given in Clarke's paper, but it is just possible to identify 20 places on the site using his schematic plans.

Comment. These are Tratman's square houses, but rather more identified. The artefacts associated are difficult to identify. Various heaps of corn and beans were recovered by Bulleid in various places on the site, and with 25 locations for Clarke's granaries almost all will be within some short distance of one of his putative structures. From Bulleid's site plans it is difficult to extract more than about 10 square structures, and most are of our Early Phase; in this we follow Tratman's ideas to some extent, as discussed earlier in this Chapter, and Gent's remarks are relevant as well (1983).

VI. Stables or byres.

Three of these were identified on site by Clarke, although he lists no Mound numbers. M85 was linked with M66 to produce a combined annexe and stable, so M85 must be the latter. The plan indicates other stables attached as lean-to structures on M65 and M4. These stables were "identified by the repeated burial of butchered horse skeletons in and around them" and artefacts included linchpins and cheekpieces.

Comment. There is no evidence whatsoever that horses were butchered and buried beneath or near these places; where Clarke got this idea from is beyond us. M85 had pelican bones under the clay, the byre area E of M65 had peas scattered around, and NW of M4 had a bobbin and a fragment of human skull. Horse bones were not abundant on the site but were found well away from any of these putative byres, and no complete horse skeleton was found. To bury a dead horse underneath a stable Floor is unlikely to guarantee a peaceful stable in any event.

VII. Sties or kennels.

These were small rectangular staked enclosures (2x1.5m) near to bake huts, granaries or ancillary huts, and Clarke's plans indicate four, possibly five: S of M65, N of M35, NW of M15, and NW of M38. Only the doghouse at M15 lasted through all Clarke's Phases. Pig bones were said to be found near M65.

Comment. There are some post settings or stake scatters in all these places, and they are part of Tratman's post-built structures. The post setting at M15 is 20x12m, that at M65 could be larger, or smaller, depending on which posts and stakes you choose to make your kennel or sty. If only stakes are to be considered, there are possibilities of plotting maybe 100 of these small enclosures, and the existence of old palisade lines can cause some congestion of posts. The pig bones were beneath Floor 1 of M65, not therefore associated with the sty area to the S, where a quantity of peas were found.

The settlement.

Clarke's provisional model was composed of structures Ia through to VII, with Major and Minor houses providing the framework for the whole complex. He believed that the settlement was built to a rigid design, first one complete unit and then more units, each placed systematically on the site. The peripheral bulges of the settlement on the S, E, NE and NW were these expansions. Each unit thus had all the components necessary for the group: two Major houses set on one-half of the space, along with a stable, courtyard, waggon stance, two workshops and open work Floors. The other half of the space had a Minor house (for female occupancy), an ancillary hut, bake hut, pigsty and granary. The whole unit provided 200 sq.m of roofed space (the houses) for a group of 15-20 persons, "an inturned, internally networked, co-operative social unit .... ancestrally linked to the unit houses...."

Clarke's sequence for the settlement began with 4 units (60 people) near the centre of the eventual site, then expanded into 5 units then 7 which was the maximum (120 people). As we have shown in this Chapter, Clarke's sequence is probably incorrect on stratigraphical grounds. He did not see much in the units to indicate "headmanship" but suspected that M42, an isolated Major house, might have been the centre of the settlement control with the initial 4 units nearby. He thought that this central area held more artefacts showing wealth, more decorated pottery, more weaving combs, more personal ornaments.

Comment. We have problems here, firstly because we do not think M42 ever had a house, nor can we demonstrate the exceptional richness of the area in the whole settlement. In Chapter 8 we will explore ideas about the site development already presented in Chapter 4, but it may be worth pointing here to the general similarity of Clarke's Phase I and our Early Phase, in the central part of the site. Where we differ is that Clarke saw three pairs of Major houses each with a Minor house related, whereas we see five individual houses placed in such a way that it is likely that only three single houses were ever in operation at the one time: M29 and M35 can hardly be exactly contemporary, M27 replaced M18, and M14 (which soon burnt down). There is also a distortion of distributions introduced in this section of Clarke's paper (1972,836). Clarke claimed that "the central area of the settlement has produced traces of especial wealth - a hoard including a bronze mirror, tweezers, two dress pins and cosmetic galena, the only coin and currency bar, a bronze cup, another mirror fragment, a glass topped pin, amber beads, the mould for bracelets - all over and above the normal complement .... (and) three other unique features .... more weaving combs than any other structure... drawn from every sector of the site ... the most comprehensive range of fine imported pottery ... the most extensive variety of bronze fibulae of all periods, including heirlooms...." By central area, Clarke implied the area on and around M42, but he also had to include the far west (M30) as here was found the possible hoard (actually a scatter of objects in the broken palisade posts); the fibulae supposedly from this Mound are labelled 'not localised' in the Black Book, and their attribution to M30 is uncertain (Bulleid & Gray 1911,201-202). For Clarke M42 and across to M30 (a distance of 50m) was the nodal area, perhaps the haunt of the wealthiest segment of the society, "the Glastonbury headman" and his followers. Yet Clarke stated in his next paragraph that his two units on the western margin (including M30) were "negatively distinguished as against the site norms"; he seems here to be having it both ways, once for richer, once for poorer. The assignment of much of the wealthy-looking material to this central area is really not justified if we look at the findspots detailed by Bulleid and Gray. The bronze cup, for example, far from being associated in or near M42 was found while Bulleid was trenching outside the palisade 9.5m SSE of M21, that is 26m from the edge of M42. We have already commented on the inability of anyone to define the distribution and character of pottery, in view of its lack of attribution to Mounds and its unstudied position up to and including 1994. It is also difficult to see how Clarke could identify weaving combs "from every sector on the site" in the total of 9 found in or near M42, in the absence of any detailed study available to him. These are niggles, we admit, but how many niggles can we disregard in the justifiable search for the broad picture, the all-embracing scheme? On the more general assertion that Clarke's central area was more wealthy than the others, with more decorated pottery, more weaving combs, more ornaments, the distributions do not support him. The real concentrations of pottery are shown in figure 2.6 , to the NW, E central and S. The spinning and weaving artefacts are concentrated in the NW, N central, E central and S (fig.6.5-6.6). The ornaments are more widely scattered, with a denser spread in the S than anywhere else (fig.6.7-6.8).

Elsewhere in his paper Clarke identified the trading connections of the settlement, and for some inexplicable reason contrasted its NW and NE sectors (with strong connections extending to the southern seaways) with the S and central units (with strong ties to the northern territories of Mendip and beyond); presumably the traders of the sectors exchanged news as they passed one another going S or N; after all, they lived only 20m apart. This exclusive relationship helped explain "the within settlement exchange of women between the extended family units", a model "supported by the physical anthropology of the skeletal remains from the house floors" (Clarke 1972,839). The first part of this sentence has entered the archaeological folklore of the early 1970s, the second part has (equally) no scientific basis one way or the other.

The economy and environment.

Clarke also provided a detailed account of the economic basis of the Lake Village, and its environmental setting. He believed the settlement was constructed upon a raised bog with reed banks around, with an ancient river flowing past the E side. To the N was a lake. To the W, through the gate, a dry road led S on to a peninsula which extended all the way to the upland of Glastonbury and its Tor. The economy was 'mixed', with wheat and barley, sheep and some cattle. 'Ditched field agriculture' was practised on the alluvium, winter-sown barley around the settlement (infield) and wheat and beans spring- sown as winter floods receded (outfield), sheep pasturing on the uplands in winter and on marshlands in summer. On the wastelands of reed and sedge some cultivation and pasturing was also possible. Clarke's diagram of infield-outfield operations, season by season, was complex and ingenious, and impossible.

Comment. (by R.A.Housley). It is clear that Clarke misunderstood Bulleid and Gray's account of the setting of the site. Reference to the village being on a raised bog is wholly wrong, and it may be that he was confusing the location of the Meare Iron Age occupation, on a raised bog, with the setting of the Glastonbury Lake Village. The alluvium spreads which Clarke took to be appropriate for his infield-outfield system did not exist in the Iron Age (see below). The channel to the E and dryland route to the W did not exist. The detailed explanations of the environmental conditions appear in Chapter 5 but can be summarised here as they apply to Clarke's model.

The reference to the presence of a river to the east of the site is misleading and would be a better description of the site in the Medieval period than in the Iron Age. Whether a river existed adjacent to the settlement is doubtful, and to refer to its existence gives a distorted view of the environment and drainage regime in the Iron Age. It is possible that a deeper water channel, within an area of shallower water, might have existed in approximately the same position as the later course of the Brue, i.e. on the eastern side. However, a better picture would be to see a shallow lake with a mosaic of fen, fen carr and tree swamp plant communities interspaced with water courses which had a sluggish, generally northward drainage flow past the village but which were by no means regularized, embanked, clearly defined or constant.

It is almost certain that Clarke's proposed western gateway could not have existed. The environmental evidence from the western end of an exploratory trench (Chapter 5) makes clear that there was no dry surface outside this gap in the palisade, not even a seasonally dry one. The presence of lake mud with floating leaved aquatics disproves the existence of any such cartway or path, whilst the presence of a peat bank would have prevented the use of wheeled transport. Both Tratman and Clarke thought that overland access to higher ground would have been possible, but the stratigraphic evidence from around the settlement makes both assertions highly unlikely. Although Lias 'islands' are now emerging out of the shrinking peat, there is still no evidence for an artificial causeway from the higher land of Glastonbury to the Lake Village, a distance of about one kilometre. The idea of driving chariots through the west entrance needs to be abandoned. Clarke's "land route from the south (forking) around the Southern sector of the settlement with an eastern branch hugging the riverside perimeter" also did not exist.

Another aspect of Clarke's model, the infield-outfield system, which was supposedly practised over a wide expanse of fertile alluvial flats and river floodplain near the village, cannot be true. The alluvial soils on which this should have happened, of great importance for medieval reclamation and grazing, had not been deposited by the late Iron Age. The prevailing environmental conditions during occupation would have made local tillage in the vicinity of the village impossible. Grazing in the immediate vicinity of the lake village was also not possible. But it is perhaps feasible that grazing could have taken place at dry periods of the year on the raised bogs to the northwest, west and southwest as well as at the margins of the peatlands. However, the amount of potential grazing land would have been much less in the Iron Age than was the case in the medieval and later periods. It seems evident that Clarke had accepted at face value the evidence for intercommoning and lowland pasturing that was well documented for the Somerset Levels in the medieval period by a variety of authors, and well-brought together in an analysis by Michael Williams in 1970; this book does not appear in Clarke's references although many of the calculations Clarke produces, on yields and movements and resources, are in that book in one place or another.

The environmental conditions and constraints on and around the Lake Village preclude acceptance of Clarke's site setting and its economic basis.

Dating.

Clarke suggested that the Lake Village existed from 150 ± 50BC to 50 ± 50BC, and was of about 100 years' duration within this span. He said that the dating was "crudely confirmed by pollen analysis, by the four to five feet of peat which accumulated during the occupation of the settlement, and by independent claims of assumptions involving the numbers of superimposed hearths and Floors, the frequency of house and granary rebuilding, and the sample numbers of surviving fibulae, querns, spindle whorls, potsherds and food debris." We need not stress the problems of modern pollen analysis of the uppermost deposits (Chapter 5), nor those of the "sample numbers of artefacts", and the 4-5 feet of peat repeated one of Bulleid's errors.

Before moving on to Clarke's model of social behaviour and late Iron Age society, we should pause here and introduce a paper that instituted the source critical analysis of the site and Clarke's influential paper.

Barrett's Critique.

In 1987 John Barrett published a short paper on the Lake Village, concentrating on a critical analysis of Clarke's 1972 paper and also presenting a few thoughts on the settlement in the light of the work going on in the Somerset Levels (at Meare and Glastonbury). Some of Barrett's criticisms of Clarke have already been noted, but he also raised several important questions independent of his analysis of Clarke's work. Among these was the post-depositional process, or processes, at work on the site following its abandonment and 2000 years of environmental effects. Barrett also drew attention to the wholly unknown quantities of Relics that Bulleid and Gray recovered but did not record in their Black Book; we hope to have answered that in part in Chapter 3. Barrett commented that Clarke, while paying lip service to post-depositional events and the excavators' partial neglect of Relics, developed his model on the basis of non-significant movement of material. Everything done on sites in the Levels since then has shown that movement does take place, mostly vertically (Orme et al 1981). An interesting concept put forward by Barrett was that in some respects, Bulleid's excavation techniques "were as good as, if not superior to, those of Pitt-Rivers" (1987,412); this is worth some analysis (by someone else, some other time). The major thrust of Barrett's paper, apart from his criticisms of Clarke's approach, was that Bulleid and Gray were digging at their point in time, and not for us in 1995 or for our particular interests; we have referred to this in Chapter 2, and will return to it again in Chapter 8. Barrett concluded his paper with the suggestions that the occupation at the Lake Village may have been seasonal, and that substantial houses may not have been abundant or even present; in discussing the evidence from M74 and M13, where Bulleid claimed houses had existed, Barrett pointed to the clay spreads overlying the wall posts and concluded that "either these structural features had collapsed or been truncated in some other way, or they had never risen as walls in the first place" (1987, 418). Therefore, "we might see many of the structural remains recovered at Glastonbury representing the underpinning and base of a crannog which .....supported seasonally erected structures on the clay, timber and rubble foundations" (1987,422). We think that the evidence assembled in Chapters 3 and 4 shows that houses were present on some parts of the site at certain periods in the site evolution, and that settlement was permanent at first and later became seasonal, and that houses were indeed swept away and replaced by open spreads of clay. But following Barrett's theme, we advance in this book our opinions on the basis of our expectations and contemporary thoughts about archaeological evidence - we can do nothing else of course. In a way, we are following Barrett's lead in this book, but attempting more and hopefully achieving a greater understanding of the Lake Village by a more exhaustive analysis.

FINAL COMMENTS AND APPRECIATIONS.

From all that we have said in this Chapter, it follows that we are not disposed to accept Clarke's "Provisional Model of an Iron Age Society and its settlement". His identifications of structural elements on the site are based on very poor factual foundations, and misleadingly so in some cases. His proposed activity areas, wealth distribution, economic base and environmental setting are all incomplete or downright wrong. There are too many uncertainties, too many misreadings of the evidence, too much neglect of Bulleid's clear statements, too much forcing of the data into the mould chosen by Clarke to explain the village. Our own mould is in Chapter 8.

Clarke did not restrict his analysis to the settlement alone. His observations and conclusions about the wider world of Iron Age societies of the south west involved a whole set of models and hierarchies. Relationships between the Lake Village and communities to north, west, south and east must have existed and a few of these can be detected in the analysis of particular aspects of the artefacts and materials (Chapter 6). Bulleid pointed to some of these in his 1911 report, and subsequent work has greatly amplified the story (e.g. Peacock 1969). Clarke tried to bring many of these aspects together in his local map (Clarke 1972,fig.217), but did not create a map for the longer-distance contacts. In a later section of his paper, however, he tried to present a model of the place of the Lake Village in the Iron Age of the south west, and its role as a marshland settlement of minor significance, "a lowly member ... a second order hamlet". That may or may not be true, or even reasonable to assume, and it is not our purpose here to explore this extended compass, to examine Maesbury (his high order market centre) or the polygonisation of the Bristol Channel region.

We likewise shy away from his seemingly uncritical use of "historical information on Celtic society preserved in the records of the classical authors and in the Irish vernacular tradition". Caesar's ethnology of certain Celtic tribes is cited to argue "a condensed but intelligible record of an important complex .... the patrilocal extended family, fraternal polygyny, and levirate" (Clarke 1972,847). All of these more intimate matters are beyond the scope and aim of our book, although in Chapter 8 we will draw whatever conclusions we think may be relevant and justified.

The contribution of D.L.Clarke in studies of the Glastonbury Lake Village, as in other aspects of archaeological thought, was influential on a generation of students and others working in the late 1960s and 1970s. The model for Glastonbury has been one of the markers for Clarke's contributions, one of those papers that emerge time and again for admiration and example. It was detailed, exhaustive, analytical, provocative and stimulating, and it has been an inspiring paper for both budding and experienced archaeologists. Many have questioned its reliability in terms of archaeological practice, but no-one will question its relevance to the development of archaeological theory.

Postscript (J.M.C.).

Although Clarke's paper has been read by the author of this Chapter many times, it is only now in late 1994 that the full impact of his fig. 21.11 is felt. This is a map of the parish of Cadbury in Devon taken from work by W.G.Hoskins (1987). It shows "A Dumnonian multivallate hill fort *c* 3 acres, its territory and settlement hierarchy". Clarke suggests that special circumstances here preserved a fossil impression of a fully developed late Celtic settlement pattern - five multilineage hamlets, twelve single lineage farmsteads and a central hill fort, preserved by boulder-built field boundaries established before the eleventh century in an area where Celtic traditions survived the Saxon penetration. This relict settlement layout includes a mill on the edge of the parish, one of the single lineage steadings; Hoskins stated that the mill existed in 1842. That "mill" is my house, built in the 18th century as two farm labourers' cottages and joined together in a restructuring act of 1842 - the date is inscribed on the wall outside my window as I write this. Was it ever a mill? There is no evidence.

Chapter 8.

Village Life

In the preceding Chapters 1-7 we have tried to set out a view of the Glastonbury Lake Village as seen from our perspective in 1994. When Bulleid and Gray published their two volumes in 1911 and 1917, they must have been well-pleased with the product. Thomas May, the excavator of Hengistbury Head and Corbridge, wrote to Bulleid in 1917:

> "it is refreshing to get a candid, careful and conscientious scientific treatise of this kind. I am more impressed with the character of the book, and the patient and accurate record of evidence, than by the speculations and conclusions of the professors and others which are more wordy, but to which I do not attach so much importance, though they are given prominent positions in the book. The latter I should hardly take the trouble to read if published separately under their own names."

It is the careful description of the evidence that has survived the 80 years or so and has both prompted and survived various re-appraisals and reconsiderations; doubtless it will survive ours. Our purpose in this book is not to re-publish the site, and we have deliberately as well as of necessity restricted ourselves to examinations of those aspects of the evidence that seemed to warrant new study. The basic evidence lies in the 1911 and 1917 books and allows us to approach the site with our own current concerns; instead of pursuing the minutiae of certain classes of artefacts, or taking a global view of the site, we have preferred to follow lines that seemed appropriate today - environment, site structure, industry and critical analysis.

Chapter 1 provides an outline of the history of the Lake Village, as expressed in the records of the years 1892-1911. It is a story of determination, hesitancy, renewal and final success. Chapter 2 is an essay into the two volumes of 1911 and 1917, using both that printed record and a wealth of other information written, illustrated and artefactual. It demonstrates how imperfect in places the record actually is, how it came to be flawed, and what proportion can be deemed reliable for further work.

Chapter 3 is documentary and the basis of all that follows. It tries to set out the physical record of the Mounds seen on the site by Bulleid and Gray, to correlate structures across the site, and to divide the period of occupation into four Phases. Chapter 3 also provides a complete listing of the finds associated or adjacent to the Mounds, providing for the first time a stratigraphic record of the artefacts on the site. Its Appendix (3.1) sets out, again for the first time, an orderly list of all the artefacts so that they can be identified as to Mound and to their publication in the 1911 and 1917 books.

Chapter 4 is restricted to a structural analysis of the Mounds. The various houses, shelters, windbreaks and open spreads, smaller built structures, palisades, pathways and entrances are identified on the site, and set into a four-Phase organisation. The settlement can be seen as one undergoing constant change, expansion and contraction, rebuilding and abandonment, alteration and maintenance. This allows estimates to be made about population, units of settlement and duration of occupation. Chapter 5 is a summary of an extensive investigation into the local and regional environments of the Lake Village, building on a series of borings across the eastern end of the Brue Valley. The precise character of the swamp in which the settlement was established, and its abutting raised bog and lake muds, now help to open questions about the economic and social purposes lying behind the Lake Village occupation.

Chapter 6 presents an overview of the material culture but does not claim to expose all of the artefacts to modern research. Several groups of the finds have been studied in depth in recent years, and others for this book, in efforts to gain a better understanding of the nature of the industries often proposed as major activities at the Lake Village. A series of distribution plans of particular groups of artefacts helps to define the extent and density of industrial or domestic activity. Chapter 7 is a critical analysis of the two best-known re-interpretations of the Lake Village, that of Tratman and his square-house settlement and that of Clarke with his modular unit approach. Both made significant contributions to the study of the Lake Village, but their specific conclusions are severely criticised, as doubtless will be our assessments in the near or distant future.

The basic problem in any attempt to analyse and interpret the site is the lack of precision in many of the records made by Bulleid and Gray. Although some of the Mounds and some of the finds have well-documented stratigraphical contexts, others do not and they therefore introduce a strong element of uncertainty in any detailed assessment. We have taken the lines of least resistance for these, in assuming contemporaneity or other relationships across the site that do not present any abrupt transformations. Nonetheless, a large number of good correlations do exist, in that clay Floors link or objects are clearly stratified, and these provide us with our best information for identifying and interpreting the patterns of occupation and activity on the site.

For Arthur Bulleid, the Glastonbury Lake Village was "the marsh village of his imagination", according to Clark (1957,68). By this, Clark was not implying that it did not exist but rather that Bulleid had dreamed of discovering such a site (Chapter 1); the expression was very close to the truth in environmental terms. Bulleid's interpretation of the discovery was never fully realised, however, as he was persuaded to resist conjecture and to adhere rigidly to the facts (Coles, Goodall & Minnitt 1992,15). His mentor, Robert Munro, had his own views, believing that the idea of settlement in a lake had somehow arrived in the north and west of Europe from its origin in Alpine Europe. With the presumed collapse of the pile-dwelling societies in Switzerland, France and Italy, carriers of the concept migrated and introduced crannog-building and terp-building to the peoples of western and northern Europe. Even so, the concept suffered as Munro made clear: "The crannogs and other lake habitations of the Iron Age are but the deteriorated remnants of a doomed system which, like every dying art before final extinction, passed through a stage of decay and degeneration" (Munro 1890,554). Bulleid never commented on such unlikely developments, but instead adhered rigidly to his original view, that of a Lake Village vibrant and successful, occupied without interruption as a permanent settlement of the late Iron Age, "industrious, and fairly civilised" (Bulleid 1894). He never questioned the intelligence of the lake dwellers in choosing such a site, nor did he waver from his view of the permanence and uniformity of the settlement. He and Gray were digging, 1892-1907, at a time when England was at some sort of peak of prosperity (for some), power and peace (not forgetting the assertion of that power in southern Africa). It was easy for them to accept the Keller-derived versions of the tranquil and easy life of the lake-dwellers of Switzerland. Today we are doubtless influenced by contemporary events in our own models of episodic variation, evolutionary unevenness, stress, competition and change. In this view the evidence of environmental variation, as much as the demonstration of site structure, helps us to advance our more dynamic model. The pity, however, is that, unlike Bulleid and Gray, we cannot test our ideas on the site by further excavation. There must have been questions, even if more simple, of which Bulleid and Gray were aware, but there is no evidence that they amended their technique or approach to answer them. We might envisage their questions to have been directed towards a better understanding of the structures on site and the industries practised.

Environment.

In Chapter 5 the immediate environment of the Village is described as a tree swamp or fen carr, thus a swamp village rather than a lake village. Standing on the site, to the west was a huge raised bog clogging the valley, and the ancient river Brue could make no impact on this; instead, it tried to flow northwards through the Godney-Garslade gap to join the Axe (fig.5.12). Here the river would encounter estuarine clays which in their southernmost spread were then mostly freshwater-based muds. To the east of the site were reedswamp, sedge fen, fen carr and open water communities, and a wide expanse of swamp, fed by the river, extended southwards to the Glastonbury upland. The fen carr selected for the settlement was probably small, and surrounded by the shallow waters of a freshwater lake. On the eastern edge of the carr was probably one of the several sluggish channels which allowed the water flow to drift northwards, and this channel may have served as the initial route to the site, the alternative routes being passable by neither boat nor foot. On the face of it, the site was basically impossible in terms of stability, dryness and land access; we will explore this "impossibility" later. But there was an advantage in terms of proximity to the resources of the swamp and its surrounds.

The concept of the "concave landscape" has been advanced for the Levels and for other wetland conditions (Coles 1978). In this the resources of both lowland wet and upslope dry can be seen to complement one another both for food and for seasonal exploitation. Figure 8.1 promotes the concept for the Lake Village, and suggests that the position of the settlement was ideal, allowing access to fertile dryland to both south and north, for arable, hoe plot and pasture as well as timber, coppice and wild animals. Downslope were reed beds,

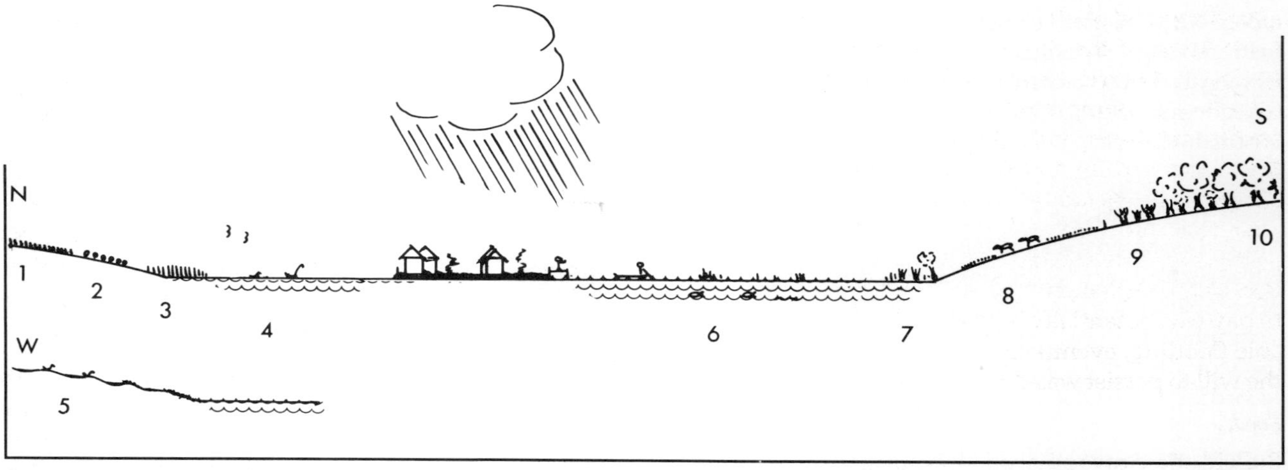

Fig.8.1 The concave landscape. 1.Arable fields. 2.Hoe plots. 3.Reed beds. 4.Wildfowl. 5.Raised bog birds and berries. 6.Fish and eel. 7.Plants of the margin. 8.Pasture. 9.Coppice. 10.Woodland timber and the hunt. JMC

Fig.8.2 Distribution of querns and food remains. JMC

abundant wild plant foods and birds. On the west the giant dome of the raised bog housed its own life of grouse and berries. The northern mud flats, periodically flooded, supported a wider variety of plants and smaller creatures, and saltmarsh grazing was beyond the island gap. In and on the shallow waters, some clogged by vegetation, were fish, eel, fowl and other resources. All were within one km of the settlement, some very close at hand. Economically then, the position of the settlement was logical, although the price to pay was potentially high in periodic yet unpredictable flooding, eventually exerting such pressure that the will to persist was diminished and then lost.

Food.

Bulleid and Gray retrieved an immense amount of evidence about these wetland and dryland resources, some relating to the industrial activities carried out on site (Chapter 6) and some reflecting the food supplies; in almost all respects the resources utilised on site were local. The interest shown by Bulleid in particular in the food plants and animals was a crucially important part of the post-excavation process, and his assembly of specialists (Chapter 1) was drawn from the highest ranks of expertise available in the country; he does not dwell on those who failed to deliver reports to him, nor did he try to edit down that which arrived, and suffered the exaggerations of Boyd Dawkins for some years (Chapter 1 and see below).

The distribution of food remains on the settlement is not accurately known but an attempt is made in figure 8.2 to show what was recorded with some degree of precision. The various wheelbarrow-loads of bones, grain and sloe stones to which Bulleid and Gray allude in their reports are probably only a reflection of

Fig.8.3 Querns. Forestier's drawing of 1911.

the more widespread distribution of smaller heaps or scatters all across the site, and outside the fences. The plot in figure 8.2. shows that querns, both saddle and rotary types, occurred in all areas of the site, more saddle querns in the south and rotary querns on the north (fig.8.3). Hardly any have recorded stratigraphic positions in the Mounds, nor do any of the iron sickles from the site. Wheat and/or barley was recovered from both areas, north and south, and legumes (mainly peas and beans) were much more widely scattered. Being more easy to see than grain in the dark peat and clay soils on site, these are probably over-represented on the plot, and cereals under-represented. Also found were fragments of "bread", unbroken wheat grains mixed with some substance (honey?) to make an unbaked cake "kneaded on the palm of one hand with the fingers of the other, the hand being small and the fingers slender". Reid thought that such cakes would be hard to eat and digest. The list of cultivated plant remains from the site consists of *Triticum vulgare, Hordeum distichum* and *hexastichum* (we use Clement Reid's terms here, in Bulleid and Gray 1917,627-628), and *Vicia* and *Faba vulgaris*. The wheat and barley were "in the state of threshed grain, only a few imperfect spikelets having been found". No flax was identified. Reid also recorded the leaves, seeds and fruits of another 40 plants recovered by the excavators, and these indicate the variety of wild plants gathered for various purposes. Some were edible, like chickweed, parsnip, goosefoot, nettle, bulrush and various berries, others were useful for fibre (matting or twine) or colour, others were probably washed or tramped in. In view of what comes later in this Chapter, some of the elements in Reid's list are listed here: crowfoot, spearwort, waterlily, mustard, chickweed, buttercup, sloe, blackberry or dewberry, rose and hawthorn, dropwort, parsley, parsnip, bogbean, bittersweet, goosefoot, orache, water pepper, bindweed, pondweed, nettle, hazel, flag, bur-reed, bulrush, sedge. Reid commented that more detailed examination of the rubbish outside the fence would have been valuable. There is not much here that relates to the estuarine environments of the north, but it is likely that some of the plants like kelp and sea purselane were within reach of the gatherers.

Were some of these local plants stored on the site? Conditions would only allow successful storage if the grain or other seeds were raised above the damp, and the various square or rectangular post-settings found on the site beside some Mounds might represent racks or containers. At these places on the site some form of rectangular setting was over or adjacent to a scatter of legumes (M40-42, M65 and M80) and this might indicate definite raised storage places (Gent 1983). It is also the case, however, that a settlement in such an advantageous position in regard to wild plant and animal foods might not need storage facilities, as there were year-round supplies of different foods, hence long-term storage was not a necessity. We think that some raised storage containers were likely to have been on the site, not perhaps for daily extraction of grain or legumes or other plants but more likely for seed storage awaiting the season of cultivation by plough or spade. It may be difficult now to envisage a reliance on wild plants for food in the eastern Brue Valley, but these were only a part (large or small?) of the overall supplies.

Bulleid and Gray were equally casual about the masses of animal bone found on the site. They recorded, in one way or another, about 3500 bones, and they noted that bones were abundant both inside and outside the fences. Bones are recorded from all parts of the site (fig.8.2) but very few have any stratigraphic position. Some came from small middens outside the fence (see below). Many bones were identified on the spot, by both men, and many were reburied in the backfilled trenches. In the 1893-94 seasons, Bulleid noted that a barrowload of bones was collected from little more than one square yard (0.85 sq.m) in some places, which must have been near the south of the site or in the central northern area. Of those bones that survived to be counted, only 2% were of wild animals. The list of domestic animals consists of sheep (88% of the total mammals), cattle (5%), pig (2%), horse (2%), dog (1%). Sheep were thus overwhelmingly predominant; they were pastured on the uplands to the south, on the islands to the north, and probably on the saltmarsh grazing just north of the Godney-Garslade gap at appropriate times of the year. Even the raised bog to the west could serve as short-term pasture in a dry summer. The cattle or horses may have been used in tillage of the fertile fields to the north, more light in soils than the clays of the south. The recent identification of several small islands of rock and sand just north of the site, exposed due to shrinkage of the peatbeds, probably shows that some of the dry fields and plots for the settlement were nearer to the site than previously suspected (fig.5.12).

Among the wild mammals, the bones of otter and beaver were more abundant than those of red deer, roe deer, boar, fox, cat, weasel, marten, polecat and hedgehog. These animals were probably hunted as much for skin, fur, tusk, teeth or antler as for meat. The wooden framing recorded from several parts of the site might have been parts of stretchers for skin as well as for textiles (fig.4.13). The deer and boar frequent marshland, and the beaver and otter reflect the watery environment. Beaver in particular may have been active in altering the flow and levels of water in the eastern Brue Valley, damming small streams and eroding the banks.

One of the remarkable records from the site is the extensive list of birds identified by C.W.Andrews. Overall, they show the existence of "a district of marsh and mere, haunted by flocks of Pelicans, Cranes, Swans and various species of Ducks" (Bulleid & Gray 1917,636). As some of the birds were very young, they were probably being bred in the vicinity of the site, unless the Lake Villagers sent out expeditions to more remote and quieter spaces. The birds most often identified were common duck, crane, whooper swan and cormorant. Other anserine birds were goose, golden eye, teal, pintail, shoveller, wigeon, tufted duck, scaup, pochard and merganser. Heron, bittern and pelican were present, and puffin may represent an inadvertent immigrant. Sea eagle, kite, goshawk and barn owl may have been prized for feathers, wings or beaks, and the lowly coot, rail, and grebe routinely collected. Most of these birds came from the great swamp and immediate environs, and many were doubtless sought for food and eggs; their feathers may have been used as decoration.

The fish bones recorded by Bulleid and Gray were fewer in number, but four species were identified by C.Tate Regan: perch, shad, roach and trout. No bones of eel were found, but these do not survive well especially if well-cooked (and eaten). Frogs were another likely source of food, and recent examinations of some bones from the site indicate their presence (Chapter 6.12). Perch must have been caught in clear moving water, probably a major channel of the ancient Brue flowing around the western edge of the Glastonbury upland. Trout also required clear water, not necessarily flowing but well-oxygenated. Shad, however, prefer more estuarine conditions, and thus come from waters to the north, at or beyond the Godney-Garslade gap. Roach are slow water fish, and could tolerate muddy and poor conditions.

On the eastern side of the settlement, the Causeway of M 47 was probably a landing stage for boats and rafts, and here were found a number of lead weights which are best interpreted as net-sinkers or line sinkers; it suggests that at some stage in the life of the settlement

Fig.8.4 The Causeway in use. Forestier, 1911.

there was sufficient water to allow water-borne craft to set out and land (fig.8.4), and that the Causeway may at times have served as a convenient fishing-platform for those inhabitants so inclined. An interesting aspect of the watery landscape around the settlement is whether or not any of it was drinkable. We do not know, but suggest that it was probably suitable at most times of the year, maybe less so in the more stagnant summer months. The springs at the Glastonbury upland (Chalice Well and the Abbey spring) may have been in use as a refreshing halt on expeditions to the fields and woodlands here.

Taken as a whole, the food remains from the Lake Village are a remarkably varied assemblage. Although little information can now be gleaned about the methods of crop cultivation, harvesting, storing or food preparation, or about the husbandry of domestic animals, the evidence is impressive in its quantity and variety. Doubtless much of the animal bone evidence did not survive the eager anticipations of the site dogs, nor the damp middens outside the fence. And the recognition of plant remains was remarkable, given the state of the site and its excavation (Chapter 2). Nonetheless, the record is extensive. It shows that the inhabitants of the Village were resourceful, experienced and persistent; they may not have consciously acknowledged conservation within their strategies for food, but they probably would not exploit any resource to the point of its local extinction. Seasonal fluctuations in a wetland like the Glastonbury swamp could be severe, with varying levels of water and different stream flows, to set alongside more predictable bird migration, varying times of planting and harvesting crops, and gathering wild foods and supplies throughout the year in different places and conditions. We should thus not think of a boring Iron Age diet of ground and cooked grain, or mutton and beef. We suggest that a selection from the menu shown here was available, perhaps prepared in even more elaborate ways than we have experienced in wetlands in the U.K. and abroad, particularly France.

Not all of these dishes were available to the Lake Village occupants, according to the evidence recovered by Bulleid and Gray. But most were potentially available, and a number of these plants and animals were identified on site, and others from environmental investigations. The Menu is designed to emphasize the wealth of resources that an environment like the great swamp and its surrounds could provide, granted the ability of people to explore, sample and exploit the whole range. Of course, personal, social and religious principles may have prevented the full use of some logical supplies, but we do not think the Lake Villagers were in any way impoverished or degenerate.

Site structure and industry.

The settlement itself has been described, and phased, in Chapter 4 and the details of Floors, spreads, houses, shelters, fences and other structures need not be reiterated here. The Early Phase had 6 houses and 15 spreads of clay, representing 42 Floors (fig.4.9). Two of the houses are likely replacements of two that burnt down. The settlement was constructed within the original fen carr woodland and was divided into two by an open area where access from the W and E was possible. Figure 8.5 is a representation of the site during this Early Phase with logboats and rafts arriving, building operations underway and (already) one house set alight. What other activities went on during this short episode of about 25-30 years? Here is where the record becomes imprecise because only a small proportion of the finds, indicative of special activities, was stratigraphically distinct, or written down. We will return to the Early Phase after a short discussion on the artefact distributions.

Domestic debris was found all across the site, seemingly in almost every Mound, between some Mounds, and occurring at all levels (fig.8.6). Pottery for example, has a wide distribution (fig.2.6) but here we can see some Mounds where pottery was very abundant. Flint is another material likely to be in general use, unspecialised, and its distribution is again widespread if we take into account Bulleid's neglect to record flint in the years 1893-1898. Personal ornaments are also likely to indicate domestic occupation and the distributions are very wide (figs.6.7 and 6.8). Some of these ornaments are phased.

More specialised artefacts may be represented by articles for spinning and weaving, woodworking, bone and antler working and metal working although almost all may well have been home-based rather than separate crafts. Spindle whorls and bobbins were widely scattered over the site (fig.6.6) while weaving combs and loom weights were more restricted to certain areas on the site (fig.6.5). Metal working as an industry required special places for the work (fig.6.1) as did woodworking for axles, wheels and spokes. Again, some of these activities can be phased. The regular use of iron billhooks is attested by the eight recovered on site, at least one dated to each of the four Phases.

The quantity of finds of all materials is very great as figure 8.6 shows; this plot excludes unnumbered pottery, bone and flint and stone, and would be very black if all these could be included. Concentrations of artefacts occur in the S, centre E, N centre and NW. Bulleid wrote about the source of the structural elements of the site: "every scrap of clay, stone and gravel, and doubtless a large proportion of the timber, was imported by the inhabitants to the site" (1911) and he could have made the same comment about the industrial materials. Transport was clearly a major aspect in the organisation of the site, and in the absence of land routes, everything came by water. Rafts carrying 0.5 tonnes of clay, stone or sand, and logboats with up to

MENU

Water cress soup made with duck stock, served with comfrey fritter

Sweet oar weed fried in nut oil and wild celery soup

Reed mace spikes and common mallow soup

Bean and duck egg salad with brooklime

Hazelnut cutlets with herb and kelp salad

Fish etc.

Tench cooked in crab apple juice with steamed laver

Smoked eel and wild celery

Pike steak and boiled marsh samphire

Terrine of eel and frogs' legs with nettle tips

Crayfish with herbs and waterlily tubers

Meat.

Filet of heron and stewed nettle with brooklime salad

*Wild boar cooked with bog myrtle berries
and served with crab apple sauce and sea kale*

*Grouse or duck (in season) and raised bog cranberry sauce
with sea beet and crab apple pickle*

Beaver tail roast with hazelnuts, peas and comfrey sauce

Saltmarsh lamb and sea purselane, with wild cabbage and meadowsweet

Roast swan with reed mace shoots and sea holly sweetmeats

Teal served with watercress and samphire

Sweet trolley

Goat cream cheese and honey

Reedmace pancakes with honey or apple jelly

Raspberries with cheeses

Bilberry crumble

Tea or coffee.

Coffee: acorn, dandelion root, goosegrass

Tea: mint, limeflower, heather flower

(served with angelica crystallised fruits)

Drinks.

Beer: nettle, heather, bog myrtle, sweet gale, crab apple cider

Wine: birch sap, oak leaf, elderflower, blackberry

Afters.

fennel seed chews, willow bark aspirin, marshmallow chews

Fig.8.5 The Early Phase. Drawn by Jane Brayne.

1.0 tonne of supplies, must have been in regular use. The water channels for these, suitable also for floating timber to the site, must have been kept open and clear at all times. The logboat from Crannel Farm, with a "deadweight capacity of 480kg at standard freeboard" (McGrail 1978,199), was almost certainly a part of the Lake Village transport system. Although the quantities of raw materials were great, the number of loads may not have been excessive per year of settlement; perhaps 10 loads of building material, and another small number with grain and game and plants. Sheep and cattle if brought to the site alive might have been led or dragged through the shallow waters, but sheep in particular would cause trouble in the wet; they probably came trussed or dead, by boat. Cattle could be made to swim if the water was deep enough. Materials for industrial use, from Mendip in particular, may have involved specific expeditions overland with final water transport to the site. The rest, bronze, iron and the like were probably imported as scrap in small quantities, and collecting antler and other materials was probably a task requiring not much heavy traffic to and fro. These comments in no way diminish the achievements of the inhabitants. They clearly had a well-organised pattern of life, exploiting a local environment very intensively, and gathering more exotic items such as glass or shale from occasional enterprises conducted with other groups to the S and E.

The Early settlement (fig.4.9 and 8.5) probably consisted of four units, each with one house, adjacent spreads of clay for more open-air activities, and various storehouses or racks. Several isolated spreads of clay may have been used for fishing, willow-work or social purposes. Metal-working was practised outside the house at the NW, some woodwork also was done at the N; other activities in the NW sector included textile work, as well as corn grinding, flint, antler and bone work. The houses at centre W were not so well-associated with activity-related artefacts at this time although there is a hint of some specialised woodworking. Across E of here was another unit where weaving is documented.

A number of Mounds had debris beneath their lowest Floors, and in some cases these represent Early Phase dumping and activity (M28,M38,M71). More enigmatic are the several post-and-stake settings under and N of M27; these have been described in Chapter 4, and they may be consecrating posts set up at the inception of the settlement. The settlement in this Early Phase was fenced only at the centre W with a trace of some sort of hurdlework at the NW.

The Early Phase therefore consists of four units, with limited activity, little specialisation, and a life span of only one generation. Our estimate is therefore a population of about 50, and a date of 250-225BC (calendar years). The hazelnuts found under the clay patch on M4 may indicate that the first occupation began in the autumn, when water levels were at their lowest.

We think that this episode was not static, but that it was only the beginning of a period of settlement that began and continued to expand. The Middle Phase represents a stage in this expansion, and was probably initiated by an influx of 'families', maybe another 4 or 5, joining their previous relations (blood or acquaintance or work) once they could see some benefit to the move. They seem to have worked hard at it, and the foundation was widened to take the new spreads of clay brought in from quarries on the Glastonbury upland, and probably from smaller islands to the north

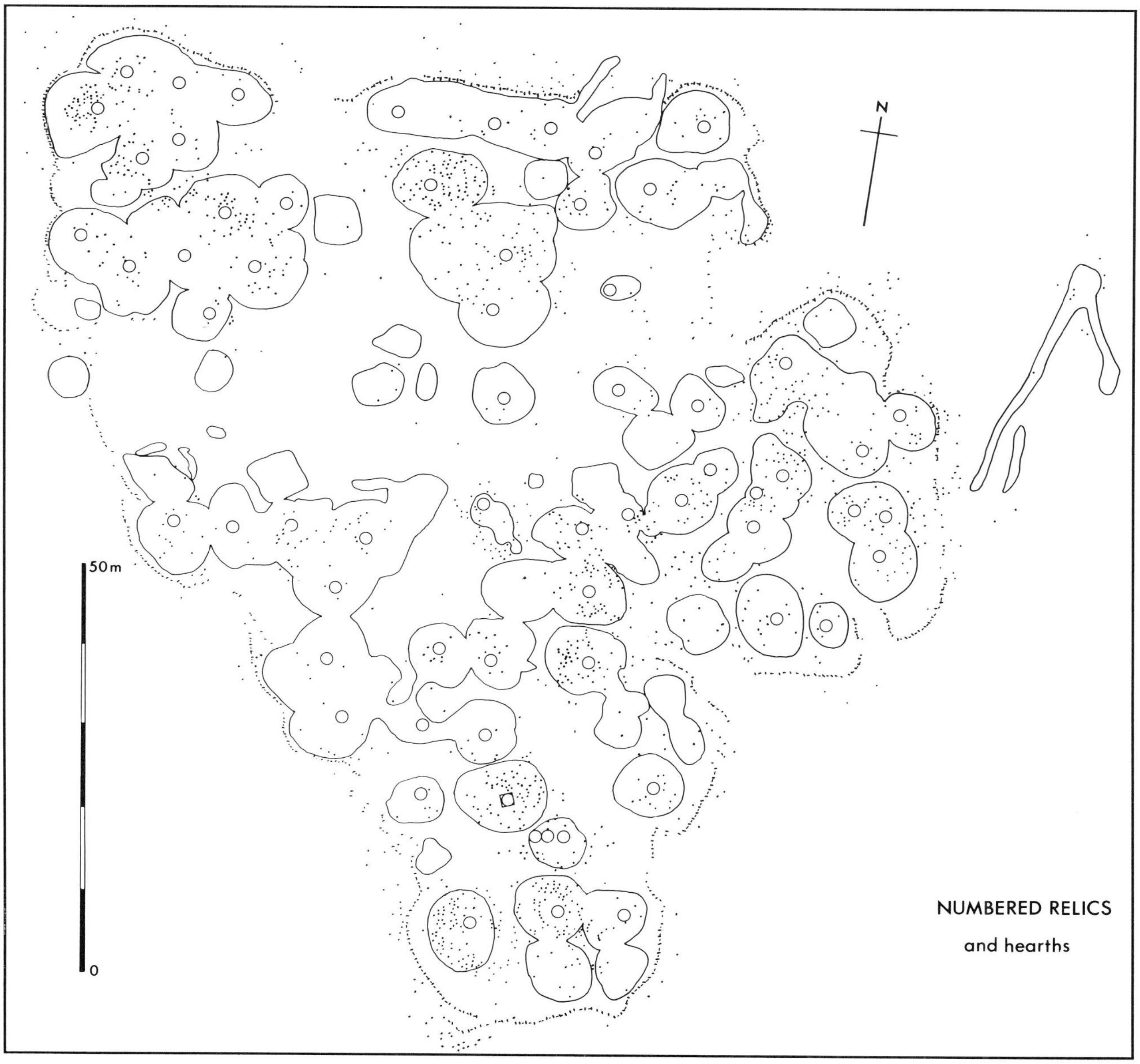

Fig.8.6 Distribution of numbered finds and hearths. This excludes most of the pottery, bone, flint and stone. JMC

as well. By the end of the Middle Phase, about 11 houses and 30 spreads had been created, with 58 separate Floors (fig.4.10). The site was now assuming its longest extent N-S, with a fence enclosing it along the W and S, and sections to NW and NE. Houses with adjoining spreads, some with hearths, were now built in the NW, the NE (of the Middle Phase site), and in the S. A large complex at the NE (M62-63-65) consisted of a house, open yard and large shelter (which burnt down). A smaller house on the NW had several sheltered areas nearby. Off to the E, beyond the fence, was a small house and larger shelter which may have been linked with the Embankment, built of stones and timber and probably serving as a primitive dock.

With an increased number of people, more resources were required, and more specialisation may have become possible, although its level was probably low. From the distribution of phased artefacts, we can detect metal working still continuing in the NW (M74 and M76) and weaving concentrated nearby (M70). Crucibles for metalwork were also part of the NE activity (M62) but at the S (M5) there was yet another area for metalwork, carried out on an open clay spread well away from any houses. For a small settlement, three separate areas for work with crucibles suggests either that these were successive, one replacing the other, or that the industry was low-level specialisation and carried out by more than one unit. On the W of the settlement some sort of woodworking area was established, and it seems likely that axle-boxes and spokes were being produced. This may well have been a specialised skill only practised by one person. Spinning of wool during this Phase took place in the central area (M16, 38-37,18) but was also more widely spread over the site. Some heavy equipment, such as antler hammers or iron pieces, were found in this central area, as well as a few ornaments (brooches). Farther S, the M5 house had several cheek pieces dated to this Phase, plus much more undated material.

The number of units in the Middle Phase was probably 10, with an expansion of the site, more significant fencing, more activity on site, but no special areas laid out for community work. Specialisation remained low and local. The structural evidence suggests that about 125 people may have lived here at any one time, and that the Middle Phase lasted for about two generations, 225-175BC (fig.8.7).

This Phase may not have got underway quite as early as 225BC if we can suggest that an outside force had a part in the substantial enlargement of population. As Baillie has persuasively demonstrated, the evidence from ice-cores and tree-rings points to a volcanic eruption in northern latitudes around 208-204BC (Baillie 1991). The effects of such a major dust-veil event, with sun dimmed, summer cold and failed harvests for several years could have prompted a re-settlement in the eastern Brue Valley, persuading a number of families to move into the already established Lake Village and to adopt its more wild resource-based practices. Another major volcanic event, at about 44-40BC, could have played a part in the final abandonment (see below).

The settlement continued to expand from 175BC for almost 100 years, into and through a Late Phase. This increase in area and units of occupation may have been natural but it is more likely that several new 'families' arrived, bringing useful labour and possibly other

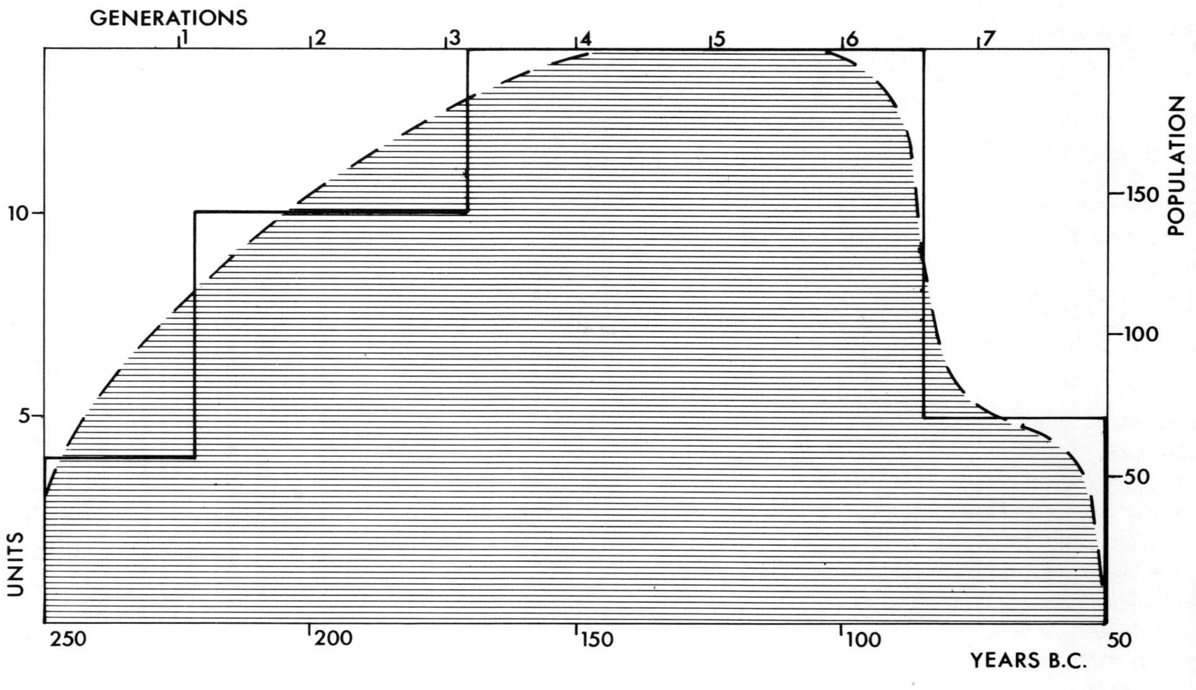

Fig.8.7 Chronology, units of settlement, generations and population. JMC

Fig.8.8 The site from the NE, Late Phase. Drawn by Jane Brayne.

things as well (see below). More houses were constructed, bringing the total on the site in this Phase to 13, with six sheltered areas and 57 spreads of clay (some with hearths) either attached or separate. There were 100 Floors of clay laid down in houses or on spreads (fig.4.11).

The fence was now completed, enclosing the old settlement area on its W and S sides and expanding E to take in an entirely new area, equally enclosed by the fence. Various entrances were now marked out and the site, giving the appearance of an enclosed settlement from a distance, nevertheless had at least six inset entries. The Embankment on the E was totally reshaped and turned into a Causeway with a hooked N end, allowing boats to glide into the stage or move around to the W face; an entry into the site was built at the S end of the Causeway (fig.4.11). The entrances appear to have been used as exits for refuse disposal, and midden-like deposits soon formed outside M48, the major and permanent E entry. The debris included bone and antler, potsherds and iron objects. Opposite M5 at the S, debris was chucked over the fence including heaps of sloe stones, bones, antler fragments, potsherds and flints. By M13, seeds, fish, bone and wood were dumped, and outside the NE entrance opposite M59-60, more bone and antler were discarded. No huge midden was found in the excavations either on or off the site. Lines of posts and hurdles in the N central area may have marked pens for temporary holding of animals and alignments leading to butchery on M34, perhaps M54 too. Several of the houses were very large (M5, M57, M65) and only two of the houses were rebuildings from the previous Phase ; this may be significant in marking a new alignment and structure to the site. The old was discarded, the site was remodelled, like a Town Planning Act come into force. Among the new features was an exit, or pair of exits, at the NW; here, two lobes of clay were laid out from the 'gap' in the fence, providing convenient places for dumping of rubbish, defecation or other activities (fig.8.8).

The activities, both domestic and industrial, on the site in the Late Phase were numerous and varied, but again we are hampered by the lack of many stratigraphic records. Much of the flintwork, for example, must belong to this Phase based on its distribution in the NE and, less surely, in the NW; dated parts of this Phase also occur on the W, S and centre. The great quantity of pottery, most of it unphased, must surely belong to the Late Phase when the settlement was at its maximum, and there is good correlation between the concentrations of pottery (fig.2.6) and the Late Phase structure (fig.4.11). On the W, some woodworking was assignable to the Late Phase, presumably using a base on M30. It is unfortunate that hardly any of the wooden artefacts were stratigraphically recorded by Bulleid and Gray (Chapter 6.10); it is likely that most of the decorated wooden vessels, as well as other fine objects, were made on this site, and probably a majority were of the Late Phase. The fact that two (X 2 and X 85) were weevil or worm eaten on site probably reflects conditions in their small middens rather than during storage in the houses.

Among other activities, weaving materials were well-represented on M74, probably on M37 as well; this latter was a very small elongated spread of clay, open, and could have been a specialised working floor. The tools for spinning and sewing were more widely scattered over the site (fig.6.6) but many whorls, bobbins and needles of the Late Phase occurred on M4; Bulleid identified this concentration as a bone tool manufactory, as many split pieces of bone were found as well. Another place for the same activity, perhaps tool-making as well as tool-using, was M63-64-65. The great mass of whorls, bobbins and points on the site are mostly unphased. Metal working on the site was still practised, with crucibles on M5, M4 and M76, but the concentrated debris on M5 was of the Middle Phase. Personal artefacts, such as brooches, rings and beads, are very poorly dated in stratigraphic terms. Those that are of this Late Phase are well-scattered across the site and only those on M5 (2 rings), and M70 (brooch), were associated with houses. Cheek pieces from M5, M4 and M9 may have been associated in use and in disposal, and a small group of cheek piece and two fasteners was found in the NE of the site.

The overall distribution of artefacts and structures of the Late Phase show a settlement at its most active and acquisitive. Debris occurred all over the site and demonstrates that a number of self-sustaining units existed. There were about 14 of these, each consisting of a house with attendant yard, some with large shelters or fenced spreads attached. There were also, for the first time, open spreads with no adjacent house or other structure; M7-8, M18, M27-38, M20, M25-44, M59-60-61 are quite evident (fig.4.11). A representation of this expansive settlement, with house units, fences, entrances and an active Causeway on the E, is shown in figure 8.9.

The effect of this Phase on the quarries, woodland and

Fig.8.9 The Late Phase. The site at its maximum. Drawn by Jane Brayne.

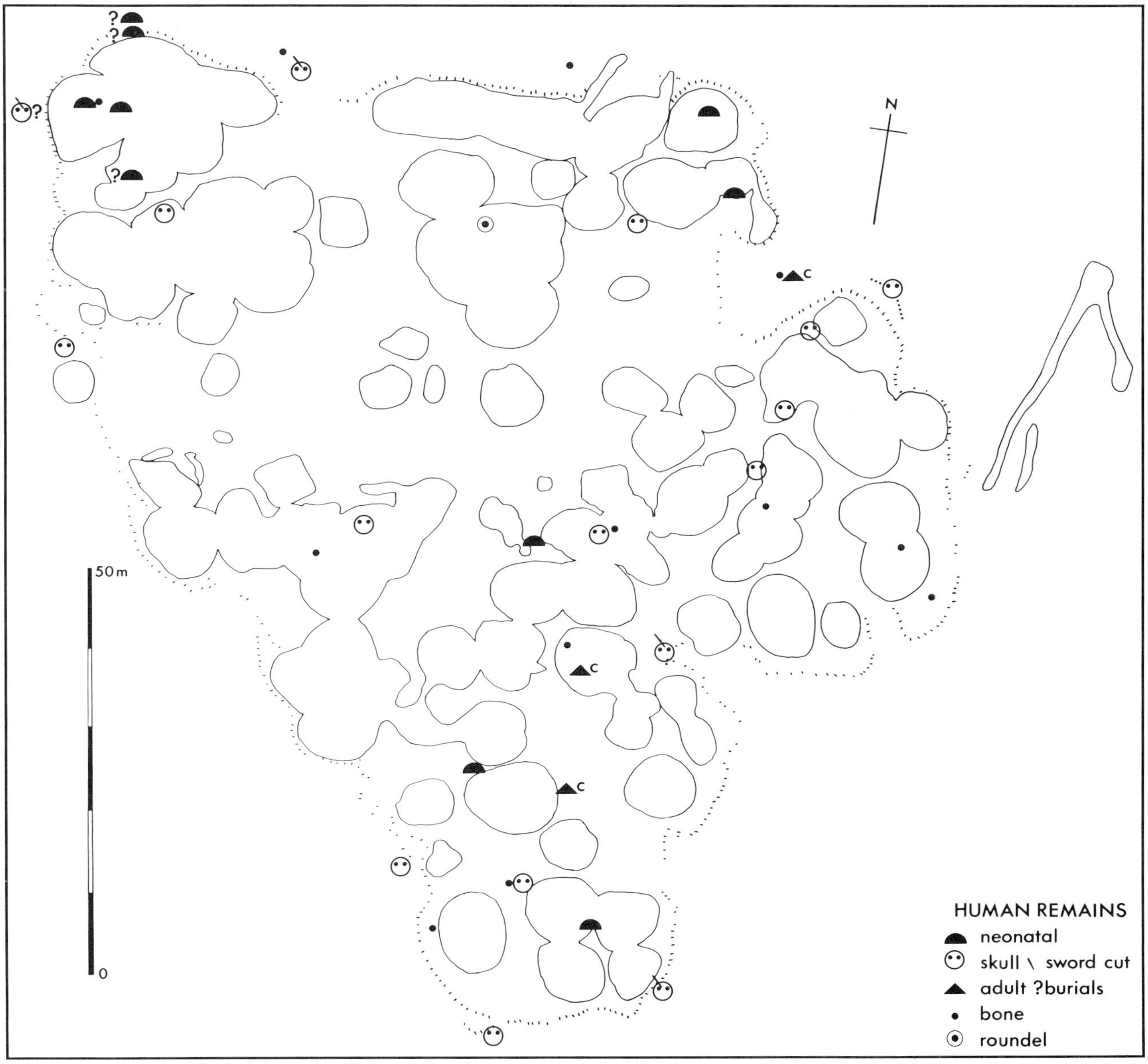

Fig.8.10 Distribution of human remains. SCM and JMC

coppices, reed beds and other sources of building materials must have been great. With such a re-organisation, the likelihood arises that it was in part if not in whole a Plan, devised by some authority and executed by the consent of the workforce. We hardly think that some great leader had emerged, but some kind of control and direction must have been applied to persuade and guide those able and willing to undertake the work. There is very little on the settlement, either phased or unphased, to indicate that it was particularly wealthy in comparison with other late Iron Age settlements. There is no especially large house, except perhaps M9 (see below), and no great wealth in artefacts. A small hoard of a bronze mirror, tweezers and 2 bone pins from outside the palisade at M30 is hardly a treasure, even if it had been deposited in a structure rather than placed outside the site. But also outside the fence, at 7 places, Bulleid and Gray recovered adult human skulls, 4 of them with cuts perhaps from a sword (Chapter 6.12, and fig.8.10). Only one skull was found at an entrance and the common image of high entrance posts with impaled skulls at Iron Age gateways may be true for other sites, but not for Glastonbury. Nonetheless, the fact that about half of the 15 adult skulls were deposited outside the fence implies some sort of ritualistic activity. Less dramatic were the burials of neonatal human remains in or beside the clay Floors (fig.8.10); only two of the 10 neonatal burials are dated to the Late Phase (one being of Middle Phase and the rest unstratified). Their distribution overall, at NW,NE, centre and S might be deliberate consecratory events at site extremes.

The small bronze hoard has been mentioned above, and Bulleid's greatest treasure, the bronze bowl (fig.8.11) was recovered from one of the entrances near M21; a fragment, perhaps of another bowl, lay between M70 and M68 at the NW of the site, in other words diagonally across from the M21 bowl. Perhaps the only other metal object that might be considered 'special' in the sense of both shape and material is a rod of tin with copper-alloy terminals believed by Gray to have once been covered by sheet gold (1911,253 and Plate XLV). This piece has been re-analyzed (Chapter 6.2), confirming the rod and terminals as tin and copper-tin-lead respectively, although no trace of the gilding survives (if it ever did exist). The 'baton' was found at the edge of M7, not far from the N end of the stone path or low bank running away from the unit of M3-4.

Fig.8.11 The Glastonbury Bowl.

There is no stratigraphic evidence that the bronze bowl (fig.8.11) or the mirror hoard or the 'baton' were of the Late Phase. By their position on the site, however, they are most likely to have belonged to this Phase (see figs.4.11 and 6.8).

One of the structures of the Late Phase is unlike the normal round houses. In the Middle Phase, M9 was an ordinary round house. It was transformed in the Late Phase, as Bulleid's plans and photographs make clear (fig.4.2). The nature of the structure itself is somewhat uncertain but we suggest it became an elongated building, walled and possibly roofed over. At the W entrance was a pathway to the spread of M12. Inside the structure, several hearths were built, successively, until they were sealed by a large clay table, called a hearth by Bulleid. This table, 1.6 x 1.4m square and 0.1m raised above the Floor, was decorated by 67 circles drawn into the surface (fig.2.2); these circles were 140mm across, with the imprint of the grooved line 9mm wide and up to 6mm deep. Presumably some round vessel, of clay or metal or wood, was used as the guide for the circles. A thin layer of ash was found on the table. Many objects were found on the several Floors of this Late Phase M9 structure, including a whorl, cheekpiece, bone point and decorated vessel. It is tempting to see this structure and its unusual furniture as a focal point for the settlement (fig.8.12), a place from where direction and control emanated, and where events and commemorations were held. If we look for some form of authority in the re-modelling and expansion of the settlement, this is where it may have been based. Much of this is not directly substantiated by the record, and it is clearly based on circumstantial evidence, but nothing contradicts it; others may well wish to dispute and substitute.

Perhaps as many as 14 units of occupation can be detected in this Late Phase, with the settlement growing fast and expanding to the E in a very substantial way. The structures and spreads, and the debris and deposits, suggest a lifespan of about 3 generations, from 175-80BC, and a maximum population of about 200, perhaps a little less (fig.8.7).

From this point in time we think the settlement encountered difficulties. In Chapter 5 the watery character of the site and its immediate environment have been stressed. What is lacking from all accounts of the site is any real evidence to explain its abandonment. We will try to advance our opinions on this later in this section. The Final Phase of occupation was marked first by a gradual and then an increasing contraction of activity, and reduction in population. Only 5 houses were built, all renewing former structures and no new positions were adopted. Many spreads of clay continued to be laid down, a large majority on the E part of the site (fig.4.12). The centre and W were almost totally abandoned, only a spread of clay at the far W and minor spreads at NW. The N perimeter was abandoned as was the major house at M5 in the S. The 'longhouse' of M9 was remodelled into a more normal round house and the decorated table was covered over by clay to make a hearth. The entrance to the site from the S end of the Causeway was closed off, and the Causeway may have been abandoned; it was not repaired. Something dramatic had occurred to cause this upheaval (fig.8.7).

The activities on site were also reduced. Only one quern is dated to the Final Phase, and that is an uncertain attribution. Weaving and spinning took place in the E sector, on open clay Floors. Metalworking is barely represented, with one crucible on M42. General debris was deposited on or near the clay spreads in the NW, M9 in the S, on the newly-laid Floors of M1-2, and on M42; the last-named was probably the focus of much of the activity on the surrounding open Floors. Two billhooks, 9 weaving combs, 2 iron knives and other iron tools, and perhaps some whorls, antler tools and other objects were recovered from the Final Phase Floor on M42. Several cheekpieces, and a set of bone beads, on the NW mark some sort of personal equipment or ornamentation but there is precious little else to mark status other than a brooch or two. The structural evidence for the Final Phase thus correlates with the finds in a general diminution of activity that left tangible traces behind. As the clay Floors of this Phase were the first to be encountered by Bulleid and Gray, we might have expected more objects to be easily attributed to the topmost Floors; we presume that Relics were rather few in number in this Phase rather than that the excavators failed to pick them up or record them; after all, that was why Gray was eager to explore all the Mounds.

Fig.8.12 Interior of a house (Mound 9?) in the Late Phase. Forestier, 1911.

What can have caused this Final Phase to be so distinct from the preceding Phase? The settlement was clearly running down, and significant areas abandoned. The changes in the centre and centre W are particularly marked but elsewhere there was a truncation of activity too. We see this as the result of a fundamental change in the eastern Brue valley. The palaeoenvironmental evidence from the deposits at the top of the sediments and those outside the settlement is truncated and affected by recent and modern soil formation, erosion, cracking and animal activity. This prevents any conclusive statements to be made about conditions at the site during its Final Phase. However, the regional picture indicates that a slow rise in water table began to occur at some point in the closing centuries BC. Any such alteration in the watery environment of the Lake Village, however small, would have an effect on the site perimeter, the channels leading to and from the site, the reed beds, swamp vegetation and animal life, and the important grazing land at the base of the uplands and islands. The reasons behind such slight but important changes are probably entirely local, and concerned with increased run-offs of water from cleared uplands, the woodlands diminished and arable land increased in extent. This is attested by the pollen record which indicates that regional forest clearance had been substantial. The resultant increase in erosion and water runoff would transport silt and clay into the streams and small rivers. When this water reached the swamp, the more or less horizontal gradient would encourage deposition of sediment, heavily waterlogged, blocking the already sluggish channels. Conditions were thus gradually created for a series of local disasters, small in area but significant to the Lake Village inhabitants. It may also be that there was a reduction in the outflow channels on the ancient river Brue as the former lake muds to the north dried-out, and it is also possible that the Axe Valley, beyond the Godney-Garslade gap, became more choked by estuarine-based clays or mere vegetation.

The effects of these changes on the Lake Village were substantial, not to the conditions on site but to the economic base. The Final Phase represented a change from a permanent settlement to an essentially seasonal occupation. Perhaps the houses at the N and S continued to be occupied all year, but the focus of activity was on the E, where many open clay spreads were laid down as bases for temporary encampments, with tent-like structures or simple windbreaks. This area was fenced on the E and entry on to the campsite was probably through the S at M19 and M21-22. A focus for the seasonal occupation was at M42. The approaches were by water, as usual, and the activities were transformed into sporadic gathering and hunting expeditions and perhaps a seasonal harvest of eggs, eel, reeds, bulrush and wildfowl. No longer were sheep and grain brought to the site and the emphasis of settlement shifted elsewhere, on to the uplands of the S and N. The Final Phase may have lasted only 30 years, one generation, from about 80BC to 50BC, and we think no more than 50 persons occupied the site either as permanent or seasonal residents during this time (fig.8.7). By 50BC even that seasonal encampment was abandoned for good.

Abandonment.

The abandonment of the Lake Village has intrigued many archaeologists, from Bulleid and Boyd Dawkins to Tratman and Godwin. In the 1917 volume, Boyd Dawkins argued that the settlement had been overrun by invaders who slaughtered the inhabitants and wrecked the site. This unlikely scenario was later transformed into an equivalent battle in which the locals won the day, sticking the enemies' heads on the fence posts. Bulleid thought that the settlement came to its end more peacefully, by flooding of the eastern Brue Valley; the inhabitants were forced out. Tratman also thought that serious flooding had been the cause of abandonment. The degree of flooding is the problem. If, from about 75BC, the settlement was being disrupted by a gradual waterlogging of the Valley, any series of heavy rainfalls or one or two bad years could essentially trigger the response to abandon both permanent and seasonal occupation. The ice-core and tree-ring evidence of a volcanic event about 44-40BC may be relevant here, but we think the settlement was already seasonal and on the brink of total abandonment by this time if not earlier. If the decision had already been taken to move elsewhere and only use the site on a seasonal basis, the final abandonment would be easy, imperceptible, undramatic. The major event had already occurred, the judgement to give up permanent occupation of the Lake Village. In proposing this sequence of events, we are aware that we are seeking to explain on the basis of incomplete environmental evidence, and neglecting the possible social and political factors that may well have influenced or forced the decisions. Some of the unusual artefacts noted above may have been deposited outside the settlement periphery as a final placatory act, at the abandonment of the permanent occupation (*circa* 80BC) or at the total withdrawal from the site (*circa* 50BC).

Why the Lake Village?

The Glastonbury Lake Village is an unusual if not unique late Iron Age settlement. It has always been singled out as an exceptional site, from the time of its discovery to the present day (e.g. Clark 1952; Coles and Coles 1986; Barrett 1987; Evans 1989). Why should this be so? It is not unusual for a settlement of this size and of this age to be discovered, nor for round houses and fences to be identified, nor for objects of great variety to be uncovered. The presence of wood, both structural and artefactual, is unusual and much attention has always been given to this material, in contrast to the more significant deposits on the site, namely, the stratified black earth, clay and peat soils that made up the Mounds. These deposits formed the basis of the site and we have devoted most of our structural analyses to them.

What is unusual about the Lake Village is its setting in a swamp. Those who decided to establish their settlement here chose to ignore the more obvious and common environmental positions of raised terrace or hillslope or hilltop. The site selected was almost deliberately difficult, difficult to establish a foundation, difficult to keep dry, difficult to maintain, and impossible to guarantee against natural disaster. The site was as far away from the dryland to N and S as possible, given the shape of the Valley (fig.1.1). Any contact or communication with those who remained on the upslopes was by definition made difficult, and water was the chosen medium of transport and travel.

The Lake Village is also unusual in its abundance of artefacts as recovered by Bulleid and Gray (fig.8.6). There are more finds per square metre than from any hillfort or other settlement that has been excavated in south-western England, even if the absolute numbers are almost impossible to work out. The artefacts are varied in material and in shape, and the site includes places of manufacture for some of the types. Some reliable sources of raw materials were clearly available, and some degree of specialised work was present. In this respect, the Lake Village is like the Meare Village occupations (both West and East Villages) which have even more artefacts than Glastonbury per square metre, but not (yet) in the total quantities recovered. Such abundances on these sites may be a reflection of the wetness of the sites and for the Glastonbury Lake Village the wetness may have been more intense than for the Meare sites. At the settlement, conditions were probably damp at best, and very damp at times. Material dropped could be lost, trampled in and then cushioned by the peaty soils, sealed by new clay spreads, covered by subsidence and shifting especially outside the fence and at the entrances. The Lake Village has no storage pits, the repositories of so much material on other Iron Age sites. Nor were the middens of the settlement ever found, even though Bulleid trenched some short distance from the fence; these middens would have augmented the yield of finds, especially those of organic material. Even without pits or middens, the site is rich in artefacts.

The Lake Village explanation is complex. Was the settlement an ordinary wetland occupation, concentrating on wild resources while still engaged in otherwise normal dryland activities - pasture, arable and woodland work? Was the settlement a normal Iron Age site, permanently occupied, exploiting both wet and dry lands, but placed in a remote and inaccessible area for security as much as for resources? Was the Village not normal at all, but a specialised service settlement for industrial work by craftsmen and women who catered for the demands of the regional settlements? Certainly the abundance of spinning and weaving appliances and tools suggests some particular expertise, but there is not much else on site that speaks strongly for full time or part time specialists; there is no glass working, some melting and forging of bronze and iron, some woodworking, and perhaps not much else. Overall, the view that this was a specialist workplace does not seem justified. Was the Lake Village even a seat of local power, wealth and prestige, its setting just another version of a withdrawn settlement - not up but down, no banks but water to define and defend and impress. There are exotic artefacts to help support this view - imported glass, cordoned pottery, shale and brooches - perhaps some measure of tribute or other acquisitive process. But these are very few in number, and as a site, the Lake Village was hardly overwhelmingly impressive. Perhaps the undefended nature of the Lake Village was part of its importance, welcoming, easily accessible by water and placed just where it posed no threat by appearance or activity to the regional Iron Age communities on the far hills. These are not mutually incompatible explanations and they reflect our own perceptions of wetland settlements in our abnormal, because unfamiliar, appreciation and distrust of a wetland existence.

The seasonal market.

In the 1987 publication of Meare Village East, of which Meare Village West has to be a part, we offered a model of the Meare sites as seasonal marketplaces for the region (Coles 1987 and Orme et al 1981). The site was placed at or near the boundaries of the territories of

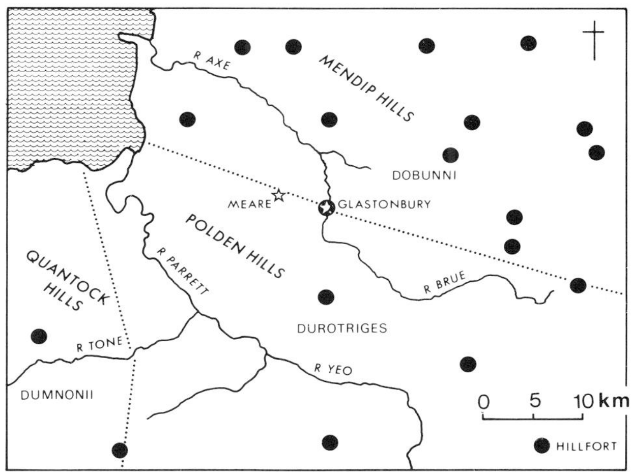

Fig.8.13 Map of the region showing the Lake Village, hillforts and probable tribal boundaries in the late Iron Age. Based on Cunliffe 1982. JMC

major Iron Age configurations - the Durotriges and the Dobunni, with the Dumnonii only a little to the west (Cunliffe 1982,60; and fig.8.13). These territories may have been closely guarded and jealously maintained, but the Brue Valley was a convenient area for a border zone, loosely and deliberately tangential to the main seats of power; this boundary zone lay in the obscurity of a wetland that no one owned. Here on the raised bog north of the island of Meare was a non-confrontational place for seasonal gatherings, where light industry could take place and some minor marketing occur, where exchanges could be made, and minor disputes settled, on neutral ground where no ascendant positions both literal and figurative could be maintained. Declaiming one's importance while balancing on a quivering clump of *Sphagnum* would be unlikely to impress.

From about 400BC the Meare occupations acted as a release for any tensions that had developed, and at the annual or otherwise regular gatherings people could affirm their presence, position, worth and intentions. Agreements could be made, promises fulfilled, debts paid and incurred, gifts and tributes exchanged, formal and informal links made or broken by consent, and all the while the ordinary industry took place both for practical purposes and as a medium for the more social intercourse. These events, or occasions like these, began to develop over 100 years before the settlement at Glastonbury was established . The evidence that the Glastonbury Lake Village was something different from the Meare gatherings is worth noting, as suggestions have been made from time to time that perhaps the Lake Villages were all the same, seasonal and impermanent.

Permanence.

The structural evidence from the Glastonbury Lake Village is more clearly identifiable than that from Meare and more positive in its interpretation. The roundness, conformity, multi-post wall lines, wattle and daub fragments, lack of clear sterile flooding lenses or washed surfaces, and fence lines, suggest more than tents, shelters or temporary roofed structures; in these respects the Glastonbury Lake Village contrasts with the far more flimsy evidence from Meare. The environmental position of the sites is also wholly different. The Lake Village is not on the edge of a raised bog as is the Meare site, and the latter would be subject to almost certain winter flooding from the lagg as well as the run-off from the bog surface. At the Lake Village, the western raised bog would cause some seasonal variation in wetness but the fen carr was less vulnerable to fluctuations, as its basin, the eastern Valley, was wide and able to respond and hopefully absorb minor episodes of flooding; the stream channels were important in this respect.

If the Meare occupations were as we suggest, the Lake Village at Glastonbury could have been established in part as a response to their existence. It may be that the Village was in effect an offshoot, but a new one, in that some of those involved in the Meare activities were no longer able or content to be only seasonally involved in the area. A more settled place was needed, one without the seasonal vibrations of the Meare bogland, but still partaking of the wetland benefits. Perhaps those who settled first on the site of the Lake Village were minor specialists, with families and support groups, who had already established their presence in the area at Meare, and who came to realise that the eastern wetland held ample resources for permanent occupation. Perhaps they felt that a more firmly-based industry was required to cater for the demand for sheep and its many products. The ease of transport, the wild resources, the fertile upland around, and the neutral position of the chosen site may all have contributed to its establishment. Here on the boundary of tribal lands the settlers could avoid the normal, or abnormal, confrontational practices or inadvertent actions that might have incurred displeasure or worse. The site was non-intimidatory, open, not difficult of access but inconvenient. It was outside the normal experiences of Iron Age contact, and emotionally strengthened by its unusual character. It had to be self-supporting because of this, and it would need satellite farms to the S and N, and possibly E as well, in order to maintain its hold on its own little territory, mostly water but important land holdings as well for cultivation and pasture. The unexplored structures at Crannel Moor, seen by Bulleid in 1893 and mentioned in *The Lake Villages of Somerset*, may be just such a satellite; a logboat from nearby is dated to the time of the Lake Village. Storage of food supplies was no problem because of the year-round supply of basics, as long as variation in food was accepted. Some of the families on the site were or became low level 'facilitators' in supplying craftsmen or women by harvesting, carrying and servicing the industries of wood, stone, textiles and perhaps metal and pottery. Others were specialists probably part time, but at certain times producing goods for the planned events at Meare and for the organised and *ad hoc* expeditions outside the wetland to adjacent Iron Age communities. The evidence from the Lake Village does not support the idea of middle or upper level specialists, full time, catering for a wide audience; it was never a leader in trade negotiations.

Wetland settlements of whatever kind, and particularly one like the Lake Village, needed some measure of control or ordering of activities. The timing of needs, and the processes to meet them, required guidance. Negotiations for payments, rewards and penalties had to be conducted. The assessment of seasonal variation and its intensity, and the encouragement of special periods of activity, had to be made firmly. The organisation and maintenance of relations with surrounding tribal configurations would be crucial in such a physically overlooked position. All these needs could be met by a strong leadership based on experience, and regularly affirmed by meetings, feastings, displays, gifts and disposals. Where on the Lake Village may we see traces of these controls and affirmations? We think the evidence for the evolution of the settlement, its maximum extent in the Late Phase, its possible focus in M9, the positions of its most valued objects, its evidence for intense and specialised operations, its wealth in resources and its lack of weaponry, all suggest leadership of a kind but at somewhere below our normal perception of a chief or priest. His or her house? M65. Specialisation? M4, M5, M30, M74. Focal point? M9 (fig.8.12, an imaginative reconstruction).

Could the Lake Village be viewed in any other way? Could it have been wholly abnormal and not even a settlement? The normality of the site lies in its houses, hearths, food remains and general debris of occupation, like the Neolithic bog settlement of Alvastra, Sweden, with its own hearths and debris (Malmer 1986) and the Iron Age fortress of Biskupin, Poland (Rajewski 1970). The abnormality of the Lake Village lies in its topographical setting, and its multitude of hearths, many of them open to the skies; the same is seen at Alvastra but not at Biskupin with its uniformity of houses in rows. Objects of great rarity and value, like the Lake Village bronze bowl, tin 'baton', mirror and perhaps decorated wooden vessels, are not normal on most sites, and the deposits of grain or animal bones could represent ritual offerings deliberately placed on or around the site. The adult human skulls from outside the fence as well as some inside the settlement may have been a part of this ostentatious disposal. Alvastra and Biskupin have equivalent deposits of grain, bones and human remains. Alvastra lies adjacent to a spring line where water is a constant force. Biskupin was placed on a prominent peninsula with wide expanses of water in front, just as the Lake Village had its swamp as a symbol of natural power. Alvastra and the Lake Village also had impressive views of high and prominent hills which would have dominated the flatness of the immediate surrounds. Alvastra is considered to be a site with a strong ritual character, while Biskupin is always viewed as a strongly organised settlement. The Glastonbury Lake Village may have combined both - a site with a domestic and ordinary purpose, but with undertones of a ritual nature.

The Lake Village was not a hidden settlement, tucked away in the swamp and deliberately obscure. It was overlooked from all quarters, the uplands to S and E, the domed bog to W, and the low islands and peninsula to N. The settlement would be visible by day, fence, rooftops and smoke advertising its presence. By night the glow of its many open fires could illuminate its existence, and dramatically enhance its bulk as people approached, gliding or poling through the still waters. Perhaps the position of the settlement was designed to attract and to draw in those who were invited, on occasion, to partake of its unusual flavours and to participate in activities not entirely domestic or purely economic. Perhaps visitors were summoned by smoke - precursor to the practice of signalling from fortlets and hilltops in the historic era. On arrival, the ceremonial activities centred in and around the M9 structure (a shrine?) could begin, involving its decorated table, the display and eventual disposal of precious objects of bronze, tin, lead, glass and wood, the currency bars and the human skulls. Could the many circles drawn on the table represent skulls? During the gathering of people, the wide and unusual variety of wetland foods could be offered, fires lit, and negotiations, ceremonies and alignments completed. This might be seen as a logical development of the seasonal and specialised activities begun at Meare six to eight generations before.

Final Comments

What we hope to have demonstrated in this book is that the Lake Village was a settlement, occupied for over 150 years as permanent home to a small community, thereafter diminished in importance. Its participation in extensive Iron Age contacts and customs was seemingly rather small, but there is enough to suggest that at some point in its existence it may have had a wider and more unusual role, its unique character both a cause and an effect of its place in Iron Age society.

Many questions remain. Bulleid and Gray left parts of the site intact, the M9 table included, and much of the lower structures survive across the site; opportunities exist for future investigations. Nonetheless, the variety and abundance of the evidence assembled in the 1911 and 1917 books, and presented here, will always pose unanswerable questions. John Morland visualised these in a letter to Arthur Bulleid in 1914 - "How one wishes they had been a lettered people." But that would have taken the fun out of the site.

Bibliography

Ambrosiani,K, 1981. *Viking Age Combs, Comb Making and Comb Makers.* Stockholm

Baillie,MGL, 1991. Marking in marker dates: towards an archaeology with historical precision. *World Archaeology* 23, 233-243

Barford,PM, 1985. Objects of stone, in Blockley,K, 1985. *Marshfield: Ironmongers Piece Excavations 1982 - 3. An Iron Age and Romano-British Settlement in the South Cotswolds.* Brit. Archaeol. Rep. Brit. Ser. 141

Barrett,JC, 1987. The Glastonbury Lake Village: models and source criticism, *Archaeol. J.* 144, 409-423

Beckett,SC and Hibbert,FA, 1979. Vegetational change and the influence of prehistoric man in the Somerset Levels, *New Phytol.* 83, 577-600

Bellamy,P, forthcoming. Worked stone, in Freeman,PW, Woodward,A and Barrett,JC forthcoming

Biek,L, and Bayley,J, 1979. Glass and other vitreous materials, *World Archaeology* 11, No.1, 1-25

Brailsford,J, 1975. The Polden Hill hoard, Somerset, *Proc. Prehistoric Soc.* 41, 222-234

Brothwell,D, 1981. *Digging Up Bones.* London

Bulleid,A, 1894. The Lake Village near Glastonbury, *PSANHS* 40, 141-151

Bulleid,A, 1895. Decorated woodwork from the Glastonbury Lake Village, *The Antiquary* 64, New Ser., 109-113

Bulleid,A, 1906. Prehistoric boat found at Shapwick 1906, *PSANHS* 52, 51-54

Bulleid,A, 1924. *The Lake Villages of Somerset.* Glastonbury

Bulleid,A and Gray,H St George, 1904. The Glastonbury Lake Village. An account of the excavations undertaken during 1904, *PSANHS* 50, 68-93

Bulleid,A and Gray,H St George, 1905. The Glastonbury Lake Village. An account of the excavations undertaken during 1905, *PSANHS* 51, 77-104

Bulleid,A and Gray,H St George, 1906. The Glastonbury Lake Village. An account of the excavations undertaken during 1906, *PSANHS* 52, 94-131

Bulleid,H and Gray,H St George, 1907. The Glastonbury Lake Village. An account of the excavations undertaken during 1907, *PSANHS* 53, 101-147

Bulleid,A and Gray,H St George, 1911. *The Glastonbury Lake Village Volume 1.* Glastonbury

Bulleid,A and Gray,H St George, 1917. *The Glastonbury Lake Village Volume 2.* Glastonbury

Bulleid,A and Jackson,JW, 1938. The Burtle Beds of Somerset, *PSANHS* 83, 171-195

Calkin,JB, 1953. "Kimmeridge Coal Money" The Romano-British shale armlet industry, *Proc. of the Dorset Nat. Hist. and Archaeol. Soc.* 75, 45-71

Clapham,AR and Godwin,H, 1948. Studies of the post-glacial history of British vegetation. VIII. Swamping surfaces in peats of the Somerset Levels. IX. Prehistoric trackways in the Somerset Levels, *Phil. Trans. R. Soc.* B233, 233-274

Clark,JGD, 1952. *Prehistoric Europe. The Economic Basis.* London

Clark,JGD, 1957. *Archaeology and Society* 3rd edition. London

Clark,JGD, 1962. *Prehistoric England* 2nd edition. London

Clarke,DL, 1972. A provisional model of an Iron Age society and its settlement system, in Clarke,DL (ed), *Models in Archaeology*, 801-869. London

Cliquet,D, Remy-Watte,M, Guichard,V and Vaginay,M, (Eds), 1993. *Les Celtes en Normandie: Les Rites Funéraires en Gaule.* Rev. Archéol. Ouest Supple. 6. Rennes

Clutton-Brock,J, 1981. *Domesticated Animals From Early Times.* London

Coles,JM, 1978. The Somerset Levels: a concave landscape, in Bowen,HC and Fowler,PJ (eds), *Early Land Allotment*, 147-148. Brit. Archaeol. Rep. Brit. Ser. 48

Coles,JM, 1987. *Meare Village East. The excavations of Arthur Bulleid and H St George Gray 1932-1956*, Somerset Levels Papers 13

Coles,JM, Coles,BJ and Morgan,RA, 1988. Excavations at the Glastonbury Lake Village 1984, *Somerset Levels Papers* 14, 57-62

Coles,JM, Goodall,A and Minnitt,SC, 1992. *Arthur Bulleid and the Glastonbury Lake Village 1892-1992.* Taunton

Cunliffe,BW, 1978. *Hengistbury Head.* London

Cunliffe,BW, 1982. Iron Age settlements and pottery 650 BC-60 AD, in Aston,M and Burrow,I (eds), *The Archaeology of Somerset: A Review to 1500 AD*, 53-61. Taunton

Cunliffe,BW, 1984. *Danebury: An Iron Age Hillfort in Hampshire. Volume 2: The Excavations, 1969-1978: The Finds.* CBA Res. Rep. 52. London

Cunliffe,BW, 1987. *Hengistbury Head, Dorset, Volume 1: The Prehistoric and Roman Settlement, 3500 BC - AD 500.* Univ of Oxford Comm. Archaeol. Monog. 13. Oxford

Cunliffe,BW, 1991. *Iron Age Communities in Britain.* London

Cunliffe,BW and Brown, L, 1987. Production, Trade and Exchange, in Cunliffe,BW, 1987, 303-321

Cunnington,ME, 1923. *The Early Iron Age Inhabited Site at All Cannings Cross Farm, Wiltshire.* Devizes

Demirjian,A, 1986. Dentition, in Tanner and Falkner 1986, 269-298

Dent,J, 1982. Cemeteries and settlement patterns of the Iron Age on the Yorkshire Wolds, *Proc. Prehistoric Soc.* 48, 437-457

Duff,KL, McKirdy,AP and Harley,MJ, 1985. *New Sites for Old: A Student's Guide to the Geology of the East Mendips.* Nature Conservancy Council

Earwood,C, 1988. Wooden containers and other wooden artifacts from the Glastonbury Lake Village, *Somerset Levels Papers* 14,84-91

Earwood,C, 1993. *Domestic Wooden Artefacts in Britain and Ireland from Neolithic to Viking Times.* Exeter

Edmonds,EA and Williams,BJ, 1985. *Geology of the Country Around Taunton and the Quantock Hills.* Memoir for Sheet 295, Brit. Geol. Survey

Evans,C, 1989. Perishables and worldly goods - artifact decoration and classification in the light of wetlands research, *Oxford Journal of Archaeology* 8, 179-201

Fazekas,G and Kosa,F, 1978. *Forensic Fetal Osteology.* Budapest

Fell,V, 1990. *Pre-Roman Iron Age Metalworking Tools From England and Wales: Their Use, Technology and Archaeological Context.* Unpublished M.Phil., University of Durham

Fitzpatrick,A, 1994. The Late Iron Age cremation cemetery at Westhampnett, West Sussex, in Fitzpatrick and Morris 1994, 108-111

Fitzpatrick,A and Morris,EL (Eds), 1994. *The Iron Age in Wessex: Recent Work.* Salisbury

Foster,J, 1980. *The Iron Age Moulds From Gussage All Saints.* Brit. Mus. Occ. Paper 12. London

Fowler,E, 1960. The origins and development of the penannular brooch in Europe, *Proc. Prehistoric Soc.* 26, 149-177

Freeman,PW, Woodward,A and Barrett,JC, forthcoming. *Cadbury Castle, Somerset: The Later Prehistoric and Roman Archaeology.* English Heritage Archaeol. Rep.

Freestone,IC, Johns,C and Potter,T, 1982. *Current Research in Ceramics: Thin Section Studies.* Brit. Mus. Occ. Paper 32. London

Freestone,IC and Rigby,V, 1982. Class B cordoned and other imported wares from Hengistbury Head, Dorset, in Freestone et al 1982, 29-42

Gent,H, 1983. Centralized storage in later prehistoric Britain, *Proc. Prehistoric Soc.* 49, 243-267

Godwin,H, 1941. Studies of the post-glacial history of British vegetation. VI. Correlations in the Somerset Levels, *New Phytol.* 40, 108-132

Godwin,H, 1943, Coastal peat beds of the British Isles and North Sea, *J. Ecol.* 31, 199-247

Godwin,H, 1955. Studies of the post-glacial history of British vegetation. XIII. The Meare Pool region of the Somerset Levels, *Phil. Trans. R. Soc.* B239, 161-190

Godwin,H, 1981. *The Archives of the Peat Bogs.* Cambridge

Gray,H, 1991 edition. *Gray's Anatomy.* London

Gray,H St George, 1902. Excavations at the Glastonbury Lake Village in July 1902, *PSANHS* 50, 68-93

Gray,H St George, 1930. Excavations at Kingsdown Camp, Mells, Somerset 1927-9, *Archaeologia* 80, 59-98

Gray,H St George and Cotton,MA, 1966. *The Meare Lake Village Volume III.* Taunton

Green,GW and Welch,FBA, 1965. *Geology of the Country Around Wells and Cheddar.* Memoir for Sheet 280, Geol. Survey of Great Britain

Guido,M, 1978. *The Glass Beads of the Prehistoric and Roman Periods in Britain and Ireland,* Soc. of Antiquaries Res. Rep. 35. London

Haevernick,TE, 1960. *Die Glasarmringe und Ringperlen der Mittel- und Spätlatènezeit auf dem Europäischen Festland.* Bonn

Haevernick,TE, 1983. *Glasperlen der Vorrömischen Eisenzeit I,* Marburger Studien zur Vor- und Frühgeschichte I. Mainz

Hallam,AD, 1934. The geology of the Hangman Grits of the Quantock Hills, *Geol. Mag.* 71, 433-446

Henderson,J, 1980. Some new evidence for Iron Age glass-working in Britain, *Antiquity* 54, 60-61

Henderson,J, 1981. A report on the glass excavated from Meare Lake Village West, in Orme,BJ et al, 1981

Henderson,J, 1982. *X-ray Fluorescence Analysis of Iron Age Glass.* Unpublished PhD thesis, University of Bradford

Henderson,J, 1985. The raw materials of early glass production, *Oxford Journal of Archaeol.* 4(3), 267-291

Henderson,J, 1986. Interaction of changes in technology and style - progress or stagnation, in Kingery,WD, Technology and Style, *Ceramics and Civilisation, volume 2,* American Ceramics Soc. 21-31

Henderson,J, 1987a. The archaeology and technology of glass from Meare Village East, in Coles,JM, 1987, 170-182

Henderson,J, 1987b. Glass and Glass working, in Cunliffe,BW, 1987, 160-163 and 180-185

Henderson,J, 1987c. Chemical and archaeological analysis of some British and European prehistoric glasses, *Annales du 10e Congrès de l'Association Internationale pour l'Histoire du Verre,* Madrid-Segovia September 1985, 13-22

Henderson,J, 1991. Industrial specialisation in Late Iron Age Britain and Europe, *Archaeol. J.* 148, 104-148

Henderson,J and Warren,SE, 1981. X-ray fluorescence analysis of Iron Age glass: beads from Meare and Glastonbury Lake Villages, *Archaeometry* 23 (1), 83-94

Hingley,R, 1990. Iron Age "currency bars": the archaeological and social context. *Archaeol. J.* 147, 91-117

Hoskins,WG, 1967. *Fieldwork in Local History.* London

Housley,RA, 1986. *The Environment of Glastonbury Lake Village,* unpublished PhD thesis, University of Cambridge

Housley,RA, 1988. The environmental context of Glastonbury Lake Village, *Somerset Levels Papers* 14, 63-82

Howard,H, 1983. *The Bronze Casting Industry in Later Prehistoric Southern Britain.* Unpublished PhD thesis, University of Southampton

Hull,MR and Hawkes,CFC, 1987. *Corpus of Ancient Brooches in Britain.* Brit. Archaeol. Rep. Brit. Ser. 168

Jackson,R, 1990. *Camerton, The Late Iron Age and Early Roman Metalwork.* London

Kidson,C and Heyworth,A, 1976. The Quaternary deposits of the Somerset Levels, *Quart. J. Engineering Geology* 9, no. 3, 217-235

Kunkel,O, 1961. Zur frage keltischer glasindustrie. Nach einer Manchinger Fundgruppe, *Germania* 39, 322-329

MacGregor,A, 1985. *Bone, Antler, Ivory and Horn.* London

Malmer,MP, 1986. Aspects of Neolithic ritual sites, in Steinsland,G (ed), *Words and Objects*, 91-110. Oslo

Maresh,M, 1955. *Linear Growth of Long Bones of Extremities from Infancy Through Adolescence.* U.S.A. Child Research Council.

McGrail,S, 1978. *Logboats of England and Wales.* Brit. Archaeol. Rep. Brit. Ser. 51

Meniel,P, 1993. Les animaux dans les practiques funéraire des Gaulois, in Cliquet,D et al, 1993, 285-290

Moberg,C-A, 1981. Two model problems: settlement change - regional parenthesis - Glastonbury - Gotland, in Moberg,C-A (ed), *Similar Finds? Similar Interpretations?.* Gothenburg

Morgan,RA, 1988. Tree-ring studies at Glastonbury and Meare, in Coles et al, 1988

Munro,R, 1890. *The Lake Dwellings of Europe.* London

Munro,R, Boyd Dawkins,W, Evans,AJ and Bulleid,A, 1895. *The British Lake Village near Glastonbury.* Glastonbury

Olivier,A, 1991. *A Study of Certain Types of One-piece Brooch in Southern Britain During the First Century A.D.: Aspects of Form, Distribution and Chronology.* Unpublished PhD thesis, University of Nottingham

Olivier,A, forthcoming. The brooches, in Freeman,PW, Woodward,A and Barrett,JC forthcoming

Orme,BJ, Coles,JM, Caseldine,AE and Bailey,GN, 1981. Meare Village West 1979, *Somerset Levels Papers* 7, 12-69

Orme,BJ, Coles,JM and Silvester,RJ, 1983. Meare Village East 1982, *Somerset Levels Papers* 9, 49-73

Peacock,DPS, 1969. A contribution to the study of Glastonbury Ware from South-western Britain, *Ant. J.* 49, 41-61

Pearson,GW and Stuiver,M 1986. High-precision calibration of the radiocarbon time scale, 500-2500 BC. *Radiocarbon* 28, 839-862

Peddemors,A, 1975. Latèneglasarmringe in den Niederlanden, *Analecta Praehistorica Leidensia* 8, 93-145

Percy,J, 1861. *Metallurgy; Fuels; Fire-clays; Copper; Zinc; Brass.* London

Rahtz,P, 1993. *English Heritage Book of Glastonbury.* London

Rahtz,P, Woodward,A, Burrow,I, Everton,A, Watts,L, Leach,P, Hirst,S, Fowler,P and Gardner,K, 1992. *Cadbury Congresbury 1968-1973: A Late/Post-Roman Hilltop Settlement in Somerset.* Brit. Archaeol. Rep. Brit. Ser. 223

Rajewski,Z, 1970. *Biskupin.* Warsaw

Ramsey,CB and Hedges,REM, forthcoming. Radiocarbon calibration and analysis of stratigraphy. *Proc. 15th Radiocarbon Conf. Glasgow 1994*

Reid,C, 1917. Plants, wild and cultivated, in Bulleid and Gray, 1917, 625-630

Renfrew,C and Bahn,P, 1991. *Archaeology. Theories, Methods and Practice.* London

Roe,FES, forthcoming. Worked stone, in Freeman, Woodward and Barrett forthcoming

Rouillard,S, 1987. The Iron Age pottery from Meare Village East, in Coles,JM, 1987, 183-221

Ryder,ML, 1993. Wool at Danebury: a speculation using evidence from elsewhere, *Oxford J. of Archaeol.*, 12, 305-320

Schoknecht,U, 1977. *Menzlin. Ein Frühgeschichtlicher Handelsplatz an der Peene.* Berlin

Schour,I and Massler,M, 1940. The development of human dentition. *Journal of the American Dental Association* 28, 1153-1160

Sellwood,L, 1984. Objects of bone and antler, in Cunliffe,BW 1984

Sharples,N, 1991. *Maiden Castle: Excavations and Field Survey 1985-6.* English Heritage Archaeol. Rep. 19. London

Sharer,RJ and Ashmore,W, 1993. *Archaeology. Discovering our Past.* 2nd edition. Mountain View, California

Silver,IA, 1969. The ageing of domestic animals, in Brothwell,D and Higgs,E (eds.), *Science in Archaeology,* 283-302. London

Smith,AJ, 1981. Flint, in Orme,BJ et al, 1981

Société Archéologique Champenoise, 1991. *La Céramique Peinte Celtique dans son Contexte Européen.* Actes du Symposium International D'Hautville, 9-11 Octobre 1987. Mémoire de la Société Archéologique Champenoise 5. Supplément au Bulletin No. 1

Stead,IM, 1991a. *Iron Age Cemeteries in Yorkshire.* English Heritage Archaeol. Rep 22. London

Stead,IM, 1991b. Many More Iron Age Shields, *Ant.J.* 71, 1-35

Stead,IM and Rigby,V, 1989. *Verulamium: The King Harry Lane Site.* English Heritage Archaeol. Rep. 12. London

Stuiver,M and Pearson,GW, 1986. High-precision calibration of the radiocarbon timescale AD 1950-500 BC. *Radiocarbon* 28, 805-838

Tanner,JM and Falkner,F (Eds), 1986. *Human Growth, a Comprehensive Treatise.* 2nd edition. New York

Theophilus. *On Divers Arts.* Translated by Dodwell,CR, 1961. London

Tratman,EK, 1970. The Glastonbury Lake Village: a reconsideration, *Proc. Univ. Bristol Spelaeol. Soc.* 12, 143-167

Tuohy,T, 1990. *Combs of Antler and Bone.* Unpublished BA dissertation, University of Exeter

Turner,WES, 1956. Studies in ancient glasses and glass-making processes. Part III. The chronology of glass-making constituents, *J. of the Soc. of Glass Technology* 40, 39T-52T

Tylecote,R, 1986. *The Prehistory of Metallurgy in the British Isles.* London

Van Arsdell,R, 1989. *Celtic Coinage of Britain.* London

Venclova,N, 1990. *Prehistoric Glass in Bohemia.* Prague

Wainwright,GJ, 1979. *Gussage All Saints. An Iron Age Settlement in Dorset.* DOE Archaeol. Rep. 10. London

Wheeler,REM, 1943. *Maiden Castle, Dorset.* London

Whimster,RP, 1981. *Burial Practices in Iron Age Britain: a Discussion and Gazateer of the Evidence c. 700 BC - AD 43.* Brit. Archaeol. Rep. Brit. Ser. 90. Oxford

Whitehead,GK, 1964. *The Deer of Great Britain and Ireland.* London

Whittaker,A and Green,GW, 1983. *Geology of the Country Around Weston-super-Mare,* Memoir for Sheet 279, Geol. Survey of Great Britain

Wild,JP, 1970. Button-and-loop fasteners in the Roman provinces. *Britannia* 1, 137-155

Williams,M, 1970. *The Draining of the Somerset Levels.* Cambridge

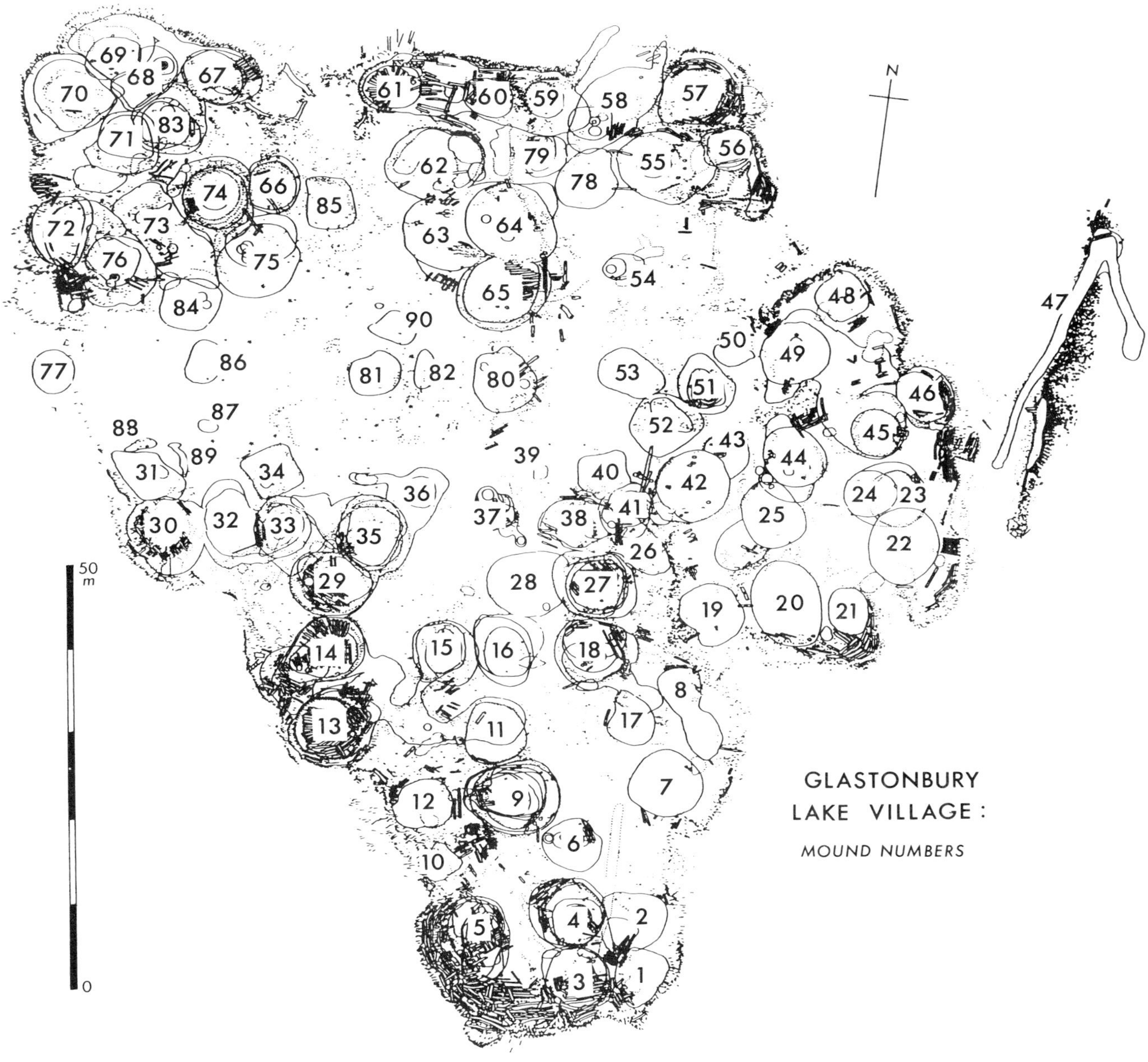

Fig.8.14 Plan of the Mounds with Bulleid's numbers, used throughout this book.